SOFTWARE PARADIGMS

SOFTWARE PARADIGMS

Stephen H. Kaisler

Senior Associate
SET Associates
and
Adjunct Professor of Engineering
George Washington University

A John Wiley & Sons, Inc., Publication

For general information on our other products and services please contact our Customer Care
Department within the U.S. at 877-762-2974, outside the U.S. at 317-572-3993 or fax 317-572-4002.

Wiley also publishes its books in a variety of electronic formats. Some content that appears in print,
however, may not be available in electronic format.

Library of Congress Cataloging-in-Publication Data:

Kaisler, Stephen H. (Stephen Hendrick)
  Software paradigms / Stephen H. Kaisler.
     p. cm.
  Includes bibliographical references and index.
  ISBN 0-471-48347-8 (cloth)
  1. Computer software—Development. I. Title.
    QA76.76.D47K34 2005
    005.3—dc22

                                2004007134

Printed in the United States of America

10 9 8 7 6 5 4 3 2 1

To my late father, E. Francis Kaisler and my mother, Dolores Kaisler
To my wife, Chryl and children, Rebecca and John

CONTENTS

ADVICE FOR THE INSTRUCTOR

This book arose out of the Graduate Master's Program core course, CS210—Software Paradigms, which is offered at the Department of Computer Science at George Washington University. When we set out to design that course, we realized that we discussed models of software development in several courses at the graduate level but had no course that tied all of the concepts together. We realized that the different models fit into a hierarchy based on scale and complexity.

Our course is intended to provide the student with an understanding of the scaling of software systems and the associated issues and problems as the application structure becomes more complex. Each topic in this book could be the subject of a course in its own right. We felt it important for the student to be exposed to all of these topics in a single course, with the attendant freedom to pursue in depth individual topics through reading courses or independent research.

This book provides introductory material for a number of the courses in the Computing Curricula 2001: Computer Science, as made available on the IEEE website, `http://www.computer.org/education/cc2001/final/cc2001.pdf`. The following table suggests a mapping from the CS Curricula courses to the chapters of this book.

CS Curricula Course	Book Chapters
CS111: Object-Oriented Programming	Parts I and II
CS112: Object-Oriented Design and Methodology	Parts I–IV
CS290: Software Development	Parts I–IV
CS396: Component-Based Computing	Part II
CS490: Capstone Project	Parts III and IV
SE12: Specialized Systems Development	Parts III and IV

STEPHEN H. KAISLER

ACKNOWLEDGMENTS

This book arose from a graduate course, CS210: Advanced Software Paradigms, which I teach at the Department of Computer Science, George Washington University, Washington, DC. This course is one of the three core courses for the Master's Degree in Computer Science. I designed this course in 1999 at the behest of Professors Michael Feldman, Curriculum Director, and Bhagirath Narahari, then Department Chair. I have taught it several times, as have Professors Adbelghani Bellaachia and Morris Lancaster, both of whom have contributed greatly to the course content and improved the course each time. Dianne Martin, Department Chair, has continued to support our approach to teaching this course, which may be unique in its integrated approach to the subject matter. I thank them all for the opportunity, their support, and their assistance without which this book would not have come into being.

Obviously, the students who have taken CS210 over the past five years have contributed greatly to improving the course content, presentation, and emphasis through their probing questions and criticisms. Several of my students in the Fall 2003 semester critiqued significant portions of the book. I thank them all for their assistance.

S.H.K

1

INTRODUCTION

Programming is about the creation of software to solve problems. Problems come in many forms: simple to complex, small to large, I/O-intensive to compute-intensive. Over the past four decades, we've tried to solve a lot of different types of problems with software. At some, we have been exceptionally successful and the solution space is well understood. For others, such as those proposed by artificial intelligence, we have only been marginally successful (and, in many cases, not at all) within limited domains.

But, programming has always been both a knowledge-intensive and labor-intensive process. As PCs became more pervasive and the demand for applications increased, a problem arose—how to develop safe, robust software quicker.

Traditionally, the software industry has focused on delivering high-quality, special purpose application software to the end-user and high-quality, general purpose development software to the professional developer. End-users are not expected to develop their own applications. Much effort has been invested in making software development more efficient for professional developers by providing huge collections of prefabricated software components. Much effort has also been invested in increasing the utility of application software by providing customizable user interfaces.

Most software development tools are too complex for end-users. The few that are simple enough to attract nonprogrammers limit the user to simple applications that can't be combined with other software. Applications have to be built from scratch; they do not scale and, therefore, are often of limited practical use. On the other hand, commercial application software offers little modifiability beyond customization of

Software Paradigms, By Stephen H. Kaisler
ISBN 0-471-48347-8   Copyright © 2005 John Wiley & Sons, Inc.

the user interface. In particular, applications do not let users modify their behavior or reuse their functionality within other applications.

The solution to this problem requires the following assumptions:

1. High-quality software applications should be producible with some skill and effort by taking advantage of functionality in software components developed by others.
2. Flexible integration of new software applications should be achievable by decomposing applications into small functional components that can be reused independently and recombined efficiently.

The first assumption requires that users focus more on gluing components together rather than developing individual components, although they will have to do some of the latter. The second assumption requires that users have standard ways of describing and representing components as well as guides for how to connect those components together.

Software developers and users should be able to build small applications fast and easily. The learning effort required to start building an application should stay in the range of hours. Nevertheless, users should expect their applications to be comparable in look and feel to commercial software.

To achieve this goal, there are four problems to be addressed:

1. How do we build more complex structures from simple parts?
2. What is the best way to integrate ("glue together") multiple parts to form a whole?
3. How can we construct parts to make them reusable, and reuse them?
4. How can we ensure that small solutions can scale to bigger problems?

This book will provide some answers to these questions. We do so through examination of different conceptual paradigms—from the small to the large for constructing software applications.

1.1 THE MEANING OF PARADIGM

Paradigm (a Greek word meaning example) is commonly used to refer to a category of entities that share a common characteristic. Numerous authors have examined the concept of a paradigm. Perhaps the foremost user of the word has been Thomas Kuhn (1996), who wrote the seminal book *The Structure of Scientific Revolutions*.

Kuhn used the notion of paradigm in the scientific process by defining it as a scientist's view of the world and the structure of his assumptions and theories, which affect that view. In his definition, he included the concepts of law, theory, application, and instrumentation: in effect, both the theoretical and the practical.

Kuhn saw a "paradigm" as emerging as the result of social processes in which people develop new ideas and create principles and practices that embody these ideas. Large software development is a social process, because it is often a team effort. Each new software application is a unique creation in its own right. Rarely, if ever, does a team of programmers set out to create a program that exactly mimics the code and structure of some other program.

Kuhn's definition has been applied beyond his original application to the history of physical science. Others believe that paradigms are the basis of normal science; indeed, the basis of established scientific tradition. In this view, the formation of a paradigm is a sign of maturity for a given science. The notion of a paradigm for programming was first expressed by Floyd (1979) as far as I have been able to discern.

We are going to apply the notion of paradigm to the investigation of programming languages and software architectures to determine how well we can solve different types of problems. The question we would like to answer takes the form: Is there a taxonomy within a particular domain that serves to organize the element of that domain? In programming languages, most computer scientists would answer "yes." In software architectures, the answer is more likely a definite "maybe." By the end of this book, we believe that you'll see the answer for software architectures is "yes."

1.2 SOFTWARE SOLVES PROBLEMS

How do we classify problems? Put another way, is there a typology of problems? If so, can we find common solutions that are widely applicable to many or all of the problems in the class? The recent emergence of patterns and frameworks suggests that there is such a typology and that we can find common solutions to them. Much work needs to be done in this area, but early results are very promising.

For a given problem class, we'd like to be able to create software that solves the problem or parts of it efficiently. There are two aspects to creating such software: the software's architecture and the choice of programming language.

1.2.1 Software Architecture

Software architecture is the structure of the components of the solution. We decompose the problem into smaller pieces and attempt to find a solution for each piece. Sometimes, the solution for a piece requires further decomposition. When we have the solutions for each of the components, we have to integrate them and make them interoperate in order to have a piece of software, sometimes called an application, that solves the problem. Integration means the pieces fit together well. Interoperation means that they work together effectively to produce an answer.

There are many software architectures. Choosing the right one can be a difficult problem in itself. It is not clear yet what metrics are suitable for evaluating software architectures. We'll address software architecture in more detail in Part III of this book.

1.2.2   Choosing a Programming Language

The second problem we face is choosing the best programming language to implement our software. There are different paradigms for programming languages that drive their syntax and semantics. There is no one programming language that is right for all problems. Alternatively, we do not know yet if there is one programming language that is best for a particular class of problems. In addition, we do not yet have the right set of metrics for deciding if this is so.

There have been a large number of programming languages. Jean Sammet (1967) counted at least 700, but most are now defunct. New programming languages continue to emerge, although less frequently than in the past. Recently, much work has focused on evolving and/or extending existing programming languages rather than creating new ones. Perhaps that is a sign of maturity in the field. George Michael (1980) once said that there will always be a Fortran, although we may not recognize today's language in it. Some features are being recognized as essential for writing good software—such as the evolution of object-oriented versions of older programming languages. Others, such as concurrency, support the way to create more efficient and better performing software.

So, faced with developing a solution to a particular problem, we have three tasks to perform (see Figure 1-1). First, we need to decide which set of features comprise our problem. This is the *requirements analysis* task. Second, we need to develop a suitable software architecture or algorithm for each subproblem and develop a software architecture for the overall problem. This is the *system design* task. Third, we need to choose a good, if not the best, programming language for each subproblem and implement the solution. This is the *implementation* task. That's not all there is to achieving a useful application, but that's the primary focus of our effort here.

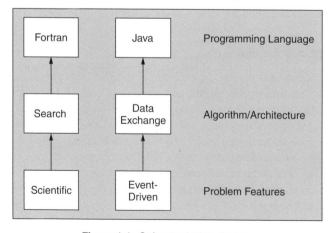

Figure 1-1. Software design phases.

It is important to distinguish between the programming language, the paradigm on which it is based, and the algorithm that is used to solve the problem. Theoretically, it should be possible to write any algorithm in any general purpose language. However, some languages offer more support for particular software paradigms than others.

The problem of architecting a software solution to a problem is a complex one. It involves multiple tradeoffs that must be decided in order to yield a successful application that meets the requirements for solving the problems and the needs of the user(s) of the system. Inevitably, some combinations of trade-offs yield programming approaches that are clearly impractical for implementing an application. We have chosen to focus our attention in this book on structural paradigms for software systems.

1.3 DESIGNING AND DEVELOPING SOFTWARE

Software was originally called "soft" to distinguish it from the machine that executed it. Software is soft in a number of ways. It is not visible when it is running. It seems to change all the time, both when it is running and when it is being built. It is difficult to describe fully all aspects of software. In other words, there is no widely known way to describe the structure of a complete software system in the same way that the structure of a complete building, or an airplane, or a chemical plant is described. We can capture the static structure of a software system fairly well in many mature tools, but the dynamics continue to elude us. Nor do many of the well-known software analysis and design methodologies provide a notation for integrating the structure of the complete system with its dynamics.

We are interested in how to solve problems. In particular, we want to develop software that repeatedly can solve the same problem over and over with new data sets. In most cases, we understand the general approach to solving the problem. We may know, in fact, all the procedures and details. But, for all but the simplest problems, the thought of working through the algorithm(s) by pencil and paper is rather daunting.

Software allows us to capture the algorithms and detailed procedures in an electronically tangible form that permits almost effortless repetition (just push the button, they say). The hard part is designing the software, developing the software, and ensuring that it is correct. This book is about software design; we leave the latter topics for other volumes.

Today, most large software systems are too complex for a single individual to understand. Most of the software development we do these days we do with others because a single person hasn't the required skill or time to solve a complicated problem alone. One way to facilitate working together is to use and reuse concepts or ideas for which we share a common understanding.

When we write our first program, it often involves an intense amount of effort. The next time we performed a similar task, it is/may be a bit easier because we learned some things that we could reuse in our next project. As we develop more experience, we not only continue to learn new practices, but we refine and hone the practices that we have already learned. Some of them become rote because we have recognized them as "best practices" for programming and software development.

When we can capture and share the things we learn each time, we can reduce the need to rediscover what we've done before and share them with others who can also save time. This leads to a very important aspect of developing software that most of us don't think much about but is basic to our success—the need for effective collaboration.

The technical literature is replete with books and technical papers on software design and the software design process. We do not intend to duplicate their efforts. We see software design as a three-pronged process: understanding the problem domain, designing the software architecture, and choosing the programming language. While addressing programming languages and problem taxonomies, our primary focus is on how to construct software.

1.3.1 Reusability

We have known for a long time that writing each new application "from scratch" is very expensive and time-consuming. There has long been an emphasis on reuse of software to mitigate some of the costs of developing new applications.

At the same time, developers felt that they could improve each succeeding application using the lessons learned from the preceding one, but that such use required

Table 1-1. A reuse taxonomy

Type of Reuse	Description
Ideas	The reuse of formal concepts such as general solutions to a class of problems
Artifacts	The reuse of software components (such as the Booch Ada components)
Procedures	The reuse of software processes and procedures
Vertical	The reuse of software within the same domain and even within the same application suite
Horizontal	The reuse of generic parts across multiple applications
Planned	The reuse of guidelines, development and testing processes, and metrics across multiple projects
Ad hoc	An informal practice in which components are selected from general libraries in an opportunistic fashion
Compositional	The reuse of existing components as the building blocks of new applications
Generative	The reuse of specifications and requirements to develop application or code generators
Black-box	The reuse of software components without any modification; usually linked together with glue code
White-box	The reuse of components by modification and adaptation

a complete rewrite of the application. By the 1990s, we realized as a community that successive applications could be built by reusing knowledge and software from earlier applications. This meant that succeeding applications could often be built faster than their predecessors.

1.3.2   Types of Reuse

At first, reuse referred just to the actual source code itself. Basili and Rombach (1988) expanded the definition to encompass everything associated with a software development project. Prieto-Diaz (1988) describes a taxonomy of eleven types of reuse as depicted in Table 1-1.

1.4   UNDERSTANDING PROBLEM PARADIGMS

A problem paradigm is a model for a class of problems that share a set of common characteristics. These characteristics serve to differentiate one problem type from another. Some problem types that you may have encountered in the past include search problems and classification problems (see Figure 1-2).

Over the past 40 years of computer science, we have identified classes of problems that share common characteristics. Problems such as search, enumeration, classification, data organization and manipulation, and sorting are encountered routinely in just about every application that is written.

When one thinks about it, there are relatively few problem structures that we encounter in computer science. However, we encounter them over and over in different contexts with different features and twists that make for interesting programming challenges.

Some of these problem paradigms have to do with the way data is structured and some with the type of processing to be applied to the data. Search, for example, is a recurring problem in many applications. But searching through a randomly ordered data set is different from searching through a known, sorted set represented as a vector or a B*-tree.

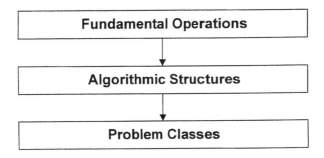

Figure 1-2. The problem paradigm.

1.4.1 Fundamental Operations

At the lowest level of computation, there are some fundamental operations that must be performed to solve any problem, no matter how they are syntactically represented. Among these are assignment of values to variables, decision making, and sequencing through instructions as shown by Bohm and Jacopini (1966). As one considers more complex programs, one realizes that other operations become fundamental as well. We would argue strongly that recursion, procedure calls, concurrency, and exception handling—to name a few—should also be considered as fundamental operations.

1.4.2 Algorithms and Architectures

An *algorithm* is a specification for how to solve a particular problem. Algorithms are ordered sets of unambiguous, executable steps that define a terminating process. The key idea is that an algorithm is deterministic. With the proper inputs to the algorithm, repeated execution of the algorithm will return the same result. In addition, an algorithm must complete (e.g., yield a result) in a finite amount of time.

Algorithms can be written in any language from English to programming languages. Recipes for how to bake a cake or make chicken cordon bleu are algorithms. These two expressions represent the same algorithm:

- The Fahrenheit temperature is nine-fifths of the Celsius temperature plus 32.
- Fahrenheit := $(9/5) * \text{Celsius} + 32$

Algorithms are translated into programs that are executed on computers. When we study algorithms, we are concerned about how much time and how much space they take to compute the result. We can derive a hypothetical result through careful analysis of the algorithm, but we are often concerned with how the algorithm performs when it is translated into a program using a specific programming language, running under a specific operating system, on a specific computer architecture.

1.4.3 Problem Classes

A *problem class* is a set of problems that are similar in nature although they may be dissimilar in their origin (e.g., the field from which they emerge). For example, checking a book or a videotape out of a public library is similar to checking a software module out of a system library. Both systems have similar fundamental operations and algorithms that characterize them. Recognizing the set of operations and the set of algorithms leads us to describe a problem class, for example, a set of operations that routinely occur in solving a particular type of problem. Some of the types of problems that we routinely encounter are search, sort, classification, enumeration, and graphics.

1.4.4 Summary

Several insights arise from this approach. First, problem paradigms are nothing magical. We have been writing programs to solve problems for over fifty years. During this period, some accepted standard solutions have emerged for given problem classes. Within the past ten years, this has been captured in the subdisciplines of patterns and frameworks, which represent problem paradigms. Second, if we can describe a problem paradigm, we can implement it on a target architecture, albeit not efficiently sometimes. Third, there is no theoretical reason why we cannot combine multiple paradigms to solve more complex problems. However, practicality is an entirely different matter. Some argue that the use of multiple patterns is just such an approach. I agree. Fourth, the target architecture has a strong influence on the way a problem paradigm is implemented. There must be a synergy between the problem paradigm and the computer architecture to obtain efficiency in execution. Fifth, any programming language can be used to implement any problem paradigm; some will do it more efficiently than others. Finally, there are numerous problem paradigms, which suggests some way of organizing them into a hierarchy or mesh-like structure according to certain properties and characteristics.

1.5   OVERVIEW OF BOOK

This was a difficult book to write. It mixes concepts from three different areas—programming languages, software architecture, and basic computer science—in an attempt to develop an interdisciplinary approach to creating software. Its interdisciplinary nature created a problem in itself: What's the best way to organize the material to make it both understandable and usable?

After some reflection, it seemed there was a natural hierarchy emerging that ran from programming languages and data constructs through more complex structures. This hierarchy is described in Chapter 2.

I have chosen to address each of these elements in a separate part within the book. Each part is composed of small chapters that address particular topics. Each chapter in itself is worthy of a whole book, but my intent here is to show how they are all interrelated. In each chapter, I suggest additional references that will allow the reader to delve more deeply into the material.

This book is divided into several introductory chapters, multiple parts, a bibliography, and a glossary.

Chapter 1, this chapter, provides a gentle introduction to the book and the topics of discourse.

Chapter 2 provides an overview of the paradigms that we will discuss in the remainder of the book. It presents a limited catalog of the types of problems that we solve with programming languages. It briefly describes the hierarchy of architectural paradigms: design patterns, components, software architectures, and frameworks.

The remainder of the book is divided into four parts, each of which consists of multiple chapters. Each part focuses on a specific paradigm. Each chapter focuses on a specific topic.

1.6 CONVENTIONS

In this book, I have used a number of conventions to simplify the reading.

I use the masculine pronoun when writing in the third person although I mean both male and female readers.

URLs for the World Wide Web are included in this text. They have been verified to be accessible as of the publication date of this book. If you find a URL that is not accessible, please notify the author. However, you should be able to search on words or phrases of that section to find other URLs pertaining to the same material.

In some chapters, I have added references for further reading for source material that is not referenced directly in the book.

I have included exercises at the end of each chapter. I hope that the answers to these exercises are not obvious: that is, you will have to do further investigation and analysis beyond the content of the chapter in order to arrive at a satisfactory answer. For many exercises, there are no right answers.

1.7 EXERCISES

I had thought about putting some summary exercises after the last chapter but eventually decided that they should be right up front where you can read and ponder them, and, hopefully, they will stimulate some comparative analysis as you read through the remainder of the book.

1.1. In Section 1.3, review Prieto-Diaz's reuse taxonomy. Then, build a table with the reuse types versus the paradigms and fill in the cells with justifying information for why a particular paradigm supports a particular reuse type.

1.2. In Section 1.3, I assert that there are large software applications today that are too complex for any single individual to understand. Indeed, this has been said about OS/MVS and succeeding releases since the early 1980s and Unix and Microsoft Windows more recently. How big, according to some unit measurement, do you think a software system has to be before it cannot be comprehended by a single individual?

1.3. Section 1.4.3 discusses the concept of problem classes. There are some well-known types of problems in computer science. Develop a taxonomy of problem classes for use in later exercises. [Research Problem]

2

PARADIGM OVERVIEW

Computation is about solving problems. Programming is about designing, developing, deploying, and executing programs that enable and support computations. There are many types of computations, and so, there are many types of programming problems. Thus, there are many ways to solve those programming problems.

When you design software, you need to design a programming model. The programming model captures the interfaces among elements of the software as well as the functionality of the elements. However, this functionality is represented at a higher level, other than the internal structures, so that the customer can concentrate on what he or she wants to do and not on how to program each element. The detailed design of the elements comes later.

A good user interface (UI) design focuses on the functionality that the UI provides to the user. That's why we can drag and drop icons into folders to manage files, and the user doesn't need to know what mechanism is being used to accomplish it. The UI presents a logical view of the functionality as opposed to the physical reality of the implementation. It describes the features and functions in a way that matches how the intended user thinks and not necessarily how the system should actually work.

A good programming model describes its functionality in a way that matches how the developer wants to think about it. It does not present internal structures, because these are the purview of the developer. Rather, it focuses on the functions of individual elements as well as the functions of elements working together.

One key to software architectures is to master their abstractions. Abstraction is the computer scientist's tool to master complexity. So we try to look at abstractions first and then focus on the implementations of those abstractions. We try to make our

Software Paradigms, By Stephen H. Kaisler.
ISBN 0-471-48347-8   Copyright © 2005 John Wiley & Sons, Inc.

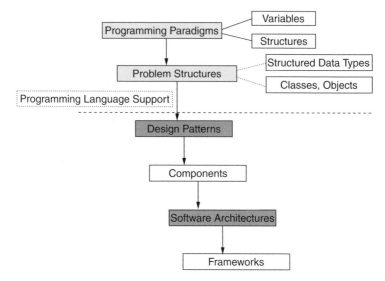

Figure 2-1. Hierarchy of structural paradigms.

implementations map closely to the abstractions of the problems, because it will make the implementations easier to understand. Figure 2-1 shows the progression of abstractions leading up to building complex systems that is used in this book.

Seasoned software developers do not write programs from scratch. They always look for patterns that best match the context of the problem they are trying to solve, and apply them to designing their software. *Design patterns* are design solutions to recurring problems in software construction.

Design patterns are often misconstrued as applicable only to programming in the large. In reality, they can be applied to solving problems in programming in the small such as implementing data structures or simple algorithms. Design patterns can be combined into components that solve larger problems.

Components are usually more complex software artifacts. A component can be based on one or more design patterns. In fact, components are often design patterns made concrete.

Within the object-oriented community, design patterns emerged as one form of programming model. But design patterns proved to be relatively simple solutions to specific programming problems. Designers realized that programmers faced complex problems that required some customization for their solution. By combining patterns and abstracting the commonality of the resulting structure, components emerged as an approach for complex problems. Finally, significant differences exist between problem domains. DARPA realized that certain domains have standard architectural structures, which could be represented by *domain-specific software architectures* (DSSAs). Each DSSA is generally comprised of multiple components plus specifications for their interoperability.

Components are often integrated into frameworks. *Frameworks*, however, have a special characteristic; they are domain-specific. That is, we develop a framework for the purpose of implementing a solution structure to a class of problems within a particular domain. Most frameworks embed one or more software architectures.

There is a natural progression in complexity from programming paradigms to frameworks. Successive layers build upon the elements below them in the hierarchy. I do not discuss programming language paradigms and problem paradigms further, as there are many excellent books that already address these paradigms.

This chapter surveys these paradigms. The remainder of the book will describe the software structure paradigms in more detail.

2.1 PROBLEM PARADIGMS

A *problem paradigm* is a model for solving a class of problems. An *algorithm* represents a solution to a problem. Specifically, an algorithm is a complete, unambiguous procedure for solving a specified problem in a finite number of steps. Algorithms may be deterministic or stochastic. The former always return the same value, while the latter do not necessarily do so.

There may be many algorithms for a particular problem paradigm. For example, there are well over 100 algorithms for sorting a set of elements (independent of the data structure used). These algorithms can be characterized in many different ways.

A *program* represents an instantiation of the algorithm for a class of problems. Specifically, the program implements a particular solution structure for problems from the class. The program may encompass all of the problems of the class or only a few.

Algorithms are embedded in programs, because a program typically does more work than just that specified by the algorithm. The basic data housekeeping and I/O are usually not specified in an algorithm but are part of the program.

Programs may incorporate just one algorithm or many. Programs are typically constructed of functions or procedures (imperative and functional programming), objects (object-oriented programming), or predicates (logic programming). A program may encompass just one function or procedure but is more likely to encompass many functions, procedures, or objects (tens to hundreds to even thousands).

Because algorithms establish the method for solving a problem, they are most often implemented using functional or imperative programming languages. Ideally, we would like to implement an algorithm in a small number of procedures. Some algorithms can be implemented in a single procedure, but more robust and complex algorithms usually require multiple procedures.

There are many ways to classify problems. Choosing a particular classification scheme reflects one's bias about the importance of certain characteristics for describing problems.

2.1.1 Sequential Versus Concurrent Problems

The basis for much software that was written up until the early 1990s was the sequential model embodied in the von Neumann random access machine. This model's basic concepts have been learned by every programmer and so affected the structure of the software developed. Beginning in the mid-1970s, we began to develop concurrent programs for several reasons: to make more effective use of then expensive hardware, to make our programs run faster, and to handle multiple simultaneous tasks at one time.

Sequential Programming   *Sequential programming* is the execution of a program one instruction at a time. Each command is processed in the order in which it is encountered. Sequential programming is usually performed on a uniprocessor. The processor speed is dependent on how fast the data can move through the hardware.

Programs contain a sequence of statements that manipulate the data structures. The main tool for abstraction is the usage of subprograms; this allows us to use the same statements at different locations and divide one task into different operations.

In most sequential programs, once the program begins running, it either prompts for input or reads its input from specified devices. If it is interactive, the user waits on the program while it computes. When it is ready for more input, the program notifies the user, who enters more data. This process iterates until the computation is complete, at which point the program terminates. This model characterizes Lisp's read-eval-print loop. Figure 2-2 illustrates this model.

The final values of the variables in a sequential program depend on the order in which statements are executed. In general, given the same input data, a sequential program will always execute the same sequence of instructions and it will always produce the same results. Thus, sequential program execution is deterministic.

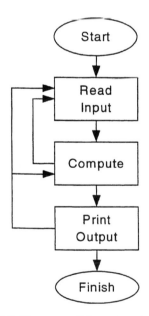

Figure 2-2. The sequential programming model.

Concurrent Programming The term *concurrent programming* (Feldman 1990) usually refers to the kind of programming required to support simultaneous activities in a software application. Put differently, concurrent programming is the set of techniques and tools used in programming activities that dynamically share information with one another. However, concurrent programming can refer to a variety of programming models. Concurrency may be apparent or real (Kaisler 1997). Concurrent programs may be executed on uniprocessors, multiprocessors, parallel processors, or distributed processors.

What is concurrent programming? A large task can either be performed serially, one step following another, or be decomposed into smaller tasks to be performed simultaneously, that is, in parallel. So concurrent programming is a strategy for decomposing large tasks into multiple smaller tasks, each of which can be executed simultaneously with the others. Concurrency is achieved by:

- Breaking up the task into smaller tasks.
- Assigning the smaller tasks to multiple workers to work on simultaneously.
- Coordinating the workers.
- Not breaking up the task so small that it takes longer to tell the worker what to do than it does to do it.

In multiprocessing, more than one processor is available to execute programs. The basic model for multiprocessing is the parallel random access machines (PRAMs) (Keller et al. 2001). The simplest PRAM assumes an unlimited number of virtual processors and an unlimited memory, all of which is accessible to each processor with unlimited bandwidth. Applying constraints to the simplest PRAM model yields other models that can exhibit interesting behavioral and performance characteristics. A basic constraint is the property of finiteness—in processors, memory size, and bandwidth—that forces some accommodation by the programmer on the software. (See Table 2-1.)

We won't delve into the PRAM model further in this book.

Parallel Programming A special form of concurrent programming is *parallel programming* in which a program is written to run on multiple physical processors. Parallel programming involves:

- Decomposing an algorithm or data into parts.
- Distributing the parts as tasks, which are worked on by multiple processors simultaneously.
- Coordinating work and communications of those processors.

Table 2-1. Classification of programs

Program	Uniprocessor	Multiprocessor
Sequential program	Sequential execution	Multiprogramming
Concurrent program	Apparent concurrency	Real concurrency

Writing parallel programs is currently much more difficult than writing sequential programs. The difficulty comes mostly from three aspects:

1. Managing the control flow along multiple threads of execution.
2. Managing the placement and access of global data.
3. Synchronizing events in such a way that program execution is deterministic and parallel speedup is achieved.

While it is possible for a programmer or end-user to explicitly develop a parallel program by indicating which tasks execute when, how tasks communicate and synchronize, and where data should be placed and how it can be accessed, such an undertaking is extremely complex.

There is not now nor will there ever be a single software paradigm that is suitable for all parallel processing applications. Coupled with the fact that 90% of all scientific and engineering computations can be parallelized, the need for the scientific/engineering programmer to understand multiple architectural paradigms is obvious.

There are several approaches to constructing parallel applications:

- Functional parallelism—different tasks done at the same time.
- Master–slave parallelism—one process assigns subtask to other processes.
- SPMD parallelism (single program, multiple data)—same code replicated to each process.

A few of these will be explored in Section 18.2.

2.1.2 Transformational Versus Reactive Programs

Another way to look at problems is how the data is handled. Most problems can be divided into transformational or reactive problems.

A *transformational program* is one in which the input data is read and processed and the results are output. Most programming skills that we teach today focus primarily on developing transformational software that will execute on sequential machines. Transformational programs can be expressed as functions over M inputs yielding N outputs. Transformational programs are exemplified by the batch processing software architecture described in Section 13.2.

Reactive programs interact with their environment while the program is executing. In general, a reactive program cannot be specified as a function. In most examples, it cannot receive new inputs while it is executing, so its behavior depends on its current state and the value of its inputs. Reactive programs are exemplified by the event handling software architecture or the blackboard software architecture, which are described in Section 16.2.

Transformational programs are a specialized kind of reactive programs—one in which the interaction usually occurs only at the beginning and end of the program.

Effects of Concurrency Transformational programs can be parallelized. Transformational programs that operate on regular data structures such as vectors and arrays are easily parallelized.

Reactive programs are inherently nondeterministic, although components of the program may be written in a deterministic manner. Some reactive programs read data at fixed points. The value(s) of the input(s) forces the processing to be performed by the program. Consider a computer chess program. At each move by the human player, the number of valid inputs is limited by the finiteness of the chess board and the current game state. However, from among the multiple possible inputs, the human player chooses one which directs the future course of the game from among the myriad possible games that can be played. The computer player calculates a set of move responses, selects one, and plays it. The outcome of any single game can only be specified at the last move by either player.

Other reactive programs can read or receive input at any time during their execution. The program may be interrupted at any point by input from the user. The input may be valid or invalid, but the program is expected to deal with it. Such programs are inherently concurrent. A good example is the modern graphical user interface for most desktop workstations.

2.2 A FUNCTIONAL CLASSIFICATION OF PROBLEMS

Yet another way to classify problems is by the type of functionality they exhibit. By functionality, we mean here the ability to perform a particular type of computation. Sorting, searching, indexing, and so on are all types of operations that can be performed on a set.

2.2.1 Search

Search is one of the oldest problems to which computers have been applied. Basically, search is the process of identifying data from some, possibly infinite, solution space (set of possible solutions). A simple search, but computationally intensive, might be to find the gazillionth prime number, where "gazillion" is an incredibly large number.

Suppose we have a collection of data items of some specific type (e.g., integers). We want to determine if a particular data item is in the collection. The particular data item we want to find is called the *key*. The task is to search the records in the data set to find one that "matches" the key.

Searching means different things to different people. Searching for the global maximum or minimum of a function is the problem of unconstrained optimization, which involves a computational aspect. Chess playing programs search for the best move to make next by using alpha-beta minimax search, which is an exhaustive search of the possible moves using a variation of backtracking. This is also a computational approach but differs in the underlying algorithmic structure.

A large number of algorithms have been proposed for searching small and large data sets with varying levels of efficiency and different data representations. We won't address algorithmic efficiency in this book, but we will try to highlight how different search algorithms are embedded in larger software structures.

2.2.2 Decision

Decision is a problem with a yes/no answer: determining whether some potential solution to a question is actually a solution or not. A particular form of decision is to determine whether some element is a member of a set, which usually devolves to a search problem. In computer science, the parsing phase of a compiler tries to decide whether or not a given string is an element of the language that the compiler accepts.

Binary decisions are usually represented as yes/no questions. Many decisions can be cast as deterministic problems.

However, there are some decisions that are nondeterministic. Some artificial intelligence problems exemplify this class of decisions. Different answers result from the order of presentation and the completeness (or incompleteness) of the input data.

If there is an algorithm that is able to correctly decide for every possible input element whether it belongs to the set, then the problem is called *decidable*; otherwise it is called *undecidable*. If there is an algorithm that can always answer "yes" when the element is in the set, but the algorithm runs forever without halting when it isn't in the set, then the language is *partially decidable*.

2.2.3 Classification

The general classification problem attempts to partition a set of objects into a discrete set of categories or classes according to a specified set of criteria. Numerous classification algorithms have been developed based on different mechanisms from pattern recognition (probability-based) to artificial intelligence (feature-based).

Classification continues to be an important research topic in computer science. Today, data mining is a primary area for research into classification methods. Such methods vary from small (kilobytes) to large (megabytes) to very large (terabytes or beyond). A good reference book is *Classification Algorithms* by James (1985).

2.2.4 Generation and Enumeration

Generation and enumeration problems focus on specifying discrete objects according to a specified set of criteria. The primary difference between these two techniques is that enumeration produces a sequential set of objects ordered according to the values of one or more attributes. Generation, on the other hand, may produce objects in any order, with the values of the attributes drawn from varying domains.

The enumeration process generally tries to produce all possible values for a given set of criteria, while generation produces a discrete number of such values. The complexity of the criteria and the computation involved can be quite large for large, complex data sets. An interesting book to consider is *Hacker's Delight* by Warren (2002).

2.2.5 Aggregation and Clustering

Aggregation is the process of evaluating a large number of objects to determine which ones share a common relationship and, usually, then to characterize that relationship through some form of description. Clustering is the problem of partitioning a set of N objects into a set of K clusters such that the objects in a cluster are more similar to each other than they are to objects in other clusters. Generally, the number of clusters K is not known beforehand.

Clustering algorithms are usually fast and quite simple. They need no beforehand knowledge of the used data and form a solution by comparing the given samples to each other and to the *clustering criterion*. The results may vary greatly when using a different kind of clustering criteria and thus unfortunately nonsense solutions are also possible. In addition, with some algorithms the order in which the original samples are introduced can make a great difference to the result. A classic book in this area is *Clustering Algorithms* by Hartigan (1975).

2.2.6 Sorting

Sorting is the process of arranging some set of objects in a specified order. It is a fundamental operation in computer science. Indeed, efficient searching of data sets often depends on whether or not the data are already sorted. Figure 2-3 briefly illustrates this, where f is the sorting function.

One can sort on the data themselves or on keys that are subsets of the data. Most algorithms are variations on these approaches. Perhaps the best book ever written on sorting and searching is by Knuth (1973), which has gone through several revisions.

Numerous sorting algorithms have been defined with varying degrees of efficiency in space and time based on the number of objects to be sorted. We won't address

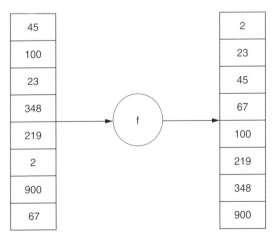

Figure 2-3. A sorting example.

algorithmic efficiency in this book, but we will try to highlight how different sorting algorithms are embedded in larger software structures.

2.2.7 Graph Traversal

The most fundamental graph problem is to traverse every edge and vertex in a graph in a systematic way. Because graphs are a powerful data organization and representation mechanism, graph traversal is a fundamental problem of computer science. Most of the operations that are performed on graphs require graph traversal, including:

- Printing or validating the contents of each edge and/or vertex.
- Copying a graph, or converting between alternate representations.
- Counting the number of edges and/or vertices.
- Identifying the connected components of the graph.
- Finding paths between two vertices, or cycles if they exist.

Any maze can be represented as a graph with each junction being a vertex and each hallway being an edge. Traversal algorithms must be powerful enough to find their way through an arbitrary maze. To do so, we must mark vertices when we have visited them. To solve many problems requires traversal of all or a large part of a graph. But we must first explore the graph to determine it breadth, depth, and connectivity. Thus, part of the traversal algorithm includes the data management for recording the structure of the graph.

A classic example of graph traversal is the Seven Bridges of Konigsberg, which are depicted in Figure 2-4.

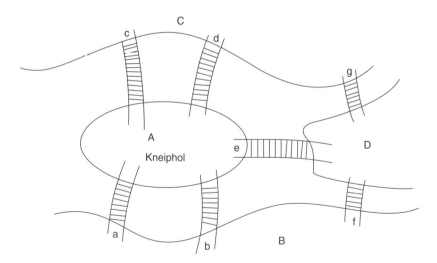

Figure 2-4. The Seven Bridges of Konigsberg.

Two good books in this area are *Graphs* by Berge (1985) and *Graph Algorithms* by Even (1979).

2.3 PROGRAMMING LANGUAGES

The principle means of composing software is to use a programming language. Features and characteristics of programming languages affect our choice and, thereby, the quality of our software solutions.

There have been many hundreds of programming languages designed and implemented—some general purpose, many special purpose. Jean Sammet (1969) listed over 700 programming languages that were being used, dying, or dead as of the late 1960s. Some that were widely used two decades ago have been superseded by newer languages with better features. The trend that keeps repeating itself is that experience with a language generates useful ideas, which are embedded in new programming languages.

One way this occurs is an attempt to eliminate conflicting goals from a programming language design. A tendency has been to put every feature that the language designer thinks is useful into a programming language. The result is that a simple and, perhaps, efficient language ends up more complex than was intended. Eventually, a user gets fed up and invents a new, streamlined language that captures the simple (original) ideas while eliminating the complexity. Java as a follow-on to C++ is a particular example. Some users or corporations will be frustrated by Java and start to add additional features to meet their needs and . . . well, you get the idea.

Programming language design is not a dead science. Over the past decade several new languages have emerged, including Perl, HTML/XML, AMPL, and Active VRML to name a few. Each of these languages meets a specialized need. For example, AMPL is used to express complex mathematical expressions, while Active VRML, derived from the CAML family, has been designed for the transmission of virtual reality scenarios across networks.

2.3.1 Programming Language Paradigms

Many programming languages are essentially similar in design. This is largely due to the influence of the von Neumann architecture for computer systems. The von Neumann architecture is based on the fetch–execute cycle; this has affected the way we store and retrieve variables in a programming language. Languages reflecting this archetype are called *imperative languages.*

Programming paradigms embody the results of people's ideas on how to construct programs and formal mechanisms for how those ideas should be expressed. People's notions of software engineering principles and practices often influence the design of programming languages as well.

Programming concepts can be expressed in many different paradigms. The choice of a programming paradigm can greatly ease the task of programming if the paradigm is appropriate to the problem at hand. But it is choosing an appropriate paradigm that is the hard part. Often, programmers learn just one paradigm and live with it throughout their programming careers. They will try to force every problem, no matter how "hairy," into that paradigm. The result is poor code that may be inefficient, unreadable, or worse.

If programmers learned different paradigms, their strengths and weaknesses, they might be better equipped to choose the best paradigm suited to a particular problem class. This begets the question of what are the best candidates for programming paradigms for a particular problem class.

Another reason for learning multiple programming paradigms arises from the emphasis on software reuse. As software systems become larger and more complex, it is more likely that subsystems will be written in different languages, which adhere to different programming paradigms. Programmers need to understand the different paradigms to be able to maintain such systems as well as to be able to properly interconnect the components and subsystems at their interfaces.

Programming languages fall into two categories: imperative and declarative. *Imperative languages*, such as Fortran, C, and Ada, enable programmers to express algorithms for solving problems. Declarative languages, such as Lisp, Prolog, and Haskell, allow the programmer to specify what has to be computed, but not how the computation is done.

Declarative languages can be subdivided into functional languages and logic languages. Lisp was the first functional programming language. Prolog is a well-known logic programming language.

Declarative languages offer three distinct advantages. First, they are inherently "high level" because they specify the logic of what is to happen, not how it will happen. The mechanics are often hidden from the programmer. Indeed, through backtracking, many thorny issues relating to iteration and recursion are avoided. Second, data may be represented both extensionally—as explicit facts—and intensionally—as a rule that describes a set of facts. Moreover, reverse reactions can be represented by a rule that reverses the extensional representation of the forward reaction. Finally, because of this ease of data representation, declarative programming languages are very useful for rapidly prototyping data structures and code to express complex ideas.

Applicative programming is a style that prohibits assignment statements or other statements that have the effect of changing the values of variables. Side effects are dealt with directly by ruling them out explicitly. Pure Lisp, as originally defined by John McCarthy, is probably the best example of an applicative language. For the purposes of this book, we will treat applicative programming like functional programming.

Every programming paradigm comes with its own terminology and metaphors. You will need to understand the terminology and the metaphors in order to understand how the paradigm works.

2.3.2 Imperative Programming Languages

Imperative programming is characterized by programming with a state and commands that modify the state. When imperative programming is combined with subprograms,

$$S_0 \times Op_0 \rightarrow S_1 \times Op_1 \rightarrow S_2 \times Op_2 \rightarrow \cdots S_{n-1} \times Op_{n-1} \rightarrow S_n$$

Figure 2-5. State transitions.

it is called *procedural programming*. In either case, the implication is clear. Programs are directions or orders for performing an action.

Imperative programming is the oldest and most popular paradigm for programming languages. It has also been called "procedural programming," although this is something of a misnomer because other paradigms also have procedures (or functions). Procedural languages are a subset of imperative languages because they incorporate constructs for modularizing source code in the form of procedures or functions, which are called with parameters and which return control to the caller.

Imperative programming languages arose from the need to program von Neumann machines in higher level abstractions that were independent of the particular machine's instruction set. At the heart of these machines is the concept of a modifiable store. Variables and assignments are the programming language analog of the modifiable store. The store is the object that is manipulated by the program. Imperative programming languages provide a variety of commands to provide structure to code and to manipulate the store. Each imperative programming language defines a particular view of hardware.

All imperative programming languages share a common conceptual approach to program design. Programs consist of sequences of statements that perform actions that cause changes of state, usually through assignment operations. In imperative programming, a name may be assigned to a value and later reassigned to another value. The collection of names and the associated values and the location of control in the program constitute the *state* of the program. The state is a logical model of storage, which is an association between memory locations and values. A program in execution generates a sequence of states as depicted in Figure 2-5. The transition from one state to the next is determined by assignment operations and sequencing commands.

Imperative programming languages are used to define algorithms through the composition of individual commands or statements representing elementary computational steps that are combined into larger units. Fine-grain composition is accomplished through control structures such as iteration, selection, and sequencing. Coarse-grain composition is accomplished through encapsulation mechanisms such as blocks, functions, and procedures.

There are a plethora of imperative programming languages. Indeed, the history of computer science for the first twenty or so years is the history of the development of imperative programming languages written large (Sammet 1969). Object-oriented programming languages borrow much from imperative programming languages.

2.3.3 Functional Programming Languages

Functional programming is so called because a program consists entirely of functions. The main program itself is written as a function that receives the program's input as its argument and delivers the program's output as its result. Typically, the main function is defined in terms of other functions, which in turn are defined in terms of still more functions, until at the bottom level the functions are language primitives.

Functional programs contain no assignment statements, so variables, once given a value, never change. More generally, functional programs contain no side effects at all. A function call can have no effect other than to compute its result. This eliminates a major source of bugs and also makes the order of execution irrelevant—since no side effect can change the value of an expression, it can be evaluated at any time. This relieves the programmer of the burden of prescribing the flow of control.

Since expressions can be evaluated at any time, one can freely replace variables by their values and vice versa; that is, programs are "referentially transparent." The value of a function is determined solely by its arguments' values.

Functional programming languages are a subset of the declarative languages. Functional programming languages (FPLs) have been developed extensively over the past thirty years. Numerous FPLs have been developed at universities as research tools for exploring new language concepts and structures. Examples include Haskell (Thompson 1999, Haskell 2002), SML (2002), and CAML (2002).

There is no general agreement on what constitutes a functional programming language. The newsgroup comp.lang.functional offers the following definition:

> Functional programming is a style of programming that emphasizes the evaluation of expressions, rather than execution of commands. The expressions in these languages are formed by using functions to combine basic values. A functional language is a language that supports and encourages programming in a functional style.

Most functional programming languages implement some nonfunctional features such as input/output.

Functional programmers argue they are an order of magnitude more productive than their imperative counterparts, because functional programs are an order of magnitude shorter. It is not completely clear why this should be. A plausible reason is that conventional programs consist of 70% or more assignment statements. In strict functional programs these are omitted! But this argument is somewhat dubious. If omitting assignment statements brought such enormous benefits in program size reduction, then Fortran programmers would have been doing it for twenty years. It is a logical impossibility to make a language more powerful by omitting features, no matter how bad they may be presumed to be.

2.3.4   Object-Oriented Programming Languages

Programming languages have traditionally divided the world into two parts—data and operations on data. Data is neither static nor immutable; the operations may change it. The procedures and functions that operate on data have no lasting state of their own; they're useful only in their ability to affect data.

Object-oriented programming is characterized by programming with objects, messages, and hierarchies of objects. Object-oriented programming shifts the emphasis from data as passive elements defined by relations or acted on by functions and procedures to active elements interacting with their environment. Emphasis also shifts from describing control flow to describing interacting objects.

Object-oriented programming collects operations and data into modular units called *objects*, each with a state and a set of operations to transform the state. It allows the combination of objects into structured networks to form a complete program. In an object-oriented programming language, objects and object interactions are the basic elements of design.

Object-oriented programming does not have to be imperative, but most successful OOPLs have been implemented on top of or influenced by imperative languages. All data are objects, all objects are treated uniformly, and all computation proceeds by passing messages between objects. Each object implements operations defined for it. Control takes the form of messages that are passed between objects. Some messages are requests to objects to transform themselves (e.g., change their state).

Object-oriented design is based on the following concepts (Hoare 1972):

- *Abstraction:* The decision to concentrate on properties that are shared by many objects or situations in the real world, and to ignore the differences between them.
- *Representation:* The choice of a set of symbols to stand for the abstraction.
- *Manipulation:* The rules for transformation of the symbolic representation as a means of predicting the effect of a similar manipulation in the real world.
- *Axiomatization:* The rigorous statement of those properties that have been abstracted from the real world and that are shared by manipulation of the real world and the symbols that represent it.

Object-oriented programming exploits two key ideas that are essential to a successful software engineering effort:

- *Information Hiding:* The ability to use language scope rules to restrict visibility of data to "local" procedures.
- *Reuse:* The ability to leverage existing types and/or code to simplify the development process by reusing rather than developing code.

Niklaus Wirth (1975) has noted "The task of composition of operations is often considered the heart of the art of programming. . . . However, it will become evident that the appropriate composition of data is equally fundamental and appropriate."

Bertrand Meyer (1992) has suggested "seven steps to object-based (oriented) happiness":

1. Object-based modular structure.
2. Data abstraction.
3. Automatic memory management.
4. Classes.

5. Inheritance.

6. Polymorphism and dynamic binding.

7. Multiple and repeated inheritance.

There's a tendency to think of objects as "actors" and to endow them with human-like intentions and abilities. It's tempting sometimes to talk about an object "deciding" what to do about a situation, "asking" other objects for information, "introspecting" about itself to get requested information, "delegating" responsibility to another object, or "managing" a process. Objects really do none of this. They are programmed to respond to events that are evidenced by method invocations. It is this active approach to execution that, viewed from a higher level, suggests that a set of objects is an active community that "converses" among its members to solve problems.

We can get carried away pursuing this anthropomorphic metaphor.

2.3.5 Logic Programming Languages

Logic programming is another form of declarative programming. Logic programming languages (LPLs) provide constructs for defining atomic relationships among values by asserting facts and rules about them in the form of "implications" in which at most one conclusion derives from the conjunction of zero or more conditions. The logic used is first order. The clauses constituting a logic program are mutually independent but cannot be treated as objects in their own right. Programs are executed by supplying a proposition and attempting to ascertain its truth. As a side effect, values are assigned to variables that can provide useful answers.

Prolog is an example of a logic programming language. It implements a subset of second-order logic (e.g., it can deal with sets as well as atomic propositions), but the language's flexibility allows propositions that lie well outside the boundaries of any classification of formal logical systems. For practical applications, Prolog seems to be the language of choice.

Prolog provides two features not present in functional languages—built-in search and the ability to compute with partial information. This contrasts with functional languages, where computations always are directed, require all arguments to be known, and give exactly one answer. A simple example of how predicates can be used to compute in several modes and with partial information is the following predicate for appending two lists:

```
append([],Ys,Ys).
append([X|Xs],Ys,[X|Zs]) :- append(Xs,Ys,Zs).
```

Append can be used not only to put two lists together, but also to take a list apart or to append some as yet unknown list to another one.

The built-in search capability makes it easier to formulate many problems. If we define what we mean by a subset of a list as the following predicate,

```
subset([],[]).
subset([X|Xs],[X|Ys]) :- subset(Xs,Ys).
subset([_|Xs],Ys) :- subset(Xs,Ys).
```

we can easily compute all subsets by asking the system to find them:

```
?- findall(Xs,subset([1,2,3],Xs),Xss).

Xss = [[1,2,3],[1,2],[1,3],[1],[2,3],[2],[3],[]]
```

Built-in search is powerful but introduces complexity in the implementation. Most LPLs provide a weak implementation of declarative programming that requires the programmer to provide some control information (cuts) for efficiency.

2.3.6 Understanding Programming Languages

Why do we need to understand programming languages, as opposed to understanding how to write programs in them? There are several reasons, but a few are reasonably obvious.

A large part of the practice of computer science involves programming. Inevitably, in some form, you will come in contact with a programming language. Indeed, it is hard to imagine how one could get a degree in computer science without doing any programming whatsoever. Thus, the practice of computer science requires that we have a good working knowledge of the programming languages we or our colleagues are likely to use.

As a program manager, you might be called upon to choose a programming language for use in a project. Before you rush blindly to choose C++ or some other popular flavor of programming language of the day, perhaps it is worthwhile to step back and ask exactly what the requirements of the project are and what programming languages might best be suited to meet those requirements. Choosing programming languages involves a number of factors: sociological, technological, economic, and, oh yes, political. We'll focus mostly on the technological issues in this book.

Much rarer, but certainly possible, is the call to design and implement a new programming language. We must understand what has been successful in the past, what the key requirements for the new language are, and what the key technological ideas driving the use and implementation of programming languages are today.

The crux of the problem we face is: What does it mean to understand a programming language? This is a difficult question to answer. If we are going to write programs in a particular language, then we need to know its syntax and semantics, but we also need to know its pragmatics. Pragmatic knowledge comes through direct experience. It is the knowledge that enables us to program effectively and efficiently in the language; but it also is the metaknowledge about the programming environment that allows us to build complex applications using the available tools. We feel that understanding is more than just syntax, semantics, and pragmatics. It is also understanding how the language can help solve problems.

2.3.7   Choosing Programming Languages for Problems

Our ultimate goal, then, is to be able to choose the best programming language for a particular problem type. But how does one go about it? And what do we mean by "best"? This leads to three assertions that are open research topics:

1. There is *no* one programming language that is right for all problems.
2. We do *not* know yet if there is one programming language that is best for a particular class of problems.
3. We do *not* yet have the right set of metrics for deciding if this is so.

Given any problem, you may just be urged to use C or, more likely, C++. But suppose the problem has severe real-time constraints. Is C/C++ the best possible choice for such a problem?

Suppose you are writing a large, complex application consisting of tens or hundreds of thousands of lines of code. What language should you choose?

2.3.8   Choosing Algorithms

Choosing a programming language is only part of the solution of a problem. You also need to choose an algorithm and, concurrently, data structures to support that algorithm. Different algorithms yield different performance. Good software engineers have one or more algorithm texts on their bookshelves. Hackers have software manuals for the latest software package, which they'll have to replace next year.

Algorithm selection can be based on a large number of factors: memory space, efficiency, number of iterations, convergence to a solution, and so on. We are often concerned with how execution time and memory space increase as the size of the data set scales. But other factors, such as ease of implementation, presentation of results, and interaction with other algorithms, also should concern us. Numerous books have been written on algorithm analysis and selection, but a particularly good one is *Handbook of Algorithms and Data Structures*, 2nd Ed. by Gonnet and Baeza-Yates (1991).

2.4   DESIGN PATTERNS

Patterns have their origin in object-oriented programming, where they began as collections of objects organized to solve a problem. There isn't any fundamental relationship between patterns and objects; it just happens they began there. Patterns may have arisen because objects seem so elemental, but the problems we were trying to solve with them were so complex.

The Gang of Four (Gamma et al. 1995) coined the phrase "design pattern." A design pattern is a proven solution for a general design problem. It consists of communicating objects that are customized to solve the problem in a particular context.

The usefulness of the solution a pattern represents has been proved in many designs. As such, it captures the design experience of experienced programmers.

A designer who is familiar with such patterns can apply them immediately to design problems without having to rediscover them. This way, design patterns make it easier to reuse successful designs and architectures. Expressing proven techniques as design patterns makes them more accessible to developers of new systems. Design patterns help you choose design alternatives that make a system reusable and avoid alternatives that compromise reusability. Design patterns can also improve the documentation and maintenance of existing systems by furnishing an explicit specification of class and objects interactions and their underlying "intent."

Put simply, design patterns help a designer get a design "right" faster. The design patterns are not about designs such as linked lists and hash tables that can be encoded in classes and reused as is. Nor are they complex, domain-specific designs for an entire application or subsystem.

2.4.1 Types of Patterns

Brad Appleton (Appleton 1999) notes that others have made distinctions in conceptual levels of patterns, such as Buschmann et al. (1996) who defines three types of patterns:

Architectural Patterns: An architectural pattern expresses a fundamental structural organization or schema for software systems. It provides a set of predefined subsystems, specifies their responsibilities, and includes rules and guidelines for organizing the relationships between them.

Design Patterns: A design pattern provides a scheme for refining the subsystems or components of a software system, or the relationships between them. It describes commonly recurring structure of communicating components that solves a general design problem within a particular context.

Idioms: An idiom is a low-level pattern specific to a particular programming language. An idiom describes how to implement particular aspects of components or the relationships between them using the features of the given language.

The difference between these three kinds of patterns are in their corresponding levels of abstraction and detail. Architectural patterns are high-level strategies that concern large-scale components and the global properties and mechanisms of a system. They have wide-sweeping implications that affect the overall skeletal structure and organization of a software system. Design patterns are medium-scale tactics that flesh out some of the structure and behavior of entities and their relationships. They do not influence overall system structure, but instead define microarchitectures of subsystems and components. Idioms are paradigm-specific and language-specific programming techniques that fill in low-level internal or external details of a component's structure or behavior.

2.4.2 Pattern Languages

The concept of a pattern language has been developed by Christopher Alexander (1977, 1979) and his colleagues in architecture and urban design. A pattern language is a network of patterns of varying scales; each pattern is embodied as a concrete prototype and is related to larger scale patterns which it supports, and to smaller scale patterns which support it. The goal of a pattern language is to capture patterns in their contexts and to provide a mechanism for understanding the nonlocal consequences of design decisions.

During the last decade, the pattern language approach has attracted a lot of interest in the field of object-oriented software design. The software patterns community focuses on using patterns to capture accepted practice and support generalization; Alexander's central concern is using patterns to achieve the ineffable "quality without a name," which characterizes great architecture.

A pattern language is not intended to be a book of patterns that is followed by rote. It is actually a metalanguage which is used to generate languages for particular problem domains. Designers modify existing patterns and create new patterns that reflect the characteristics, constraints, methodology, and practices of the designer's community.

2.5 COMPONENTS

Patterns are abstract concepts that describe solutions to problems. Patterns are instantiated as components—concrete implementations of abstract concepts.

There are many definitions for the term "component." Here are a few selected definitions:

> A software component is a unit of composition with contractually specified interfaces and explicit context dependencies only. A software component can be deployed independently and is subject to third-party composition.
>
> —Clemens Szyperski

> A component is a non-trivial, nearly-independent, and replaceable part of a system that fulfills a clear function in the context of a well-defined architecture. A component conforms to and provides the physical realization of a set of interfaces.
>
> —Philippe Krutchen

> A run-time software component is a dynamically bindable package of one or more programs accessed through documented interfaces that can be discovered at run time.
>
> —Gartner Group

We see component software as an object-based software model aimed at efficient and incremental software development. The main idea is to break monolithic applications into reusable, binary components that can be developed, distributed, and upgraded independently. To accomplish this, we need to provide standard mechanisms for interoperability between applications and components. If components can interoperate, they can be combined to build larger applications in a flexible and incremental way.

We believe that component-based software development will improve programmer productivity and software quality because:

- Less new code must be written to produce the same results.
- Off-the-shelf components should be "well-seasoned" and therefore more reliable than code written from scratch.

More and more individualized components are being developed (and tested and deployed). These components are combined by users to fulfill specific tasks, replacing large monolithic applications. As the usage of components increases rapidly, the importance of component interoperability and configuration management will also increase rapidly. A component must be compatible and interoperate with a whole range of other components.

2.5.1 Component-Based Software Versus Object-Oriented Development

Leeb (1996) has suggested that component-based development differs from object-oriented programming in several ways. First, components interoperate at runtime and can therefore be integrated in applications in a flexible and dynamic way. Second, interface descriptions are separated from the actual implementation of a component, which makes it possible to develop and update components independently. To implement code that refers to a component, only the interface specification of that component is needed.

Leeb also notes that components have several disadvantages. First, developing a component is a complex task and usually requires several months, perhaps years, of background training, even for professional programmers. Second, components provide little support for dynamic modification. They typically have a specific functionality that cannot be modified or extended. Their interfaces are determined at compile time and are immutable.

Finally, in order to build applications that use components, one has to use a conventional programming tool. Even the more user-friendly tools that support component integration, for example, Visual Basic, require at least several weeks of learning and are therefore too complex for the average end-user. Furthermore, users depend entirely on developers for component functionality. For one, in the growing market of components it becomes hard to find out what's available. On the other hand, because available components will usually not fit exactly the requirements of a specific application, a lot of customizing and glue programming are often required to make their behavior appear slightly different. Finally, new versions of the development platform may not support older components, because the component standards are constantly evolving.

2.5.2 Interconnection

As the size and complexity of software systems grow, the interconnection dependencies among various pieces of a system have become responsible for an increasingly important part of the development effort. A variety of interconnection relationships exist such as communication, data translation, resource sharing, and synchronization relationships.

At the implementation level, software systems are sets of source and executable modules in one or more programming languages. Although modules come under a variety of names (procedures, packages, objects, clusters, etc.), they are all essentially abstractions for components.

Programming Language Support   Most programming languages directly support a small set of primitive interconnection mechanisms, such as procedure calls, method invocation, or shared variables. Few programming languages support the notion of components or frameworks as a first class citizen of the language definition. Rather, they leave this concept to be handled by the development environment.

These mechanisms are not sufficient for managing more complex dependencies. Complex dependencies require the introduction of more complex managing protocols. Because modern programming languages do not provide support for these protocols, the programmer is forced to embed additional code into components, including multiple interconnection mechanisms, to emulate them. Thus, two components may have to conduct a dialogue in order to exchange the necessary information for a complex interaction. Alternatively, the syntax and semantics of the protocols become increasingly complex and specialized to the communications between pairs of components.

Dependencies Among Components   Some possible dependencies that may exist among components include:

- *Flow Dependencies:* Flow dependencies represent relationships between producers and consumers of resources. Coordination protocols for managing flows decompose into protocols that ensure accessibility of the resource by the consumers, usability of the resource, as well as synchronization between producers and consumers.

- *Sharing Dependencies:* They encode relationships among consumers who use the same resource or producers who produce for the same consumers. Coordination protocols for sharing dependencies ensure proper enforcement of the sharing properties, usually by dividing a resource among competing users, or by enforcing mutual exclusion protocols.

- *Timing Dependencies:* Timing dependencies express constraints on the relative flow of control among a set of activities. Examples include prerequisite dependencies and mutual exclusion dependencies.

Interoperability Issues   Two main issues arise with respect to interoperability information: how to express interoperability information and how to publish this information.

Interoperability information must be specified at three levels:

1. *Interface Level:* The interface level provides information about the syntax of a component's interface. This may be expressed using an interface description language such as OMG's CORBA IDL, but it does not contain much information about the meanings of the interface described. It addresses the question: Do the components fit together structurally?

2. *Originator Level:* The originator level enhances the interface information by including information from the software development process where the component originated. This includes version information and dependencies of components. It specifies exactly the context in which the component was developed, including which versions of other components it requires, and which documentation and other information are associated with it. During development, this information is often available, as the developer needs to investigate interoperability issues, but subsequently it gets lost again. The originator level relies on the developer to provide this information in the development process. It addresses the question: Which types and versions of components work together?

3. *Semantic Level:* The semantic level provides a description of a component's functionality. No general established way of describing complete semantic information about components exists. Its implementation, the source code, is often the only existing formal description of a component's semantics. The ideal case of a complete formal specification of the semantics that is sufficiently abstract and independent from the implementation rarely exists. Solutions are available only for specific classes of problems, for example, which may be described by finite automata or by algebraic specifications. This level addresses the question: Do the components work together on a specific semantic level?

The interface level is not sufficient for a proper employment of a component, as it does not provide complete information about how to correctly use it (Brown and McDermid 1991). The semantic level, on the other hand, provides full information about the meanings and behavior of a component. In order to access this information, its implementation would need to be studied in-depth, but the source code is rarely published and is not easily understandable. However, a component's user often is not interested in the implementation details, but only in a more abstract description of what it does. Unfortunately, no general established and understandable abstract way to describe component semantics exists yet.

2.6 SOFTWARE ARCHITECTURES

An architectural paradigm is a way of thinking about computing systems, for example, their configuration and design. By computing systems, we mean the hardware, the software, and the telecommunications components. A set of components gathered together does not provide us with a problem solution. We must impose a topology for interaction and communication upon them—an architectural style—and ensure that the components both integrate (physically communicate) as well as interoperate (logically communicate).

Software architecture focuses on a high-level description of the system. We view the structure of the system and its functionality as a whole, including its dynamic functionality. We can assess the architecture for the nonbehavioral requirements: performance, security, reliability, scalability, and extensibility, among others.

Certain design methodologies do lead to certain types of components, but many types of components may be identified that are common to many methodologies. The use of standard models of software components supports reusability. If components are to be procured and reused in the context of different design methodologies, then the conceptual model of a component should be independent of the notation, terminology, and so on associated with a specific design methodology or a specific architecture.

2.6.1 Software Architecture Patterns

Based on the extensive experience in developing large and complex software programs over the past several decades, practitioners have come to realize that some architectural structures repeat themselves—software architecture patterns. A number of these patterns have been described in Garlan and Shaw (1994), who refer to them as software architecture styles, and analyzed in the literature. Part III discusses these patterns in detail. See Section 2.8 for additional references.

2.6.2 Software Architecture Description Languages

According to Clements and Kogut (1995), an architecture description language (ADL) is a set of notations, languages, standards, and conventions for an architectural model. An ADL is a language that is designed specifically for the representation and analysis of software architectures. An ADL defines a formal syntax for expressing architectures and assigns a semantic interpretation.

Several software architecture description languages (SADLs) have been developed to describe collections of components, their interconnections, and the protocols that control information exchange and control flow among them (Kogut and Clements 1994). Different languages define interconnections in different ways.

Rapide (Luckham and Vera 1995) connections are mappings from services required by one component to services provided by another component. Unicon (Shaw, DeLine, and Klein 1995) connectors define protocols that are inserted into the system in order to integrate a set of components.

SADLs are discussed further in Section 19.1.

2.7 FRAMEWORKS

One concept closely related to design patterns and components is a *framework*. Many authors agree that an object-oriented framework is a reusable software architecture comprising both design and code, but no generally accepted definition of a framework and its constituent parts exists.

We'll define it as follows: a *software framework* is a reusable miniarchitecture that provides the generic structure and behavior for a family of software abstractions, along with a context of metaphors that specifies their collaboration and use within a given domain. Software frameworks are also referred to as *application frameworks*.

A framework is usually not a complete application: it often lacks the necessary application-specific functionality, although it may include considerable domain knowledge embedded in its definition. Instead, an application may be constructed from one or more frameworks by inserting this missing functionality into the plug-and-play "outlets" provided by the frameworks. Thus, a framework supplies the infrastructure and mechanisms that execute a policy for interaction between abstract components with open implementations.

The Gang of Four defined a framework as "a set of cooperating classes that make up a reusable design for a specific class of software." A framework provides architectural guidance by partitioning the design into abstract classes and defining their responsibilities and collaborations. A developer customizes a framework to a particular application by subclassing and composing instances of framework classes. Again, note the obvious influence of the object-oriented paradigm, although this is not required to use the concept.

Appleton (1999) notes the following:

> The difference between a framework and an ordinary programming library is that a framework employs an inverted flow of control between itself and its clients. When using a framework, one usually just implements a few callback functions or specializes a few classes, and then invokes a single method or procedure. At this point, the framework does the rest of the work for you, invoking any necessary client callbacks or methods at the appropriate time and place. For this reason, frameworks are often said to abide by the Hollywood Principle ("Don't call us, we'll call you.") or the Greyhound Principle ("Leave the driving to us.").

Frameworks first appeared in the literature in conjunction with Smalltalk-80 (Goldberg and Robson 1983). The Smalltalk user interface framework, Model-View-Controller (MVC), is a widely used framework for developing GUI-based applications that has transcended its Smalltalk origins. Apple Computer was one of the first vendors to make extensive use of the framework concept with its MacApp software development environment (Schmucker 1986). Subsequent frameworks focused on user interfaces also, particularly Interviews (Linton et al. 1989) and ET++ (Weinand 1988). Taligent, an IBM and Apple subsidiary, later an IBM subsidiary, and now folded into IBM Corporation, developed a set of object-oriented development tools that is known as the CommonPoint framework.

2.7.1 Design Patterns Versus Frameworks

Design patterns may be employed both in the design and the documentation of a framework. A single framework typically encompasses several design patterns. In fact, a framework can be viewed as the implementation of a system of design patterns. Thus, design patterns and framework are distinctly different entities. As Appleton notes, "a framework is executable software, whereas design patterns represent knowledge and experience about software. In this respect, frameworks are of a physical nature, while patterns are of a logical nature: frameworks are the physical realization of one or more software pattern solutions; patterns are the instructions for how to implement those solutions."

To summarize, the Gang of Four notes the major differences between design patterns and frameworks as follows:

1. Design patterns are more abstract than frameworks. Frameworks can be embodied in code, but only examples of patterns can be embodied in code. A strength of frameworks is that they can be written down in programming languages and not only studied but executed and reused directly. In contrast, design patterns have to be implemented each time they are used. Design patterns also explain the intent, trade-offs, and consequences of a design.

2. Design patterns are smaller architectural elements than frameworks. A typical framework contains several design patterns but the reverse is never true.

3. Design patterns are less specialized than frameworks. Frameworks always contrast; design patterns can be used in nearly any kind of application. While more specialized design patterns are certainly possible, even these wouldn't dictate an application architecture.

2.7.2   Using Frameworks

Developing a framework is an intensive effort, so frameworks should only be developed where many similar applications will be implemented and where the time and effort invested can be recouped.

To develop a framework, you need examples from the application domain. However, you can't have too many examples or your framework will never be completed. Once you get the first version of your framework done, you can develop and test more examples.

A good rule of thumb is to pick three applications that your framework should support and develop these sequentially. Ideally, these applications should be deployed to actual users to garner the necessary feedback to improve the next application. It is difficult to generalize the proper abstractions from a single example, or even two examples if they are not all that different. Three examples should provide enough variety to find many of the common abstractions.

2.7.3   Building Frameworks

Building frameworks is a difficult job. It requires considerable domain analysis. People think concretely, not abstractly. So abstractions must be found bottom-up, by examining multiple concrete examples and generalizing common features and characteristics from them.

Generalization is an iterative procedure. The more examples that you examine the better your abstraction will be. As you consider each example, your abstraction will improve. But improvements will often consist of lots of small changes interleaved with a few big changes that represent major ways of viewing the problem domain.

Here are just a few hints for generalizing:

- Find things that are given different names but are really the same.
- Parameterize to eliminate differences.
- Break large things into small things so that similar components can be found.
- Categorize things that are similar.

There are many other heuristics that can help you in the process of formulating abstractions. They are better explained in a book on software design.

2.7.4 The Role of OLE and CORBA

Microsoft's OLE and OMG's CORBA are two component framework environments that allow users to develop application frameworks. Component frameworks enable the interoperation of independently developed components by limiting the kinds of allowed relationships and by providing a standardized infrastructure for managing them. Only components explicitly written for a framework can interoperate with one another.

There have been many interoperability mechanisms proposed for combining components. Two of the earliest were Apple's OpenDoc (Apple Corp. 1994a, 1994b) and Microsoft's OLE (Brockschmidt 1994). OpenDoc has been subsumed into IBM's SOM technology (Campagnoni 1994), while OLE has been superseded by Microsoft's DCOM technology. Beyond COM/DCOM, Microsoft has developed the .NET framework for software development. A competing framework is Sun Microsystem's J2EE Java-based framework.

2.8 FURTHER READING

Software Architecture Patterns

Buschmann, F. et al. 1996. *Pattern-Oriented Software Architecture—A System of Patterns.* John Wiley & Sons, Hoboken, NJ.

Fowler, M. 2002. *Patterns of Enterprise Application Architecture.* Addison Wesley, Reading, MA.

Jones, C. 2002. Software Architecture Patterns. Master's Thesis, Software Engineering, De Paul University, Chicago, IL.

Schmidt, D. et al. 2000. *Pattern-Oriented Software Architecture: Patterns for Concurrent and Networked Objects.* John Wiley & Sons, Hoboken, NJ.

2.9 EXERCISES

2.1. Smalltalk is usually considered the definitive object-oriented programming language. However, since object-oriented programming became popular, there have been object-oriented extensions made to functional languages (like Lisp), imperative languages (like C), and logic languages (like Prolog). Is object-oriented programming a programming paradigm of the same sort as logic programming, functional programming, and imperative programming?

2.2. It has been said that object orientation is an additional model of computation that can be added on top of an existing paradigm. For example, we might think of Smalltalk as using the object model between objects and the imperative programming model within each class. Can we implement logic programming mechanisms on top of imperative or functional programming languages in an efficient way?

2.3. Is there a problem that cannot be implemented in one of these programming paradigms? Describe it. What are its characteristics?

2.4. Describe the characteristics of an ideal software architecture definition language. Should it look like an existing programming language? [Research Problem]

I

DESIGN PATTERNS

Design patterns have been heavily researched and documented since the Gang of Four (GoF) published their seminal book in 1995. They initially proposed 23 different patterns. Subsequently, other patterns have been developed by such researchers as Schmidt (Schmidt et al. 1996), Lea (1996), and Coplien (Coplien and Schmidt 1995). In addition, the notion of design patterns has widely been extended beyond computer science to other disciplines such as program management and education.

Design patterns, as described in the technical literature, are models of partial solutions. Most often they have been associated with object-oriented programs, although this does not preclude them from occurring in programs based on other paradigms. Typically, a design pattern is defined as a collection of abstract classes, which are specialized relative to a particular problem. They are useful because they allow us to give names to common problems that continually recur in the applications and systems we build.

Design patterns are not designs. A pattern must be instantiated. This means the programmer must write code and, in the process of writing code, make evaluations and trade-offs about how to perform certain operations. A common mistake in using design patterns is to think that patterns will solve your problems. Unfortunately, they don't. You still have to write the functionality.

Design patterns are not components. Components are instantiated building blocks. As noted above, patterns must be instantiated. Patterns are building blocks from the design viewpoint, but not from the implementation perspective.

Patterns are not frameworks. Frameworks, as noted in Chapter 1, are skeletal designs for large problems. Many patterns may be contained within a framework. Because frameworks are usually associated with specific domains, critical design decisions may have already been made about the design and the use of patterns.

Software Paradigms, By Stephen H. Kaisler
ISBN 0-471-48347-8   Copyright © 2005 John Wiley & Sons, Inc.

Frameworks can be extended through subclassing or other mechanisms. Indeed, frameworks are often amalgams of components and design patterns.

This section of the book will examine several design patterns in different ways. We will examine a few design patterns chosen from the GoF book in order to give a flavor of their approach. However, the reader is referred to that book as well the *Pattern Languages of Program Design* (PLoP) books for additional patterns and details (Coplien and Schmidt 1995) We will also look at patterns on a small scale as objects, based on Noble's work, and on a larger scale as algorithms.

3

OVERVIEW OF
DESIGN PATTERNS

Design patterns are a recent software engineering problem-solving discipline that emerged from the object-oriented community. A design pattern is an abstract solution to a problem. As we note later, design patterns arose from the work of Christopher Alexander, but also derive from the success of the Model-View-Controller (MVC) pattern used by Smalltalk-80 for GUI design. Today, there are many categories of design patterns across many technical and nontechnical disciplines. Design pattern definition has become a cottage industry in its own right.

3.1 A BRIEF HISTORY OF PATTERNS

Although patterns have been used for hundreds of years in other disciplines (rug-making, cross-stitch, architecture, etc.), it is only within the past ten years that patterns have become a discipline to be studied within computer science. In 1987, Cunningham and Beck (Beck 1997) used Chris Alexander's (1977, 1979) ideas to develop a small pattern language for Smalltalk-80. Smalltalk-80 was a good choice for this effort because it represented the only pure object-oriented programming language. By 1990, the Gang of Four had begun compiling a catalog of design patterns independently through work on their dissertations. In 1991, Bruce Anderson conducted the first Patterns Workshop at OOPSLA. In 1993, Kent Beck and Grady Booch organized the first meeting of a continuing series that is now known as the Hillside Group. In 1994, the First Pattern Languages of Program Design (PLoP)

Software Paradigms, By Stephen H. Kaisler
ISBN 0-471-48347-8   Copyright © 2005 John Wiley & Sons, Inc.

conference was organized (Coplien and Schmidt 1995). PLoP conferences have led to a continuing series of books that continue to enrich the patterns literature. Finally, in 1995, the Gang of Four published their design patterns book and, as they say, the rest is history.

3.2   WHY PATTERNS?

Designing systems is a hard problem. We can ameliorate the need for design by reusing existing designs—in whole or in part. But the ability to reuse designs requires that we learn something about them. Communicating information about designs is a problem almost as hard as the act of design in the first place.

Communication is difficult because existing design descriptions almost always focus on the "what" of the design but rarely capture the "why." However, the "why" of a design is absolutely crucial for deciding whether a particular design is applicable and determining how to customize it to the problem at hand. Improving our ability to communicate the "why" of designs is essential to improving our ability to reuse them.

The study of patterns is not unique to computer science. The importance of patterns has long been recognized in many of the physical and social sciences. Herbert Simon (1973) observed that "hierarchic systems are usually composed of only a few different kinds of subsystems in various combinations and arrangements." Put another way, complex systems are often based on common ways of doing things. These patterns may be small or large and may occur across a small number of systems or a large number of systems. Indeed, in "The Sciences of the Artificial," Simon illustrates how these patterns manifest themselves in social and biological systems, and how the existence of such patterns helps to simplify their inherent complexity.

Carl Linnaeus [1707–1778] (http://www.ucmp.berkeley.edu/history/linnaeus.html) helped organize the field of botany by recognizing that there were patterns to be found in the structure and behavior of animals and plants. The fields of comparative botany and zoology, which arose from his work, look for similarities and differences in order to classify and understand the characteristics of new species.

3.3   PATTERN SPACES

We will characterize a set of patterns applied to a particular domain or discipline as a *pattern space*. Numerous pattern spaces have been developed. Table 3-1 depicts the pattern space originally presented by the GoF (Gamma et al. 1995).

Of these 23 patterns, four—Factory Method, Adapter, Interpreter, and Template Method—were class patterns, while the remaining 19 were object patterns. A class pattern focused on the static relationship between a class and its subclasses, while an object pattern dealt with dynamic relationships that could be managed at runtime.

Table 3-1. The Gang of Four pattern space

Purpose	Design Patterns	Aspect(s) that Can Vary
Creational	Abstract Factory	Families of product objects
	Builder	How a composite object gets created
	Factory Method	Subclass of object that is instantiated
	Prototype	Class of object that is instantiated
	Singleton	Sole instance of a class
Structural	Adapter	Interface to an object
	Bridge	Implementation of an object
	Composite	Structure and composition of an object
	Decorator	Responsibilities of an object without subclassing
	Facade	Interface to a subsystem
	Flyweight	Storage costs of objects
	Proxy	How an object is accessed; its location
Behavioral	Chain of Responsibility	Object that can fulfill a request
	Command	When and how a request is fulfilled
	Interpreter	Grammar and interpretation of a language
	Iterator	How an aggregate's elements are accessed, traversed
	Mediator	How and which objects interact with each other
	Memento	What private information is stored outside an object, and when
	Observer	Number of objects that depend on another object; how the dependent objects stay up to date
	State	States of an object
	Strategy	An algorithm
	Template Method	Steps of algorithm
	Visitor	Operations that can be applied to object(s) without changing their class(es)

The GoF patterns were divided into three categories: creational, structural, and behavioral. *Creational patterns* focused on creating objects—whether through subclasses or other objects. *Structural patterns* use inheritance to compose classes or specify ways to assemble objects. *Behavioral patterns* use inheritance to describe algorithms and flow of control or to describe how a group of objects can cooperate to perform a task that no single object can carry out alone.

Since the early 1990s, numerous disciplines have been subjected to the process of identifying and describing patterns, including analysis patterns (Fowler 1997), organizational patterns (Coplien 1997), and configuration management (Hunt and Tichy 1994).

3.4 TYPES OF SOFTWARE PATTERNS

Patterns can also be classified based on their level of abstraction. Riehle and Züllighoven (1996) suggest three types of software patterns:

Conceptual: Patterns whose form is described by using terms and concepts from an application domain. Such patterns may exhibit a complex design for an entire application or subsystem.

Design: Patterns whose form is described using software design constructs such as objects, classes, and modules. Such patterns provide solutions to general design problems in a particular context.

Programming: Patterns whose form is described by means of specific programming language constructs. Such patterns provide reusable components such as linked lists and hash tables.

The GoF patterns lie in the middle category. Table 3-1 depicts the 23 GoF patterns arranged in three categories: creational, structural, and behavioral. Creational patterns focus on object creation. Structural patterns focus on the composition of classes and objects. Behavioral patterns focus on the interactions between classes and objects.

The GoF uses C++ to describe examples of their patterns. Thus, their notion of classes and objects is somewhat different from that presented by Cunningham and Beck.

Coplien suggests a different approach. He categorizes patterns as either non-generative or generative. Patterns that we observe in a system that has already been built are termed nongenerative, because they are descriptive and passive. Although these patterns are discernible, there may not be any rationale behind them; some of these patterns don't lead to useful results. Generative patterns, on the other hand, help us to design and build systems by specifying the shape of software architectures. They are prescriptive and active; they exert a positive influence on the structure of the software we build.

3.5 DESCRIBING PATTERNS

There are numerous ways to describe patterns. Descriptive schemes range from the simple to the complex. The GoF suggested four essential elements for describing patterns:

Name: A descriptive phrase that captures the main characteristic of the pattern; finding good names is hard to do.

Problem: Describes the typical problem to which the pattern applies.

Solution: The specification for how to solve the problem, including a description of the elements that make up the design pattern, the relationships between these elements, and the responsibilities of each element to the others.

Consequences: When and how the pattern can be used, for example, the situation in which the pattern is most likely to be applicable; may also provide information on understanding the cost and benefits of applying the pattern.

They also suggested additional elements that would enhance the reader's understanding of the pattern:

Applicability: The constraints on when the pattern's problem description matches a real situation.

Examples: Some actual uses of the pattern to solve real problems, sometimes accompanied by the actual code.

Sample Code: An example of an implementation of the pattern in a particular context.

Rationale: A brief explanation of why this solution applies (and is useful) to the problem described.

Related Patterns: Other patterns that may be used with this pattern; they may share a context or constraints and may be used conjointly.

Berczuk (1994) has called this the Alexandrian style of pattern description because it closely follows the approach used by Christoper Alexander. The solution section provides guidance for developing an actual instantiation of the pattern for specific problem solutions. Both the GoF and Buschmann et al. (1996) provide detailed instructions for implementing their patterns.

Design pattern descriptions should be independent of programming language or implementation details because a design pattern is like a template that can be applied in many different situations. Nevertheless, many design pattern descriptions are accompanied by sample source code (where applicable) to indicate how they would be implemented.

3.6 HOW DO WE DISCOVER PATTERNS?

Since design patterns reflect lessons learned over a period of time, each captures the experience of an individual in solving a particular type of problem.

The first thing you need to do to discover patterns is to build things yourself. As you do so, you need to make notes about how you solve problems—a programmer's notebook, if you will. As you gain experience, you will encounter the same types of problems again and again. Recognizing that you have encountered a similar problem before will lead you to your notebook to see how you solved it in the past. Each time you encounter a type of problem and consult your notebook, you annotate your notes to reflect what's different, what's the same, and how you solved it. Eventually, you will build up a standard way to solve that problem that you will continually use. That's a design pattern!

You should also watch and ask other individuals how they solve problems. This is harder to do because you don't know how much they reveal about their thinking about the problem and its solution(s). A particular methodology called *protocol analysis* can facilitate this process. The basic idea behind protocol analysis is that you watch a sequence of actions or interactions and attempt to discern within that sequence a set of common activities, decisions, or operations. Newell and Simon (1972) provide a good description.

As you solve different types of problems, you need to ask yourself into what kinds of categories they fit. The GoF suggested three basic categories, but this is not the only way to classify patterns. If necessary, make up your own categories. Each time you think you have a pattern, add its name to a category. Periodically, review the categories—especially in light of additional information you may have collected—redistribute patterns across categories, if necessary, and try to determine the common characteristics of the set of patterns in each category.

Finally, write your patterns down and distribute their descriptions for others to review, use, and comment upon. Teach your patterns to others when you have the opportunity. Also, ask others what patterns they have discovered and can provide to you.

Shull et al. (1996) describe a more detailed method for discovering patterns from object-oriented applications using inductive methods. Smith and Stotts (2003) describe a set of automated tools for analyzing source code to extract patterns.

3.7 USING PATTERNS

Using patterns is a personal discipline, not something that can easily be taught. You—the programmer—must want to use patterns as part of your personal design toolkit in order for them to be useful to you. You—the programmer—must also consciously look for patterns that meet the requirements for problems that you need to solve. Let's address a few of the issues that arise in using patterns.

3.7.1 How We Use Patterns

Meijers (1996) describes three ways to use patterns:

Top-Down: Given a pattern description, the programmer generates the necessary components to implement the pattern. The class structure implementing the pattern can be used to create instances of the pattern within the application.

Bottom-Up: Given a number of components from an application, the programmer uses a pattern to bind them together, perhaps to coordinate their actions. This may involve writing some glue code or additional components to complete the pattern description.

Hybrid: This approach differs slightly from the bottom-up approach in that some key components of the pattern description may be missing and must be created.

This occurs when the programmer realizes the collection of components nearly matches the pattern description.

When we are developing software, we will use all three approaches. Some parts of the application design are well thought out and we can recognize what patterns to use immediately. In others, we need to begin coding to understand how the design should proceed and only later do we recognize that we match an existing pattern.

While the ideal situation is to say that we keep all our patterns in our head, this is rarely the case. In fact, most programmers I know don't begin designing with patterns, but instead try to lay out the overall software architecture. As they decompose the upper levels, they encounter problems they have solved before—part of their experience for which, usually, they have their own private toolkit. When they encounter problems they haven't solved before, they look for patterns and components that meet their needs.

Schmidt (1995b) describes one approach to using design patterns for evolving software from the Unix operating system to Windows NT operating system.

3.7.2   Learning New Patterns

Good programmers are not averse to recognizing and learning new patterns. However, it may take several repetitions of the same problem for a new pattern to become part of one's private toolkit. Just because your solution isn't documented in the technical literature doesn't mean it's not a pattern. Although patterns have been widely discussed for many types of problems, you should remember that patterns— whichever ones you choose to use—are part of your personal toolkit.

Learning new patterns will occur most effectively if you remember that a pattern is a model that needs to be adapted to a situation. Understanding the object-oriented approach to design and programming can ease your introduction to and learning of design patterns. From learning how to describe individual objects, you can learn how to describe collections of objects working together, since most patterns involve collections of objects. You should focus on the services provided by a design pattern, not its potential implementation. Depending on the complexity of the pattern, the blocks in a pattern description may yield multiple objects in implementation. Flexibility, scalability, and maintainability all arise from not committing early to specific details of these blocks.

3.7.3   Ensuring Consistency

As we use patterns, we must be careful to ensure consistent usage. As we design with patterns, we may add or subtract methods from the comprising classes, or move methods from one class to another in the interests of efficiency, understandability, or ease of use. However, we need to be aware of the constraints on pattern usage and ensure that any of these actions do not violate the constraints. Its okay to do them, but we must realize that we may then be creating a new pattern, which needs the proper documentation if others are to understand what we did and be able to reuse it later. For example, for efficiency, we may collapse a class hierarchy, but we must ensure that we are preserving the semantics of the class hierarchy.

Particular operations that involve semantic changes are often useful in adapting a pattern to a particular design problem. For example, you may add a new factory to an Abstract Factory implementation or replace a class in a pattern with a subclass. These types of operations make patterns useful to specific problems without violating the constraints imposed by the pattern usage. With experience, in describing your patterns, you will also recognize where pattern-specific operations can be performed that allow the pattern to be adapted to different situations.

3.8 FURTHER READING

Ambler, S. 1999. *More Process Patterns: Delivering Large-Scale Systems Using Object Technology.* Cambridge University Press/SIGS Books, New York.

Hay, D. A. 1995. *Data Model Patterns: Convention of Thought.* Dorset House Publishing, Dorset, England.

Lea, D. 1999. *Concurrent Programming in Java: Design Principles and Patterns*, 2nd Ed. Addison Wesley, Reading, MA.

Penker, M. and H-E. Eriksson. 2000. *Business Modeling with UML: Business Patterns at Work.* John Wiley & Sons, Hoboken, NJ.

Rising, L. 2000. *The Pattern Almanac.* Addison Wesley, Reading, MA.

Vlissides, J. 1998. *Pattern Hatching: Design Patterns Applied.* Addison Wesley, Reading, MA.

3.9 EXERCISES

3.1. Stepping outside computer science for a minute, pick a discipline, such as something associated with one of your hobbies, and try to identify five patterns in the processes that you use in practicing the hobby.

3.2. What are the challenges facing design pattern developers? [Research Problem]

3.3. Examine the code you have written. Are there any patterns that you have used in developing software? Describe and categorize the ones that you have used. Can you identify any patterns that are unique to you?

3.4. Start a working group on patterns at your school or workplace. Over three months, how many patterns can you and your colleagues identify and describe? Compare these with published patterns.

4

SOFTWARE PATTERNS

The field of software design and development is rich in patterns. Indeed, one of the hallmarks of an expert software designer is his personal library of code modules that he uses time and again in developing programs.

We'll begin our investigation of design patterns by reviewing a few of the design patterns originally described by Gamma, Helms, Johnson, and Vlissides—the Gang of Four (GoF). These patterns have been described elsewhere in substantial detail, but examining a few in detail is worthwhile to set the stage. I've picked patterns that are both simple and interesting.

We'll wrap up this chapter with an examination of some other software patterns by reviewing the work of James Noble, who has described how to solve some common problems in object-oriented design using patterns.

4.1 SINGLETON

The Singleton pattern is one of the most often-cited design patterns that were included in the GoF book. We start with it because it is one of the simplest patterns and, therefore, easy to understand (Maclean 1997). Sometimes it is necessary, and often sufficient, to create a single instance of a given class or object. Restricting the number of instances may be necessary or desirable for technological or business reasons, such as a GUI application must have a single mouse, an active modem needs one and only one telephone line, an operating system can have only one window manager, and a PC is connected to a single keyboard.

Software Paradigms, By Stephen H. Kaisler
ISBN 0-471-48347-8   Copyright © 2005 John Wiley & Sons, Inc.

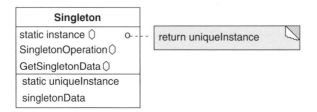

Figure 4-1. The Singleton pattern.

The Singleton pattern applies to the many situations in which there needs to be a single instance of a class—a single object. An important consideration in implementing this pattern is how to make this single instance easily accessible by many other objects (Gamma et al. 1995). Figure 4-1 depicts the UML representation for a singleton.

The requirements for a singleton are:

- Ensure a class has only one instance and provide a global point of access to it.
- Have an encapsulated static variable holding the single instance of a class.
- Provide a static get-operation that creates the single instance once and returns it from then on.

Using a global object ensures that the instance is easily accessible but it doesn't keep you from instantiating multiple objects—you can still create a local instance of the same class in addition to the global one. The Singleton pattern provides a solution to this problem by making the class itself responsible for managing its sole instance. The sole instance is an ordinary object of its class. The class is written so that only one instance can ever be created. Thus, you guarantee that no other instance can be created. Furthermore, you provide a global point of access to that instance. The Singleton class hides the operation that creates the instance behind a static member function. This member function, traditionally called Instance(), returns a pointer to the sole instance.

Obviously, you don't need to name your class Singleton. You can name it to reflect the object for which you are trying to create a single instance. So the name might be Mouse, or FileSystem, or WindowManager.

4.1.1 Describing the Singleton Pattern

In Section 3.5, we described how to document design patterns. Using the Alexandrian approach, we can describe the Singleton design pattern in an abbreviated form as follows (after `http://home.earthlink.net/~huston2/dp/ singleton.html`).

Singleton

Intent: Ensure a class has only one instance and provide a global point of access to it.

Problem: Application needs one, and only one, instance of an object. Additionally, lazy initialization and global access are necessary.

Discussion: Make the class of the single instance object responsible for creation, initialization, access, and enforcement. Declare the instance as a private static data member. Provide a public static member function that encapsulates all initialization code and provides access to the instance.

The client calls the accessor function (using the class name and scope resolution operator) whenever a reference to the single instance is required.

Singleton should be considered only if all three of the following criteria are satisfied:

- Ownership of the single instance cannot be reasonably assigned.
- Lazy initialization is desirable.
- Global access is not otherwise provided for.

If ownership of the single instance, when and how initialization occurs, and global access are not issues, Singleton is not sufficiently interesting.

The Singleton pattern can be extended to support access to an application-specific number of instances.

Structure: See the diagram above.

Example: The Singleton pattern ensures that a class has only one instance and provides a global point of access to that instance. It is named after the Singleton set, which is defined to be a set containing one element.

The Office of the President of the United States is a good example of a Singleton pattern. There can be at most one active president at any given time. Regardless of who holds the office, the title "The President of the United States" is a global point of reference to the individual.

Rules of Thumb: Abstract Factory, Builder, and Prototype can use Singleton in their implementation (Gamma, et al. 1995, p. 134). Facade objects are often Singletons because only one Facade object is required (Gamma et al. 1995, p. 193). State objects are often Singletons (Gamma et al. 1995, p. 313).

4.1.2 Implementing the Singleton Pattern in C++

A simple approach to this situation is to use static members and methods for the "singleton" functionality. For these elements, no instance is required. The class can be made final with a private constructor in order to prevent any instance of the class from being created.

Here is how a generic Singleton class would look in C++:

```
class Singleton
   {
   public:
      // gives back the instance
      static Singleton* Instance();
      // proof that the object was made
      static proof(void);
   protected:
      // constructor
      Singleton();
   private:
      static Singleton* _singleton;
   };
```

The implementation looks something like this:

```
Singleton* Singleton::_singleton = 0;

Singleton* Singleton::Instance()
   {
      if (_singleton == 0)
         {
         _singleton = new Singleton;
         }
      return _singleton;
   }
```

To ensure that users can't create local instances of the class, Singleton's constructor, assignment operator, and copy constructor are declared protected. The class also declares a private static pointer to its instance, _singleton. When the static function Instance() is called for the first time, it creates the sole instance, assigns its address to _singleton, and returns that address. In every subsequent invocation, Instance() will merely return that address. Any attempt to create an instance without using this function will fail because the class constructor is protected. Instance() uses lazy initialization, which means it returns a value that is created when the function is accessed for the first time.

Here are three ways to create a singleton using the code above:

```
Singleton *i1 = Singleton::Instance();
Singleton *i2 = i1->Instance();
Singleton &iref = *Singleton::Instance();
```

The source code shown above creates but a single instance. However, with some minor modifications, you can adapt it to create a limited number of instances. Thus, the basic model can be simply extended to apply to other problems where a finite number of instances are required.

- A *procedural wrapper* is a program that acts as a "back end" to a legacy application, transforming its functional interface into an object interface.

- A *combination wrapper* is a program that instantiates one or more objects, all of which act as back ends to a legacy application, transforming its functional interface into an object interface.

Object Wrappers   An object wrapper is an object that encapsulates a legacy application, transforming its functional interface to an object interface. Methods for the wrapper are written and packaged as an object-oriented class in the particular programming language. Other programs can reuse existing legacy programs by instantiating objects from the object wrapper class or its descendants. The functional interface and data structures of the legacy application are hidden from other programs, and it looks and acts like another object in the system.

This type of wrapper is often useful when a legacy program becomes the server in a client–server application. Consider a legacy program that has a command-line user interface. To use the program in a client–server environment, a graphical user interface (GUI) is added, written as an object-oriented program. This GUI program acts as the client program and the legacy program becomes the server program, responding only to requests. But the objected-oriented GUI program sends messages and passes large blocks of data, neither of which the legacy program may be properly equipped to handle.

The object wrapper solves this communication problem by serving as the "translator" for both the messages and the data structures. The object wrapper must establish data structures for:

- Data passed from the object-oriented program.
- Data passed to the legacy program.
- Data returned from the legacy program.
- Data returned to the object-oriented program.

So, how do we write an object wrapper? There are two steps. First, set up the necessary data structures. Determine all the data that must be passed between the object-oriented and the legacy programs. Divide the data into two categories: the data that are always needed, regardless of the task, and the data that are specific to a particular task. The data that are always needed are defined as instance data in the wrapper. The data that are specific to a particular task are coded as temporary variables of the appropriate method in the wrapper program.

Second, perform a task analysis of the legacy program to determine all of its functions. Usually, each task corresponds to a method in the object-oriented wrapper. The code in a typical method:

1. Contains local variables necessary for the method to perform its task.
2. Contains variables necessary for passing parameters and return values.
3. Parses or translates data items passed from the object-oriented program.

4. Calls the legacy program. (This can be a call to the main program, a subprogram, or an entry point.)

5. Parses or translates data items returned from the legacy program.

6. Returns to the object-oriented program.

Procedural Wrapper   A procedural wrapper is a program that reconciles a legacy application's functional interface to an object interface. Modules are written and packaged as entry points in a program, which is the procedural wrapper. Existing legacy programs can reuse object-oriented programs by calling the appropriate entry point in the procedural wrapper. The invocation interface and data structures of the object-oriented application are hidden from the legacy application, which sees a functional interface that looks like another subroutine in the system.

Legacy programs must frequently continue to be the main, or client, programs. Frequently, a legacy program needs either an existing function changed or a new function added, but this function is a subprogram, or server, to the legacy program. Often the function can be modeled as a class, resulting in an object-oriented program. The legacy program is trying to invoke the function modeled by the class, but the object instantiated from the class responds only to messages.

This problem can be solved by a procedural wrapper if the following conditions are true:

- The number of methods in the class is predictable. The object-oriented program is stable; methods are added or deleted either rarely or not at all. The hierarchy of subclasses is stable and the probability of adding new subclasses is very low. This results in a stable procedural wrapper that can be used by multiple legacy applications.

- A small number of data items are shared between the legacy program and the object-oriented program. The number of temporary variables in the procedural wrapper depends on how many different types of data items must be passed as parameters. If there are many different types of data items, a combination wrapper should be considered.

A procedural wrapper allows the legacy program to continue as the main program by answering procedure calls from the legacy program and sending messages to the object-oriented program.

To write a procedural wrapper:

1. Identify all the data items that must be passed between the legacy and object-oriented programs. The data are coded as local variables of the wrapper program.

2. Match each method in the object-oriented program to an entry point in the wrapper program. The code after the entry statement:
   a. Creates an instance of the object.
   b. Parses or translates data items passed from the legacy program.

  c. Invokes the appropriate method.

  d. Parses or translates data items returned from the object-oriented program.

  e. Frees the instance of the object.

  f. Returns to the legacy program.

3. Add other data items and code to complete the wrapper. Include:

  a. A class definition.

  b. One or more object reference variables to hold object handles.

Combination Wrapper   A combination wrapper is a program that instantiates one or more objects, all of which reconcile a legacy application's functional interface to an object interface. The combination wrapper is made up of two parts: the procedural portion and the object-oriented portion. Modules are written and packaged as entry points in a program, the procedural portion. Methods are written and packaged as object-oriented classes, the object-oriented portion. Existing legacy programs can reuse object-oriented programs by calling the appropriate entry point in the procedural portion, which creates the appropriate objects in the object-oriented portion. The invocation interface and data structures of the object-oriented application are hidden from the legacy application. As with the procedural wrapper, the object-oriented applications look like another subroutine to the legacy application.

4.2.2   Simple Wrappers

The simplest wrapper provides an alternative interface to an existing object's interface. This alternative interface may just extend the current interface, rename some of the operations, or extend/reduce the number of parameters to be provided. This approach is often used when an existing object must be integrated into a federation of objects that were developed independently.

A schema must be created for the federation of objects. The wrapper maps the new object to the schema. In Figure 4-2, a set of objects have a uniform interface,

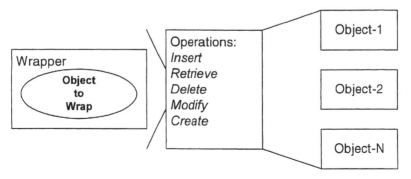

Figure 4-2. Wrapping objects to map to schemas.

which may itself be defined as a wrapper. A new object is mapped to that uniform interface by means of a wrapper. This allows the new object to be integrated with the existing system.

This approach has been used successfully to provide semantic gateways among different relational databases. For example, DB2 may provide a semantic gateway that makes it look like Sybase.

To support this kind of integration, we must capture some metadata about the target system and the interface. This meaning can be captured in different ways—each of which has implications for reusability:

- Internally to each constituent of the system, but this promotes diversity of implementation and makes the overall system harder to maintain.
- Relating the new constituent to an existing one yields a set of pairwise connections that are also difficult to maintain.
- Relating the constituent to a reference definition maintained outside the system minimizes the number of pairwise connections and increases reusability.

4.2.3   Data Wrapping

Data wrapping allows legacy data to be accessed using a different interface or protocol than those for which the data was designed initially. Data wrapping improves connectivity and allows the integration of legacy data into modern infrastructures.

Some of the simplest data wrappers are used to wrap fundamental data types. For example, Java has a complete set of classes that wrap the primitive data types (e.g., for char—java.lang.Char). These classes allow data types to be passed polymorphically.

An example of a data wrapper is a database gateway. A *database gateway* is a type of software gateway that translates between two or more data access protocols used by different database management systems (Altman et al. 1999). Three specifications have emerged as industry-accepted standards: ODBC, JDBC, and ODMG. Open Data Base Connectivity (ODBC) is Microsoft's standard for accessing data in a heterogeneous environment of relational and nonrelational database management systems. It is included in the SQL-1999 specification (NCITS 2002). Java Database Connectivity (JDBC) is a standard defined by Sun for database-independent connectivity between Java applets/applications and a broad range of SQL databases. ODMG is the standard of the Object Data Management Group for persistent object storage. It builds upon existing database, object, and programming language standards to simplify object storage and ensure application portability.

4.2.4   Providing Single Interfaces to Different Objects

We can use the Wrapper pattern to provide a single interface to a multitude of objects. In many drawing programs, each type of object to be drawn has a

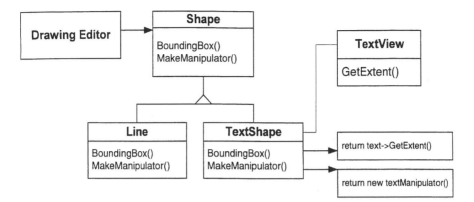

Figure 4-3. Using wrappers for multiple objects.

common set of attributes and functions. But the implementation of those functions differs with the type of object. For example, we can draw either a line or a block of text in a pane of a window. We'd like to call one function and give it the object to draw. The object implements its own drawing behavior. This can be depicted as in Figure 4-3.

Here, lines, textshapes, and many other types of drawing objects share the attributes of a bounding box, which defines the screen area they will occupy. Calculating the bounding box differs for lines and textshapes. We call the BoundingBox() method for each object, but the implementation and the result are determined by the object.

4.2.5   Object Fusion

Wrapping provides a mechanism for fusing information from multiple objects into a single object. The client only needs to call one set of operations to retrieve the data or invoke specific behaviors. And it is insulated from source idiosyncrasies and data transformation operations. A similar effect can be achieved using mediators, which are not described in this book, but see Papaconstantinou et al. (1996).

When the objects represent different databases, the client needs to formulate only one set of queries. The fused object constructs the queries to each of the dependent databases and then transforms and aggregates the results for presentation to the client.

Object fusion requires a federated schema across the set of objects to be included in the system. Once this schema is known, a mapping must be created from each constituent object to the federated schema. However, additional metadata are required to implement the fused system:

- Rules for which objects are to be included.
- Rules for how values from participating objects are to be fused.
- Descriptions of the objects themselves to support self-reflection.

Fusion is useful for distributed objects that communicate within and across different machines. The intent of object fusion is to remove communication overheads from collaborating sets of objects and to enable optimizations across object boundaries.

4.2.6 Implementation Issues

A number of implementation issues arise when considering the use of the Wrapper class.

Object wrappers have been presented as a way to allow legacy applications and object-oriented applications to work together. Object wrappers do not always solve the interoperability problem for legacy applications, such as those written in COBOL. The conflict between legacy and object-oriented applications arises from their method of operation. The COBOL legacy application is a linear block of code with a sequence of PERFORM and CALL statements. The object-oriented application is usually implemented as a data-centered collection of classes. It creates object instances and directs messages to their methods, requesting service.

4.2.7 Principles for Wrapping

Wrapping requires substantial data to ensure both integration and interoperation. Some principles for gathering the data necessary to support the creation of wrappers are:

- Capture syntactic, semantic, and representational information about the attributes of the objects in order to support the development of transformation operations.
- Capture information on the parameters and messages used to invoke operations in the objects, including requirements for presence or absence of certain values.
- Modularize the information into small groups to maximize reusability and minimize the creation of large fused objects.
- Use reference definitions to capture and maintain commonality across many participating objects.

In general, the following principles should be observed when using wrapping to integrate objects or programs:

- All members in the Wrapper class have the same attributes (Name, Data type, Scope, etc.) as the members they wrap.
- Properties are wrapped using read and/or write access methods to access the wrapped property.
- Fields are also wrapped using read and write access methods to access the wrapped field.

- Events are wrapped by events, using read and write access methods to access the wrapped event rather than event handlers.
- Methods are wrapped by methods, which simply pass on the call and parameters to the wrapped class, returning whatever the wrapped method returned.

4.3 THE ABSTRACT FACTORY PATTERN

The Gang of Four (Gamma et al. 1995) developed the Abstract Factory pattern to help create instances of other classes. Factories often have methods that produce instances of several related classes, but all in a compatible way. Each of the instances then implements the operations in its own way. Factories can also create subclasses, which then decide which instances to create.

Factories have a simple function to perform: produce new objects. Obviously, a factory is not needed to make an object. A simple call to `new` (in Java or Ada95) will do it for you. However, the use of factories gives the programmer the opportunity to abstract the specific attributes of an object into specific subclasses that create them. An Abstract Factory pattern is depicted in Figure 4-4.

As you see in Figure 4-4, the CreateProduct() function of the Client class uses the AbstractFactory classes' CreateProduct() function to create an object of the AbstractProduct class. Because there is no direct connection between the Client and the ConcreteProduct class, the ConcreteProduct can be any derived class of AbstractProduct.

Antonio Garcia has made a useful analogy to pasta makers (`http://exciton.cs.oberlin.edu/JavaResources/DesignPatterns/FactoryPattern.htm`). A pasta maker can produce different types of pasta by inserting different metal disks

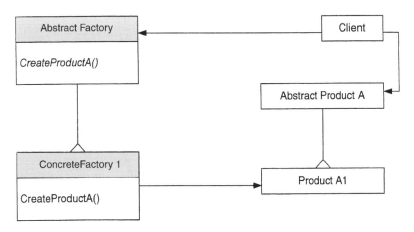

Figure 4-4. An Abstract Factory pattern.

between the dough and the extrusion point. All disks have common properties that allow them to fit into the pasta maker. The pasta maker acts as the Abstract Factory and the disk as the Factory. The pasta maker doesn't care what the disk is doing, nor should it. You turn the handle on the pasta maker, and the disk makes a specific shape of pasta come out. Each individual disk contains the information of how to create the pasta, and the pasta maker does not.

There are two types of Abstract Factory. The simple version is an abstract class defining methods to answer instances of concrete subclasses, such as depicted in Figure 4-4. The second version is an abstract class defining a common protocol of methods. Concrete subclasses of the Abstract Factory implement this protocol to answer instances of the appropriate suite of classes.

For example, we could create an Abstract Factory class *WindowFactory* defining methods like #createButton. We would subclasses *MSWindowFactory* and *MacWindowFactory*, which implement #createButton to answer instances of MSButton or MacButton, respectively. A window painter can then be given an instance of MSWindowFactory or MacWindowFactory. Sending it the #createButton message will result in an instance of MSButton or Macbutton. Assuming they respond to the same protocol, the client can remain ignorant of the class of the resultant button.

4.3.1   Example: DBFactory

The Factory pattern can be used to decouple an application from its data storage facility, such as a relational database. This decoupling minimizes changes in the underlying facility without requiring changes to the application. Consider an application that uses a standard set of operations to access a relational database, such as DBTransaction, DBQuery, and DBReport.

Different implementations of these operations may be required for different DBMSs. However, some functionality may be common across all implementations and can be factored out. Each of these operations can be specialized to work with a different relational database management system (RDMS), because most RDMSs provide additional parameters—to tune their SQL for performance. Thus, an application would have to be aware of which RDMS it is using, say, Oracle, in order to generate the appropriate SQL code and parameters.

One approach would be to subtype each operation, for example, DBQuery-ForOracle, for which specific parameters are required. The choice of which version to use can be resolved at compile time through the use of switches. However, a change in one subsystem (e.g., the database) would require the application to be recompiled. Dynamic SQL generation would require that each version be present at runtime, thus increasing the size of the application in order to provide portability.

A solution to this problem is to use the Factory pattern to create objects that interface to the appropriate data storage facility as depicted in Figure 4-5. Suppose the system is required to work with DB2. DBDefaultFactory creates a DB2 object, DBFactoryDB2, and returns it to the application.

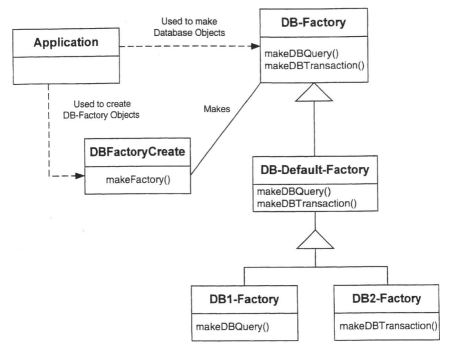

Figure 4-5. Using the Factory pattern.

4.3.2 Implementing the Abstract Factory

Abstract Factory takes advantage of polymorphism to provide a common interface that is used for creating objects that are removed from the underlying implementation.

The Abstract Factory Class The code in Figure 4-6a depicts a possible implementation of the Abstract Factory pattern as a Java class. The class AbstractFactory defines the creation functions for each of the products that a factory will be able to create. The main program creates a new instance of a factory and invokes it creation functions. In this example, invocation of the printing functions of each of the product creation methods will print a short message to demonstrate operation.

```
import java.io.*;

abstract class AbstractFactory
  {

  public abstract ProductA createProductA(int i);
  public abstract ProductB createProductB(int i);
```

Figure 4-6a. Abstract Factory pattern as a Java class.

```
public static void main(String args[])
     {
     ConcreteFactory factory0 = new ConcreteFactory(0);
     factory0.prt();
     ( factory0.createProductA(0) ).prt();
     ( factory0.createProductB(0) ).prt();
     }

  }
```

Figure 4-6a. (*Continued*)

The Concrete Factory Class   The code in Figure 4-6b implements a Concrete Factory as a Java class.

```
Class ConcreteFactory extends AbstractFactory
{
  public ConcreteFactory(int id)
     {
     _identification = id;
     };

  public ProductA createProductA(int I)
     {
     return(new ProductA0(i));
     }

  public ProductB createProductB(int I)
     {
     return(new ProductB0(i));
     }

  public void prt()
     {
     System.out.println("ConcreteFactory: "+_identification);
     }

  class ProductA0 extends ProductA
     {
     public ProductA0(int I)
        {
        _i=i;
        }

     public void prt()
        {
```

Figure 4-6b. The Concrete Factory class.

```
    System.out.println(" ProductA0:  "+_i);
    }
  private int _i;
  }


class ProductB0 extends ProductB
  {
  public ProductB0(int I) {_I=I;}
  public void prt()
    {
      System.out.println(" ProductB0:  "+_I);
    }
  private int _I;
  }


private int _identification;
}
```

Figure 4-6b. (*Continued*)

4.3.3   Example: Component Object Model

Raj (2000) describes a use of the Factory pattern with COM objects. The Creator is played by a COM interface called the *IClassFactory* and the Concrete Creator is played by the class that implements that interface. COM alleviates the need for the COM runtime to know about all the possible object types that it needs to create ahead of time. Typically, Object creation may require acquisition of system resources, coordination between several Objects, and so on. With the introduction of the IClassFactory interface, all the details of object creation can be hidden in a Concrete derivation, manifested as a Class Factory. This way, it is only the class factory that has to be explicitly created by the COM support system.

4.3.4   Analysis of the Abstract Factory Pattern

Abstract Factory is one of the most widely used design patterns because of its extensibility and its generality.

Abstract Factory appears very similar to the Prototype pattern (Gamma et al. 1995). As Vlissides (1998) points out, Prototype will work wherever Abstract Factory will work. Indeed, Vlissides suggests that Prototype has more flexibility, but at a runtime performance penalty. If you are willing to trade off performance, Prototype will create fewer abstract classes than Abstract Factory.

In Figure 4-6b, ConcreteFactory has to be configured with a method to produce a concrete product. For an Abstract Factory to produce multiple products, it must have an abstract product definition for each product and ConcreteFactory needs the appropriate code to produce instances of that product. If this is done at compile time, then Abstract Factory is limited just to those predefined products. But if new product creation methods can be bound at runtime, then a particular Abstract Factory can be extended dynamically. Of course, support for dynamic extension is much more complex than the statically defined version.

One benefit of Abstract Factory is that it abstracts the object creation process. This prevents hard coding of object creation in client code. The other benefit we achieve is extensibility. Whenever we need new kinds of products to be created we can make new concrete factory classes.

The Abstract Factory provides the product creation interface, which is implemented by the concrete factories. Each product has an abstract class, which provides the product interface. Abstract Factory uses the factory method pattern to delegate the real object creation task to the concrete factory classes. This pattern makes exchanging product families easy by simply changing the concrete factory object in the code. Clients manipulate instances through their abstract interfaces so that the concrete product classes are isolated.

Extensibility has a problem, however. Multiple product types can be difficult to maintain, especially if they share some common features. We would generally like to avoid a parallel hierarchy of concrete factories with respect to products.

4.4   OBSERVER PATTERN

The Observer pattern allows one entity to keep track of the activities of one or more other entities. It defines an interface for observed objects to notify the observer when an event occurs. It also stores state information about one or more of its observable entities. And it provides a mechanism for attaching and detaching observables to an observer.

The Observable entity is the object to be observed. It stores the information about the state of interest to the Observer entity. And it sends a notification to the Observer when its state changes. The Observer pattern is depicted in Figure 4-7, as presented in Gamma et al. (1995).

There is usually minimal coupling between the observer and its observable entities. This allows the observable entities to be reused in other applications without reusing their observers and vice versa. Observers can be added without modifying the observable, because all the observable knows is a list of its observers. Each observer only needs to implement the update interface, so the observable needs to know nothing about the observer. A simple example is a hand-held calculator where entering data and pressing the function keys results in updates to the display.

The Observer pattern allows event changes to be broadcast to many different locations in an application because the observable can send the event notification to all observers. Since observers can be added and/or removed at any time, the amount and type of notification can be controlled based on the overall application requirements.

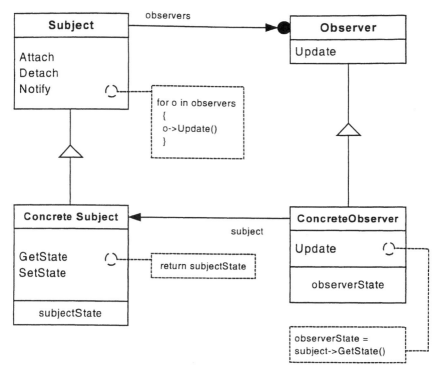

Figure 4-7. The Observer pattern.

4.4.1   Implementing the Observer Pattern

The Observer pattern is implemented using *callback* functions. A callback function is a function that is made known by one entity to another to be used at a later time (like a return phone call) when a given event occurs.

Callback functions are often used in GUIs. In fact, callbacks were first introduced extensively in the X Windows System (Scheifler and Gettys 1986). In Java's AWT, when a button is pressed and released, it generates an action event that is sent to all registered listeners. Listeners must implement the ActionListener interface and implement the actionPerformed() method. Pressing the button causes the actionPerformed() method of the listener object to be invoked.

A simple example for a GUI will illustrate the use of callbacks. The little GUI in Figure 4-8 has just two buttons: a "Start" button and a "Stop" button.

Notice that updates are triggered by the observable. An observable should update its own state before sending an event notification to the observer. In the event of system failure, the true state resides with the entity that actually performs the work.

```java
import java.awt.*;
import java.awt.event.*;

public class SHK_App extends Frame implements ActionListener
  {
  // Some GUI buttons
  public button stopButton = new Button("Stop");
  public button startButton = new Button("Start");

  // SHK Application constructor
  public SHK_App()
     {
     super("My Application");
     setupWindow();
     }

  // Setup the GUI
  private void setupWindow()
     {
     Panel bottomPanel = new Panel();
     bottomPanel.add(stopButton);
     bottomPanel.add(startButton);

     // Register this window as the actionListener
     // for these buttons
     stopButton.addActionListener(this);
     startButton.addActionListener(this);
     pack();
     }

  // Handle callbacks here
  public void actionPerformed(ActionEvent event)
     {
     Object src = event.getSource();
     if (src == startButton)
       start();
     else if (src = stopButton)
       System.exit(0);
     }

  // Main method for application
  public static void main(String[] argv)
     {
     SHK_App app = new SHK_App();
     app.setVisible(true);
     }
  }
```

Figure 4-8. An Observer example.

The amount of information that is transmitted in an update notification depends on the implementation model—either *push* or *pull*. In the push model, a large amount of information may be transmitted because the observable sends as much information as possible in a single update notification. In the pull model, a minimal amount of information is usually sent. But then the observer and the observable must engage in a dialogue to allow the observer to retrieve additional information. Usually, this occurs through the observer calling additional methods in the observable.

4.4.2 Java's Observable Class

Consider a Java Observable object and its Observer objects. Each Observer implements the Observer interface and provides an implementation of the update() interface method. As far as the Observable is concerned, it essentially has a pointer to an update() method to callback when Observers should be notified.

We implement the Observer in the following way:

```
public class myObserver implements Observer
  {
  public void update(Observable object, Object arguments)
    {
    << myObserver code >>
    }
  << additional methods >>
  }
```

The Observable is implemented in the following way:

```
public class anObservable extends Observable
  {
  public void setName(String name)
    {
    this.name = name;
    setChanged();
    notifyObservers(name);
    }
  << additional methods >>
  }
```

4.4.3 Implementation Issues

A number of implementation issues arise when using the Observer pattern. Because observers can be added or removed at any time, the possibility of collision among notifications arises. Observers may not necessarily be aware of each other, especially if they have been added from different parts of the application. Thus, one observer may notify another observer, which may have already been notified either directly or indirectly. This cascade of notifications must be managed carefully so that updates are not triggered more than once and duplicate information is recorded. Similarly, one must avoid circular dependencies among observers that cause one observer to be notified of the event that it itself notified other components about.

An observer may keep track of more than one observable. When it receives an update notification, it must determine which observable sent it the update. Thus, in the Java Observable class, the event notification includes the name of the observable providing the update.

Because the Observable must call the update() method of each Observer, the performance of the Observable is tied to the performance of the update() methods in each Observer. Care must be taken that state changes do not overrun the number of observers to be notified, for example, the total time required to complete the notification process for all observers is longer than the interval between state changes of the observable.

Reusability may be difficult because the `notify()` procedure must be inserted everywhere a state change occurs. Otherwise, the observable must gather all state changes and periodically send them to every observer that should be notified. This increases the complexity and data handling responsibilities of the observable component.

4.5 EXERCISES

4.1. Describe two examples for each of the following wrappings:

    a. Wrapping an object while adding new methods.

    b. Wrapping an object while adding new attributes and methods.

    c. Wrapping an object while hiding several methods.

    d. Wrapping an object but neither adding nor removing methods.

4.2. Look at the descriptions of event-based systems in Section 16.2 and blackboard systems in Section 17.2. How would you use the Observer pattern in each of these software architectures?

4.3. Take the code for the Singleton pattern and modify it to create code for a Doubleton pattern, for example, a pattern that allows no more than two instances of a given class to exist in an application.

4.4. Develop a procedure for creating a component from a design pattern (after reviewing Chapter 8. How would you specify a set of tests to ensure that the component faithfully implements the design pattern?

4.5. Would you ever create a wrapper that has the same interface as the object which it adapts? Would your wrapper then be a Proxy? [Refer to Gamma et al. (1995).]

4.6. What are the properties of a system that uses the Observer pattern extensively? How would you approach the task of debugging code in such a system?

4.7. Is it clear to you how you would handle concurrency problems with the Observer pattern? Consider an Unregister() message being sent to a subject, just before the subject sends a Notify() message to a ChangeManager (or Controller).

4.8. How does the Abstract Factory promote loosely coupled code?

5

HUMAN–COMPUTER INTERFACE PATTERNS

A particularly rich domain for developing patterns is the boundary between the human and the computer, the so-called human–computer interface (HCI). The academic and technical literature is replete with good information on user interface design. Common lessons have been discussed by many authors, such as direct manipulation, immediate feedback, judicious use of sound, and gentle error messages (Tidwell 1999). But, as Tidwell points out, novice designers find it hard to remember all these pieces of wisdom, much less apply them effectively.

One of the earliest HCI researchers to recognize the utility of patterns was Donald Norman (1988) in his book, *The Psychology of Everyday Things*. Norman acknowledges the influence of Alexander's book. The first version of Apple's Human Interface Guidelines (Apple Computer, Inc. 1992) also noted Alexander's influence in environmental design.

5.1 STYLE GUIDES

One of the first ways to describe HCI patterns was through the use of style guides, which prescribed how to design user interfaces to guarantee the same look-and-feel. Some were issued by vendors, such as Apple's Macintosh Style Guide (Apple Computer, Inc. 1992) and Microsoft Windows Design Guide (Microsoft Corp. 1987); others were issued by large corporations trying to ensure organizational uniformity, and others by academic institutions in the interests of knowledge dissemination.

Software Paradigms, By Stephen H. Kaisler
ISBN 0-471-48347-8   Copyright © 2005 John Wiley & Sons, Inc.

The problem with style guides is they are often tied to particular operating systems or design toolkits. These programs evolve and, sometimes, disappear. The knowledge is often very specific to the system and is often difficult to transfer to another system.

But there's a pitfall. You can limit your creativity and expressiveness by mimicking what other designers have done or by not fully exploring the design space alternatives. For beginners, mimicry is not bad because it can help to limit the mistakes they make—if they pick the good designs to emulate. Another pitfall is that if you are a software developer restricted to using specific tool suites, then you are also restricted to the tool suites' authors' choices of design patterns for user interfaces (or for software problems, for that matter).

Reinventing techniques is not practical much of the time, because designers don't have the time to thoroughly test out their ideas before they have to deliver a working application. But it is not a bad thing either—since new tools often elicit new insights into how to implement existing techniques. Good designers draw on deep experience to apply principles and techniques to the problems on which they work. With experience comes skill, good judgment about what works and what doesn't—across different media contexts—and how to adapt good ideas to work in new contexts.

5.2   AN HCI PATTERN LANGUAGE

Tidwell proposed developing an HCI-oriented pattern language. Because it would utilize the vocabulary of HCI, it would be more meaningful to HCI designers. User interfaces exist in many fields—book design, automobile dashboards, the myriad of appliances we use in everyday life, and video games. Today, we are still visually and textually oriented for many of our user interfaces, but recent advances in technology suggest that whole-body tactile suits, speech technology, and other mechanisms will readily be available in the next few years. As Tidwell (1999) notes: "By isolating the qualities that make certain trendy metaphors, idioms, and widgets work so well, we can learn from them and move beyond them, without losing their lessons from our collective memory."

As we develop more integrated user interface environments that combine several technologies, the HCI community will need to develop patterns across several technologies. Interactions will be multisensory and multifaceted.

Jennifer Tidwell's first attempt at human–computer interaction patterns was entitled Common Ground (`http://www.mit.edu/~jtidwell/common_ground.html`). She suggested that such a pattern language would help designers by:

- Capturing the collective wisdom of other designers in a way that can be used immediately, even by less-experienced designers.
- Providing a common language to speak with fellow designers, with interdisciplinary design teams, and with customers.

- Encouraging designers to think "outside the toolkit."
- Focusing on essential features and properties.
- Expressing design invariants that can support portability of the user experience over many similar applications.

Similarly, such a pattern language would allow the HCI community to capture common lessons learned from diverse fields requiring user interfaces such as automobiles, aviation, and consumer electronics. These lessons can provide valuable information about why interfaces do and do not work. And they provide information for developing new HCI toolkits.

5.2.1 Motivation

Tidwell focused on the patterns that would support high-quality interaction between a user and a software artifact, whatever its manifestation. The artifact might support one or more activities, ranging from passive ones such as gathering or absorbing information, to the hands-on creation of new entities and artifacts. Some of the complex kinds of software artifacts we interact with today include:

- Current desktop GUI software.
- Web sites.
- Palmtops and hand-helds.
- Video games.
- Multimedia educational software.
- Graphics and visual arts design tools.
- Scientific visualization.

There's a wide diversity of goals engendered in these artifacts. Some are more interactive than others, while others trade off verbal (textual) versus manipulative factors. But Tidwell suggests that many of them bear strong resemblance to traditional media. What this means is that we carry the comfortable things from the past forward to new technologies, new applications and artifacts, and new mechanisms for interaction.

Tidwell (1999) also notes that all software is similar in its basic purpose. All the best software artifacts provide a satisfying experience to their users, by doing one or both of these things well:

1. They shape the user's understanding of something, through a stylized presentation that unfolds the content to the user in an appropriate way.
2. They enable a user to accomplish a task, by progressively unfolding the action possibilities to the user at an appropriate pace as the user interacts with the artifact.

Table 5-1. Content-related primary patterns

Pattern	Possible Artifacts
Narrative	Books—fictional or nonfictional—news articles, linear and verbal articles such as web pages that appear, for example, in `http://www.about.com/`.
High-Density Information Display	Maps, charts, and tables—including spreadsheets—that provide a big picture view and allow the user to drill down to the specific details.
Status Display	Any artifact presenting time- or performance-oriented information such as a wall clock, a dashboard, or a VCR display, which monitors the state of something that will change.

As Tidwell notes, these two purposes are almost orthogonal: (1) an artifact that provides a set of actions has to present the choices for the set of actions in a comprehensible way; and (2) an artifact that provides a set of facts or information has to provide users with actions to interact with and manipulate them. Much of HCI design and the patterns that represent the accumulated experience of the HCI community is trying to achieve a balance between these two purposes.

5.2.2   Primary Patterns

Tidwell proposed a set of primary patterns divided into two categories, which I'll call *content-related* or *action-related*. Content-related patterns focus on unfolding the content, either through successive interactions or through textual or visual narratives. (See Table 5-1.)

The action-related patterns focus on a cascading set of actions—actions arising out of other actions, or a sequential flow of actions that must be performed to accomplish an overall task. (See Table 5-2.)

5.3   WEB DESIGN PATTERNS

The human–computer interface (HCI) domain is replete with patterns. A website has been devoted to HCI patterns (`http://www.hcipatterns.org`) with links to specific authors. Martin Welie (`http://www.welie.com/patterns/`) has documented a large number of patterns in the Web, GUI, and mobile domains. Jennifer Tidwell created a website in 1998 for user interface patterns (`http://timetripper.com/uipatterns/`). Linda Rising (1998) published a handbook of user interface patterns.

Table 5-2. Action-related primary patterns

Pattern	Possible Artifacts
Form	There are many examples of forms such as tax forms and on-line ordering forms (e.g.,Amazon.com). With interactive forms, the user is expected to provide preformatted information. Most user actions are prescribed and limited.
Control Panel	These are used to set the state of one or more things or processes. Light switches are simple examples, but VCR controls are much more complex. Cultural constraints or functionality often limit the available actions.
WYSIWYG Editor	These support textual development through visual interfaces. MS Word, MS Powerpoint, and the Visual Basic forms designer are examples.
Composed Command	Commands were the earliest form of interaction with operating systems and other programs. Commands occur in many contexts from one person directing another to verbal commands to the computer in Star Trek (by Scotty). These follow linguistic patterns as opposed to the graphic patterns of the WYSIWYG Editor. Usually, immediate feedback is provided to the user.
Social Space	We all exist in social spaces—water cooler chat groups, news and mail groups, and so forth. The artifact is a mediator between a group of people as opposed to an active participant or provider of content. Usually, it provides very stylized actions limited by cultural constraints.

5.3.1   Welie's Patterns

Welie has divided his UI patterns into three categories: Web, GUI, and mobile. Within the first two categories, he has further subdivided the patterns based on their usage. Table 5-3 depicts the breakdown of patterns.

Welie's (2001) patterns focus on making a website navigable in the belief that an easily navigable website will attract reader's time and again because of the ability to locate and peruse information. Navigational patterns help users to traverse the information structure of the website and tell them where they have been and where they can/have to go. Most websites are hierarchical, so the navigation patterns have to help users go up and down the tree as well as cross from one branch to another.

As Welie notes, a site's main navigation is almost never the only access to information. Site maps allow users to reach information, to find out what can be found on the site, and how it is organized. Also, the site map should give users an indication of where they are and where they go. Search engines can drop a user into the middle of a site based on the search criteria entered. So site navigation and information structure need to go hand in hand (e.g., be designed at the same time).

Table 5-3. Welie's interaction patterns

Category	Usage	Patterns
Web	*Navigation*	Bread crumbs; Double tab; Meta navigation; Outgoing links; Split navigation; Repeated menu; Progressive filtering; Teaser menu; Combined menu; Fly-out menu; Directory; Scrolling menu
	Page Elements	News box; List builder; Tabbing; Paging; Wizard; Parts selector; Language selector
	Searching	Simple search; Advanced search; Site map; Search area
	e-Commerce	Shopping cart; Identify; Product comparisons
GUI	*Modes*	Automatic mode switching; Helping hands; Mode cursor
	Selection	Magnetism; Continuous filter; Contextual menu; Focus!; Unambiguous format; Preview; Setting attributes; Command area; Managing favorites; Preferences
	Guidance/Feedback	Shield; Hint; Warning; Progress; Undo
	Navigation	Wizard; Soft keys; Navigating spaces; Container navigation; List browser
	Presentation	Grid layout
	Physical Interaction	Like the real world . . . ; Media slot
Mobile	*WAP/WML*	

Site Navigation Mechanisms   Welie suggests several ways to provide site navigation mechanisms:

- *Top:* Usually a horizontal bar with several clickable items placed at the top of the page. The bar is present on every page. The selected item is highlighted. For example, move your cursor across the top bar in Netscape 7.0 or Internet Explorer 6.0.
- *Left:* A vertical bar at the left of the window has clickable items that allow the user to jump to other pages. Because of scrolling, it allows almost an unlimited number of items to be displayed.
- *Top-Left:* A combination of the previous two mechanisms that allows additional information to be displayed in the left bar once a general item has been selected using the top bar.
- *Bread Crumb:* Clickable items may be placed anywhere in the window, but as you select an item, its icon is displayed and the next set of choices is presented for your attention. As you navigate down the hierarchy, each level leaves its icon behind. This allows you to return to any level merely by clicking on its icon.

- *Split:* For large sites with a deep page hierarchy and many choices per level, Welie suggests a "split" approach, where one mechanism is used for certain levels and another mechanism for different levels.

- *Matrix:* In complex websites, pages may fit into multiple levels in the hierarchy or the mesh, depending on how they are linked from other pages. The page exists only once but is cross-linked from many different places. If you think of all the page references as forming a mesh, then you jump to different parts of the mesh by following page links.

I did not intend to delve deeply into website design here, but to give you a flavor for how patterns occur and reoccur in other domains.

5.3.2   Tidwell's Web Patterns

More recently, Tidwell has developed an extended set of patterns available at `http://time-tripper.com/uipatterns/`. Most of the early patterns, especially those first described in the Gang of Four book (Gamma et al. 1995), were based on research performed on user interfaces. However, these patterns focused primarily on solving software design problems. Tidwell, like Welie, has focused on developing patterns that make the user experience more manageable and productive, especially when dealing with complex websites.

Many of Tidwell's patterns are complementary to Welie's patterns, but some express a different viewpoint of the same problem. Let's explore a few.

Card Stack   This pattern is familiar to most GUI users, especially those using Microsoft's internet Explorer for Windows. Tidwell suggests using this pattern when you have too much information to display on one page. The information is distributed across several pages and allows the user to select the appropriate page using a tab (as depicted in Figure 5-1).

The labeled tabs partition the information into chunks that can be visually grasped quickly. Tabs are familiar to users and the cards are compact. Before constructing your card stack, split the information into categories, then select the labels

Figure 5-1. Microsoft's internet Explorer property card stack.

based on the categories. If you split the information up wrong, users will have to flip back and forth between cards to access the necessary information.

5.4 FURTHER READING

Borchers, J. 2001. *A Pattern Approach to Interaction Design.* John Wiley & Sons, Hoboken, NJ.

Van Duyne, D. K., J. A. Landay, and J. I. Hong. 2003. *The Design of Sites.* Addison Wesley, Reading, MA.

Van Welie, M. and G. C. van der Veer. 2003. "Pattern Languages in Interaction Design: Structure and Organization." In *Proceedings of Interact '03,* 1–5 September, Zürich, Switzerland; M. Rauterberg, M. Menozzi, and J. Wesson, (eds.), pp. 527–534. IOS Press, Amsterdam, The Netherlands.

A Visualization Pattern Language. 2003. A set of patterns for visualization by Barry Wilkins. `http://www.cs.bham.ac.uk/~bxw/vispatts/index.html`.

User Interface Design Patterns. 2003. A set of 21 patterns written by Laakso, Laakso, and Saura of the University of Helsinki. `http://www.cs.helsinki.fi/u/ salaakso/ patterns/`.

5.5 EXERCISES

5.1. Consider a meeting room in which collaborative work can be accomplished among a study group. For example, read about the Xerox COLAB project, which was designed to facilitate person-oriented creative meetings. It pioneered the concept of WYSIWIS (What You See Is What I See). Develop full specifications for at least five UI patterns based on this material. `http://www2.parc.com/ istl/members/steWk/colab.htm`.

5.2. Apple developed the Hypercard stack as a way to organize and present information. It was easy to use and program using a simple scripting language (the forerunner of AppleScript). It was the forerunner of today's web pages. Research the Hypercard application. Compare and contrast its capabilities with those of today's HTML-based (or XML-based) web pages.

5.3. Consider the body glove as developed by Jared Lanier for virtual reality navigation. What kinds of design patterns might you use in a 3D environment?

5.4. Consider an interactive holographic display (the Star Trek HoloDeck comes to mind). What kinds of design patterns might you use to implement some of the simulations that operate on the HoloDeck?

5.5. Examine one or more of the games currently available for the Playstation, Nintendo, or the Xbox. Identify five design patterns that you find in the user interface to such games.

6

OTHER
PATTERN DOMAINS

As we noted in the opening paragraphs of this part, patterns have widely been applied to many different domains—some removed from computer programming directly. However, if we stay within the boundaries of computer science, we still find ample use of the design pattern concept in various nonprogramming domains.

6.1   COPLIEN'S PATTERNS

Jim Coplien, who has been instrumental in pushing the process of pattern definition, documentation, and adoption, has focused on creating a Common Pattern Language. He proposes to do this, not by a formalized mechanism, but by creating an electronic sandbox in which other authors can come and play. In this sandbox, authors can try different structures for patterns. They can obtain feedback and comment on others' work. Through this collaborative process, he hopes that a new pattern language will evolve that incorporates the collective experience. The electronic sandbox is found at the website `http://i44pc48.info.uni-karlsruhe.de/cgibin/ OrgPatterns`.

In particular, Coplien is focused on organizational patterns, for example, patterns about how organizations work and interact. Currently, over 100 organization patterns can be found at the website. A graphic map of the organizational patterns can be found at `http://www1.bell-labs.com/user/cope/Patterns/Process/ OrgPatternsMap.html`. The table of patterns is found at `http://www.bell-labs. com/cgi-user/OrgPatterns/OrgPatterns?OrganizationBookPattern Table`. Some patterns contain other patterns and some are contained within others.

Software Paradigms, By Stephen H. Kaisler
ISBN 0-471-48347-8   Copyright © 2005 John Wiley & Sons, Inc.

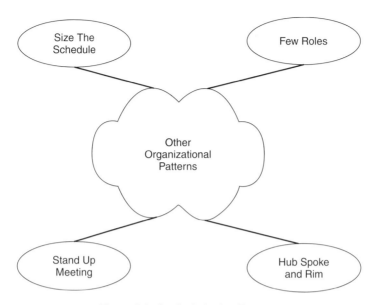

Figure 6-1. Coplien's Anchor Patterns.

Interestingly enough, four patterns anchor the map: two at the top—*Size the Schedule* and *Few Roles*—and two at the bottom—*Stand Up Meeting* and *Hub Spoke and Rim* (see Figure 6-1).

Coplien's table contains over 40 patterns that distill a large amount of project management and organizational structure knowledge. This repository is recommended for readers who are or intend to become project leaders or project managers. We'll briefly review these in the following sections to give you a flavor for organizational patterns.

6.1.1 Size the Schedule

Schedule is one of the three critical factors in any project: cost, schedule, and functionality (Rechtin 1991). An overly aggressive or an overly generous schedule can cause problems. If the schedule is too aggressive (ambitious), the developer begins to miss deadlines because they have not sized the work properly. Similarly, a generous schedule often leads to coxmplacency and the decision to put off either easy or hard parts of the problem (depending on personal preference). Ultimately, the schedule catches up with the work and the project falls behind. The most common solution has always been to throw more people at the problem, but as Fred Brooks (1995) notes, "adding people to a project makes it later."

The alternative, as Rechtin notes, is to cut the functionality to what you can deliver within the remaining time frame. However, the customer may accept a cut in functionality with the promise of having the as yet undelivered functionality at some future date. Projects without schedule deadlines tend to go on forever, or spend too much time refining already developed functionality that is either irrelevant or doesn't serve customer needs.

Coplien suggests two approaches:

1. Reward the developers for proposing and complying with schedules.
2. Keep two schedules: one for the marketers and one for the developers.

The external schedule is negotiated with the customer and is usually several weeks longer than the schedule negotiated with the development staff.

6.1.2 Few Roles

As projects get organized, personnel assume different roles based on project needs, individual preferences, skills, and organizational relationships. The people occupying these roles must communicate for the project to succeed, but if the number of roles is very large, the overhead associated with this communication—through inclusion or hierarchy—can overwhelm the progress it is intended to facilitate.

The number of communication paths increases with the number of roles in a project. So five roles have ten communication paths, but the number of paths jumps to 45 with ten roles. As the number of roles and paths increases, people can't talk to each other directly. So information reaches some people indirectly, but this increases latency and overhead.

Thus, keeping the number of roles small—between 10 and 16—keeps the communication paths and latency down and can improve productivity and efficiency.

6.1.3 StandUp Meeting

Information ages quickly in projects that change quickly. Everyone needs the same information in order to be able to make both individual and consensus decisions and mitigate risk. The need for change may be due to early decisions based on incomplete information or on stress or crisis within the project. Quick response demands a coordinated effort because things go wrong badly when people operate from different and stale information. Short, daily meetings where each project manager stands up and describes technical progress and risk issues are encouraged to ensure dissemination of information among the project team's leadership. These meetings should be held to 15 minutes or less to encourage brevity.

6.1.4 Hub, Spoke and Rim

Many development processes can be partially or fully automated, but many more require some human intervention at crucial steps. Some mature processes still need additional mechanisms to integrate the various stages. Process stages should be decoupled to reduce the communication associated with handoffs. This helps to promote independence between stages. However, independence creates opportunities for parallelism and increased throughput and can hamper information flow. Link each independent stage to a hub process, which coordinates actions and ensures the work is done efficiently while the work is done at the rim processes. The spokes provide communication channels to the hub. However, the hub process must be discouraged from micromanaging with respect to the actions of the rim processes in accomplishing their tasks. By analogy to the current airline route system, several people have noted that the hub-and-spoke system contributes to congestion.

6.2 OBJECT-ORIENTED PATTERNS

An object-oriented program (OOP) is comprised of a collection of objects. Generally, these objects will communicate via their interfaces. This interface may be standardized or ad hoc, for example. defined by the programmer for a particular set of objects. By using an object's interface, other objects may invoke behavior in the target object, thus treating it as a server. Similarly, an object may invoke another object's methods through its interface in the role of a client. James Noble (1996a) has shown how to use objects to solve some frustrating problems in subprogram invocation. The following sections summarize some of his work.

6.2.1 Object-to-Object Communication

Objects communicate with one another through their interfaces. Other objects can use an object as a server by invoking its method and, thus, accessing its behavior. Similarly, an object can be a client of other objects. The key element to successful communication is implementing an effective protocol. However, one protocol cannot fit all instances of an object's usage within an application. As a result, Noble (1997) has shown how to introduce flexibility into object communications through patterns for O-O protocols.

Noble distinguishes two types of patterns: patterns about arguments and patterns about results (Figure 6-2). His basic premise is that the design of an object-oriented program can be improved by introducing additional objects into the program. This seems somewhat counterintuitive because the idea of OOP is to simplify the program design by limiting the number of objects. As Noble notes, these patterns simplify a program locally but impose global changes.

The Argument Object   Some subprograms have argument structures that are regular but require numerous arguments. An inspection of the X Windows code will show that many functions share a sequence of common arguments. For example, a graphical View object will provide an interface for drawing many types of objects in

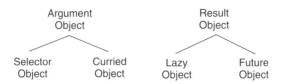

Figure 6-2. Argument and Result Object patterns.

many different ways, but almost every message will take arguments that specify the color and line thickness to use when drawing. The same combinations of arguments may occur across many methods. As a result, many arguments may be passed in parallel through many messages and across many objects.

An interface with many methods is easy to use because it provides flexibility to its clients through a richness of methods, but it is also difficult to use because the programmer must learn and understand the nuances of many individual methods, some of which may vary in only a single parameter. Large interfaces are more easily changed through addition of new methods but are also difficult to change because the probability is relatively high that some method is being used by some client requiring the specific functionality.

As Noble notes, quoting Alan Perlis (1982), "if you have a procedure with 10 parameters, you probably missed some." The challenge is to reduce the number of parameters that are replicated in each method and simplify the method invocation structure.

Noble suggests that an Argument Object be created, which has one attribute for each common argument that appears in multiple methods. The object has the appropriate get and put methods for each attribute created in the Argument Object. And each method then has the appropriate arguments replaced by one argument, the Argument Object.

The Selector Object   No doubt you have run into the situation where you have multiple methods performing the same function but varying in the number of arguments they take. Languages such as Common Lisp handle this fairly well, but imperative and O-O programming languages—even with polymorphism—often have difficulty. Noble suggests capturing the different methods in a Selector Object.

6.2.2   Object Relationship Patterns

Noble (1996b) notes that relationships among objects are very important in object-oriented programming languages. Most OOPLs do not support relationships formally, but leave it to the programmer to define them. Some of the kinds of relationships include unidirectional or bidirectional, one-way or multiway associations, or timed relationships. Most relationships are supported through attributes whose data types map to the handles of other objects (Figure 6-3). Usually, these are one way but—with polymorphism—they can accommodate a hierarchy of objects.

Table 6-1, adapted from Noble (1996b), presents brief descriptions of these patterns. It depicts how some weaknesses in current OOPLs can be surmounted by

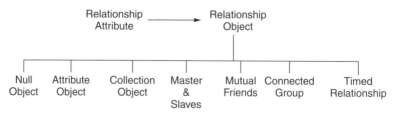

Figure 6-3. Object Relationship patterns.

Table 6-1. Object Relationships

Pattern	Description
Relationship Object	A relationship object represents an association between two or more objects. Remove any attributes and methods from the participating objects and place them in the relationship object. This effectively decouples the participating objects from each other: as an example, modeling the relationship between airlines flights and cities using a timetable—a many-to-many relationship.
Attribute Object	An attribute object represents a one-to-one association based on a single attribute. It has two methods: an accessor and a settor. While this leads to additional objects, it makes it easier to implement different methods for each variable.
Collection Object	A collection object models directed, one-to-many relationships (e.g., a container). An example is an insurance policy with many endorsements attached. There is one policy, but many elements to it. The collection can be implemented in many different ways based on behavioral requirements.
Mutual Friends	A mutual friends pattern models a bidirectional relationship among two or more objects. One-to-one and one-to-many are directly supported in OOPLs, but many-to-many is not. So the object implements and maintains pairs of one-to-one or one-to-many relationships internally. The extra burden is to keep these consistent. It is a difficult pattern to implement because of the synchronization requirement.
Masters and Slaves	Many relationships are not symmetrical, for example, they are initiated from one direction. An example is a broadcast of a task to be completed by multiple server objects. Participating objects implement messages to establish and dissolve the relation, and receive tasking. In Java's AWT, for example, a window manages all of its panes.
Null Object	Some relationships are zero-to-one or zero-to-many relationships. A null relationship can be represented by a null value in an attribute, but it is difficult to manage consistency. A null object replaces a real object and implements the same methods, but does not respond to them. For example, an owner may have zero, one, or many dogs. A nullDog would look like a realDog except it would not respond to any messages.
Timed Relationship	Temporal relationships change over time, including existing or not existing or changing from describing future state to current state. A timed relationship object is a complex object that maintains both a current and an historical representation, including dates and times when the state of the object has changed.
Connected Group	A connected group manages a set of relationship objects whose behavior and relationships are interconnected, for example, changing one object causes changes in one or more other objects. A connection manager object mediates the changes across the set of other objects. This is a relatively complex object to implement because of the consistency and behavioral requirements to be met.

using object-oriented principles to decouple the relationship information from the participating object implementation.

6.3 ANTIPATTERNS

Patterns are intended to show good solutions to problems—things that people do over and over again because they work. However, there are also patterns of behavior or solutions to problems that will make the situation worse rather than better. These are called antipatterns (Mowbray et al. 1998) because they tell how to go from a problem to a bad solution. According to Jim Coplien, a good antipattern describes something that looks like a good idea, but which backfires badly when applied (like a Pyrrhic victory).

As an example, the most interesting task for a school mathematics teacher is working out how a particular pupil gets it wrong. Most cognitive errors are systematic rather than random—so if Johnny cannot do long division, there must be a specific step in the process that he is getting wrong, or a specific axiom or principle that he hasn't properly understood.

Many patterns can be expressed in a negative form: avoid XYZ. Experienced engineers have a personal set of negative patterns (or design pitfalls) that they search for when evaluating or testing other people's designs. Some of these negative patterns have a corresponding positive pattern: "avoid XYZ, do PQR instead."

As of this writing, a partial antipattern catalog is maintained at `http://c2.com/cgi/wiki?AntiPatternsCatalog`. These have been grouped into the following categories: architecture, development, management, and other. In Sections 6.3.1 through 6.3.3, we'll briefly review one pattern from the first three categories to give you a flavor for what they entail. Then we'll look at a couple of examples from other areas.

6.3.1 Design By Committee

DesignByCommittee, an architectural antipattern, describes the situation in which no one person has enough clout to present a design for a system and get it approved. This makes it difficult to get actions accomplished because too many people have to concurrently agree in order for any activity to occur.

One often-cited example is the development of Ada. In the early 1970s, the DoD did not believe that existing programming languages did not provide large-scale programming support, encapsulation, or other features that designers had decided were required to build complex, large-scale applications. No one had the force of personality or vision to drive through a language description or mandate the choice of a particular language. In essence, there was no Grace Hopper. The DoD formed a committee to solve the problem. The committee battled over the requirements and features to be included in the new language because each member had their own vision of what was right. Because there was no unifying vision, the result was a mixture of features meant to appease as many members as possible. Further discussion of how Ada was developed can be found at `http://www.adapower.com/lab/adafaq/8.html`.

Rightly or wrongly, Ada has been criticized for some of the features it contains or lack of features it does not contain. Most critics attribute this to its design-by-committee approach.

6.3.2 Feature Creep

Feature Creep (or CreepingFeaturitis), a development antipattern, is the situation in which more and more features are added to a system—not necessarily in the design phase—in order to satisfy customer wants. It is often initiated by the desire to do the best possible job for the customer and, concurrently, build the best possible system. Sometimes it is an outgrowth of DesignByCommittee. Everybody believes they need to add just one more feature in order to make the application sing, dance, do tricks, or anything else that will amaze and astound the customer.

It can occur at any stage—Analysis, Design, or Development. However, during development, it is often manifested by individual programmer decisions to add just another feature.

6.3.3 Paralysis Through Analysis

Analysis Paralysis, a management antipattern, is a term given to the situation where a team of otherwise intelligent and well-meaning analysts enter into a phase of analysis that only ends when the project is cancelled. The analysts continue to analyze and model to exacting detail in order to determine every requirement exactly. Thus, analysis is never complete, and development work never begins.

Frequently, in such situations, designers and developers are staffed but have no work to do. They are often assigned busy work and training to keep them occupied but unproductive. As a result, resources are consumed without results and eventually the project appears headed for an overbudget, overschedule situation, which is not recoverable. This often results in project cancellation.

Some of the reasons for the occurrence of this situation are:

- Insistence on completing all analysis before beginning design.
- Increasingly conflicting goals.
- Creative speculation where discovery and definition are required (e.g., no access to the necessary data to complete the analysis).
- The Big Project Syndrome: this design will handle all the problems if only we can get all the detail.

A few solutions to avoiding or overcoming AnalysisParalysis include:

- Constrain the analysis to just the critical requirements; work out the details during development.
- Employ an incremental evolutionary development model such as the Boehm spiral model or extreme programming, both of which force delivery of partial functionality.

- Employ a software/systems architect to drive the vision, but who does not develop; he has sole responsibility for functional decisions in each phase.

6.3.4   A Medical Example

Medicine offers a rich environment for generating patterns. For example, a disease mutates and evolves: new flu viruses, more virulent forms of tuberculosis, the evolution of HIV. As the human immune system and/or the drug companies develop resistance (e.g., drugs) to one form of disease, another form appears, which elegantly evades our best defenses. What we observe is the immune system and/or the drug resisting the impact of the disease.

6.3.5   A Programming Example

Once upon a time, computer programmers could easily recognize spaghetti code by the presence of one word: GOTO. It was considered harmful; programming languages were developed in which GOTO was unnecessary or impossible; generations of programmers were trained to resist anything that resembled a GOTO (Dijkstra 1975).

But the pattern mutates and reappears in a new form, designed to bypass our programmed resistances. Large complex computer systems are now being developed; each software component may be impeccably designed and coded, but these software components are wired together (using some form of scripting language or middleware) into something that we can only regard as a new manifestation of spaghetti code.

6.3.6   Some Architectural Antipatterns

Christopher Alexander (1964) identified a number of negative patterns from the (building) architecture domain, some of which are depicted in Table 6-2.

Table 6-2. Alexander's negative patterns

Negative Pattern	Corresponding Positive Pattern(s)
Bedrooms make no sense since we occupy them less than 30% of the day.	Bedroom alcoves Dressing rooms
High buildings sometimes make people crazy.	Four-story limit
Outdoor spaces that are merely "left over" between buildings will, in general, not be used.	Positive outdoor space
The artificial separation of houses and work creates intolerable rifts in people's inner lives.	Scattered work
The homogeneous and undifferentiated character of modern cities kills all variety of lifestyles and arrests the growth of individual character.	Mosaic of subcultures

6.4 FURTHER READING

Adamczyk, P. 2003. The Anthology of Finite State Machine Patterns. Available at `http://jerry.cs.uiuc.edu/~plop/plop2003/`.

Brown, M. A. and E. Tapolcsanyi. 2003. Mock Object Patterns. Available at PLoP 2003: `http://jerry.cs.uiuc.edu/~plop/plop2003/`.

Fortier, A., J. Cappi, and G. Rossi. 2003. Interception Patterns. Available at `http://jerry.cs.uiuc.edu/~plop/plop2003/`.

Lampson, B. 1983. Hints for Computer System Design. Available at `http://research.microsoft.com/~lampson/33-Hints/Acrobat.pdf`. A good application of patterns, although Lampson calls them hints, is to computer system design. In this paper, he summarizes two decades of experience in designing a variety of computer systems at the Xerox Palo Alto Research Center and synthesizes the many lessons learned.

Weiss, M. 2003. Patterns for Web Applications. Available at `http://jerry.cs.uiuc.edu/~plop/plop2003/`.

6.5 EXERCISES

6.1. Assess your organization and try to develop at least one pattern and one antipattern based on your personal experience.

6.2. Define the Builder and the Abstract Factory patterns in some detail. Discuss the differences and similarities between them.

6.3. Many patterns show structural similarities. If you factor out these similarities, do they constitute patterns, minipatterns, or something else? (Consider abstract coupling, for example.)

6.4. Research real-time programming problems and environments. Such environments often have very strict timing constraints for problem solving and computation. How would you modify the basic design pattern description to account for the specification of additional information necessary to support real-time programming?

6.5. Read forward into Part II of this book. Then come back and answer the following. How would you develop an algorithm for converting a design pattern to a component?

6.6. While a design pattern is an abstract concept, designers still need guidance for ensuring the "ilities" are met in the resulting software. What types of information might you specify in a design pattern to assist in specifying data for the "ilities" and ensuring that they are met?

7

PATTERN DESIGN

We've only touched a small part of the extensive literature on using and developing design patterns. Numerous books and papers have been written on applying the design pattern concept to different domains. At the end of this chapter, I'll point out various sources in the technical literature for further reading and exploration.

At this point, I'd like to synthesize some lessons learned about design patterns and look at some of the issues associated with using design patterns. As you read across the literature, you may be struck—as I have—with some observations about design patterns. One such observation is: I've done it that way! Or to phrase it more cynically: What's so new about that? Well, the answer in a large majority of the cases (better than 95%) is: Not much. This is not to say that we don't ever discover anything new or that you won't ever discover a new way to represent a data structure, code an algorithm, or solve a problem. But many of the solutions that we find to software design problems have probably already been found by some other programmer.

7.1 DESIGN PATTERN ISSUES

In applying design patterns in software development and other domains, a number of issues arise that can impact our success. I expressly did not use the term "problems" because I don't think they lead to bad consequences. But, if we are not careful, some choices can lead to less than effective solutions in any domain.

Software Paradigms, By Stephen H. Kaisler
ISBN 0-471-48347-8   Copyright © 2005 John Wiley & Sons, Inc.

7.1.1 Structural Similarity

After reading patterns for awhile, you'll probably think that many of them seem to have a similar structure. And you won't be far wrong. For example, the GoF Prototype pattern can be implemented using Abstract Factory (Vlissides 1998). So some patterns can implement other patterns. Similarly, a pattern may have multiple implementations such as Adapter or Wrapper.

What we learn from this is that just describing the structure of a pattern isn't sufficient. We need also to describe the semantics—what the pattern does and what its intent is. The intents of Prototype and Abstract Factory are different even if their structure is the nearly the same. Consider the Observer pattern: there are always an observer and a subject. The observer needs to notify the subject when an event happens, but it is not required that the observer do this by directly communicating with the subject. Many types of intermediate objects, including proxies, can be used to mediate, buffer, or manage the communication.

Patterns always have participants who are related through the pattern structure. This leads to the observation that we can create different patterns by varying the type and features of the participants. In fact, we can create a family of patterns from one pattern by understanding how to substitute different participants into a pattern.

Another aspect of structural similarity is that we may be able to factor out the common similarities among a set of similar patterns. Thus, there may be smaller building blocks that can be used to comprise design patterns. These building blocks are larger than objects and classes. For example, abstract coupling, which Noble (see Section 6.2.1) describes, is an interaction between abstract classes where the actual interaction is accomplished by subclasses that have concrete functionality.

7.1.2 Patterns as Building Blocks

We view patterns as building blocks for software design. A similar notion is applicable in other domains. There are some implications of this observation.

A pattern that solves a particular problem in some way can be replaced by a pattern that solves the problem in a different way. Class objects can create instances or they can implement prototypes. What do we need to know and what constraints must we satisfy to perform this one-for-one substitution? Some of the answers to this question underlie the domain of component technology, which is addressed in Part II.

A pattern imposes constraints on the design. For example, the Observer pattern requires that all observers must implement the update method. Similarly, a pattern forces the maintenance of certain relationships among the participants. An Abstract Factory relates the Factory with the Products. When we introduce a new Product, the Factory must be able to produce the Product. Coupled with the ability to substitute one pattern for another, we can impose as rigid or as loose constraints as we wish on different participants by selecting the pattern that we specify in some part of the design.

Given an application, we can examine and analyze it to discern the patterns that lie therein (and there will be some!). Knowing these patterns, we can then determine whether it is reasonable and feasible (e.g., cost effective) to replace one pattern with another and, thereby, obtain some benefit such as improved performance, reduced memory requirements, or simpler interface.

7.2   SOME SIMPLE PATTERN DESIGN PRINCIPLES

The plethora of articles and books describing design patterns have produced an equally large set of design principles for how to create design patterns—too numerous to replicate here. Using a programming language that provides object-oriented features makes the job of developing and implementing design patterns much easier because of inheritance support. However, a few key principles have emerged that should be mentioned.

The Open, But Closed, Principle   Meyer (1997) suggests that we design our objects to be open to extension, but closed to modification. We should be able to change what our patterns do, without modifying them. Abstraction is the key to this principle, as it is to the concept of design patterns.

Program to an Interface, Not an Implementation   A class that inherits from a parent class has access to all of the methods of that parent class. It also has access to all of its nonprivate variables. Using a complete, working class as the root of an inheritance hierarchy may restrict flexibility for redefining methods in subclasses. In addition, you carry along all the method code even if you do not use it in every subclass. You should define the top of any class hierarchy with an *abstract* class, which implements no methods, but simply defines the methods that class will support. In your derived classes you have the ability and flexibility to implement each method in a manner that best suits your application's requirements.

There are many implementations of the GoF patterns available on the Web in many different programming languages. When you write applications using design patterns, write your invocations based on the interface specifications. As long as the implementation conforms to the interface specification, your application should work correctly, because it is unaware of the underlying classes used for the implementation.

If you were programming a brokerage account application, your set of stocks could be represented by different implementations. You merely write

```
Collection stocks = new <some subclass>;
Stocks.add(aStock);
```

Once you've settled on a pattern, you want to keep the implementations relatively consistent. Abstract classes/Java interfaces (as examples) fix the interface, but allow you freedom of implementation (see Figure 7-1).

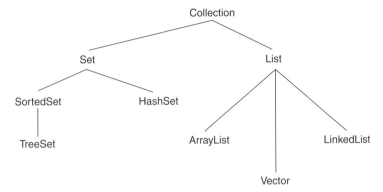

Figure 7-1. Java interface for collection.

Subclass Substitution Subclasses should be substitutable for their parent classes using the property of polymorphism. Meyer (1992) formulated this principle as part of his design by contract approach to specifying APIs. Any client of a parent class should continue to function if one of its subclasses is substituted for it. The contract defined for the parent class should be enforced in each of the subclasses. Most of us have experienced this principle in geometry, where we learned that a circle is just a degenerate form of an ellipse.

Partition the Interface for Flexibility Different clients may require different interfaces. Rather than having one large general-purpose interface with lots of parameters, design multiple interfaces—one per unique client—to improve flexibility. This prevents clients from invoking methods not intended for them since they can see all exported methods from a class. This approach is used widely in Microsoft's COM (see Section 10.3). Note that this does not require that every client have its own unique interface, only that the number of interfaces is designed to lessen the parameterization of the interface methods.

7.3 LIMITATIONS OF DESIGN PATTERNS

If you have searched the Web semiexhaustively, you will be convinced that there exist a plethora of design patterns. As we noted in Chapter 3, the definition of a design pattern is a well-tested solution to a recurring problem. And the goal is to disseminate this knowledge to as many practitioners as need or want to use it. But the terms "well-tested" and "recurring" are somewhat subjective, so the result is a possibly endless stream of design patterns of varying utility. This problem is exacerbated by the PLoP and other conferences.

Eventually, the number of design patterns will be too large to be either maintainable or comprehensible. Individual programmers will not be able to grasp the problem being solved by the varying patterns, and it will become laborious to search for a specific pattern that best fits the design problem at hand. So we can either limit the number of new patterns that are created and posted by placing restrictions on them—not a really good idea since we may intentionally miss a very useful design pattern—or we can reevaluate the design patterns already posted and determine which, according to some strict criteria, should really be design patterns or not. In the larger patterns community, this approach will meet with strong resistance. But as a personal endeavor, this may yield a reasonably sized library of patterns that you can use to solve problems that you encounter.

The problem with the latter approach, of course, is determining the criteria to use to help winnow the pattern set to something smaller, more usable, even more intimate. Bosch (1998) has noted the following limitations on implementing design patterns:

- *Traceability:* A design pattern generally cannot be traced in the implementation since the programming language does not support a corresponding concept.
- *Self Problem:* The implementation of several design patterns requires the forwarding of messages. Once the message is forwarded, the reference to the object originally receiving the message may no longer be available.
- *Reusability:* Since design patterns generally specify part of the behavior of a group of objects, patterns have no first class representation at the implementation level. Hence, the implementation of a design pattern cannot be reused.
- *Implementation Overhead:* Implementation of a design pattern often requires several methods with only trivial behavior, for example, forwarding a message to another object or method.

7.4 FURTHER READING

Coad, P. 1992. "Object-Oriented Patterns." *Communications of the ACM* 35(9):152–159.

Coplien, J. and D.C. Schmidt (eds.). 1995. *Pattern Languages of Program Design.* Addison Wesley, Reading, MA.

Kotula, J. 1996. "Discovering Patterns: An Industry Report." *Software—Practice and Experience* 26(11):1261–1276.

Lea, D. 1996. *Concurrent Programming in Java—Design Principles and Patterns.* Addison Wesley, Reading, MA.

Pattern Languages of Programs (PLoP) website with on-line conference proceedings, http://jerry.cs.uiuc.edu/~plop/.

Pree, W. 1994. *Design Patterns for Object-Oriented Software Development.* Addison Wesley, Reading, MA.

Riehle, D. and H. Züllighoven. 1996. "Understanding and Using Patterns in Software Development." *Theory and Practice of Object Systems* (*TAPOS*) 2(1):3–13.

Vlissides, J., J. Coplien, and N. Kerth (eds.). 1996. *Pattern Languages of Programs 2.* Addison Wesley, Reading, MA.

7.5   EXERCISES

7.1. Develop your own personal set of criteria for evaluating design patterns that you encounter. Select a dozen patterns and evaluate them using your criteria. Refine your criteria using the results and how you feel about the individual evaluations.

7.2. Does the order in which you apply or compose patterns matter? Find two examples and two counterexamples and describe them.

7.3. Patterns have been applied to many domains. Pick two domains other than the obvious ones mentioned in this book and discuss what additional description is required for patterns within those domains.

7.4. Suppose you have collected a large set of patterns from a number of colleagues and other expert sources. What criteria would you use to winnow that set down to something manageable?

II

COMPONENTS

Components are building blocks for information systems. The best analogy is the Lego building block system (http://www.lego.com) in which each block, of whatever shape, has a standard interface that allows it to be stacked and/or connected to other blocks (Figure II-1). These little blocks are standardized with plugs on one side and sockets on the other. A designer can draw on many different shapes, each plug-compatible with the others to form amazingly complex structures.

Unlike Legos, however, components may have varied functions, so the standard interfaces vary with the component. Nevertheless, the component's interfaces must adhere to certain standards in order to support integration of components into a large system structure. However, just as with Legos, the scale of the system can vary from small to large. My son has built multithousand block Lego structures that are truly complex. Systems can attain even greater complexity because of the diversity of components and the added requirement of interoperability.

Unlike design patterns, components may be partially or wholly instantiated objects. Partial instantiation may require parameterization (with recompilation and linking) and/or development and integration of customization code. Wholly instantiated components can be introduced into a system through plug-and-play mechanisms, such as the loading of "plug-ins" in Netscape Navigator.

Component-based software engineering (CBSE), which has arisen as a specialization of software engineering, focuses on the explicit use of components to create large, complex systems. The SEI has extended the component concept to the assembly line process through its product line architecture and engineering process.

Component engineering has taken two tracks. In one track, there is an emphasis on using components to build new, large applications. There are critical questions associated with integration, interoperability, interface matching, and so on. This track also

Software Paradigms, By Stephen H. Kaisler
ISBN 0-471-48347-8   Copyright © 2005 John Wiley & Sons, Inc.

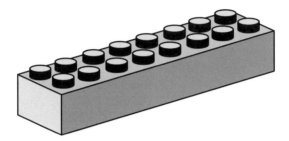

Figure II-1. Prototypical Lego block.

emphasizes the use of frameworks to help guide and direct the software architecture of the resulting applications. On the other track, there is an emphasis in extending existing applications and products with plug-in components that provide additional functionality. Here too, there are critical questions associated with integration, interoperability, and interfaces. Examples include Adobe Photoshop, Netscape, and Microsoft's Visual Basic.

This section begins by examining the basic definitions and concepts of components. It also addresses some of the issues associated with using components. The remainder of the section looks at various types and examples of components. Obviously, a book of this size cannot examine every type of component. We have tried to make a judicious selection of component types to examine in more detail that exemplify the fundamental concepts of components.

8

COMPONENT CONCEPTS

A *component* is a reusable software building block: a prebuilt piece of encapsulated application code that can be combined with other components and with additional code to produce a custom application. Components may be simple or complex. There is no general agreement on what is or is not a component. Components come in a variety of shapes and sizes. A component can be very small, such as a simple GUI widget (e.g., a button), or it can implement a complex application service, such as a network management function.

The commonly accepted notion of a component is a so-called "binary component," which is a compiled software artifact that is integrated into the application at runtime. Source code is usually not available, so the components cannot be modified. If they are implemented using an OOPL, they can be extended though inheritance or delegation. Examples of binary component systems include Microsoft's Windows 9x/NT Dynamically Loadable Library (DLL), Apple's OpenDoc, the Taligent CommonPoint system, and the Microsoft Foundation Classes (MFC).

An application is composed of a collection of components. Applications provide an environment, including some glue code or a code skeleton, into which components are plugged. Components interact with their environment and may interact with the operating system of the particular computer on which they are executed. Components also interact with each other through an interface. Changing a component's interface may require changing the components that use that interface. Changing a component's implementation should require no changes to the clients of that component.

Software Paradigms, By Stephen H. Kaisler
ISBN 0-471-48347-8   Copyright © 2005 John Wiley & Sons, Inc.

8.1   WHAT ARE SOFTWARE COMPONENTS?

A *software component* is an independently deliverable package of reusable software services in its most general sense. Philippe Kruchten of Rational Software believes that a component is a nontrivial, nearly independent, and replaceable part of a system that fulfills a clear function in the context of a well-defined architecture. A component conforms to and provides the physical realization of a set of interfaces. On the other hand, Szyperski (1998) sees a software component as a unit of composition with contractually specified interfaces and explicit context dependencies. A software component can be deployed independently and is subject to third-party composition. Thus, a business component represents the software implementation of an autonomous business operation or process.

8.1.1   Component Facets

A component has three facets, as depicted in Figure 8-1:

- A *specification*, which describes the services, for example, what the component does and how the clients should use it.
- An *implementation design*, which describes how an implementer has chosen to design and construct the software and data structures to meet the intended specification.
- An *executable* code, which delivers the component's capability on a designated platform through a designated interoperability standard.

The *interface* summarizes how the client should interact with the component but hides the underlying implementation details. The client, in turn, can depend on the interface to provide access to the proper services. But the specification model for an

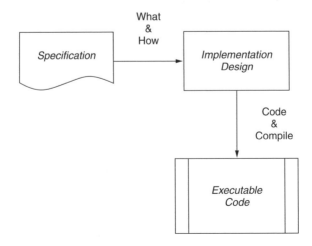

Figure 8-1. Component parts.

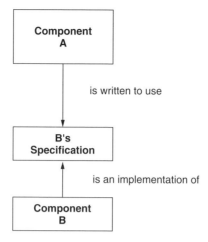

Figure 8-2. Relationship between two components.

interface is not an implementation design. The interface has no information about how the data is stored or organized. No access to the implementation of the component is provided or allowed by the interface.

We depict how two components are related in Figure 8-2.

Component B has a specification that is implemented in some programming language. Component A adheres to the API contained within B's specification when A invokes functionality provided by Component B.

Ideally, component implementations would be written in different programming languages and would execute on different software technology platforms from that used by the client program. However, today much component programming is still done in a single programming language.

Independently deliverable components must be unaware of the context in which they may be used. This does not mean that components have no dependencies on one another. For example, a component to perform spell checking may require the services of a dictionary manager component. We will need both components in the final application. However, we may be able to get the dictionary manager from several different sources. Knowing exactly which components work together will be a key requirement for exploiting component-based design.

8.1.2 Describing Interfaces

An interface is "a set of semantically related functions implemented on an object" (Brockschmidt 1994). An *interface* summarizes the behavior and responsibilities that any component will have to adhere to if it is to participate as part of an assembly that represents some application. The interface specifies the API used by clients of the component to request services from the component, but does not specify the implementation. This separation makes it possible to replace the implementation of a service without changing the interfaces and to add new services without changing the existing implementation.

Consider an automobile in motion. This is a system composed of an automobile and a human being. There is a collaboration between the steering wheel, the driver, and the vehicle. Let's consider how a driver drives an automobile. When the driver turns the steering wheel clockwise the car turns right, and when he turns it counterclockwise it turns left—relative to its present course, of course. The angle of deviation of the car is dependent on how far the wheel is turned in either direction. When the wheel is not turned, the car stays on its present course.

From this description we can identify certain terms: clockwise, counterclockwise, hold wheel steady, present course, angle of turn. Three operations spring to mind immediately: turn wheel clockwise, turn wheel counterclockwise, and hold wheel steady. Each of these becomes a method or procedure in the description of the steering wheel component of the moving automobile system. Each must be presented in the interface of the steering wheel component.

Now, consider a component called Membership Manager. Its function is to look after memberships. It could be used for many different types of organizations such as a sports club, a video store, or a library. Let's specify a few of its operations, such as these basic ones:

addMember(in aPerson)
removeMember(in aPerson)
paySubscription(in aPerson, amount)
getTotalMembers(out number)
getCurrentBalance(out amount)

Now, let's apply this to an example:

addMember(Sam)
addMember(Bill)
paySubscription(Sam, 100)
addMember(Anne)
paySubscription(Bill, 200)
getCurrentBalance() → 300
getTotalMembers() → 3

We need the notions of a set of CurrentMembers, a running count of the totalMembers, and a running total of the current Balance. These can be expressed in an interface specification box as depicted in Figure 8-3.

The component specification describes both the attributes and the interface of the component. The interface specification describes the method signatures. Various notations are used to specify public versus private methods.

Interfaces defined using standard techniques, such as interface definition languages (IDLs), are good at defining functional properties but cannot define behavioral properties such as accuracy, availability, or security.

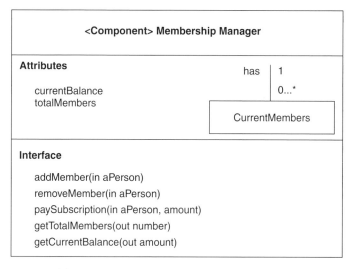

Figure 8-3. Interface specification for a component.

8.1.3   Are Components Objects?

A question that is often asked (by my students, at least) is: Are components objects? The short answer is no, but objects may be simple components. Many objects may comprise a component.

This question has been addressed in previous forums, including Henderson-Sellers et al. (1999) and DeSouza and Wills (1998). Let's recap what an object is. Conceptually, an object is an abstraction of a real-world entity characterized by a unique and invariant identifier, described by a class to which it belongs, and a state represented by a simple or complex value. The class defines the behavior of the object through its method definitions. The state of an object does not change spontaneously, but only as a result of the operations performed upon it through invocation of its methods. Many objects may be created from a class. Objects interact by invoking each other's methods.

Both components and objects support encapsulation and access through well-defined interfaces. Encapsulation is a function of the programming language's semantics for objects (weak—C++; strong—Ada 95) and a function of the runtime system for components. Kaisler (1997) defines strong encapsulation as "an object which has no external access to its attributes except through appropriately defined methods."

Both components and objects are abstractions of real-world entities, while components are often used to model more complex structures. We can use either objects or components to model a real-world entity, so this argument doesn't resolve the issue. One might consider a big object (e.g., many state variables and methods) as equivalent to a small component.

A significant difference is one of roles. An object is used to describe a real-world entity while a component is used to describe the services of a real-world entity. Put another way, objects are useful for describing the domain structure, while components describe its functionality. When an object requests a service, it does not know what other objects are providing that service. Since components must provide services to many different objects—often anonymously—it does not maintain state information unless that is a characteristic of the service it provides. This requirement must also flow through to the objects that make up the component.

Suppose we have a hardware driver that provides access to a set of similar devices, but each device has some unique characteristics. If a program does not care which device it gets service from, it can request the service from a component and let the component determine which device to use. The component invokes the appropriate methods in an object associated with a specific device. On the other hand, if the program knows exactly which device it needs service from, it might invoke either the component with the particular device specification or the specific object associated with the device.

To summarize, components provide services. Components are comprised of objects that, working together, implement the service provided by components.

8.1.4 Ada Packages as Components

Ada 95 packages were designed with component-based design and development as a primary goal. Each package consists of two parts: the package specification and the package body. The package specification describes the interface, for example, the operation signatures—both public and private, that the package supports. In Ada, the package specification is used at compile time to provide information about the public package variables and methods to other packages that intend to use them. The package body provides the implementation of the specification. The executable file is the compiled version of the Ada 95 package that is available to be bound into an application. The code in Figures 8-4a and 8-4b depicts an Ada 95 package for a buffer.

```
--
-- Programmed by:
--
-- Steve Kaisler
-- George Washington University
--
-- POS_BUFFER.ADS
--
-- This file written to provide a buffering capability
   between two
-- or more tasks
--


with Simple_IO; use Simple_IO;

with System.Address_to_Access_Conversions;
```

Figure 8-4a. Buffer specification.

```
with System; use System;

package buffer is

type Buffer_Record is
  record
    Task_ID: System.Address;
    Task_Message: System.Address;
  end record;

task type Buffer_Task is
  entry init(buffer_size: in Positive);
  entry clear;
  entry put(ID: in System.Address; MSG: in System.Address);
  entry get(ID: in System.Address; MSG: out System.Address);
  entry search(ID: in System.Address; ret: out Boolean);
  entry finalize;
end Buffer_Task;

type Buffer_Pointer is access all Buffer_Task;
subtype Buffer_Handle is Buffer_Pointer;

type Buffer_Record_Pointer is access all Buffer_Record;
subtype Buffer_Record_Handle is Buffer_Record_Pointer;

type Buffer_Array is array (Positive range <>) of
Buffer_Record_Handle;

type Buffer_Array_Pointer is access Buffer_Array;
subtype Buffer_Array_Handle is Buffer_Array_Pointer;

private

--procedure buffer_message(STR: in String);

Buffer_Space_Error: exception;

end buffer;
```

Figure 8-4a. (*Continued*)

```
--
-- Programmed by:
--
-- Steve Kaisler
-- George Washington University
--
-- BUFFER.ADB
```

Figure 8-4b. Buffer implementation.

```
--
-- This file written to provide a buffering capability between
   two
-- or more tasks
--

package body buffer is
  task body Buffer_Task is
    buffer: Buffer_Array_Handle;
    buffer_length: Positive;
    flag: Boolean;
    exit_flag: Boolean;

begin
  loop
    select
      accept init(buffer_size: in Positive) do
        --
        buffer := new Buffer_Array(1 .. buffer_size);
        --
        for i in 1 .. buffer_size
        loop
          buffer(i) := null;
        end loop;
        --
        buffer_length := buffer_size;

        exit_flag := False;
      end init;
    or
      accept clear do
        --
        for i in 1 .. buffer_length
        loop
          buffer(i) := null;
        end loop;
        --
      end clear;
    or
      accept put(ID: in System.Address; MSG: in
      System.Address) do
        --
        flag := False;

        -- Find an empty slot

        for i in 1 .. buffer_length
        loop
```

Figure 8-4b. Buffer implementation.

```
if (buffer(i) = null)
          then

              buffer(i) := new Buffer_Record;
              buffer(i).Task_ID := ID;
              buffer(I).Task_Message := MSG;

              flag := True;

              exit;

          end if;
        end loop;
        --
        if (flag = False)
        then
          raise Buffer_Space_Error;
        end if;

     end put;
   or
     accept get(ID: in System.Address; MSG: out
     System.Address) do
        --
        for i in 1 .. buffer_length
        loop
          if (buffer(i) = null)
          then
            null;
          elsif (buffer(i).Task_ID = ID)
          then
            MSG := buffer(i).Task_Message;
            buffer(i) := null;
            exit;
          else
            null;
          end if;
        end loop;
     end get;
   or
     accept search(ID: in System.Address; ret: out Boolean)
     do
        --
        ret := False;
        --
        for i in 1 .. buffer_length
        loop
          if (buffer(i).Task_ID = ID)
```

Figure 8-4b. (*Continued*)

```
        then
           ret := True;
           exit;
        end if;
      end loop;
    end search;
 or
   accept finalize do
      exit_flag := True;
   end finalize;
 end select;
 exit when exit_flag = True;
end loop;
--
end Buffer_Task;
--
end buffer;
```

Figure 8-4b. (*Continued*)

Now, is this a component? Yes, but a small component with a few methods. It provides a mediating service between two or more clients that enables the clients to proceed independently.

We should note that there is no constraint on the size of components. Some commercially available components have tens or hundreds of methods and thousands of lines of code.

8.2   WHY USE COMPONENTS?

Today, more and more software is being based on components. Until recently, most software continued to be built for a specific purpose and was frequently implemented and deployed as complex, monolithic systems that were incapable of change. This has been changing as the larger software vendors and large system development and consulting firms recognize that significant profits can be made by entering the components market.

Currently, about 70% of the spending of IS organizations is devoted to maintaining existing systems. Often, this maintenance includes making enhancements to these systems. The cost of maintenance increases with the time an application has been in use. An older application will require additional maintenance due to increasing size, complexity, and the number of integration points with other applications. Also, maintenance is usually performed using a methodology other than the one used for the original development. So components may tend to exhibit a patchwork structure over time. Also, maintenance itself requires additional maintenance, so that more resources are consumed by maintenance over time. Thus, many large organizations are precluded from any significant redesign of their mission-critical systems.

In many organizations, there are mission-critical applications that are as much as ten or more years old. Many of these use outmoded or obsolete technology. Despite the cost of maintenance, organizations often keep legacy systems in place as the best low-cost and low-risk approach. The maintenance cost and risk for legacy systems are a significant factor in the replacement decision because of how this software has evolved over its life cycle. Each round of maintenance will increase the size and interrelation of systems elements leading to the "n to n − 1" integration problem.

One solution to these problems is to use components. Components can be packaged to be usable by a domain expert, who is not necessarily an expert programmer, to design new applications. A component can capture a level of abstraction without exposing the end-user to this terminology. Components allow software vendors to build visual software development environments in which the concept of plugging together "software modules" forms the basis of any new development effort. Typically, the components of interest are imported and customized without explicit coding. Finally, they are wired together to form an application.

One of the major benefits of component-based construction is that manufacturers and developers can specialize in what they know best. Let's draw an analogy with the hardware domain. Seagate and Quantum can concentrate on designing the best hard disk drives possible, and compete with each other to do so. Similarly, Matrox and STB can ignore the issues that concern disk drive design and concentrate on producing good graphics cards. PC companies like Compaq, Dell, and Gateway can pick and choose the best components for their systems and can work out any problems that might arise when the components are plugged together.

In summary, the advantages of using components are as follows:

Increased productivity gained by reuse of design and implementation.

Increased reliability by using well-tested code.

Lower maintenance costs because of a smaller code base.

Minimization of effects of change since black-box programming tends to rely on interfaces as compared to explicit programming.

Provision of a well-encapsulated mechanism to package, distribute, and reuse software.

8.2.1 Component Composition

A key benefit of using components is that we can combine two or more components to produce a new component. Generally, we assume the new component encapsulates the enclosed components in a black box. This is an application of the Wrapper and Adapter design patterns discussed previously.

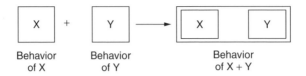

Figure 8-5. Understanding the behavior of composed components.

Any component assembly can become a part of a larger assembly. All assemblies are potential subsystems. Because components provide services, we must assess and predict the emergent behavior of a collection of components working together. Often, this cannot be predicted just from an analysis of the interactions of the components.

When we compose components, we can simplify some of our understanding about how an application will work. For example, suppose we are given two components, call them X and Y. If we understand how X and Y work individually and separately, then we must be able to deduce their combined behavior when encapsulated in another component (Figure 8-5).

If we look at the hardware industry today, component composition is the norm rather than the exception. Not long ago, computer hardware manufacturers made almost every component of a computer system, right down to the monitors and printers (e.g., read about Digital Equipment Corporation or IBM Corporation). But, just recently, a friend of mine went to a computer show and bought the components for a Wintel computer system from six different vendors. When he got home, he plugged them all together, loaded the Windows XP operating system, and had a working computer system for his son!

Today, we cannot generally do this with software, although there are many instances of software applications that allow plug-ins, such as the Netscape Browser. The question we must ask ourselves is: Why not? The corollary question we must ask is: Why does it work for hardware manufacturers, but not for software vendors? The answer seems to be that we still do not have standard component definitions for commonly provided services. And even when there are standards, vendors routinely provide "enhancements" that lead to incompatibilities.

The problem stems, in part, from our inability to know a priori that the security of a component composed from components A and B can be determined from knowledge about the security of component A and the security of component B. The security of the resulting component is more than just the sum of the security of the individual components because of the interactions between the two components.

In general, we can characterize the problem as follows. Assess the functional correctness of a composed component $f(A \times B) = f(A) \times f(B)$ for some "ility," such as security, reliability, or availability. Consider A to be an operating system and B an intrusion detection system (IDS) at an Internet boundary. The operating system has a built-in authentication mechanism and the IDS has a mechanism for detecting known patterns of events that might presage an attack. The security of the entire system depends on the security of the individual components. The IDS may fail to recognize a particular type of attack, but the operating system may be able to prevent access.

The question, I suppose, is: Which, if any, of the "ilities" are easy to compose? The answer, I think, is there are no "ilities" that are easy to compose, but there are some that are harder to compose than others. Let me make an analogy for you. In physics, there is the so-called N-body problem. Various characteristics of two-body problems can be solved, but three-body problems are not generally tractable and must be solved with significant simplifying assumptions. The larger N is, the worse the problem becomes. I suggest a similar problem besets us in composing multiple components.

8.2.2 Component Integration

We combine components through integration to develop an application that solves a class of problems. As we'll see Part IV, frameworks are a structured collection of components, some of which must be instantiated by the application developer.

Component integration is a "wiring together" process. Connections between components must be made by setting attribute values in components and developing glue code to couple them together. As we'll see in Part III, some predefined wiring schemes have proved their utility and versatility over large classes of problems.

One of the key problems is architectural mismatch as described by Garlan et al. (1995):

> Architectural mismatch stems from mismatched assumptions a reusable part makes about the structure of the system it is to be part of. These assumptions often conflict with the assumptions of other parts and are almost always implicit, making them extremely difficult to analyze before building the system.

They point out four types of structural assumptions that must be addressed during application development:

1. The nature of components (infrastructure, control model, and data model).
2. The nature of connectors (protocols and data models).
3. The architecture of the assemblies (constraints on interactions).
4. The runtime construction process (order of instantiations).

The remainder of this part will address assumption type 1 as we discuss components in more detail. Assumption types 2 and 3 will be addressed in the software architecture part. Assumption type 4 is outside the scope of this book, but investigation of current frameworks, such as .NET or J2EE—both mentioned in Part IV, will highlight some of the problems that are encountered in initializing an application built on a framework.

8.2.3 Component Substitution

The basic idea of components allows us to substitute one component for another—often to improve performance. A component Y can be substituted for a component X if all applications that work with component X will work with component Y. Syntactically, we can replace one component with another if the new component implements at least all of the interfaces of the old component, or the interface of the new component is a subtype of interface of the old component.

In elementary school geometry, we learned that a square is just a degenerate rectangle. Both have four sides: the rectangle's pairs of sides may be of unequal length, while the square's sides must all be of the same length. To accommodate both square and rectangle, we might have to do something like the following:

```
class Rectangle
  {
  public:
    virtual void SetWidth(int w)
      {
      itsWidth=w;
      }
    virtual void SetHeight(int h)
      {
      itsHeight=h;
      }
    int GetHeight()
      {
      return itsHeight;
      }
    int GetWidth()
      {
      return itsWidth;
      }

  private:
    int itsHeight;
    int itsWidth;
  };

class Square : public Rectangle
  {
  public:
    virtual void SetWidth(int w);
    virtual void SetHeight(int h);
  };

  void Square::SetWidth(int w)
  {
    Rectangle::SetWidth(w);
```

```
    Rectangle::SetHeight(w);
}

void Square::SetHeight(int h)
{
Rectangle::SetHeight(h);
Rectangle::SetWidth(h);
}
```

With this code, we can use a Square object wherever we use a Rectangle object. The Rectangle remains a rectangle and the Square remains a square with the appropriate attributes properly set.

8.3 COMPONENT MODELS

A *component model* defines the basic architecture of a component and specifies the structure of its interfaces and the mechanisms by which it interacts with its environment and with other components. A component model provides guidelines to create and implement components that can work together to form a larger application.

Every component must have two basic attributes: encapsulation and a well-defined interface. *Encapsulation* means that its inner workings must be hidden from the outside world. Computer system vendors like Compaq and Gateway do not concern themselves with the inner workings of disk drives they install in their workstations as long as they adhere to a standard interface and provide the level of performance and reliability required. The component must also provide a documented, well-defined *interface* to the world by which other components can interact with it. This interface must conform to an accepted standard in order to ensure that the component can interoperate with other components. Ideally, components will also incorporate the object-oriented property of inheritance so that they can be extended and instantiated.

We'll briefly discuss three component models: CORBA, Web Browsers, and the Macintosh OS in the following sections. Microsoft's COM/DCOM specification, described in Section 10.3, is also a component model.

8.3.1 The CORBA Component Models

The CORBA component model (CCM) is a distributed object-oriented model that describes an architecture for defining components and their interactions, including both client and server-side components. The CCM extends the CORBA framework (see Section 10.1) by defining features and services that enable application developers to implement, manage, configure, and deploy components that integrate commonly used CORBA services, such as transaction, security, persistent state, and event notification services, in a standard environment. It provides a framework for specifying various nonfunctional attributes including life cycle, (de)activation, security,

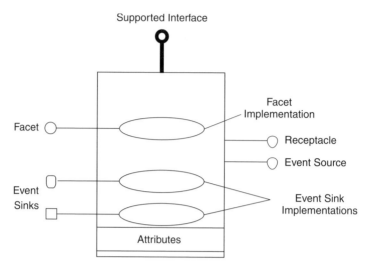

Figure 8-6. CCM component structure.

transactions, persistence, and event handling. It promotes interoperability with Enterprise JavaBeans (see Section 10.4.3) and provides multilingual executables. In effect, the CCM enables a CORBA "plug-and-play" architecture. A CCM component consists of attributes and ports as depicted in Figure 8-6.

A *port* is one of three types: a facet, a receptacle, or an event source/sink. A port mechanism specifies different views and the required interfaces that a component exposes to clients.

The *supported interface* is the set of methods inherited from superclasses of this component. Each component either redefines these methods or uses a method definition in some superclass. A *facet* is an interface provided by the component, which can be varied from client to client and invoked either synchronously or asynchronously. Facets allow CCM components to expose different interfaces to different clients based on the IDL used to describe the component.

A *receptacle* is a connection to another component that allows a component to delegate work, for example, invoke a method in the other component. To access the other component, the calling component must have a handle of the component to be called, which is stored in the receptacle.

Event sinks allow components to respond to asynchronously occurring events. They are based loosely on the Observer pattern described by the GoF (Gamma et al. 1995). A component declares its interest to publish or subscribe to events by specifying *event sources* and *event sinks* in its definition.

The CCM allows an existing component to be replaced by a new component that extends the original component definition by adding new interfaces *without affecting existing clients* of the component. Moreover, new clients can check whether a component provides a certain interface by using the CCM `Navigation` interface, which enumerates all facets provided by a component.

A typical CCM architecture consists of:

- CCM containers.
- The CORBA components that run in these containers.
- The Portable Object Adapter (POA).
- The Object Request Broker (ORB).
- Other CORBA services as needed.

An application server provider creates and sells an application server along with the CCM containers that run on this server. CCM providers develop components that run on these servers. Application developers use the prebuilt CORBA components to build their applications. This environment is depicted in Figure 8-7.

A client uses a CCM component to obtain a service. They find the service through CORBA lookup services and acquire the CCM Container name. The client calls the CCM container methods, which invoke the CCM component methods to provide the service.

The application server implements a virtual machine, which runs on top of a specific operating system. It provides basic execution services, such as multiprocessing, device access, and naming and transaction services, and makes the containers visible to potential clients.

The *CCM containers* act as proxies or adapters to interface between the CORBA component and the external environment. A CCM client never accesses a CORBA component directly. Any component access is performed through container-generated methods, which in turn invoke the component's methods. Containers are either transient or persistent. *Transient containers* may contain components whose states are not saved at all, while *persistent containers* may contain components whose states are saved between invocations.

A CCM component may have multiple interfaces. As the IDL is defined for each component, the interfaces (also called facets) that it provides and the interfaces that it uses have to be specified. Similarly, the events that it generates and the events that it consumes have to be defined in the IDL. The ability to use an interface is facilitated by declaring it as a receptacle. Event generation declarations are used to define an event

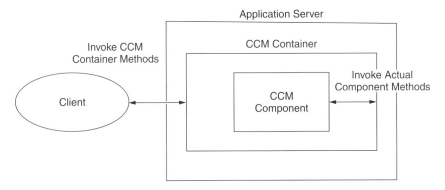

Figure 8-7. CCM architecture example.

source. Event consumption declarations are used to describe event sinks. Facets provide for synchronous invocation while event sinks provide for asynchronous invocation of services. Facets, receptacles, event sources, and event sinks are collectively called Ports.

Table 8-1 depicts the four types of CCM components.

Like EJB, CCM uses XML descriptors for specifying information about packaging and deployment. However, CCM has an assembly descriptor, which contains metadata about how two or more CCM components are wired together.

8.3.2 Other Component Models

Component models exist for many applications and systems that use components as the basis for their implementation. A few are described briefly below.

Web Browser Component Model   Web browsers are powerful interpreters that dynamically generate environments (the displayed pages) based on specifications presented to them serially. HTML-based languages treat Web applications as collections of files linked to one another via `<a href>` and `<form>` commands coded inside the files.

Table 8-1. CORBA component model types

CCM Component Type	Description
Service	A Service component is usually associated with one CCM Client. Its lifetime is restricted to one single operation request (or a single method call). Each Service component is created and destroyed by the particular CCM Client with which it is associated. Service components do not survive an application termination.
Session	A Session component is usually associated with one CCM Client. A Session component is created and destroyed by the particular CCM Client with which it is associated. A Session component can either have states or they can be stateless. However, Session components do not survive an application termination. A Session component is very similar to a Session EJB.
Process	A Process component always has a state. Each Process component may be shared by multiple CCM Clients. Their states can be persistent and stored across multiple invocations. Hence, they can survive application termination.
Entity	An Entity component always has a state. Each Entity component may be shared by multiple CCM Clients. Their states can be persistent and stored across multiple invocations. Hence, they can survive application termination. Each Entity component can be identified uniquely by its Primary Key. An Entity component is very similar to an Entity EJB.

HTML is a language for describing Web pages that are displayed through a Web-enabled application such as the Netscape, Mozilla, and Microsoft Internet Explore browsers and Microsoft's Word. Page structures are described using a set of predefined tags. However, to make a browser more of an application container, a good component model was needed to incorporate components dynamically. Dynamic HTML (DHTML) provides the mechanism for linking components that are downloaded into the browser.

Macintosh OS Component Model   Early in its development, Apple determined that the Macintosh operating system could not provide every service that every application needed by itself. External support for certain kinds of services would be required. So Apple built into the MacOS an extensibility feature that allowed third party vendors to provide extensions that either enhanced existing services or provided new types of services. Extensions are stored in the Extensions folder in the System folder. When the MacOS is loaded, all of the extensions in the Extensions folder are also loaded. Each extension provides additional functionality that the MacOS did not originally include. However, most of these extensions are specific to vendor applications.

8.3.3   Component Model Elements

What should a standard for component models specify? Table 8-2 suggests some elements for generic as well as distributed components.

Table 8-3 briefly describes the generic model elements.

From a syntactic viewpoint, the interface specification of the "used" components must allow the "using" components to get the services they need. When both sets of components are written in the same programming language or programming language paradigm, this property is easy to satisfy. However, different programming language paradigms introduce transformation and translation problems that can overwhelm the benefits of using components. For example, attempting to directly

Table 8-2. Component model elements

Generic	Distributed System
Properties	Transaction Model
Constraints	Persistence Model
Event Model	Concurrency Control
Introspection	Security
Customization	Quality of Service
Composition	Manageability
Reliability	
Packaging and Installation	

Table 8-3. Generic component model elements

Element	Description
Properties	The component model must provide an abstract view of the externally visible state of a component. This view is typically available through the API. Clients must be able to set component properties through the API as well. For example, Java Server Pages use the jsp:setProperty method.
Constraints	The model must provide a means of specifying constraints on property values and cross-property constraint specifications. Internal to the component should be the constraint-checking mechanisms that prevent incorrect values from being assigned to the property. Cross-property constraints should be embedded in internal methods but publicly disclosed in the component specification.
Event Model	The model must provide a mechanism for specifying the propagation of occurrences of activity. A specific activity could be a change in the value of a property. The model must specify what happens when an event occurs.
Introspection	The model should provide a means of reflecting on the component's capabilities. Introspection is hard to build into a component because it requires a metadata structure that captures information about the component itself. This requirement makes maintenance doubly difficult—not only must the programmer maintain the code for the methods of the components, but he must also maintain the information about those methods in the metadata structure.
Customization	The model must provide a means for customizing the behavior of the component through inheritance or delegation.
Composition	The model must provide a means of making complex components by putting together simple ones. This mechanism should support both syntactic and semantic interoperability.
Reliability	The model should provide a way for a client to determine how reliable a component is from which it will request services or to which it will send messages. Assessing and ensuring the reliability of a component are two difficult tasks. Similarly, the component developer must find a way both to ensure his component's reliability given different operating environments and to provide a means to convey that reliability to potential clients. This is an open research issue in developing component technology.
Packaging and Installation	The model should provide a mechanism for putting a component together for software distribution and then using a component package in building an application.
Security	Security is primarily a combination of access control, intrusion detection, authentication, and encryption. Controlling the communication process allows us to encrypt communications, reliably send user authentication from client to server, and check the access rights of requests, all

Table 8-3. (*Continued*)

Element	Description
	independent of the actual application code. These mechanisms can all be imposed on a component-based system by controlling its communications, whether security is a server-side consideration alone or needs to be specified outside this realm.
Quality of Service	Quality of Service (QoS) encompasses a variety of requirements for getting things done within time constraints. The real-time community recognizes two varieties of real-time systems: *hard real-time* and *soft real-time*. Hard real-time systems have tasks that must be completed at particular deadlines, or else the system is incorrect. To achieve hard real-time systems, one can either reserve resources and plan consumption or use some kind of anytime algorithm. Hard real-time requires cooperation throughout the processing chain, because the promise of a particular service can be abrogated in too many places. The entire system is designed with hard real-time constraint and operation in mind. Soft real-time systems seek to allocate resources so as to accomplish the most important tasks. Soft real-time systems are often amenable to the underlying communication control. Much of the recent work in communication protocols is dedicated to improving the quality of service of communications systems.

call components written in Prolog or Common Lisp from a Java program is a difficult problem. Invoking them through a process is less difficult but introduces other problems.

Composition has a requirement for interoperability as well. Not only must components be able to request services and pass data, but there must be some cognizance on the part of the calling component of characteristics of the service. For example, if the using component will make repeated calls to another component, it needs to know if the data it has passed is persistently stored or not. In the latter case, more data may need to be passed with each successive call, necessitating repetitive processing inside the called component.

Table 8-4 depicts the distributed component model elements.

Configuration management is partially an issue of component life cycle and partially an issue of the operating environment. In the former, procedures must be in place to ensure that the right version(s) of the component is distributed to the right location(s). In the latter, communication control must ensure that knowledge of the right component is made available (somehow) to clients and that messages are properly directed to the right version of the component at the right location.

Table 8-4. Distributed component model elements

Element	Description
Transaction Model	A mechanism for handling protected interactions among components distributed across multiple systems.
Persistence	A mechanism for ensuring a persisting state of a component.
Concurrency Control	A mechanism for handling concurrent execution of multiple components on the same computer system.
Security	A mechanism for ensuring security across multiple systems for communicating and interoperating components.
Quality of Service	A mechanism for ensuring appropriate responsiveness to client requests.
Manageability	The OSI model defines five elements to system manageability: performance measurement, accounting, failure analysis, intrusion detection, and configuration management. The first four of these are handled during application execution, usually through generation of the proper events and messages to the appropriate recipients—whether other processes or human operators.

8.4 USING COMPONENTS

Components may be statically or dynamically bound. Basically, the binding problem can be expressed as: What do we know about a variable and when do we know it? Today, much component usage still occurs through static binding, for example, the Edit-Compile-Link-Execute (ECLE) model. However, plug-and-play or dynamic linking environments are becoming more prevalent as dynamic binding technology evolves. Dynamic binding allows new objects and code to be interfaced with or added to a system without affecting existing code.

8.4.1 Static Binding

The basis for static binding is the ECLE model. The ECLE model can be depicted as shown in Figure 8-8.

A source code unit is opened with an editor for creation or revision. After editing, a revised version of the source code unit is emitted to be stored (usually) on the file system. Next, a source code unit is compiled to create an object module. If compilation errors occur, the source code unit must be re-edited.

Multiple object modules are linked along with language and system libraries to form a load module. If linking errors occur, source code units must be recompiled or re-edited, depending on the nature of the error. Sometimes, additional library units must also be specified.

The load module is loaded by the operating system and executed. If execution errors occur, the source code units must be recompiled or re-edited, or object modules must be relinked.

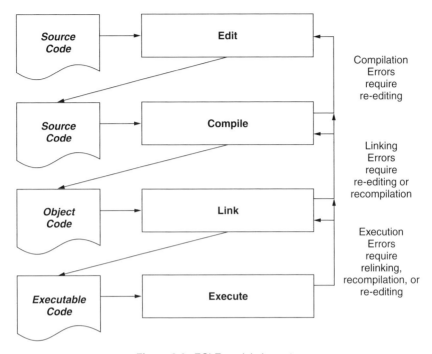

Figure 8-8. ECLE model elements.

In this model, the resulting executable code contains a copy of every procedure required by the application. Thus, the exact code to be executed is known before execution starts. If the contents of any source code unit are changed, it must be edited, recompiled, and relinked to form a new load module. Similarly, if system or language libraries change, the load module must be relinked with new libraries.

8.4.2 Dynamic Binding

In dynamic binding, linking of load modules is deferred until execution time. Load modules may be loaded on-demand and bound as required by the application's execution.

Dynamic binding occurs in three forms: control, data, and function. Control binding involves the use of an event-based model to support asynchronous notification of events. Data binding involves the use of a semantic markup language, such as XML, to determine the meaning based on the context in which the data is used. Function binding uses polymorphism to determine which version of a function to execute based on the data passed to the function.

Control Binding   In *control binding*, an adapter provides the mechanism for effecting communication between the two components (Figure 8-9). The adapter provides a known, static interface through which the components are coupled. The

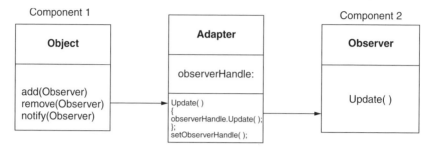

Figure 8-9. Control binding.

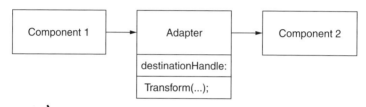

Figure 8-10. Data binding.

Wrapper, Proxy, and Adapter design patterns are examples of such mechanisms. However, the adapter maintains a handle variable of type Observer to which can be assigned the handle of any known observer component. The adapter's setObserverHandle(...) method is called to assign the handle of an Observer component to the variable at runtime.

Data Binding   In data binding, a formatted message is passed between two components possibly using an Adapter to transform the message. Recently, XML has emerged as a formatting scheme because it can carry the specification for transformation with it, such as the name of an applet. In Figure 8-10, Component 1 sends a message to Component 2 through an Adapter. The Adapter reviews the message, determines if a transformation is required, and, if so, performs it, then sends the message to Component 2. Component 2 does not need to know the message has been transformed. This is a flexible coupling mechanism, but the message transformation process may require considerable time.

Function Binding   Function binding is based largely on the notion of polymorphism. Component 1 invokes a function in Component 2 to handle the event based on the type of event. Multiple copies of the event handling function, each oriented to a particular event type, are defined in Component 2 using polymorphism. The specific function dispatched depends on the event type passed as an argument (Figure 8-11).

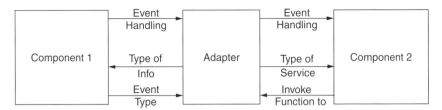

Figure 8-11. Function binding.

8.5   COMPONENT REUSE

A major motivation for using components is the ability to reuse them in other applications. During the design of an application, you should already be thinking about which components might be reusable in other similar applications. Although it is possible to design with reuse as an objective, you must be careful not to design components that are not reusable. Reusability solutions emphasize simplicity; you can build the complexity in when you reuse the component.

Reusable software components as a practice apply the power and benefit of reusable, interchangeable parts, as practiced in other industries, to the field of software construction. Other industries have long profited from interchangeable, reusable components, because of standard interfaces. Reusable electronic components, such as resistors and power supplies, are found on circuit boards. A typical part in your car can be replaced by a component made from one of many different competing manufacturers, not necessarily the original manufacturer. Whole industries have been built around parts construction and supply in most competitive fields.

The component reusability problem is depicted in Figure 8-12. The client expects a component to have an interface defined by type specification X. The component implements type specification Y. The critical question concerns conformance between type specification X and type specification Y. Table 8-5 depicts the degree of conformance.

When X implements an API that is a subset or equivalent to Y's API, then the component is conformant with the client. But when Y's API is less than what X expects, errors may occur. However, X may properly use Y and thus avoid errors.

8.5.1   Properties of Reusable Components

The properties of reusable components vary with the author. Here's a list with which I feel comfortable.

- *Additivity:* Able to combine components with minimal side effects and without destructive interaction.
- *Correct:* Allows correctness conditions to be stated and component combination to preserve key properties of components.

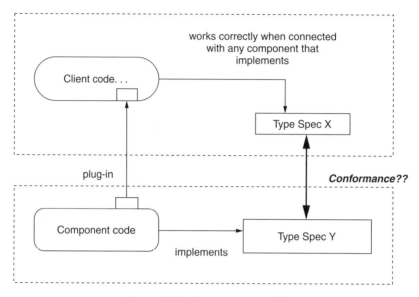

Figure 8-12. Component reusability.

Table 8-5. Degree of conformance

Type Spec X	Type Spec Y
<	OK
=	OK
>	Errors may occur

- *Self-contained:* Each component embodies only a single idea.
- *Easily Describable:* Easy to understand.
- *Programming Language Independent:* Not unnecessarily specific about superficial language details.
- *Verifiable:* Easy to test that the component provides the advertised services.
- *Simple Interface:* Minimal number of parameters passed and parameters passed explicitly.
- *Easily Changed:* Easy to modify with minimal and obvious side effects.
- *Reusable:* Has high reuse potential; likely to be usable in many systems.

8.5.2   Guidelines for Reusability

If the component that you build for reusability is too complex, it will either be unusable or only a small portion of it will be reused. A key rule of thumb is to design just as much as you need and no more.

There are three concepts that you should keep in mind when designing for reusability:

1. *Design Interfaces for Common Behavior*: A component's public interface should reflect the common behavior that can be reused in other applications. Its private interface is used to capture application-specific behavior. Of course, the common behavior is encoded in a set of subprograms or methods that do not contain application-specific data or code.

   Different components may provide the same interface, albeit with different typing. This is a form of specification reuse. Specific functionality is obtained by calling a particular component object. For example, suppose there are different ways to order a product—by phone, mail, web, email, and so on. The order must be received from the individual or system ordering the product but is ultimately entered into the ordering system. You can design a common interface for order entry that receives its input from other components, each of which services a particular mode of receiving an order.

2. *Generalize Functionality for Reusability*: As you think about functionality, think also about its generalization. A hierarchy of components—especially in object-oriented systems—can support generic interfaces with application-specific functionality provided through inheritance in subclasses and component objects.

   The top-level component will have very simple generic interfaces. In many cases, these will resemble the database CRUD operations. For example, many GUIs define a window component with just a few basic operations. Subclasses of the window component add more functionality and more detail such as scroll bars and menus.

3. *Use Facades to Hide Other Interfaces*: As noted by Gamma et al. (1995), a facade is a type of interface that passes control to other interfaces. It may reformat, extend, or reduce the arguments to the underlying interfaces. Facades also allow one component to connect to multiple underlying, more specialized components as determined by the application you are building.

8.5.3 Rolling Your Own Components

So you've decided to develop your own components. This is always an option. Most programmers feel they can develop software better than anyone else. This hubris can lead to disaster—a "can't see the forest for the trees" syndrome. Table 8-6 lists some tips that you should consider when designing and creating your own components.

Clearly, this list is idiosyncratic. You may have your own list.

8.5.4 Component Reuse Metrics

If we practice reuse, we need to measure how good we are doing. Without quantifiable measures, we do not have a basis for improvement. Table 8-7 provides some reuse metrics that you might find useful.

Table 8-6. Component design tips

Use code inspection and tools to develop your code.

Avoid implicit initialization; for example, clearly define and document default state.

Define a single header file that contains the complete interface for your component.

Don't write error messages to standard output.

Return an error code for each kind of problem.

Throw explicit exceptions.

Never exit from a component; always return to the caller.

Define each function to do something reasonable in any state.

Build components that fit in with standard frameworks; document assumptions about the infrastructure in which the components will operate.

Understand that you can't control how others will use your component(s), so plan accordingly (i.e., program defensively).

Table 8-7. Component reuse metrics

Metric	Definition
Commonality	How frequently a component recurs across a set or family of systems.
Reuse threshold	Indicates the minimum number of times a reusable component must be reused to pay back the investment in creating or preparing it for reuse.
Reuse merit	A measure of the reusability of a component relative to the average reusability of a component of the same type.
Reuse creation cost	A measure of the cost of creating or preparing a component for reuse. This includes the costs of purchasing the component, identifying it via domain analysis, and preparing it for reuse.
Reuse usage cost	A measure of the user-related costs incurred each time the component is reused. This includes the costs of finding, understanding, modifying/specializing, and integrating the reusable component.
Reuse maintenance cost	A measure of the costs of supporting a reusable component.
Degree of commonality	A measure of the proportion of an application's components that are common with other applications.
Degree of reusability	A measure of the proportion of an application's components that are reusable.
Reuse target level	Indicates the minimum proportion of an application's components that is reusable.
Reuse merit	A measure of the proportion of an application that is reusable relative to the average proportion for an application across the entire organization.

Table 8-8. Identifying reusable components

Is the component functionality required in future applications?
How common is the component's function within the domain?
Is there duplication of the component's function within the domain?
Is the component platform-independent (e.g., both hardware and software)?
Does the component remain unchanged between implementations?
Are there common elements used by multiple components that can be removed to
  another component?
Is the component customizable?
Are there nonreusable components that could be parameterized to make them reusable?
Can the component be made reusable with minor modifications?
Can a nonreusable component be decomposed to yield some reusable components?

8.5.5 Identifying Reusable Components

In order to be able to reuse components, we must describe them in such a way that the potential use can understand what the component does and how to use it. Table 8-8 provides a number of questions to help guide you in identifying reusable components.

8.6 EXERCISES

8.1. What kinds of qualities should component or subsystem developers predict about their software artifacts? (*Note*: By "predict" we mean a description of the component's behavior under a specific set of environmental assumptions.)

8.2. What kinds of reasoning should a component or subsystem developer apply to attempt to predict the emergent behavior of a subsystem of composed components? Do you think the number of components has any influence on the emergent behavior? [Research Problem]

8.3. Define the following five properties of components and describe a procedure for measuring and certifying each property: performance, accuracy, reliability, security, and maintainability.

8.4. In Section 8.2.1, I made an analogy to the N-body problem in physics. Pick an "ility" and try to describe how you would characterize the composed behavior for two, three and an arbitrary number N of components. [Research Problem]

8.5. Rechtin (1991) has remarked that many problems in software architectures occur at the interfaces. These problems arise due to assumptions about environment and protocols. Describe a general procedure for assessing, evaluating, and testing the interface of a component using other test components.

8.6. Legos (see image at beginning of this part) are a great learning experience for all ages. What kinds of design patterns can you create with Lego blocks? [Research Problem, non-computer science]

8.7. Consider the code in Section 8.2.3 for a rectangle and a square. Suppose we inserted an assertion of a postcondition into the following function, which uses the Rectangle class:

```
void makeRectangle(Rectangle& rect)
  {
  rect.setWidth(6);
  rect.setHeight(5);
  assert(rect.getWidth() * rect.getHeight() = 30);
  }
```

What happens if we substitute a Square object for the Rectangle object?

9

TYPES OF COMPONENTS

There are many types of components available—commercially, academically, and as freeware/shareware. The types and number of components often depend on the application domain. For example, Table 9-1 depicts some of the component types available for the Apple QuickTime multimedia application (Apple 2001).

9.1 EVENT-BASED COMPONENTS

One category of components is event-based components (EBCs), that is, components that handle events of different types. This leads to a software architecture called event-based computing (see Section 16.2).

Event-based communications are asynchronous compared with the request/ response communications used in the standard client–server model for distributed systems. Many application areas can use event-driven operation as the most natural paradigm: interactive multimedia presentation support; telecommunications fault management; credit card fraud; disaster simulation and analysis; mobile programming environments; and location-oriented applications, among others.

An EBC usually implements a variation of the Observer design pattern (Gamma et al. 1995). Java implements delegation using the Observer design pattern. The basic idea is that certain objects are "observers" and certain objects are "observable." Observable objects describe events that occur in a specific and well-defined way. Observers are interested in when certain events occur to some set of observable

Software Paradigms, By Stephen H. Kaisler
ISBN 0-471-48347-8   Copyright © 2005 John Wiley & Sons, Inc.

Table 9-1. QuickTime component types

Component Type	Services
Movie controllers	Displays movies and provides playback controls.
Media handlers	Interpret and manipulate media sample data.
Video digitizers/Sequence grabbers	Convert analog video data to digital form. Confer the ability to obtain digitized data from external sources.
Data exchange	Imports and exports data from nonmovie sources and nonmovie formats.
Compressors/Decompressors	Provide compression and decompression services for media (such as sounds and image sequences).
Transcoders	Translate data from one compressed format to another.
Video output	Sends video to devices (such as DV Cameras) that are not recognized as displays by the computer.
Graphics importers	Display still images obtained from data in various file formats.
Graphics exporters	Store still images in the same format that graphics importers handle.
Preview	Creates and displays previews.
Tween	Performs interpolation between values of various data types.
Effects	Provide real-time effects and transitions.
Text channel	Imports and exports text between movies and external text handling applications such as word processors.
Clock	Generates timing information and schedules time-based callback events.
Real-time streaming	Allows the reception of movies and live video in real time without downloading large files.
Media presentation	Supports development of custom graphics importers, sound components, or music synthesizers.
Media capture	Supports creation of new Video Digitizer, image compressor, or image compressor dialog component.
Media handling	Handlers for video, sound, text, sprite, 3D, vector graphics, and between media. QuickTime includes base components for media handling, effects, and transitions and musical instruments.
Utility tasks	QuickTime includes data exchange components, sequence grabber channel and panel components, video digitizers, video output components, image transcoders, data handlers, streaming components, clock components, music components, and note allocators.

objects. In Java applications, GUI components play the role of observables, while your program plays the role of observer.

Figure 9-1 depicts the Observer design pattern. Each observer registers with the observable object. When a change occurs to the observable objects, it notifies all of its registered observers by calling their update() methods. Both the observable object and the observers are instantiated as concrete entities within the application.

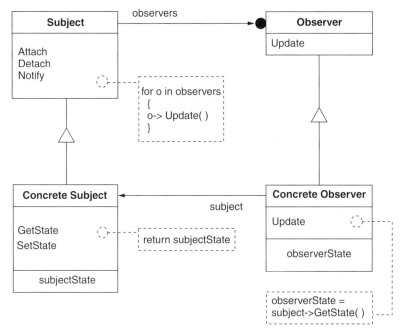

Figure 9-1. Observer design pattern.

9.1.1 Event Terminology

An *event* is something that happens that we might want to know about and possibly react to. Specifically, an event is defined as the occurrence of some interaction point between two computational objects in a system. In GUIs, visible events are mouse clicks and key presses as well as moving the cursor. Events may reflect internal changes to the system or external changes recognized by the system.

An *input event* is an event generated by user manipulation of an input device such as a joystick, mouse, or key. Events from devices attached to the computer system are usually referred to as *interrupt events* although they may ultimately transfer data into an application.

Raising an event is similar to a procedure call except that (1) the destination is unknown (who will handle the event); (2) normally, one cannot return from an event; and (3) it is not done to support local processing.

Event handlers are application modules that respond to events. In Java, event handlers are called *listeners*. Each Listener handles events of a certain type by implementing the appropriate interface.

9.1.2 Event-Based Component Integration

Event-based component integration allows components to be asynchronously coupled through the posting, dispatching, and handling of events. Figure 9-2 depicts the generic model.

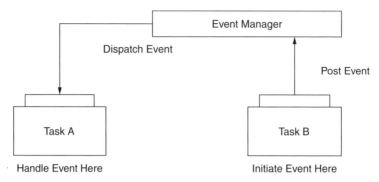

Figure 9-2. Event-based component integration.

Task B initiates an event and posts it to an event manager. The event manager dispatches the event to another task, which contains an event handler, that is, a capability to process the event. As discussed previously, the two tasks must register with the event handler to either post events or receive events.

9.1.3 Event Models

Each programming language or window system that supports events provides a specific way to describe and use events. This is called the *event model*. The Java event model is based on delegation. In delegation, events are associated with a specific component (source) and that component is charged with "delegating" responsibility for handling the event to other objects in the program.

There are two primary models for event-based communication: the *pull model* and the *push model*. In the pull model, event handlers regularly check with the event dispatcher to see if new events have occurred. In the push model, the dispatcher informs all event handlers that have registered that type of event that a particular event has occurred.

Under the *pull model*, an event handler requests a new event to process once it has completed processing an event. If an event of that type exists, it is dispatched to the requesting event handler. If not, the event handler waits an appropriate period of time and makes another request. This approach can balance the event processing load across the number of event handlers created for a specific type of event. However, if the number of events of a particular type is larger than the number of event handlers, events may be missed because all of the event handlers are busy.

Under the *push model*, an event handler is interrupted to receive notification of an event each time an event of any of the types it has registered for occurs. The event dispatcher begins the notification process until it finds an event handler that is free for that type of event. If the event dispatcher finds no event handler able to take the event, it has to queue it or discard it. In either case, the event may not be processed within the requisite time period. If the frequency of events of a particular type is large, the event handler may take a long time to complete processing of the event. In fact, it may not process the event satisfactorily because it runs out of time. This situation may cause errors in the system due to missed data or specific actions not being taken.

9.1.4   Web Services

A new application has evolved as a result of the Internet known as *Web services.* They look a lot like the client–server architecture that we will discuss in Section 14.2. The dynamic nature of Web services is partially based on a clear-cut division between *service requesters* and *service providers.* The provider can offer a Web service and the requester can look up, bind to, and invoke that Web service. The process is unidirectional: one component makes the call and the other responds. Though the communication is flexible, the stateless process is fixed. Normally, there is a request followed by a synchronous response.

Web services interfaces can be described using the Web Services Description Language (WSDL), an XML-based vocabulary whose data types and structures can be realized in multiple programming languages. It also uses the Observer design pattern to decouple the interaction between the requestor and the provider. Figure 9-3 depicts how the Observer pattern is adapted for the Web services application (Geysermans and Miller 2003).

The observer is initially the service requester and the subject is initially the service provider. However, the subject and observer become both clients and servers of each other when they are implemented using Web services. During the `update()` call,

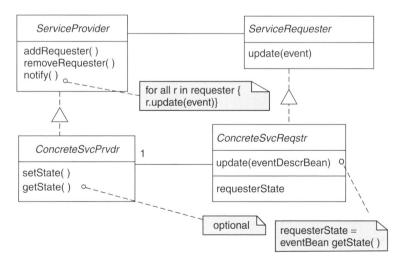

Figure 9-3. Web services using Observer pattern.

the subject is initiating a callback to the observer. At that point, they switch roles and the subject is the service requester and the observer is the service provider. Each component is a service requester at some points in the process and a service provider at others. By implementing the observer callback pattern using Web services, this provides a new mechanism for an asynchronous architecture over a synchronous infrastructure.

9.2 JAVA EVENTS

Java implements an event model as a first class element of the programming language. Events are objects in the Java object hierarchy. The Java event model was developed under the Advanced Windowing Toolkit (AWT). Swing uses the AWT event model almost entirely (which is why you must always import the `java.awt.event` package). However, Swing adds new events of its own.

The Java event model follows the client–server model. Each component acts as a server, which responds to or generates events in response to client actions. Some objects act as clients. They must register with the server object to be notified when an event is generated. Clients must implement certain methods defined by the server. When the client registers with the server object, it agrees to respond to method calls issued by the server object. In Java, we say the client "listens" for an event generated by the server.

An *event listener* is an object to which a component has delegated the task of handling a particular kind of event. Event listeners implement appropriate listener interfaces, which contain methods appropriate for handling the particular kind of event at hand. Table 9-2 lists the standard listeners implemented in Java.

If you implement an instance of WindowListener, you must define all seven methods even if some of them only have empty bodies. On the other hand, you may want to hand off event handling to another class. To do so, you need only implement an Adapter class (the middle column), which defines the methods for each listener. An object of the Adapter class then implements only those methods in another class that you want to handle the event. Other methods are stubbed out.

9.2.1 Types of Java Events

Java has made event handling a primary focus of its support for GUI programming in both the Advanced Windowing Toolkit (AWT) and the Swing classes. In GUI programming, the program reacts to the user's interaction. For example, the user moves the mouse and presses its button or presses a key.

An input event is dispatched to the Java component having the input focus when the user interacts with some input device. In games, input events are essential to handling user responses to game situations. User response handling establishes the feel of the game. Altering the means by which the system provides user response can significantly alter the "play" of the game.

Table 9-2. Java standard listeners

Listener Interface	Adapter Class	Interface Methods
ActionListener	*None*	actionPerformed
AdjustmentListener	*None*	adjustmentValueChanged
ComponentListener	ComponentAdapter	componentHidden componentMoved componentResized componentShown
ContainerListener	ContainerAdapter	componentAdded componentRemoved
FocusListener	FocusAdapter	focusGained focusLost
ItemListener	*None*	itemStateChanged
KeyListener	KeyAdapter	keyPressed keyReleased keyTyped
MouseListener	MouseAdapter	mouseClicked mouseEntered mouseExited mousePressed mouseReleased
MouseMotionListener	MouseMotionAdapter	mouseDragged mouseMoved
TextListener	*None*	textValueChanged
WindowListener	WindowAdapter	windowActivated windowClosed windowClosing windowDeactivated windowDeiconified windowIconified windowOpened

Java generally supports keyboard events and mouse events. Keyboard events are generated by pressing one or more keys on the keyboard. Key presses actually generate two events: key down and key up. Mouse events are generated by mouse button clicks and mouse movements. Mouse button clicks generate two events: mouse button down and mouse button up. An additional event is generated by mouse dragging: pressing a mouse button and moving the mouse.

All event objects inherit from AWT Event. Table 9-3 shows some of the types of Java events.

Table 9-3. Some Java event types

Event Type	Responds To
ComponentEvent	Moving, Resizing, Showing, Hiding
FocusEvent	Keyboard focus given or taken away
KeyEvent	Key pressed or released
MouseEvent	Motion, Dragging, Clicking, Entering, Leaving
ActionEvent	A ButtonComponent is pressed
AdjustmentEvent	Scrollbar Changes
ItemEvent	Choicelist and Checkbox Events
Others....	

9.2.2   Java Event Handling

Each event type is associated with a specific listener interface, which implements the methods that an implementing object must provide. We define the object as follows:

```
class A extends B implements ActionListener
  {
  ...
  }
```

A class may implement the listener interface for more than one type of event, which means that it may handle multiple types of events.

`ActionListener` specifies the method `actionPerformed(...)`, which takes an event as its argument. Instances of class A will provide handling for specific events. A particular instance may test the type of event and dismiss itself if it does not provide handling for that type of event.

Components provide a means for registering and deregistering interest in certain types of events. Examples include `addMouseListener(...)` and `addKeyListener(...)`.

9.2.3   Generic Listener Example

The generic form of a listener in Java is

```
public interface ActionListener
  {
  public void actionPerformed(ActionEvent e)
  }
```

Any class that implements ActionListener must provide a definition for the actionPerformed method.

```
public class MyActionListener implements ActionListener
  {
  public void actionPerformed(ActionEvent e)
```

```
      {
      // deal with event "e"...
      }
    }
```

A simple example of how to use a listener is depicted in the following code, which shows how to create a simple frame in Java with a few components:

```
import java.awt.*;
import java.awt.event.*;

/**
* Creates a Frame, add a few components, and sets up event-
handling.
* Event-handling will be done by the SimpleFrame
*/

public class SimpleFrame extends Frame implements
ActionListener
   {
   private static final int FRAME_HEIGHT = 100;
   private static final int FRAME_WIDTH = 200;

   // FIELDS

   private Button commandButton;
   private TextField infoField;
   private Label outputLabel;

   // METHODS

   public SimpleFrame()
      {
      // Create the button, add its listener
      commandButton = new Button("Click me");
      commandButton.setBounds(20,20,70,30);
      commandButton.addActionListener(this);

      // Create the text field, add its listener
      infoField = new TextField();
      infoField.setBounds(100,20,80,30);
      infoField.addActionListener(this);

      // Create the output label
      //
      outputLabel = new Label("NO EVENTS YET");
      outputLabel.setBounds(50,50,150,30);

      // Use absolute positioning to add components to frame
      setSize(FRAME_WIDTH, FRAME_HEIGHT);
```

```
    setLayout(null);
    add(commandButton);
    add(infoField);
    add(outputLabel);
    }

/**
  * Decide which component was the source of the event, do
  whatever
  * is necessary to deal with that event.
  */

  public void actionPerformed(ActionEvent e)
  {
  if (e.getSource() == infoField)
     {
     // If enter text and press return, put that text in the
     label
     outputLabel.setText(infoField.getText());
     }
     else if (e.getSource() == commandButton)
     {
     // If press the button, just put a message in the label
     outputLabel.setText("button clicked");
     }
  }
```

Method main() creates the frame and makes it visible. Referring to the class SimpleFrame above, we see it creates a command button and a field.

```
//
// Main Module
//
public static void main(String[] args)
   {
   Frame frame = new SimpleFrame();
   frame.setVisible(true);
   }
}
```

See Section 9.5 for some additional references on the Java event model.

9.3 DISTRIBUTED COMPONENTS

A *distributed system* (DS) is a collection of autonomous, geographically dispersed computing entities (hardware and software) connected by one or more communications systems. A *distributed application* is one that executes on a distributed system, where parts of the application execute on these autonomous entities. *Distributed computing* involves the design and implementation of applications as a set of cooperating software entities (processes, threads, objects). The network connectivity may be implemented by a LAN, MAN, or WAN. For example, the World Wide Web has made client–server computing an ubiquitous architecture through thin clients. A click on a button in an HTML page can activate a program on a server that resides next door or halfway around the world. To build a distributed application, one needs to integrate (possibly) heterogeneous software components executing on (possibly) heterogeneous distributed hardware components.

9.3.1 Distributing Components

To build a distributed system, the designer has to resolve a number of design issues related to integration and interoperability:

- *Location:* Each DS component must have a means of finding out about other components in the system.
- *Usage:* Components must have a means of invoking the functionality of other components.
- *Failure Handling:* Components must be able to continue to operate in the event of failure of other components (whether due to the components themselves or the systems they run on). Failure in a distributed system can occur because a component performs the service wrong (e.g., gives wrong results) or the component ceases to exist, because of hardware, software, or network failure.

Generally, the mechanisms for resolving the design issues are partially or wholly embedded in the communications infrastructure. Distributing components requires an infrastructure to support the communication among the components.

Static distribution assigns specific software components to specific hardware components either during compilation or linking. In this scheme, location, usage, and failure handling issues can be resolved prior to execution of the application. But static distribution provides the least flexibility and may yield complete application failure if any hardware component fails.

Dynamic distribution allows the assignment of software components to hardware components at runtime. Software components must register with some well-known "broker" so that other components can locate them. CORBA provides such a capability.

Two primary methods exist for implementing this infrastructure: (1) remote procedure calls and (2) message passing. Others are variants of these primary methods.

Both advantages and disadvantages accrue to using distributed computing. Among the advantages are improvements in performance, scalability of the application, resource sharing, and fault tolerance. Among the disadvantages are increased communications latency, synchronization issues, and increased potential for partial failure of the application.

9.3.2 Design Issues

In designing and developing distributed systems, we need to consider several issues. First, distributed systems introduce complexity into the software development process. Programmers often have a hard time figuring out the behavior of a centralized, serial system. The effort to keep track of multiple concurrent activities exacerbates the debugging process. In fact, there is no good model available yet for debugging a distributed system.

Second, it is also difficult to plan how to distribute the resources given an initial set of conditions for service and a set of constraints on the available servers. This may be easier in homogeneous than heterogeneous systems. And it is difficult to schedule activities to ensure that actions occur at appropriate times.

Third, distributed systems are prone to incomplete failures. Leslie Lamport has noted that a distributed system is one where the failure of a system you didn't even know existed can impact your work. In uniprocessor systems, a failure terminates the program. However, in distributed systems, the failure of a processor terminates only the processes running on it. A process may try to perform an action on another process and have it not happen or only partially happen. The invoking process is still running. It needs mechanisms to detect the failure of other processes and to take remedial action when such failures are detected.

Fourth, true distributed systems must run on a variety of hardware and operating system platforms. Middleware makes this possible. So does the concept of a virtual machine, such as Java's VM, which masks the underlying hardware and software platforms.

Finally, distributed systems can be less secure. Many distributed systems communicate over public channels, such as the Internet. There are significant opportunities for intrusion, subversion, unauthorized modification of information, or denial of service. Getting security right is a task that eludes many so-called security experts, much less the average application programmer.

9.3.3 Interoperability

Distributed systems involve multiple applications running on different computer systems. These applications need to communicate in order to cooperate, which raises the issue of interoperability. Interoperability can be defined as the ability of two or more entities to communicate and cooperate despite differences in the implementation language, the execution environment, or the model abstraction.

Interoperability involves the exchanges of messages between system elements in an agreed upon manner. It involves both information sharing and synchronized operation among the two systems. Interoperability depends on the complexity of the communicating elements. Simple elements—with simple APIs—are likely to be more successful at communication than complex elements.

As Putnam (1997) notes, a system engineer must consider several issues in distributed systems interoperability:

- Interactions between one application and another.
- Interactions between an application and its operating environment (OE).

- Interactions between a service within an OE and the service or services of a target (different) OE.
- Agreement on the interfaces, in terms of name, syntax, and semantics (such as side effects).
- Architecture of the components and their interactions.
- Distribution transparency or identity transparency.

Common Hardware and Software   When two applications interact with each other on common hardware and software, the key issues are the nature of the interface, the behavior of the API, and how to invoke the API. Syntactic interoperability is well-defined and understood; middleware vendors have made significant progress toward establishing different standards at this level, such as CORBA, EJB, and DCOM.

At the semantic level, things are much different. Some effort has been devoted to attempting to prove the behavioral properties of components. But for large applications, the increasing complexity makes it impractical. Semantic interoperability should go beyond operational semantics or behavioral specifications of components. Agreements on names and meaning of shared concepts (ontologies) are also needed, as well as context dependencies, quality of service information, and nonfunctional requirements (Heiler 1995).

We assume that both applications use similar services from the operating environment and conform to the conventions imposed by the operating environment. Interoperability issues are therefore minimized, as depicted in Figure 9-4.

Common Operating Environment   For a particular operating environment, the application is bound to that OE's services API. To make the application portable, its access to required OE services needs to be independent of the OE. The DoD has taken this approach through implementation of a common operating environment

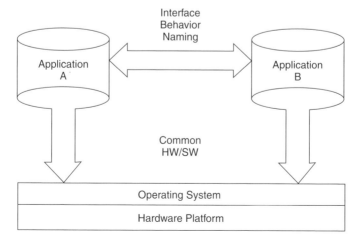

Figure 9-4. Two applications on common hardware and software.

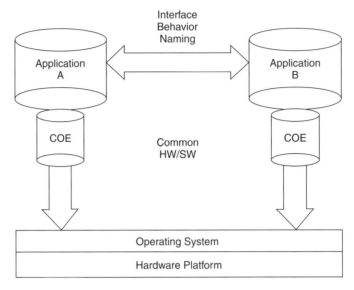

Figure 9-5. Application using a common operating environment.

(COE) through which an application acquires OE services. The COE is then mapped to individual OEs as depicted in Figure 9-5. POSIX is one example of a COE.

The Department of Defense's Defense Information Infrastructure (DII) has developed a COE that allows different applications to be ported to different hardware and software platforms. More information can be found on the COE's home page at `http://diicoe.disa.mil/coe/`.

The key to interoperability is transparency. It enables the client to be shielded from the servicer by encapsulating the activities of the servicer. Transparency minimizes the knowledge needed by the client and, thereby, minimizes the interface information that must be maintained by the servicer. There is a trade-off, however. Interoperability is more achievable the more two systems know about each other. But the more knowledge that is required, the more complex the set of possible interactions, the harder it is to replace either system, and the less robust the overall system will be.

Different Hardware and Software   As we see in Figure 9-6, the risk of distributing components to different target hardware and software platforms can be mitigated if the applications utilize a COE for their service interfaces.

Two different implementations of the COE are used because the host operating environment is different. All three application use the COE's API to request services. However, for communication between Application B and Application C, additional consideration must be given to the services each will provide the other and the architecture of the individual systems in ensuring interoperability.

The enabler for interoperability is a standard for the interfaces of each of the applications. Both parties to interoperability must agree on the same standard, including the same mandatory services, syntax and semantics of the transfer protocol, and a means in the protocol to identify the standard in use. Although different products may be

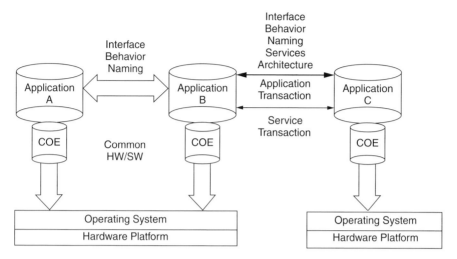

Figure 9-6. Distributed applications using COE.

compliant with a standard, interoperability across two different products using the same "standard" interface does not guarantee interoperability, because the services may be different even though the names appear to be the same. To ensure interoperability, products compliant with a standard for the interface must also comply with the use of the standard services, or have an agreement on how to handle the differences.

For example, until recently there were many TCP/IP products that conform to the basic TCP/IP standard. However, as with many standards, optional services were left up to the implementer's discretion. Some products could not interoperate because, although they conformed to the standards, they did not implement all or some of the optional services or implemented them in different ways.

9.3.4   Advantages and Disadvantages of a Distributed System

There are many advantages to distributed systems, but the following are the primary ones:

- Reliability.
- Sharing of resources.
- Aggregate computing power.
- Openness/scalability.

There are several disadvantages to distributed systems, but the following seem to be the primary ones:

- Security—local and global.
- Physical distribution of resources versus demand.
- Limited computing power of nodes.

9.4 TRANSACTION PROCESSING

Business computing depends on transactions. A transaction groups one or more changes to a data unit into a single operation, such that either all of the changes occur or none of the changes occur. Transactions as a medium of interaction between components have been incorporated into the Microsoft Transaction Server (MTS) and Enterprise JavaBeans (EJB) by Sun Microsystems. Transactions are managed by a transaction processing monitor (TPM) such as IBM's CICS, Tivoli, and NCR's Encina.

9.4.1 Transaction Concepts

A component can interact with a server through transactions. The component accesses the server through a transaction coordinator or TPM. The TPM provides services to define the begin, end, and abort of a transaction. The implementation of the transaction (e.g., the packaging) is transparent to the client. The server receives transactions and implements a transaction protocol (e.g., two-phase commit).

9.4.2 Transaction Properties

However, in both MTS and EJB, transaction processing is integrated with the inter-component communication.

A good transaction system possesses four key properties—the ACID properties. ACID stands for atomicity, consistency, isolation, and durability.

- *Atomicity* means that either a transaction is performed completely or no modification to the database is performed. Transactions have a beginning and an end. The client must inform the TPM of the transaction boundaries—usually through specific APIs. The beginning of a transaction is a rollback point if the transaction must be aborted.
- *Consistency* ensures that after a transaction all resources remain in a consistent state. During a transaction, inconsistencies may arise, but these must be resolved before the end of the transaction. Transactions are aborted if the TPM cannot resolve the inconsistencies.
- *Isolation* means that each transaction accesses resources as if there were no other concurrent transactions. Modifications performed by the transaction are not visible to other transactions until the transaction completes.
- *Durability* means that a completed transaction's results are always persistent, for example, the database has been permanently modified.

In MTS, every component has a transaction attribute that signals the beginning of a transaction when the first method is called in a component. MTS checks this attribute and establishes the environment for intercomponent communication. Values for this attribute allow MTS to always, never, or sometimes establish a transaction processing environment for method invocations. A client component specifically signals when a transaction is to end and whether it is successful or aborted.

9.5 FURTHER READING

Java Event Model

Event Handling. `http://java.sun.com/docs/books/tutorial/uiswing/overview/` `event.html`.

Java AWT Event Model. `http://java.sun.com/products/jdk/1.1/docs/guide/` `awt/designspec/events.html`.

Lea, D. 1999. *Concurrent Programming in Java: Design Principles and Patterns*, 2nd Ed. Addison-Wesley, Reading, MA.

Palmer, G. 2001. *Java Event Handling*. Prentice Hall PTR, Englewood Cliffs, NJ.

Zukowski, J. K. 1997. *Java AWT Reference*. O'Reilly & Associates, Sebastopol, CA.

Transaction Processing

Bernstein, P. A. 1990. "Transaction Processing Monitors." *Communications of the ACM*, 33(11):75–86.

Bernstein, P. A. and E. Newcomer. 1996. *Principles of Transaction Processing for the Systems Professional*. Morgan Kaufmann, Los Altos, CA.

Elmagarmid, A. K. (ed.) 1993. *Database Transaction Models for Advanced Applications*. Morgan Kaufmann, Los Altos, CA.

Gray, J. and A. Reuter. 1993. *Transaction Processing: Concepts and Techniques*. Morgan Kaufmann, Los Altos, CA.

Jagodia, J. and L. Kerschberg (eds.) 1997. *Advanced Transaction Models and Architectures*. Kluwer Academic Publishers, Norwell, MA.

Smolenski, J. and P. Kovari. 2003. "Transactions in J2EE." IBM Redbooks Paper, IBM Corp., White Plains, NY.

9.6 EXERCISES

9.1. Research and compare at least three algorithms for distributing processes across multiple hardware/software platforms. Identify, define, and use five criteria in your analysis.

9.2. Is it possible to define a general model for handling failure in a distributed application? Argue both pro and con with supporting evidence from the technical literature. [Research Problem]

9.3. Develop a formula for how you would characterize the aggregate computing power of a distributed system. Is it different for homogeneous versus heterogeneous platforms? What parameters do you need to consider? (*Hint*: Begin with a formula for a symmetric multiprocessor.) [Research Problem]

10

COMPONENT TECHNOLOGIES

Today's applications are large and complex—time consuming to develop, difficult and costly to maintain, and risky to extend with additional functionality. Many applications are still developed as monolithic entities, prepackaged with a wide range of features, most of which cannot be upgraded independently.

Over the past twenty years numerous component technologies have been developed. Some have succeeded temporarily, only to be subsumed into other products; some have not succeeded at all. And some have succeeded by virtue of market dominance. But none have succeeded due to technological innovation. We are still searching for the ideal way to integrate components to yield good applications.

Component technologies are mechanisms for implementing software components. We seek easy ways to define and describe components, their interfaces, their semantics and interactions, and their packaging. A general solution for the latter two elements has proved difficult to find.

10.1 CORBA

As software applications become more complex, there is a need for software components to communicate with each other using "standard" mechanisms and "open" interfaces for effective interoperability to occur. The Common Object Request Broker Architecture (CORBA) is a conceptual "software bus" that allows applications to communicate with one another, regardless of who designed them, the platform they are running on, the language they are written in, or where they are

Software Paradigms, By Stephen H. Kaisler
ISBN 0-471-48347-8   Copyright © 2005 John Wiley & Sons, Inc.

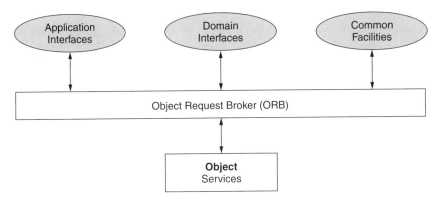

Figure 10-1. OMG reference model architecture.

executing. CORBA also enables the building of a plug-and-play component software environment. This environment is depicted in Figure 10-1.

CORBA was designed by the Object Management Group (OMG), a consortium of over 800 members to support the goal of making the development and use of integrated software systems easier. In particular, OMG members believe that the object-oriented approach to software development best supports this goal. The goal of CORBA is application integration. CORBA solves the problem of interoperability among objects through the notion of the "CORBA bus."

But OMG did not stop there. It also defines an Object Management Architecture (OMA), which allows applications to be built in a standard manner using basic building blocks and thus enables enterprise integration. OMA standardizes the component interfaces that facilitate a plug-and-play software development approach based on object technology. OMA broadly consists of two major components: the CORBAservices and the CORBAfacilities. We will describe these components in this section. However, the benefits of a software architecture will become apparent in Part III: Software Architectures.

10.1.1   CORBA Concepts

The CORBA software bus enables the implementation of a plug-and-play methodology for constructing software applications. The principal components of CORBA are the Object Request Broker (ORB) and the auxiliary services. Any component that adheres to the ORB API can use the ORB to communicate with other compliant components.

The ORB   The ORB is used to instantiate objects, to establish communications between objects, and to invoke one object on behalf of other objects. The ORB is responsible for delivering method invocations to target objects, marshalling and unmarshalling arguments and return values, and translating between different architectural representations (e.g., big-endian vs. little-endian).

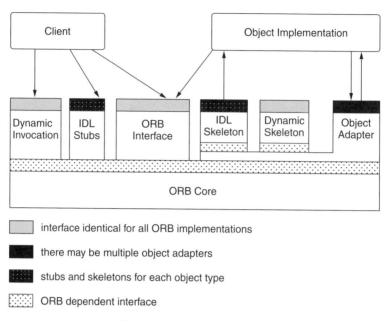

Figure 10-2. ORB architecture.

The ORB is the middleware that establishes the client–server relationships between two or more components. Using an ORB, a client can transparently invoke an object on a server, which can be on the same machine or across a network, as depicted in Figure 10-2.

The client is the program entity that invokes an operation on an object implementation. Accessing the services of a remote object should be transparent to the caller. Ideally, it should be as simple as calling a method on that object. The remaining components in Figure 10-2 help to support this level of transparency.

The object implementation defines operations that implement a CORBA IDL interface. Object implementations can be written in a variety of languages including C, C++, Java, Smalltalk, and Ada.

Interfaces Interfaces to CORBA objects are specified through an Interface Definition Language (IDL), a metalanguage that is then compiled to a particular target programming language. Consequently, CORBA is language-independent (but the IDL compiler is language-dependent). Objects can use CORBA concepts for any programming environment for which there exists an IDL compiler and an ORB implementation. The CORBA specification does not presume any object-oriented features. However, programming environments that do not possess object-oriented features may yield complex and awkward implementations of CORBA.

An ORB is a logical entity that may be implemented in various ways (such as one or more processes or a set of libraries). The CORBA specification defines an abstract interface for an ORB to decouple applications from implementation details. This interface provides various helper functions such as converting object references to strings and vice versa, and creating argument lists for requests made through the dynamic invocation interface described below.

IDL stubs and skeletons serve as the glue between the client and server applications, respectively, and the ORB. The transformation between IDL definitions and the target programming language is automated by a CORBA IDL compiler. The use of a compiler reduces the potential for inconsistencies between client stubs and server skeletons and increases opportunities for automated compiler optimizations.

The Dynamic Invocation Interface (DII) (Schmidt and Vinoski 2002a) allows a client to directly access the underlying request mechanisms provided by an ORB. Applications use the DII to dynamically issue requests to objects without requiring IDL interface-specific stubs to be linked in. Unlike IDL stubs (that only allow RPC-style requests), the DII also allows clients to make nonblocking deferred synchronous (separate send and receive operations) and one-way (send-only) calls.

The Dynamic Skeleton Interface (DSI) (Schmidt 2002b) is the server side's analog to the client side's DII. The DSI allows an ORB to deliver requests to an object implementation that does not have compile-time knowledge of the type of object it is implementing. The client making the request has no idea whether the implementation is using the type-specific IDL skeletons or the dynamic skeletons.

The Object Adapter (Schmidt 1997) assists the ORB with delivering requests to the object and with activating the object. More importantly, an object adapter associates object implementations with the ORB. Object adapters can be specialized to provide support for certain object implementation styles (such as OODB object adapters for persistence and library object adapters for nonremote objects).

Services CORBA services are defined through two major components: CORBAservices and CORBAfacilities. CORBAservices provide basic infrastructure functionality that is of use across a broad spectrum of applications, such as the Naming Service, Event Service, and Object Trader Service. CORBAfacilities provide higher-level functionality at the application level, such as user interfaces and task management, as well as domain-based functionality.

10.1.2 CORBA Benefits

CORBA can provide multiple benefits to an organization in several ways. Immediately, it provides standard tools and libraries that do not need to be developed: they can be bought off the shelf and are usable almost immediately with minimal effort. This means developers can concentrate on application development. Code can be reused and interchanged as necessary and when required.

CORBA provides interoperability across a wide range of heterogeneous hardware and software platforms. With CORBA, it is possible to express data using a variety of data types, including integer, floating point, enumerated types, characters, strings, arrays, and structs. CORBA handles the translation of data representations between differing computer architectures. The impact on application development is that the

CORBA specification of the data format can be read and interpreted by machines and humans, and many of the programming steps for handling new data formats are completely automated.

With CORBA, it is easy to define new interfaces. If the system is properly implemented, it is also easy to create new code modules to plug into the system. CORBA provides language bindings for a number of high-level languages, including C, C++, Ada, Smalltalk, and Java. A particular ORB will support one or more of these bindings.

Because CORBA is platform-independent, it can be implemented on different platforms using different programming languages and support applications written in different programming languages. If there is an ORB available for a particular hardware–software platform, an application's interfaces can be up and running with limited effort.

10.1.3 Handling Distribution

CORBA provides the Name Service to perform location determination of distributed components. The Name Service associates a logical name with a reference. References to CORBA objects, which may be transient or persistent, are stored in the Name Service. References are accessed only by names, which are stored as strings. The Name Service returns the reference associated with the name upon request. There is no mechanism for handling stale references, for example, where the objects have ceased to exist. Because the name is logical, it is the only location-independent reference provided by CORBA.

A server creates a binding of an object to a name by calling the bind method of the naming service. Normally, only one object can be bound to a name in a particular context at a time. However, since OMG only specifies the API of a naming service, implementers can modify this constraint to allow multiple bindings as long as they provide a means of selecting only one reference to return to the client. Barth et al. (2000) show how to implement load distribution across multiple objects by modifying the naming service to allow multiple bindings.

10.1.4 CORBA Performance Issues

There are many factors that can affect the performance of a distributed system. However, three factors are of particular importance in evaluating performance in a CORBA-based system:

- The number of remote invocations that are made within the system.
- The amount of data that is transferred with each remote invocation.
- The marshalling/unmarshalling costs associated with each IDL data type used in the application.

Some applications do not need all of the services provided by CORBA, yet they pay the price for having those services available.

10.2 SYSTEM OBJECT MODEL

IBM developed the System Object Model (SOM) (Campagnoni 1994) as a library packaging technology that enables languages to share class libraries regardless of the language in which they were written. This ability to share class libraries between various object-oriented languages is intended to solve some interoperability and reuse problems between object-oriented and non-object-oriented languages as well.

SOM was developed as part of IBM's joint venture with Microsoft to develop a successor operating system to Windows. When the joint project dissolved, IBM renamed its operating system OS/2.

SOM was never intended to provide compound document functionality. OpenDoc (see Section 10.2.3), which was developed by Apple Corporation [actually Component Integration Laboratory (CIL), an Apple subsidiary], provides a framework specifically designed for building components or "parts" that can be integrated into compound documents.

Using SOM, vendors can:

- Create portable shrink-wrapped binary components.
- Create class libraries in one language that can be accessed and used by other languages.
- Subclass from binary components even if they were written in a different language.
- Add new methods and override existing methods without recompilation of the application.
- Insert new classes into the inheritance hierarchy without recompiling the application.

In order to promote independence from the suite of object-oriented programming languages (OOPLs), SOM provides a distinct object model. Specific OOPL models are mapped to SOM. SOM can also work with traditional, non-O-O procedural languages as well. This provides an object model for those programming languages that do not incorporate one into their syntax.

SOM includes an Interface Definition Language, an IDL compiler, a runtime environment with procedure calls, and a set of enabling frameworks. The SOM IDL does not correspond to CORBA's IDL. IBM incorporates this technology into OS/2 and licenses it to other vendors.

10.2.1 SOM Objects

SOM objects are derived from a root object that defines the essential behavior common to all SOM objects. Factory methods (Section 4.3) are used to create SOM objects at runtime. These factory methods are invoked on a class object in the SOM runtime environment.

Once created, an object will exist until explicitly deleted or until the process that created it no longer exists. A SOM object must make use of a persistence mechanism in order to exist beyond the life of the process that creates it.

Each object may have a state. The state is accessed through published interfaces to an object. Invoking operations on objects may cause state changes. SOM objects have private data that is not externally accessible through the interface operations.

SOM provides the following object services:

- Objects can be distributed and deployed in binary form. Thus, class library developers do not need to supply source code to allow users to create their objects. This allows application developers to utilize an object at any level, without modifying or recompiling the source code.

- Objects can be used, including full subclassing, across languages. It should be possible to build an object using one language, invoke the object using another language, and use that result to build an application in yet a third language. Users of class libraries will want to modify and build applications from these classes in their preferred language, but not necessarily the one in which the class was originally written.

- It provides for the subsequent updating of these components without having to recompile preexisting clients that use them (upward binary compatibility). This is essential because applications dependent on system libraries cannot be rebuilt each time a change is made to a component in the library.

An object in SOM is defined using the IDL. The interface language is then "compiled" into a language-specific form. For instance, if one were using C to implement the object, the SOM compiler would be used to produce .C, .IH, and .H files. The language-specific form created by the SOM compiler has function stubs that the programmer would fill in. These stubs are the bodies to the methods defined in the IDL.

SOM objects can be packaged in DLL or EXE files. Using these objects in a DLL offers great flexibility since they can be referenced by any program that loads the DLL.

Classes Versus Objects   SOM has a root class that serves as a metaclass that defines the essential behavior common to all SOM classes. The SOM metaclasses define factory methods that manufacture objects of any class for which they are the metaclass.

A class defines both an interface and an implementation for objects. The interface defines the signature of the methods supported by objects of the class, and the implementation defines what instance variables implement the object's state and what procedures implement its methods.

SOM classes support attributes. An attribute can be thought of as an instance variable that has accompanying "get" and "set" methods. The get and set methods are invoked the same way as other methods.

New classes are derived by subclassing from previously existing classes through inheritance and specialization. Subclasses inherit their interfaces and implementations from their parent classes unless they are overridden. New methods can be added and old methods can be overridden. Methods can also be relocated upward in the hierarchy without requiring recompilation of the application.

In SOM, all classes are real objects. SOM supports a class object that represents the metaclass for the creation of all SOM classes. The SOM metaclass defines the behavior common to all class objects. Since it inherits from the root SOM object, it exists at runtime and contains the methods for manufacturing object instances. It also has the methods used to dynamically obtain information about a class and its methods at runtime.

SOM supports multiple inheritance; that is, a class may be derived from multiple parent classes.

Operations and Methods   A SOM object has an interface definition that specifies the operation signature. An operation signature consists of an operation name and the argument and result types. Operations are performed by methods that implement an object's behavior. A client requests a service by specifying the object name and operation name along with pertinent arguments. An object can support multiple operations. Some programming languages support polymorphic forms of operations.

A method is a procedure invoked on a SOM object. Generally, the operation signature matches the method's calling sequence. SOM provides three different method dispatching mechanisms: offset resolution, name resolution, and dispatch function resolution.

The *offset resolution* mechanism uses a static scheme for typing objects. It is roughly equivalent to the C++ virtual function concept. It generally offers quick access for SOM method resolution at the cost of some loss in flexibility. It supports polymorphism that is based on the derivation of the object's class.

Name resolution supports access to objects whose class is not known at compile time and permits polymorphism based on the protocols that an object supports, rather than its derivation.

The *dispatch function resolution* is a feature of SOM that permits method resolution to be based on arbitrary rules known only in the domain of the receiving object. It is a dynamic mechanism that permits runtime type checking and open-ended forms of polymorphism.

Communication Model   SOM assumes that an operation occurs in a single thread within a single process. However, SOM code permits concurrent execution by multiple threads on systems where SOM can access the underlying threads model. Thus, multithreaded programs can use mutual exclusion mechanisms to serialize updates to SOM objects with confidence that critical sections in SOM are thread-safe.

SOM does not prohibit interobject communication that crosses process boundaries. However, standard interprocess communication mechanisms supported by the underlying operating system must be used to create this capability.

Implementation When SOM creates an object, it returns a handle to that object. Higher level abstractions must define and implement such operations as identity, equality, and copy.

SOM is designed to work with a variety of programming languages. SOM supports an interface definition language to define interfaces and data. The IDL is then compiled and linked with the application. This does not preclude the use of a language's object model in the same application.

The use of SOM with a procedural language provides that language with object-oriented capabilities.

10.2.2 DSOM

Distributed SOM (DSOM) is a set of SOM classes (shipped with the SOMobjects Toolkit) that extends the method dispatch mechanism provided in the SOM runtime engine to allow methods to be invoked, in a programmer transparent way, on SOM objects that exist in a different address space from the caller [usually on a different (virtual) machine]. The DSOM class library is compliant with the Object Management Group's (OMG's) Common Object Request Broker Architecture (CORBA) specification.

DSOM is a framework built using the SOM technology that allows developers to construct distributed object applications. DSOM does not implement a separate object model or runtime since DSOM is built with the SOM and runtime.

10.2.3 OpenDoc Technology

Like Microsoft (see Section 10.3), Apple devoted substantial effort to standardizing object representation and communication. Apple formed a consortium called the Component Integration Laboratory (CIL) that included Lotus, IBM, Novell, Adobe, and Taligent. (It is interesting to note that both Lotus and Taligent have now been incorporated into IBM.) CIL's application model is based on the generic concept of a document. A document represents an object, possibly complex, that is manipulated by the application code. CIL sought to generalize this concept further by developing OpenDoc, a component library, that would enable independently developed components to interact and interoperate to create complex applications.

OpenDoc (Apple Corp. 1994a, 1994b) was a cross-platform, component software architecture that would enable developers to evolve current applications into component software or to create new component software applications. OpenDoc was built on top of IBM's System Object Model (SOM). Both SOM and OpenDoc were written in C++. Most components that were developed were also written in C++.

During the early 1990s, Apple sold the rights to OpenDoc to IBM. IBM has incorporated many of the OpenDoc concepts into extensions to SOM as well as its Visual Age product lines. So OpenDoc began with SOM and ended with SOM.

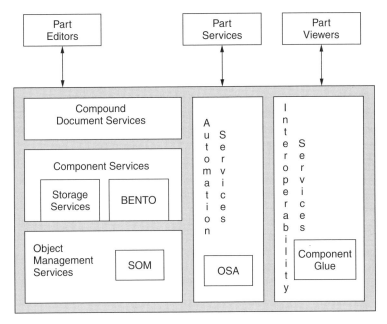

Figure 10-3. OpenDoc software architecture.

BENTO   Apple separated the communication mechanism from the standard for documents. It formed a consortium with other vendors to define a multivendor structured definition for documents. OpenDoc integrated three standards: (1) System Object Model (SOM), which was IBM's CORBA-compliant standard for interapplication message exchange; (2) BENTO, which standardizes the format of structured documents; and (3) the Open Scripting Architecture that is part of Apple's ICA (see below). These are depicted in Figure 10-3.

BENTO defines the standard elements for structuring documents in OpenDoc. BENTO documents are stored in containers, which are collections of objects. BENTO objects are organized as a collection of properties, which have values of some data type. An object has a persistent ID that is unique within its container. The values are where data is actually stored and their types describe the corresponding formats.

OpenDoc had a simple idea: documents are composed of heterogeneous objects that are managed and manipulated using a set of specialized software components. Rather than thinking of an application as a monolithic block of code or a full-fledged application such as Microsoft Word or Excel, Apple viewed applications as dynamic entities that could be evolved by the user as necessity demands. More importantly, the user did not need to know the details of every object in the document, only those that were added to the document.

How OpenDoc Works   OpenDoc emphasized a task-centric rather than application-centric environment. The key element of an OpenDoc entity was the compound document, which managed disparate types of data. A compound document had two elements: a container for holding parts and the parts themselves. Users placed into the document OpenDoc parts, which were the fundamental building blocks. Each part had a part handler consisting of a part viewer and a part editor.

Part handlers represent the applications in a document. A part handler is responsible for the following functions:

- Displaying the part (both on-screen and printing). The part handler may be asked to display the part on a dynamic medium such as a screen or a static medium such as the printed page.
- Editing the part. The part handler must accept events and change the state of the part so that the user can edit and script the part.
- Storage management (persistent and runtime) for the part. The part handler must be able to read the part from persistent storage into main memory, manage the runtime storage associated with the part, and write the part back out to persistent storage.

Part viewers could display data held in the part, while part editors allowed users to manipulate the parts. Parts could be obtained from Apple or third-party vendors or could be created by the users themselves.

Building a document was easy: users could drag-and-drop parts into an open document window. The part would then automatically embed itself in the document. OpenDoc supported irregularly shaped parts, as opposed to the standard rectangular entities, and supported multiple concurrent parts working together. Parts could be linked together so that if data in one part changed, the second part was notified to change its data as well.

Parts represented the boundaries in a document where one type of data ended and another one began and were displayed in frames within the window representing the document, as depicted in Figure 10-4.

In this sample OpenDoc document, we see the following parts:

- The root part is an object-style graphic editor.
- In the upper left corner, there are two content objects—a rectangle and an ellipse.
- A clock part has been embedded in the top right corner.
- Toward the center and bottom left, a chart part overlaps a table part.
- In the right center, a text part is embedded.
- A button part is embedded in the text part.
- A second button part is embedded in the graphics part, at the bottom center of the document.

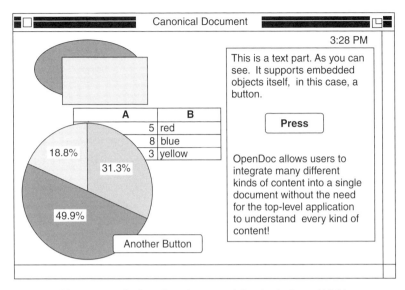

Figure 10-4. An OpenDoc document (after Apple Corp. 1994b).

The on-screen representations of parts were mouse-sensitive and could yield different behaviors or bring up different menus depending on the specific part the mouse hovered over.

OpenDoc Part Hierarchy   The OpenDoc part hierarchy provided a complex environment for composing and rendering complex documents. An extract from this hierarchy is depicted in Figure 10-5.

Figure 10-6 depicts the relationships between the core OpenDoc elements.

Each part handler implemented a set of methods based on its position in the part hierarchy. Figure 10-7 depicts a few part handlers with the methods that they must implement as part of the basic interface in OpenDoc.

Building an OpenDoc Component   Building an OpenDoc component requires four steps:

1. An ".idl" source file is created using the SOM Interface Definition Language. It specifies the interface to the component. The new component inherits from a generic OpenDoc object called ODPart 60 methods that define its behavior. However, you only need six methods to define a simple OpenDoc part.

2. This interface file is compiled by the SOM compiler to produce a C or C++ API. Compilation produces several binding files plus some glue code for the SOM runtime environment.

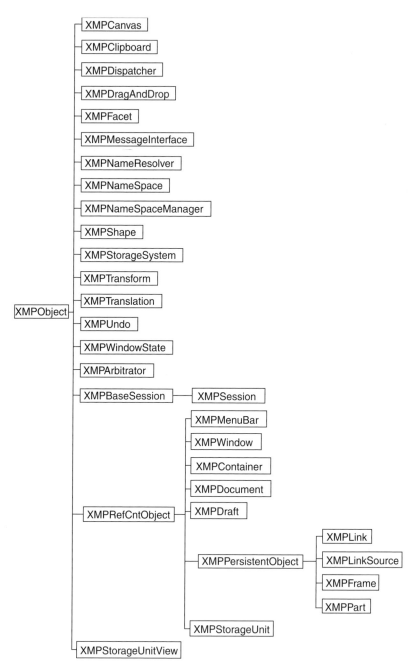

Figure 10-5. OpenDoc part hierarchy (partial view).

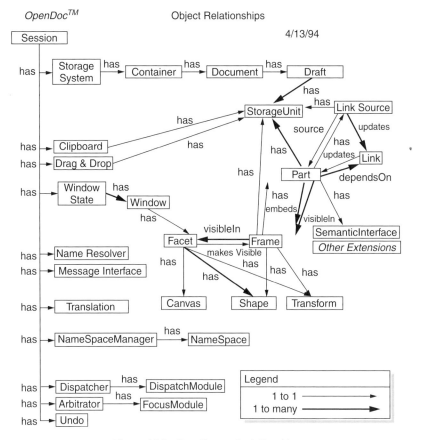

Figure 10-6. OpenDoc part relationships.

3. C++ source code is written to implement the functionality of the component. This code forms the body of the methods that were declared in the ".idl" file.

4. Compile and link the implementation file. This creates a shared library, which includes classes from the SOM library and any other components that were created.

Apple provided a tool called PartMaker to simplify the first two steps of the above process because most simple objects had the same interface methods. Programmers then only needed to focus on writing the C++ code. However, if you wanted to inherit from some component other than ODPart, you had to perform the first two steps yourself.

The Interapplication Communication Architecture Apple developed the Interapplication Communication Architecture (ICA) as a standard mechanism for

XMPPart
```
void Draw(     XMPFacet* facet, XMPShape* invalidShape);
XMPBoolean HandleEvent(     XMPEventData event,
                    XMPFrame* frame,
                    XMPFacet* facet);
void InitPartFromStorage(XMPStorageUnit* storageUnit);
void Externalize();
void Open(XMPFrame* frame);
void UndoAction(XMPActionData actionState);
void RedoAction(XMPActionData actionState);
void DragEnter( XMPStorageUnit* dragInfo, XMPFacet* facet,
XMPPoint where);
void DragLeave( XMPFacet* facet, XMPPoint where);
void DragWithin(XMPStorageUnit* dragInfo, XMPFacet* facet,
XMPPoint where);
XMPDropResult Drop(   XMPStorageUnit* dropInfo,
                    XMPFacet* facet,
                    XMPPoint where);
void DropCompleted(   XMPPart*   destPart,   XMPDropResult
dropResult);
void FulfillPromise(XMPStorageUnitView*promiseSUView);
XMPLink* CreateLink( XMPPtr data, XMPULong size);
void LinkUpdated(     XMPLink* updatedLink, XMPChangeID id);
```

XMPClipboard
```
XMPBoolean Lock(     XMPULong wait, XMPClipboardKey* key);
void Unlock(XMPClipboardKey key);
XMPChangeID GetChangeID();
void Clear(XMPClipboardKey key);
XMPStorageUnit* GetContentStorageUnit(XMPClipboardKey key);
void ExportClipboard(XMPClipboardKey key);
```

XMPContainer
```
XMPStorageSystem* GetStorageSystem();
XMPContainerID GetID();
XMPContainerName GetName();
void SetName(XMPContainerName name);
void Release();
XMPDocument* GetDocument(XMPDocumentID id);
```

XMPDocument
```
XMPContainer* GetContainer();
XMPDocumentID GetID();
XMPDocumentName GetName();
void SetName(XMPDocumentName name);
void Release();
```

Figure 10-7. OpenDoc part handler methods.

communication among Macintosh OS applications. ICA had four goals:

1. Exchange data through copy-and-paste operations.
2. Read and write data blocks from and to other applications.
3. Send and respond to Apple events.
4. Be controlled through scripts.

Apple events are standard high-level messages that can be generated by any application or software module and responded to by other applications. An application uses an Apple event to request a service from or provide a service to another application. A *client application* is an application that sends an Apple event to request a service, while the application that provides the service is the *server application*. The client and server applications can reside on the same machine, or on different machines connected to the same network.

The ICA consists of four subsystems, which are depicted in Figure 10-8:

1. The *Edition Manager* provides support for copy-and-paste operations among applications and updating information automatically when data in the source document changes.
2. The *Open Scripting Architecture* defines the standard mechanisms that allow for the external control of single or multiple applications. OSA is comparable, to some extent, to Automation in OLE 2.0. OSA is not tied to any specific scripting language. Each scripting language has a corresponding scripting component that translates the scripts into events.
3. The *Event Manager* provides the support that allows applications to send and receive events. The Event Manager defines a standard architecture for event handling and the elements of the Apple messaging backplane.

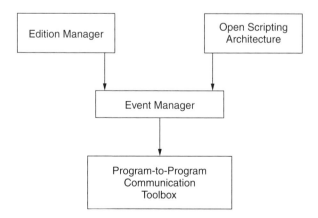

Figure 10-8. ICA elements.

4. The *Program-to-Program Communication Toolbox* provides low-level support that allows applications to exchange blocks of data in an efficient way. The Edition Manager and the Open Scripting Architecture provide the user level support. They both rely on the Event Manager to exchange data and messages across applications. The Event Manager, in turn, relies on the Program-to-Program Communication Toolbox to transport data.

Relationship to OLE2 Apple realized the dominant market position of Microsoft operating systems and their constituent software. So it made OpenDoc able to accept any OLE2 component as an OpenDoc part. This allowed developers to preserve their investment in OLE2 components, while taking advantage of OpenDoc technology.

Additional information on the OS/390 implementation of SOMobjects can be found in Section 10.5.

10.3 MICROSOFT'S COM/DCOM

Microsoft has developed a component object model (COM) that defines a language-independent notion of what an object is. Components developed using this model can be used and reused consistently, no matter what language is used to access them. COM underlies much of the Microsoft Windows environment. Microsoft's Visual Basic (VB) programming environment makes many COM-related calls, but these are mostly hidden by VB.

COM refers to both the specification and the implementation developed by Microsoft, which provides a framework for integrating components. This framework supports interoperability and reusability of objects by allowing programmers to build systems by assembling reusable components from different vendors, which communicate via COM.

COM defines an application programming interface (API) to allow for the creation of components for use in integrating custom applications. To interact, components must adhere to a binary structure specified by Microsoft. As long as components adhere to this binary structure, components written in different languages can inter-operate.

Distributed COM is an extension of COM that allows network-based component interaction. While COM processes can run on the same machine but in different address spaces, the DCOM extension allows processes to be spread across a network.

We consider COM and DCOM to be a single technology that provides a range of services for component interaction, component integration, and component communication across heterogeneous distributed platforms. COM and DCOM provide a foundation on which higher-level services are built such as ActiveX, MTS (Microsoft Transaction Services), and, recently, .NET.

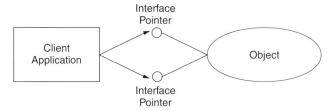

Figure 10-9. COM object.

COM is principally supported on the Microsoft Windows operating systems (95/98, NT/2000, XP, CE). Restricted versions have been developed for the Macintosh operating systems to support the Microsoft Office products on those machines and for various Unix platforms. The Open Group has delivered an open source version of COM (http://www.opengroup.org/comsource/).

10.3.1 Component Object Model

COM defines a programming language-independent binary standard for the interface between a client and an object providing services. Any object conforming to this standard is a legitimate Windows Object, no matter what language is used to implement it. A COM object, depicted in Figure 10-9, can support any number of interfaces, each of which is a collection of methods.

Services implemented by a COM object are presented through a set of interfaces that represent the only point of contact between the client and the COM object. COM defines a binary interface such that applications and objects written in any language can communicate as long as their compilers can yield code compliant with this binary standard. A COM object can support any number of interfaces. This allows developers to provide interfaces of greater or lesser complexity for different types of client applications.

COM Objects COM objects and interfaces are specified using the Microsoft Interface Definition Language (IDL). Every COM object runs under control of a server. A server may support one or more COM objects.

A Windows object is any object, in whatever form, that supports at least one predefined interface, called *IUnknown*. Every object must implement this interface in order to support garbage collection. Interfaces whose reference count is 0 can be unloaded without impacting the application's stability. Note that the other two functions defined here increase and decrease reference counts.

As part of the IUnknown interface, OLE defines a standard function, called *QueryInterface*, through which the user of one interface of an object can obtain a pointer to another interface of the same object. QueryInterface takes as input a pointer to an interface identifier (IID) for the desired interface, and either returns an error (and a NULL pointer), meaning the object does not support the interface, or a valid pointer to the new interface. The IUknown interface is depicted as follows:

```
interface IUnknown
{
  virtual HRESULT __stdcall QueryInterface(const IID& iid,
                                           void** ppv) = 0;
  virtual ULONG __stdcall AddRef() = 0;
  virtual ULONG __stdcall Release() = 0;
};
```

Operations resemble standard C++ functions and are defined as part of interface definitions. A client requests an operation, which resembles calls to C++ functions, but functions are always called indirectly, through interfaces. The methods that implement operations are essentially equivalent to C++ functions.

There are a number of ways to create a Windows object. One way is to use a *class factory object*. A class factory object represents a specific class identifier, is obtained by a specific OLE function, and supports an interface named *IClassFactory*. The IClassFactory interface contains a function named *CreateInstance*, to which is passed an identifier of the desired interface to that object. The expression *IClassFactory::CreateInstance* is the logical equivalent of C++'s *new* operator.

In C++, an object is destroyed by calling the delete operator on an object pointer (which ultimately causes the object's destructor function to be called). The corresponding function that frees a Windows Object (and essentially calls its destructor) is a function called Release. This function is part of the IUnknown interface and is thus present in every interface. However, calling Release does not necessarily destroy the object. Internally, the object maintains a count of how many references exist to any of its interfaces. Creating an interface pointer increments the reference count, whereas Release decrements it. When the count is reduced to zero, the object frees itself, calling its own destructor.

COM does not support the notion of inheritance. Rather, inheritance is a language-specific tool. COM provides a limited notion of inheritance through the containment mechanism. The object being used remains entirely self-contained and operates on its own instance of data. The containing object also works on its own data and calls the other object as necessary to perform specific functions, for which it can be passed the data on which to operate.

To implement what corresponds to a subclass Y of a class X using containment, class Y completely contains an X object and implements its own version of the X interface, which it exports to clients. This makes Y a simple user of X, and X need not know about its use within Y. This is useful when Y needs to override some aspect of X's behavior. Since all external calls go to the Y implementation first, Y can either override selected behavior or pass the calls directly through to X.

Interfaces   The Component Object Model uses the word "interface" by itself to refer to the definition (signatures) of those functions. An implementation of an interface is an array of pointers to functions. Any code that has a pointer to that array can call the functions in that interface. A Windows object implements one or more interfaces, that is, provides pointers to function tables for each supported interface.

Unlike C++, where objects are defined using class definitions that generate user-defined types, Windows objects are defined in terms of the interfaces they support. Since all objects support at least one interface (IUnknown), all Windows objects are at least of type IUnknown and can be treated as being of another type by using a different interface. Because of this mechanism, there is no single user-defined type associated with a Windows object class, as there is with a C++ class. In fact, there is no specific way to identify a specific object. This is because object references (pointers) to Windows objects are not references to the object itself, as in C++, but rather are pointers to one of the object's interfaces.

Given a pointer to an interface, the user can access only functions contained in that interface. The user can never have a pointer to the whole object (because there is no direct user-visible concept of "whole object"), so there is no direct access to state, and no concept of "friend" as in C++. Through the IUnknown interface, a user can obtain pointers to other interfaces that the object also supports, but this means obtaining a different pointer that refers (indirectly) to the same object. Each pointer to an interface points to a function table associated with the object, and each table contains only functions for a specific interface. Because a pointer to a Windows object always points to a function table, such a pointer can also be used from within programs written in languages other than C++, such as VB or assembly code. Figure 10-10 depicts this access structure.

Once an interface is defined, it should not be changed. New methods should not be added, and existing methods should not be modified. This restriction on the interfaces is not enforced, but it is a rule that programmers should follow. Adhering to this restriction removes the potential for version incompatibility. If an interface never changes, then clients depending on the interface can rely on a consistent set of services. If new functionality has to be added to a component, it can be exposed through a different interface, which may include the methods of other interfaces.

A Windows object class is identified as such only through a class ID that associates an object with a particular DLL or EXE in the file system (e.g., the application

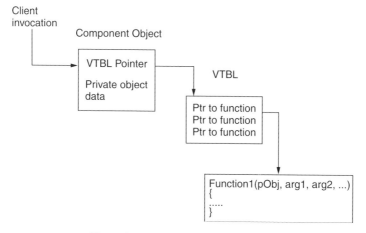

Figure 10-10. COM function invocation.

that implements the object). The class ID is stored in a registration database, along with information that defines where the object "lives" and characteristics that a potential user may wish to know without having to actually instantiate the object.

10.3.2 Interobject Communication

Microsoft provides two standards for communication between objects: DDE (Dynamic Data Exchange) and OLE (Object Linking and Embedding). DDE supports communication only among objects that reside on the same computer. Microsoft also defined ODBC (Open Data Base Connectivity) as a communication mechanism between applications and databases, where one could view a database as a very complex object.

DDE DDE provides data exchange between two objects based on the client–server model. A *client* is any object that initiates a DDE connection. After establishing a connection with a server object, a client will request some data. The connection can be characterized as one of three types based on how data is updated on the server side: cold, warm, or hot (Figure 10-11).

In a *cold* connection, the server plays a passive role, waiting for the client to request or "pull" the data. When a request is received, it retrieves and returns the data requested. In a *warm* connection, the update responsibility is shared between the client and the server. The server notifies the client when data has been updated, but the client must request the updated data. In a *hot* connection, the server "pushes" the updated data to the client as it is received. Clients and servers may be linked to multiple entities.

Although DDE is primarily used for data exchange, it does provide a limited capability for executing commands on the server side. This capability can be used to implement a limited remote messaging capability.

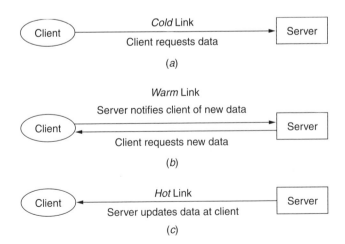

Figure 10-11. DDE connection types.

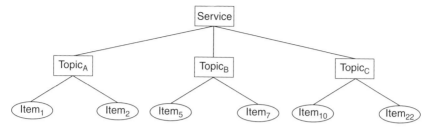

Figure 10-12. DDE service hierarchy.

Most Microsoft products support DDE. Each client specifies the *topic* of the connection, that is, the type of data it wants to retrieve. Microsoft Word ".doc" files are valid topics for a connection. A client retrieves an *item*, which is an instance of a topic, such as a Word document, with a DDE request. A server provides a hierarchy of topics and items for which it can handle requests or push updates to the client as depicted in Figure 10-12.

OLE Microsoft's Object Linking and Embedding (OLE) technology is a software architecture that allows applications to be built from binary software components. It is much more complex than DDE, because Microsoft sees it as the foundation for implementing distributed objects. OLE 2.0, the current version, relies on COM for its object representation.

A key feature of OLE 2.0 is the definition of structured documents. Structured documents contain *storages* and *streams* that are organized in a similar way to traditional file systems: *streams* are analogous to files while *storages* act as directories. So *storages* contain either *streams* or *storages*. Storages and streams provide support for structured or composite documents that are organized in a hierarchical structure. OLE 2.0 provides a standard definition for the document's structure and also a set of functions that support the standard operations on structured documents.

An OLE container is any application that can incorporate OLE objects. *Containers* display the OLE objects and accept commands for them. However, *containers* are not intended to process the objects. Objects retain an association with *server* applications that are responsible for servicing the requests addressed to the objects. The idea here is that clients do not need to be aware of the internals of the objects they contain. The object (data) together with its associated server corresponds to the usual notion of object in object-oriented terminology, which encapsulates both data and operations on the data. *Servers* accept commands, called *verbs*, that correspond to actions that can be applied to the objects. An interface is the set of operations that can be applied to an object via its server.

OLE 2.0 offers two ways to integrate an object into a compound document: *linking* and *embedding*. Embedding is used most frequently. The *container* application owns and stores each embedded object, but the server retrieves the object. The server plays an anonymous role by processing the object on behalf of the container application. Alternatively, an object can be linked into a document. A linked object belongs to a given document (and is stored in that document's file), but it is referenced in another document. In this way, several *containers* can share a single linked object.

OLE 2.0 provides a standard for data transfer called Uniform Data Transfer (UDT) and a standard for scripting called Automation. Automation allows objects associated with one application to be directed from another application, or to perform operations on a set of objects under the control of a macrolanguage.

ODBC Open Data Base Connectivity (ODBC) is an application programming interface (API) that allows a programmer to abstract a program from a database. When writing code to interact with a database, you must include code that talks to a particular database using a proprietary language. If you want your program to talk to Access, SQL Server, and Oracle databases you have to code your program with three different database languages.

When programming with ODBC, you only need to issue requests using the ODBC language (a combination of ODBC API function calls and the SQL language). The ODBC Manager will figure out how to interact with the type of database you are targeting. ODBC emphasizes the isolation of the application from the database. Because databases provide a mechanism for object persistence, they are useful for maintaining state information between invocations of an application. ODBC provides:

- A standard way to connect to a database.
- A set of function calls that allows an application to connect to one or many databases, execute SQL statements, and retrieve the results.
- A standard representation for data types.

The ODBC architecture is depicted in Figure 10-13.

Each database management system (DBMS) implementing a database has its own database driver. When an application requests access to the database, a driver manager residing in the database server loads the appropriate database driver to facilitate the

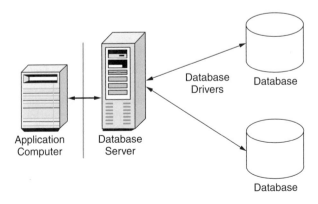

Figure 10-13. ODBC architecture.

access. The drivers are responsible for adapting to the specific syntax of the individual DBMSs.

10.3.3 Access to COM Objects

COM objects may be accessed in three different ways by a client:

1. *In-Process Service:* The client and the service are bound in the same process through a library that provides function calls to access the COM services (Figure 10-14).
2. *Local Object Proxy:* The client, running in one process, may access the server, running in another process, through interprocess communication mechanisms, such as a lightweight remote procedure call. When the client and server are in different processes, COM must format and package the data in order to transfer it via the remote procedure call (Figure 10-15).

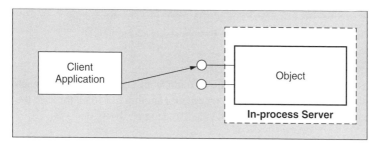

Figure 10-14. Same process accessibility.

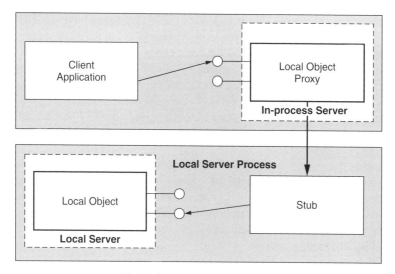

Figure 10-15. Local object proxy.

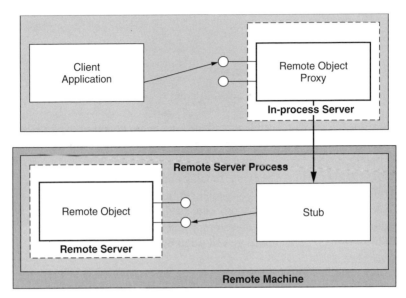

Figure 10-16. Remote object accessibility.

3. *Remote Object Proxy:* The client, running in a process on one machine, can access the server, running in a process on another machine, through the DCOM interprocess communication mechanism (Figure 10-16).

Marshalling As noted earlier, interprocess communication requires that the data to be transmitted be formatted and packaged in a canonical form. This process is called *marshalling*. It is accomplished through a "proxy" object and a "stub" object that handle the cross-process communication for any particular interface. COM creates a "stub" in the object's server process to manage the real interface pointer. COM also creates the "proxy" in the client's process and connects it to the stub. The proxy supplies the interface pointer to the client.

The client calls the methods of an interface of the server through the proxy, which marshals the parameters and passes them to the server stub. The stub unmarshals the parameters and makes the actual call inside the server object. When the call completes, the stub marshals return values and passes them to the proxy, which in turn returns them to the client.

The same proxy/stub mechanism is used when the client and server are on different machines. However, the internal implementation of marshalling and unmarshalling differs depending on whether the client and server operate on the same machine (COM) or on different machines (DCOM). Given an IDL file, the Microsoft IDL compiler can create the default proxy and stub code that performs all necessary marshalling and unmarshalling.

Using a COM Object All COM objects are registered with a component database maintained by the Windows operating system. This allows client applications to find COM objects when they need them. A client application creates and uses a COM object as follows:

1. It invokes the COM API to create an instance of a COM object.
2. The COM API within Windows locates the COM object description and initiates a server process for that object.
3. The server process creates an instance of the object and returns an interface pointer to the COM object.
4. The client accesses the instance of the COM object through the interface pointer.

COM objects have no identity, that is, no name. The sole access to a COM object instance is through the interface pointer.

10.3.4   Distributed COM

Because objects are self-contained, they can be distributed across multiple machines that communicate via network facilities. Microsoft extended COM to support communication among distributed objects, DCOM (Microsoft Corp. 2001). DCOM was introduced with the advent of Windows NT 4.0 in mid-1996. It was later added to Windows 95 and subsequent Windows operating systems.

As depicted in Figure 10-16 in the previous section, communication among distributed objects uses a remote procedure call (RPC) mechanism. DCOM is built using technology from X-Open's Distributed Computing Environment (DCE).

DCOM provides features and services that are similar to CORBA's. DCOM's usage, however, is largely limited to Win32 API environments.

The following discussion is extracted from an MSDN article by Horstmann and Kirtland (1997).

DCOM Architecture   DCOM serves as the middleware that allows components on different machines to communicate with each other. Figure 10-17 depicts the basic DCOM architecture.

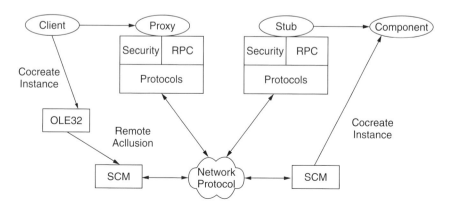

Figure 10-17. Basic DCOM architecture.

DCOM provides the communications mechanisms that mediate the transfer of data between two machines.

Activating Objects Remotely A client must be able to locate and activate a COM object instance on a remote machine. On a local machine, each COM object is given a globally unique identifier (GUID), which is unique to that local machine. The GUID is a large (128 bit) integer that provides a collision-free namespace. When the GUID refers to a class of objects, it is called a class identifier (CLSID).

To create an instance of a COM object, the programmer calls one of several creation functions in the COM API. To create objects on other machines, both the server identifier and GUID/CLSID of the object must be known. When the creation function is invoked, the service control manager (SCM) on the local machine communicates with the SCM on the remote machine to request creation of the object.

Monikers Once a remote instance has been activated and methods have been invoked, the remote instance has established an internal state that is (probably) unique from any other instance of the same object. But what is returned from instance creation is an interface pointer. So clients need a way to refer to a specific instance. The naming mechanism implements a "moniker" for a COM object instance. A *moniker* is a COM object itself but contains the code necessary to locate the COM object instance to which it refers. They can also recreate and reinitialize an instance if there is no running instance, such as after a component termination. The interface to the moniker is a standard interface called IMoniker.

A COM object instance is usually in charge of naming itself, that is, creating the moniker and distributing it to those that request it. Object instances also register their monikers so that they can be found at a later time. Each Windows implementation maintains a table called the Running Object Table (ROT) in the registry that contains a list of all the active object instances.

Moniker objects use the ROT to find the pointer to the instance to which they refer. If they do not find a running instance, they use the object creation method described earlier to create an uninitialized instance of the object. The moniker is then responsible for restoring the instance's state through some mechanism appropriate to the object, the specified instance, and the moniker's capabilities.

If the object's instance has some persistent information, it must be stored on a file or in a database on some server. The moniker needs to keep track of the location of this data so that it can restore the object if it must recreate it. An object may be created on the server where its persistent data is stored so that it can readily be initialized. This limits performance bottlenecks and network inefficiencies by eliminating the movement of large amounts of data that may be needed to reinitialize the object instance.

Moniker Types Several types of monikers are predefined within DCOM. The file moniker encapsulates the file: protocol and maps names to the URL file: protocol. A sample name might look like `file:c:\myfiles\afile.dat`. This protocol is used for accessing persistent data through the native file access mechanism provided by the Windows Win32 API.

The initialization protocol between the moniker and an object is IPersistFile: as the moniker creates an object it calls QueryInterface for IPersistFile and passes the file name to the object. The object in turn uses native file APIs to access the file.

Several standard Internet protocols are also included as monikers: http:, ftp:, gopher:. Each of these maps the moniker object to the corresponding standard URL protocols. Typical display names for URL monikers are `http://www.microsoft.com` or `http://www.netscape.com`. The protocol used to access the persistent data depends on the Internet protocol being used.

A moniker can support multiple initialization interfaces with its target COM object. The moniker can use different interfaces based on the location and type of the object and the persistent data. With URL monikers, a client can bind to objects whose persistent state is stored on the Internet without ever having to worry which Internet protocol is being used.

Marshalling and Unmarshalling   To call an object in another address space, the parameters to the method call must somehow be passed from the client's process to the called object's process. The client places the parameters on the stack. For remote invocations, the parameters must be read from the stack and written to a flat memory buffer so they can be transmitted over a network. This "flattening" process is called marshalling. Parameter marshalling is nontrivial because parameters can be arbitrarily complex—they can be pointers to arrays or pointers to structures. Structures may contain arbitrary pointers and many data structures also contain cyclic pointer references. In order to successfully invoke a method call remotely with complex parameters, the marshalling code has to traverse the entire pointer hierarchy of all parameters and retrieve all the data so that it can be reinstated in the object's process space.

The counterpart to marshalling on the remote server is the process of reading the flattened parameter data and recreating a stack that looks exactly like the original stack set up by the caller. This process is called "unmarshalling." Once the stack is recreated, the object can be called. As the called method returns to the client, any return values and output parameters need to be marshalled from the called object's stack, sent back to the client, and unmarshalled into the client's stack.

COM uses the OSF DCE standard Network Data Representation (NDR) for the relevant data types. COM needs to know the exact method signature, including all data types, types of structure members, and sizes of any arrays in the parameter list in order to marshal/unmarshal parameters correctly. This description is provided using an interface definition language (IDL), which is built on top of the DCE RPC standard IDL. IDL files are compiled using a special IDL compiler [such as the Microsoft IDL (MIDL) compiler, which is part of the Win32 SDK]. The IDL compiler generates C source files that contain the code for performing the marshalling and unmarshalling for the interface described in the IDL file. The client-side code is called the "proxy," while the code running on the object side is called the "stub." The MIDL-generated proxies and stubs are COM objects that are loaded by the COM libraries as needed.

Microsoft extended the IDL to handle the interface pointers that COM returns when it creates an object instance. In certain cases, an object can override the standard mechanism and provide custom proxy and stub objects to perform the marshalling/unmarshalling chores.

Integrating Legacy Transports The ability to specify custom marshalling/unmarshalling routines allows a programmer to integrate a legacy RPC transport with DCOM. The remote object must act as a server for the non-DCE RPC transport and provide the appropriate marshalling/unmarshalling routines at its endpoint. The remote object must provide some sort of string or handle to the client in order to enable it to determine which custom proxy object to use to perform marshalling/unmarshalling at its end. This also works in reverse where the client may be a legacy system attempting to invoke COM objects.

10.3.5 Security Support

With distributed applications, one of the major issues is providing security among the communicating objects. Some of the issues include: Who can access which objects? Which operations are objects allowed to perform? How can administrators manage secure access to objects? How secure does the content of a message need to be as it travels over the network?

DCOM provides security-related mechanisms to support secure applications distributed across a network. These mechanisms must interoperate with different security mechanisms on other platforms, especially non-Wintel platforms. To enable distributed security, they must provide a means of identifying a security principal (typically a user account), a means of authenticating a security principal (typically through a password or private key), and a central authority that manages security principals and their keys. If a client wants to access a secured resource, it passes its security identity and some form of authenticating data to the resource and the resource asks the security provider to authenticate the client (see Table 10-1).

Access Security Remote servers need to prevent against unauthorized access to objects stored in their address space. A fundamental question is: Who can connect to

Table 10-1. Fundamental aspects of security

Aspect	Description
Access security	Which security principals are allowed to call an object?
Launch security	Which security principals are allowed to create a new object in a new process?
Identity	What is the security principal of the object itself?
Connection policy	Integrity—can messages be altered?
	Privacy—can messages be intercepted by others?
	Authentication—can the object find out or even assume the identity of the caller?

an object? Sometimes, only authorized users are allowed to do so, while at other times (or all the time), unauthorized users can connect to an object. Typically, these latter users are limited in the functionality they can invoke.

DCOM enforces access security on every method call on an object. If the process does not programmatically override security settings, DCOM reads a security descriptor from the registry. When a client's invocation arrives at the object, DCOM authenticates the caller (using whatever security provider is configured) and obtains an access token. It then performs an access check on the security descriptor with the access token.

Launch Security   Since all COM objects on a machine are potentially accessible via DCOM, unauthorized users must be prevented from creating instances of these objects. This protection has to be performed without any involvement of the object itself, since the mere act of launching the server process could be considered a security breach and would open the server to denial of service attacks.

COM performs special security validations on object activation. If a new instance of an object is to be created, COM validates that the caller has sufficient privileges to perform this operation. The privilege information is configured in the registry, external to the object.

Launch security is enforced whenever a new process needs to be created as part of object activation. DCOM finds the application's identifier corresponding to the activation request and reads a security descriptor from the registry. It then authenticates the activator and checks the activator's access token against the security descriptor.

Security Identity   Since an object performs operations on behalf of arbitrary callers, it is often necessary to limit the capabilities of the object. Also, the object must be able to verify the identity of clients for specified operations.

Connection Policy   Both clients and objects are often concerned about the transport of data over uncontrolled networks (e.g., they do not have the ability to control who accesses or uses the network). Thus, they must have a mechanism for ensuring that data are neither altered nor intercepted by third parties.

Physical data integrity is usually guaranteed by the low-level network transport. If a network error alters the data, the transport automatically detects this and retransmits the data. It is the upper layers of the Internet protocols, particularly the TCP/IP protocols, where the problem becomes more acute.

The overhead in terms of machine and network resources increases with the level of security. DCOM therefore lets applications dynamically choose the level of security they require.

For secure distributed applications, data integrity really means being able to determine if the data actually originated from a legitimate caller and if it has been logically altered by anyone. The process of authenticating the caller can be relatively expensive, depending on the security provider and the security protocol it implements. DCOM lets applications choose if and how often this authentication occurs.

Data integrity implies that each and every data packet contains authentication information. But data integrity does not imply that no one can intercept and read the data being transferred.

10.3.6 Summary

COM's symmetric communication model allows bidirectional communication between clients and server objects. Indeed, the roles of "client" and "server" can change dynamically during the execution of an application. For example, a client passes an interface pointer to a server; the server can use this interface pointer to send notifications or data back to the client. This is the COM equivalent of callback interfaces, which were used extensively in X Windows.

Interface pointers also allow transitive communications to take place. A client invokes an object method, which returns an interface pointer to yet another (perhaps remotely located) object. Now, the client can communicate directly with the third object without going through the intermediate object that provided the interface pointer.

See Section 10.5 for further reading on COM and DCOM.

10.4 JAVABEANS

The JavaBeans architecture defines a reusable software component model based on the Java programming language.

A JavaBeans component (a bean) is a specialized Java class that can be added to an application development project and then manipulated by the Java IDE. A bean provides special hooks that allow a visual Java development tool to examine and customize the contents and behavior of the bean without requiring access to the source code. Multiple beans can be combined and interrelated to build Java applets or applications or to create new, more comprehensive, or specialized JavaBeans components.

10.4.1 The Concept of JavaBeans

Reusable software components are simple things like push buttons, text fields, list boxes, scrollbars, and dialogs in a GUI. But, more recently, third-party vendors have been marketing more complex components such as calendars, calculators, control panels, and spreadsheets.

Reusable components add standardized interfaces and object introspection mechanisms to GUI widgets, allowing builder tools to query components about their properties and behavior. Software components need not be visible in a running application; they only need to be visible when the application is constructed. The main difference between JavaBeans and native platform controls, such as OLE or ActiveX, is that they define a design-time interface, which allows application designer tools or builder tools to query components and ask them what kinds of properties they define, as well as what kinds of events they can generate or respond to.

Beans have properties, which are attributes. Visual properties might include color or screen size. Other properties may have no visual representation: a BrowserHistory Bean, for example, might have a property specifying the maximum number of URLs to store. Beans expose *setter* and *getter* methods (called "accessor methods") for their properties, allowing other classes or development environments to manipulate their state. Customization is the process of configuring beans for a particular task.

JavaBeans provides support for introspection. Tools that recognize predefined patterns in method signatures and class definitions can "look inside" a Bean to determine its properties and behavior. A Bean's state can be manipulated at the time it is being assembled as a part within a larger application. The application assembly is referred to as design-time in contrast to runtime. In order for this scheme to work, method signatures within Beans must follow a certain pattern in order for introspection tools to recognize how Beans can be manipulated, both at design-time and runtime. In effect, Beans publish their attributes and behaviors through special method signature patterns that are recognized by beans-aware application construction tools.

JavaBeans support customization. The programmer can alter the basic appearance and behavior of a bean.

10.4.2 The Java Application Framework

The Java Application Framework (JAF) is a framework for using JavaBeans to develop flexible applications. JAF provides a set of standard services to determine the type of an arbitrary piece of data, encapsulate access to it, discover the operations available on it, and instantiate the appropriate bean to perform those operations. It is particularly useful in browsers, which can obtain an object from a site, determine the type of object, say, a JPEG image, and dynamically create and provide a mechanism for viewing and manipulating that image.

The success of JAF has instigated a number of competitors in industry and academia who support its basic functionality but extend it with additional capabilities. An open source version is being developed through SourceForge (`http://sourceforge.net/projects/atrisframework/`).

The framework is platform-neutral, so it is a good choice for developing portable Java applications for a heterogeneous environment.

10.4.3 Enterprise JavaBeans (EJB)

Enterprise JavaBeans™ is a technology for the development and deployment of reusable Java server components. It extends JavaSoft's JavaBeans component model to support scalable, transactional, multiuser secure enterprise-level applications. The EJB model supports a number of implicit services, including lifecycle, state management, security, transactions, and persistence.

Lifecycle: Individual enterprise beans do not need to explicitly manage process allocation, thread management, object activation, or object destruction. The

EJB container automatically manages the object lifecycle on behalf of the enterprise bean.

State Management: Individual enterprise beans do not need to explicitly save or restore conversational object state between method calls. The EJB container automatically manages object state on behalf of the enterprise bean.

Security: Individual enterprise beans do not need to explicitly authenticate users or check authorization levels. The EJB container automatically performs all security checking on behalf of the enterprise bean.

Transactions: Individual enterprise beans do not need to explicitly specify transaction demarcation code to participate in distributed transactions. The EJB container can automatically manage the start, enrollment, commitment, and rollback of transactions on behalf of the enterprise bean.

Persistence: Individual enterprise beans do not need to explicitly retrieve or store persistent object data from a database. The EJB container can automatically manage persistent data on behalf of the enterprise bean.

The EJB Server architecture that implements these services is depicted in Figure 10-18.

A typical EJB architecture would consist of the following:

- EJB Server.
- EJB containers that run on these servers.
- EJB clients.
- Auxiliary components.

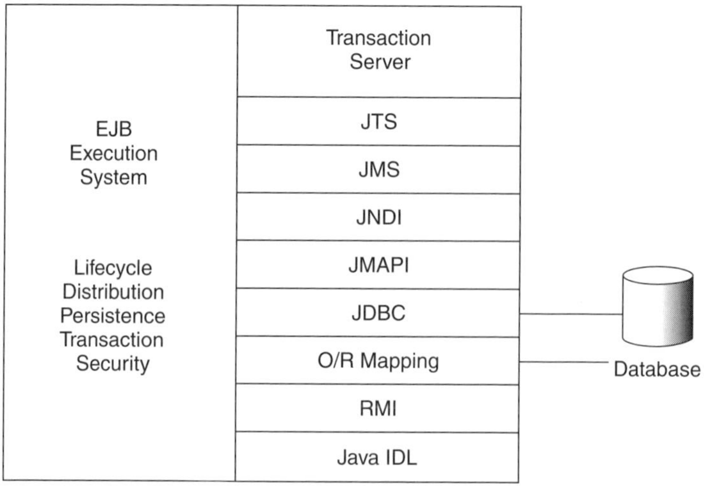

Figure 10-18. EJB Server architecture.

EJB Server   The EJB server provides an environment that supports the execution of applications developed using Enterprise JavaBeans technology. It manages and coordinates the allocation of resources to the applications. An EJB server provides a standard set of services to support enterprise bean components. Enterprise JavaBeans components are transactional; therefore, an EJB server must provide access to a distributed transaction management service. The EJB specification does not specify how to implement the EJB server.

EJB Container   An EJB is wrapped in a container. A container can hold multiple beans. The container provides services to each bean requesting them. The EJB specification describes a minimal set of services, which each container must provide. This allows beans using only those services to move among different containers. Specialized containers can provide more services than required by the specification, but developers must be wary of using such services as they can inhibit portability.

EJB Types   Enterprise JavaBeans contains the components that you write to encapsulate business or application logic. Transaction services to the EJB are provided by the container and the server.

Enterprise JavaBeans technology supports both transient and persistent objects. A transient object is called a *session bean*, and a persistent object is called an *entity bean*.

Sessions Beans   A *session bean* is created by a client and, in most cases, exists only for the duration of a single client–server session. A session bean performs operations on behalf of the client, such as accessing a database or performing calculations. Session beans can be transactional, but they are not recoverable following a system crash. Session beans can be stateless, or they can maintain conversational state across methods and transactions. The container manages the conversational state of a session bean if it needs to be evicted from memory. A session bean must manage its own persistent data.

Entity Beans   An *entity bean* is an object representation of persistent data that is maintained in a permanent data store, such as a database. Entity beans are persistent across client sessions and the lifetime of the server. A primary key identifies each instance of an entity bean. Entity beans can be created either by inserting data directly into the database or by creating an object (using an object factory Create method). No matter when or where you get a reference to an entity bean with a given identity, the bean should reflect the current state of the persistent data it represents. Multiple clients can access an entity bean at the same time. Entity beans are transactional, and they are recoverable following a system crash.

Entity beans can manage their own persistence, or they can delegate persistence services to their container. If the bean delegates persistence to the container, then the container automatically performs all data retrieval and storage operations on behalf of the bean. This saves you the trouble of adding JDBC calling code in your bean code. But the automated persistence support is limited. Some beans require more management and, so, must write their own persistence mechanisms using JDBC calls (Flanagan et al. 2002).

10.4.4   The Need for EJB

On the front end, there are many different types of clients (desktops/browsers, PDAs, Web phones, thin clients, different platforms). On the back end, there are many types of platforms (Unix, Windows, Mac) and data repositories (RDBMS, ODBMS, Mainframe). Java middleware can connect the two. EJB provides the glue between clients and applications by providing a mechanisms for implementing the business logic.

EJB can eliminate low-level system programming concerns and thus allow developers to focus on the business logic. The developer can code the EJB as if it was to be used only by a single client. EJB provides for server-side components whose API is available to all clients. Thus, there is motivation for developers to provide both off-the-shelf server-side components that can serve a wide number of different clients. Because EJB follows the Java object-oriented model, it can be extended and specialized as necessary to provide additional functionality. One use is to have the EJB translate relation data to objects.

EJB has some limitation that enhances its utility as middleware objects. EJB cannot start new threads or terminate the running thread or use thread synchronization primitives. EJB can only use static fields as read-only fields. The limitations ensure portability and the ability to service any client that can access EJB's APIs.

10.4.5   Java Distributed Object Model

The distributed object model extends the Java object model to remote objects. A *remote object* is an object whose methods can be accessed from another address space. Remote objects are described by an interface that declares the methods of the remote object. These methods are invoked by Java's Remote Method Invocation (RMI). Clients access the remote objects through the interface.

The Java object model is supported for remote objects with a few exceptions. For example, remote object handles are passed by reference rather than value. And cloning of remote objects is prohibited. Moreover, the exact types of arguments to remote objects need not be known at compile-time; polymorphism is fully supported. Finally, a remote object must declare an additional exception for each remote invocation: RemoteException.

Enterprise JavaBeans uses Java's Remote Method Invocation (RMI) technology to provide communication among distributed Enterprise JavaBeans. RMI is a high-level programming interface that makes the location of the server transparent to the client. The RMI compiler generates a stub object for each remote interface. The stub object is installed on the client system and provides a local proxy object for the client. The stub implements all the remote interfaces and transparently delegates all method calls across the network to the remote object.

Unlike CORBA, everything using RMI must be implemented in Java as the mechanisms are Java-specific. In one sense this yields better performance since there is no need to introduce a common object model to support or integrate components from other programming languages. On the other hand, interoperability with components written in other languages is not easily possible.

10.4.6 Jini

Jini (Waldo 2001) extends the idea of distributed computing by replacing peripherals and applications with network-accessible services. This network-centric approach makes the network the central connecting mechanism for distributed systems. As Waldo (2001, pp. 76–82) notes:

> Jini allows anything with a processor, some memory, and a network connection to offer services to other entities on the network or to use the services that are so offered. This class of devices includes all the things we traditionally think of as computers but also most of the things we think of as peripherals, such as printers, storage devices, and specialized hardware. The definition also encompasses a host of other devices, such as cell phones, personal digital assistants, and microprocessor-controlled devices, such as televisions, stereo components, and even modern thermostats.

Furthermore, Jini assumes that the network components and the interactions among those components may be constantly changing. While the network has a persistent presence, the entities comprising the network, its services, and its clients may all be short-lived.

Jini was designed to extend the Java RMI communication mechanism to handle ad hoc communications among distributed components, for example, ones that are unplanned, transient, or opportunistic. Distributed applications, such as mobile computing or wireless phones, are dynamic in that they are only transiently connected. The duration and time of connectivity is highly dependent on the application and may or may not be predictable.

Because Jini is implemented as a set of Java classes, objects inheriting from Jini classes attain new capabilities to support location, usage, and failure handling. Jini provides simple mechanisms for discovering, connecting to, and detaching from other objects. Since new components are added and old ones are decommissioned routinely, Jini provides a mechanism based on Java's reflection package that allows components to determine and use the interfaces of new objects. Additionally, Jini provides a mechanism for handling failure based on the lease concept.

Each component of the Jini system is a logical extension of the corresponding Java functionality. But Jini adds the discovery service, which enables an entity to find a lookup service, and the lookup service. A comparison of Java and Jini is depicted in Table 10-2 (after Waldo 2001).

Lookup Service   The Jini Lookup Service handles location determination of distributed components. It is based on the notion of a ServiceItem, which has a unique

Table 10-2. Java versus Jini comparison

System	Infrastructure	Programming Model	Services
Java	Java VM Java RMI	Beans SWING	Enterprise Beans Java Naming Directory Services Java Transaction Service
Jini	Discovery Lookup Service	Leasing Transactions Distributed Events	Java Spaces Transaction Manager
Jini extension	Objects find and communicate with each other	Support remote object location and communication	Everything else is a service

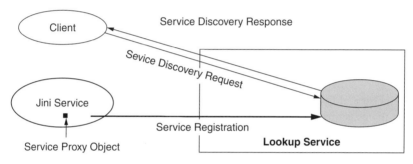

Figure 10-19. The Jini Lookup Service.

identifier, a set of attributes, and an object that implements the interfaces of a service that allows a Java class to be registered with the Lookup Service. In this way, a client gets all the code it needs to invoke a particular service from the Lookup Service without knowing about the location of the service component or the communication protocol to be used between them. In effect, the ServiceItem implements a device driver that allows the client to request a service and the Lookup Service to find a component to provide it to which the client can be connected. The object implementing the interfaces has a standard interface. When the client requests a service from the Lookup Service, the object (e.g., its byte code) is transferred to the location of the client for execution (Figure 10-19).

Leases A Jini lease is a contract between two parties. One party, the lease grantor, is willing to grant some of its resources to the other party, the lease holder. The contract is valid for only a limited amount of time. Before granting access to the resource, the amount of time is negotiated between the two parties. Upon expiry of a lease, the resource can be freed by the lease grantor and can be assigned to another client. If a lease holder wants to extend the period of time it is allowed to use a resource, it can ask the lease grantor to renew the lease and set a new expiration time. The lease grantor may extend the expiration time of the lease, but there is the possibility of not extending the lease. If a lease holder is finished using a resource before the associated lease ends, rather than waiting for the lease's expiry it can explicitly cancel the lease.

When a service component registers with the Lookup Service, it is granted a lease for a specified period of time. During that period, it must honor requests for service. When the lease expires, it is removed from the Lookup Service. The Lookup Service does not have to validate registered service components on a periodic basis. A simple detection mechanism enables it to check if a lease has been granted and has not yet expired. Services can revoke their lease at any time or they may request to extend it indefinitely.

Refer to Section 22.5 for additional references on J2EE.

10.5 FURTHER READING

SOMobjects Manuals

IBM Corp. 1997. *SOMobjects Object Services*, 2nd Ed. SC28-1995-01, Poughkeepsie, NY.

IBM Corp. 1997. *SOMobjects Programmers Guide*, 4th Ed. GC28-1859-03, Poughkeepsie, NY.

IBM Corp. 1997. *SOMobjects Programmers Reference, Volume 1*. SC28-1997-01, Poughkeepsie, NY.

IBM Corp. 1997. *SOMobjects Programmers Reference, Volume 2*. SC28-1998-01, Poughkeepsie, NY.

IBM Corp. 1997. *SOMobjects Programmers Reference, Volume 3*. SC28-1999-01, Poughkeepsie, NY.

IBM Corp. 1997. *SOMobjects Getting Started*, 2nd Ed. SC28-1995-01, Poughkeepsie, NY.

IBM Corp. 1997. *SOMobjects Messages, Codes and Diagnosis*, 2nd Ed. SC28-1996-01, Poughkeepsie, NY.

COM/DCOM

Gregory, B. 2000. *Applying COM+*. New Riders Publishing, New York.

Nathan, E. 2002. *.NET and COM: The Complete Interoperability Guide*. Pearson Education, Upper Saddle River, NJ.

Sanke, J. 2000. *COM Programming By Example*. Miller Freeman, San Francisco, CA.

Tapadiya, P. 2000. *COM+ Programming*. Prentice Hall, Englewood Cliffs, NJ.

Javabeans

Harold, E. R. 1998. *Javabeans*, John Wiley & Sons, Hoboken, NJ.

Monson-Haefel, R. 2000. *Enterprise Javabeans*, 3rd Ed. O'Reilly Associates, Cambridge, MA.

Pew, J., L. Cable, and J. Cable. 2001. *Core Java Beans*. Prentice Hall, Englewood Cliffs, NJ.

Watson, M. 1997. *Creating Java Beans—Components for Distributed Applications*. Morgan Kaufmann, Los Altos, CA.

10.6   EXERCISES

10.1. Jini is Java-centric. Review the Jini services described in this chapter and consult some of the publicly available Jini documentation. Pick another programming language and discuss how you would implement Jini-like services in that language (e.g., consider Ada, C++, Concurrent Eiffel, or Common Lisp).

10.2. The CORBA specification implicitly assumes an object-oriented environment. Review the CORBA specification and discuss what features are required for a programming language to implement an ORB.

10.3. What elements are common to the four component technologies discussed in this chapter? Develop a table depicting them and describe each according to the technology.

10.4. Compare and contrast the Jini approach with the CORBA approach to remote method invocation using the criteria of scalability, reliability, and ease of programming. [Research Problem]

10.5. Compare Microsoft's Transaction Server with Sun's Jini service. Both focus on transaction processing for distributed environments.

10.6. Identify the steps that are necessary to create a set of JavaBeans and to use those beans to develop a particular Java application or applet. Explain what is happening in each step, why it is necessary, and what is required to accomplish that step.

10.7. Compare Microsoft's ActiveX components with Sun's JavaBeans technology.

11

COMPONENT-BASED SOFTWARE ENGINEERING

Software component development seeks to develop a set of reusable software components that satisfy particular asset specifications. This is generally done either by developing the components from scratch or through "reuse-based" reengineering of legacy artifacts. Most of the current work in component-based development is focused on infrastructure development and the accompanying middleware to connect independent components to provide system-level functionality.

Component-based software engineering (CBSE) is an approach to application software development in which prefabricated, pretested, and reusable pieces of software are assembled together to form flexible applications that are built rapidly. A good metaphor for CBSE is children's Lego blocks. CBSE is sometimes referred to as component-based software development, but this term omits the critical element of component design and specification, which must precede the development.

CBSE has existed in one form or another for a number of years. The idea of constructing modular software has long been recognized as advantageous within the software community, even dating back to the early days of Fortran programming with subroutines and libraries serving as "components." Early work on components was performed by Grady Booch (1987) for Ada 83 and Bertrand Meyer (1997) for Eiffel.

CBSE is drawing a lot of interest because of the emergence of enabling architectures and SDKs such as ActiveX, JavaBeans, .NET, and the Web. But CBSE goes beyond just technology. Suppose an application designer could draw on a pool of software objects whose form and function were as obvious as Lego blocks. Then

Software Paradigms, By Stephen H. Kaisler
ISBN 0-471-48347-8   Copyright © 2005 John Wiley & Sons, Inc.

applications would be as easy to build as "snapping" together the software modules. An organization could move from *application* development to *application* assembly. Unfortunately, it is not so simple.

11.1 DEFINING CBSE

Component-oriented programming aims to replace traditional monolithic software systems with reusable software components and layered component frameworks (Szyperski 1998). The frameworks provide an execution environment for plugging in components developed by third parties. These components must conform to the interfaces specified by the framework and implement or extend framework functionality.

CBSE is a coherent engineering methodology: it incorporates both a process and a technology description. The process, emphasizing reusability, includes system design, project management, and system life cycle concerns. The technology description, based on some of the definitions of components given in Chapter 8, enables the creation of applications.

CBSE is based on three principles:

- *Separate Component Specification from Its Design and Implementation:* This allows independent implementation of the component, including multiple implementations that can support a plug-and-play architectural approach.
- *Focus on Interface Design:* Interfaces provide a contract between clients and servers that allows encapsulated behavior that is independent of other components.
- *Formal Specification of Component Semantics:* Associated with the interface specification is a semantics specification that helps to guide the implementer in developing the component.

While CBSE has often been linked with object-oriented programming (OOP), OOP is not a prerequisite for practicing CBSE. We can build components using programming languages that do not support object-oriented behavior as long as we define an appropriate methodology for how these components are designed and used.

11.2 PROBLEMS WITH CBSE

CBSE requires much work before we can rise to the level of flexibility and ease of use associated with Lego blocks. Five problems must be addressed:

- Building components.
- Finding components.
- Using components.

- Testing components.
- Harvesting components for re-use.

11.2.1 Building Components

How does a designer build a reusable component? This is, perhaps, the thorniest problem facing CBSE. What is reusable to one designer is an obstacle to another.

A key question is whether software can be designed in isolation of its intended use. For low-level components, the answer is fairly obvious. The C++ Standard Template Library and Booch's Ada components are good examples of reusable components. But these components are data structure components rather than functional components for a specific domain.

Let's look at another aspect of the problem. Suppose we could design reusable components. How would we describe them in such a way that potential clients could find them, determine that they are useful, and assess whether they would cause any problems in the intended application? Moreover, how could they be customized and how is that described to the potential user?

A corresponding question, but one that has commercial and legal ramifications is: How can we ensure that these components would be used properly?

Suppose we are building reusable components. Does using an object-oriented programming system (OOPS) guarantee that the components will be easier to reuse and customize? Can we build extensible components (e.g., customizable, as well) if we do not use an OOPS? To the latter question, the answer is most likely yes since programming languages such as Ada are object-oriented and provide some limited extensibility.

Reusability implies an adherence to standards. For Lego blocks each plug and each socket has a standard diameter such that plugs fit into sockets. Moreover, plugs and sockets are laid out on each block in a uniform, standard way.

With software, it's a different story. A number of standards that promote interoperability and interaction have been developed, including CORBA, SOM, and DCOM. Unfortunately, many of these standards are not interoperable among themselves. So a designer building for one standard will not produce components usable with another standard unless he creates a duplicate set oriented to the second standard.

Lack of a uniform interoperability and interaction standard is one of the great obstacles to truly reusable components.

11.2.2 Finding Components

Suppose we have a collection (or even several collections) of reusable components. How do we, as users, find the components that are right for us? The finding process is more than just locating an exact match. We want to find similar components, because if a component must be redeveloped for the target application, an example similar to the desired component can reduce the effort and eliminate many defects.

Suppose the components are described in a catalog just like Lego blocks, automotive parts, and integrated circuits. How do we determine that a particular component is a good fit to the requirements we have? One aspect of this is determining exactly what the component will do and, equally as important, what it will not do. A significant obstacle to reusable components is the lack of standardized descriptions that enable potential clients to match up their requirements with the capabilities of the component. So we need a standard for describing components that is susceptible to automation. While the model used to describe design patterns is a good start, it does not capture all the information we need, particularly about implementation.

Another obstacle is that components become less and less reusable the more specific they become. It becomes increasingly difficult to find an exact match for the user's detailed requirements. Solving the description problem is only part of the solution, because we still need to figure out how much detail about each component we provide for matching. If we can factor out the specificity, we can reduce the size of the search space considerably.

11.2.3 Using Components

Suppose we have found the components that we need to build our application. We have three tasks to perform. First, we must understand the components. Second, we must modify them if we need additional functionality. Third, we now have to assemble them into an application.

Understanding the component(s) is required whether or not we intend to modify them, but it is especially required if we do intend to modify them. The user needs a mental model of the component's computation to use it properly. This is a fundamental problem that limits our reuse of components. Lack of understanding and comprehension is due to many factors, but poor documentation and awkward code are two that come to mind.

Some components, of course, cannot be reused right out of the box. Some modification is required—most likely extensions and specializations of the component. The problem, of course, is how to write code such that components can be substituted for an alternative and changes can be made to the code when both new requirements arise and new components are available with minimal disturbance to the whole application.

Modification is a key process in software reusability. Modification varies with the programming language paradigm. This is largely a human skill, as there are almost no tools that provide any measure of automation of components.

The composition and assembly process is the most challenging one. On the one hand, we need to be able to specify the structure of the application and the generic components that comprise it. But we must also be able to specify the requirements for each concrete component that becomes part of the application. The problem is that component composition has both global and local effects, where the former are much harder to characterize and describe.

Do the components have an easy to use interface, like Lego blocks, that allows us to snap them together? If not, additional work is required to "glue" the components together, which may include writing additional software ("glue code") to perform data translation, data restructuring, or additional computations. This may require skilled IT professionals to develop applications, a scenario that components were originally intended to largely avoid.

11.2.4 Testing Components

Testing is a crucial software development activity that is used to determine if a software artifact has errors. Testing is used to assess the compliance of the implementation with the specifications. Two problems arise:

1. *Test Effectiveness:* What is the best selection of test data?
2. *Test Adequacy:* How do we know that sufficient testing has been performed?

Methodologies for testing software artifacts are addressed comprehensively in Beizer (1983), Hetzel (1988), and ANSI/IEEE (1989). Software testing requires both detailed knowledge of the specification and knowledge of the implementation. However, since we cannot observe the source code of a component, any testing that we do will be limited. So we must assess the testing of commercial off-the-shelf (COTS) components, which we cannot fully test ourselves.

At best, we can test the COTS component for domain compliance knowing the domain for which it was developed. Typically, we do not have access to the component's specification. We must use the component's interface description and accompanying documentation to guide any testing we want to do of the component.

Domain testing evaluates two properties of a component: its observable behavior and its controllable behavior. Observable behavior requires that every distinct input produce a distinct output. So by giving the component distinct inputs, we can determine the mapping of inputs to outputs. Controllable behavior requires that we can obtain a desired output value by specifying an input that yields the output. A key aspect is determining the sequences of inputs that yield particular outputs.

11.2.5 Harvesting Components for Reuse

While the concept of reuse is generally accepted as a good idea, few organizations have really attempted it on significant scale. In part, this is because few software projects have anything that is readily available to reuse.

The current investment in software may yield some components that can be reused in other applications. The challenge is to identify, extract, and package those components for reuse. Organizations need to create a pool of components to reuse. To do so, they must analyze existing software projects—one by one—to determine what might be reused.

Ideally, the reusable components should be managed through a catalog so that they are susceptible to searches as described in Section 11.2.2. The catalog is built by extracting metadata from individual components for entry into the catalog. You must define a classification scheme for the catalog that enables you to represent the characteristics of components to be represented there such that you can find components that will be useful to you.

The harvesting process for components has three steps:

1. Analyze existing applications and software projects to determine data structures and components that occur in a similar form across multiple systems.
2. Determine which of these recurring structures and components can be used to build future systems.
3. Reengineer and repackage existing components for reuse; enter their metadata in the catalog.

11.3 PROBLEMS IN USING COMPONENTS

Although we have been dealing with components for over ten years, we are still learning how to build component-based systems and frameworks. There are several problems that we'll discuss that affect using components. The principal problem is the glue: How do we wire components together? Software architectures, described in Part III, help to solve part of this problem.

11.3.1 Interoperability

As components are used to build more complex systems, it is no longer sufficient that components just be integratable. They must also be interoperable. Interoperability can be defined as the ability of two or more components to communicate and cooperate despite differences in the implementation language, the execution environment, or the abstraction model (Wegner 1996).

In order to solve the problem of describing interoperability, we need to know what information is required about interoperability. Two types of information are required: syntactic (static) interoperability and semantic (dynamic) interoperability.

Syntactic Interoperability   Before components can interoperate, they must, of course, integrate. What do we need to know to integrate components? Primarily, we need to know the syntax of the interface to the component, for example, the syntax of the API. This syntax can be described using a formal method or a description language such as the CORBA IDL. Syntax enables structural integration, but not functional integration. So syntactic interoperability is the ability of two components to work together if properly connected; that is, data and messages passed between them are understood by each component.

Additional information is required to help potential users understand how to use the component and its provenance. This includes version information and dependencies of components. It specifies exactly the context in which the component was developed, including which versions of other components it requires, and which documentation and other information is associated with it. While this information is available during development, it is often lost once components are packaged and made available for deployment. This information allows the potential user to determine what types and versions of components work together.

Semantic Interoperability   Interoperability also requires that we have semantic information about a component's functionality (Heiler 1995). This type of interoperability means that the behavior provided by a component should be in accordance with the behavior expected by its clients. One approach has been Bertrand Meyer's (1997) "design by contract."

No general established way of describing complete semantic information about components exists. Its implementation, the source code, is often the only existing formal description of a component's semantics. Software engineering is replete with semantic mismatches that lead to system failures such as the Ariane crash and the Mars Polar Lander (Huckle 2003).

Let us consider interoperability through an example using Figure 11-1.

Figure 11-1 depicts two processes that communicate. Process 1—consisting of components X1 and X2—communicates with process 2—consisting of components A1 through A4. The communication is effected from component A1 to component X2.

The two processes could be "owned" by different developers. Process 1 could represent a library that is used by process 2. A2 and A3 are other components used by A1, while A4 is used by A2 and A3. A2 and A3 may have been acquired commercially and brought along A4. If A2 and A3 were acquired from different sources, the developer needs to ensure that the versions of A4 are compatible and needs to choose one for inclusion in the system.

There are two levels of semantic interoperability that must be considered. The first is data interoperability. The two components can exchange data through some mechanism (such as RPC or messaging). This allows data to be shared by different objects and procedures independently of the programming languages or hardware platforms used. The type model is defined using the specifications based on the structures of the objects, and type compatibility is achieved by overcoming representation differences

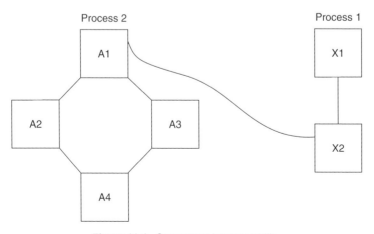

Figure 11-1. Component interoperability.

(such as byte ordering and floating point format) in how machines implement such objects, usually by translation into and out of a universal representation format. Most systems today provide application programming interfaces (APIs) to encapsulate such differences when various programs must interoperate in a networked environment, at least at the level of simple data types intrinsic to most popular programming languages (Howie et al. 1996).

The second level of interoperability is behavioral interoperability in which metadata about the data must be exchanged. This allows the participating components to understand how each interprets the data that is exchanged. For example, if a client or user agent were to search for information about a specific book from a set of distributed library resources, it would include an explicit indication that the search criteria is to be interpreted within the context of the library discipline. The search criteria could specify that the usage of a search term be restricted to a specific author or time period, the context restricted to within a copyright notice, and the authority restricted to a well-known discipline thesaurus. The client may also specify that the retrieved metadata be based on the library discipline. The requested search results may thus be restricted to retrieving the author's name, the time period of the book, the location of the original work, the location of reproductions, and a list of related books.

Two key questions arise:

1. How does one express interoperability information?
2. How does one publish this information so others can find it?

Both of these must be resolved before semantic interoperability can become independent of a particular implementation or technology.

One approach to this problem is the Z39.50 search and retrieval protocol, which has been designed to achieve semantic interoperability among heterogeneous data sources. Z39.50 has predefined a global set of search criteria and metadata, but it also offers a means for specialized disciplines to define their own set of search criteria and metadata. A number of disciplines have already established agreements, including Bibliographic Data, Government Information Resources, Scientific and Technical Data, Earth Sciences and Data, Digital Library Collections, and Museum Information (St. Pierre 1996).

Protocol Interoperability   A third type of interoperability is called protocol interoperability (Yellin and Strom 1997), which addresses the relative order in which methods should be called in a component, the order in which it calls methods in other components, and the rules that govern component interactions. Two components are compatible if the restrictions imposed on the interaction of each component when they call each other are preserved; that is, their protocols match each role they share, and their communication is deadlock free.

Protocol interoperability impacts whether or not we can substitute one component for another. Suppose component A is to be replaced by component B. We must check two properties of the replacing component. First, all messages accepted by A (i.e., supported operations) are also accepted by B. Also, all of B's invoking messages, issued when implementing A's services (i.e., both the replies and the required operations), are a sub-set of the outgoing messages of A. This allows B to provide additional services beyond A's, but it must at least provide A's services. Second, we must test that the relative order among the incoming and outgoing messages of both components is consistent.

11.3.2 The Impact of Hidden Assumptions

Every developer of components makes some assumptions as he designs and implements the components. Such assumptions include decisions about garbage collection, persistence, concurrency, and sequencing of invocations to component services. A key problem is how to make these assumptions known to the users of components. Note that this does not mean revealing the internal implementation of the component, but providing to the user some indication of the performance characteristics of the component.

Every user of COTS components must deal with several uncertainties. First, there is uncertainty over the safety and security of the component. Second, you are unaware of the vendor's assumptions about how the component will be used. These assumptions may be in conflict with characteristics of your environment. These two concerns are further amplified by a concern over testing. Most COTS components are tested using the black-box method; white-box testing is not an option. Also, components provide little or no malleability for end-users to make improvements. Few components provide parameters that you can set that allow you to make precise improvements in the performance and/or behavior of the component. Finally, shrink-wrapped component licenses offer you only a "take it or leave it" option, which provides you with little recourse in the event of software failures.

11.3.3 Component Configuration Management

Users need to be able to find out about the components in order to find a suitable and consistent set of components for a given problem.

11.3.4 Dependability of COTS Components

Commercial off-the-shelf (COTS) software is software that is acquired from an independent, third party and is used on an "as is" basis. This definition encompasses a wide variety of items from utilities to DLLs to operating systems. Much COTS software comes shrink-wrapped, so that it can be installed right out of the box.

Using COTS components involves accepting and mediating a number of risks, including:

- Given a set of COTS components, fitting the application to them may be a significant challenge.
- Detailed specifications for the COTS components are often unavailable.
- The application developer may have questions about the components that cannot be answered, so the developer makes assumptions about what a component does.

- Some required functionality may be missing (e.g., it does 80% or 90% of what is needed).
- Some existing functionality may need to be masked (e.g., by wrapping).
- Unanticipated limitations and faults may arise in certain environments.
- You don't control the maintenance and evolution of the components.

A major problem we face when using a COTS component is how to ascertain its dependability. This has a number of ramifications: legal, ethical, and technical. From a legal standpoint, consider the following question: If an information system sold or delivered by you contains defective COTS components, will your clients absolve you of blame for system failures? Similar questions arise in the ethical arena. From a technical standpoint, the literature cites an average of between 0.5 and 2.0 defects per thousands of lines of code (KSLOC). As a vendor, can you live with this level of software defect in your product?

So what do you do? In most cases, the option of avoiding COTS by "rolling your own" is not acceptable. It takes too long, you miss urgent deadlines, and you still have many of the same testing and dependability issues. You could do an audit at the vendor site, but this is impractical because you can't afford to do it at every vendor's site that you might use. There will be some vendors whose products you have tested who you do not choose to use. They probably benefit more than you do in this case.

So what do you do? You can practice defensive programming by analyzing the ways a COTS component might fail in your system and surrounding it with wrappers to mitigate those failures. Reread the discussion on the Wrapper design pattern of Section 4.2 to see how this might be used in your environment.

11.4   PROBLEMS WITH GLUE CODE

Building applications from predefined software components requires some mechanism for connecting those components together in such a way as to enable them to collaborate and communicate. This mechanism is commonly known as *glue code*. As noted previously, the most difficult problem in using component technology is the glue. In this section we address some of the problems with glue code. The role of glue code is depicted in Figure 11-2.

In order for glue code to assist in implementing applications, it must be configured through parameterization to integrate two or more components.

11.4.1   Mapping Between Object Models

Object-oriented technology does not have a standard specification. Different vendors implement object-oriented programming in different ways—at the programming language or component level. For example, the Smalltalk model is different from the C++ model which is different from the CLOS model—yet all purport to be object-oriented technologies.

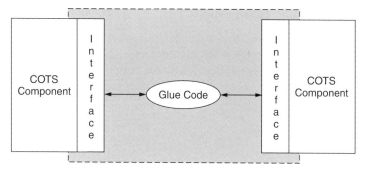

Figure 11-2. The role of glue code.

Glue code must translate, if necessary, between the different object models. CORBA provides such a feature, as does COM, although the latter uses a common calling sequence from different languages coupled with the COM interface mechanism. So CORBA supports (almost) general heterogeneity, while COM/DCOM only supports it within the Microsoft environment.

11.4.2   Adapting Between Incompatible Policies

Components may be developed with different types of policies related to security, interaction, storage, and so on. These policies must be made known explicitly in the component documentation in order for the programmer to understand and adhere to them, and understand the consequences of ignoring them. Glue code can assist in translating between policies, including masking out certain policies of the recipient component by providing default parameters.

11.4.3   Bridging Interaction Styles

Components also have different interaction styles. Ideally, one should be able to invoke component services in any order. However, realistically and practically, most components require that some methods be invoked in a certain order. Again, these requirements need to be made explicit in the component documentation. Glue code, acting as a wrapper, can accept method calls and reformat them into a different sequence of method calls in order to meet the requirements of the serving component.

11.4.4   Hooking into Legacy Components

Glue code also acts as a wrapper when interfacing with legacy components, perhaps written in other programming languages. It performs data translation, method or procedure argument arrangements, and sequencing of method calls for the legacy components.

11.4.5 Determining Good Glue

One of the problems we need to solve is determining what are good glue "abstractions." This is an open research problem in the sense that we need to develop good models for formally representing components in both client and server roles. Then we need to examine scenarios for different types of components and their features and properties.

11.5 EXERCISES

11.1. What is the best way to define a component in order to certify its properties? [Research Problem]

11.2. What component-related programming language features are needed to best support multiple, different implementations for the same abstract component, so as to enable plug-and-play?

11.3. What is the best way to define a component to allow client programmers to control the component's performance? [Research Problem]

11.4. Given a particular programming language, which language features should be aggressively used—and which should be avoided—when designing components to be composable, certifiable, efficient, reusable, and tunable? [Research Problem]

11.5. Compare and contrast C++'s constructor and destructor operations, with Ada 95's initialization and finalization operations in support of component instantiation.

11.6. Some authors have suggested that system integration productivity tends to decrease if the number of COTS components is increased. Give three reasons why you think this is so and justify your answer.

SOFTWARE
ARCHITECTURES

We design and implement information systems to solve problems and process data. As problems become larger and more complex and data becomes more voluminous, so do the associated information systems. The number of elements increases and the organization and structure of those elements in the information system become more complex.

We rarely develop information systems to solve single problems anymore. Today, we design and implement information systems that solve classes of problems—what we call a *problem space*, albeit the problems are related.

A *software architecture* describes the structure of a solution set to a problem space. A software architecture results from decomposing a problem space into smaller pieces, identifying commonalities among the pieces, finding a solution for a set of pieces having common properties, and associating component(s) with each of those pieces. The problem space encompasses a set of problems having mutual characteristics. So the architecture should provide a solution set for how to solve a set of problems.

Concretely, a software architecture describes how a system is composed from its components. It specifies the characteristics of the components, the interactions between components, and the communications topology among the components. As Garlan (2000) notes, a software architecture serves as a bridge between the requirements for a system and its actual implementation, as depicted in Figure III-1.

As the problem size and complexity increase, algorithms and data structures become less important than getting the right structure for the information system. Specifying the software architecture of the information system becomes a critical design problem itself (Garlan and Shaw 1994). So a software architecture describes not only the structure of the solution both abstractly and concretely, but the set of decisions made about the software architecture (e.g., what's in and what's out).

Software Paradigms, By Stephen H. Kaisler
ISBN 0-471-48347-8   Copyright © 2005 John Wiley & Sons, Inc.

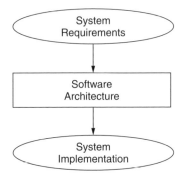

Figure III-1. Software architecture is the bridge.

There are many different software architectures. Choosing the right one for a problem space can be a difficult problem in itself. There is no algorithm (that I know of) for deciding what the best (optimal?) software architecture is for a particular problem domain (although some heuristics do exist). In fact, this may very well be an undecidable problem. Moreover, we don't have a good set of metrics yet for assessing problem domains and how well different software architectures map to them.

In this section we'll discuss the characteristics of software architectures, examine some specific software architectures and the problems to which they can be applied, and discuss how to describe them.

12

OVERVIEW OF SOFTWARE ARCHITECTURES

There are many definitions for software architectures. One of the earliest is proposed by Perry and Wolf (1992): "a set of architectural elements that have a particular form." They propose three types of elements: processing, data, and connecting. Connecting elements distinguish one architecture from another. The form of the architecture is given by enumerating the properties and relationships of the different elements.

Garlan and Shaw (1994, Shaw and Garlan 1996) propose the following definition: "a collection of components and connectors together with a description of the interactions between those components and connectors."

Finally, Bass, Clements, and Kazman (1998) offer the following definition: "Software architecture is the structure of the structures of the system, which comprise software components, the externally visible properties of those components, and the relationships among them."

Other definitions are given by Hayes-Roth (1994), Tracz (1994), and Boehm (1986).

All software architectures can be implemented as sequential programs. However, greater productivity and less time to solution are often achieved through concurrent implementations. Throughout the following chapters, we will discuss some of the concurrent variations of software architecture models. This work is based primarily on work by Greg Andrews (1991), Andrews and Schneider (1983), and Mattson and Bosch (1999).

Software Paradigms, By Stephen H. Kaisler
ISBN 0-471-48347-8   Copyright © 2005 John Wiley & Sons, Inc.

12.1 SOFTWARE ARCHITECTURE ELEMENTS AND DESCRIPTION

A *software architecture* is comprised of elements. A software architecture is described by an architectural description. The architectural description is not the architecture. This seems too obvious to say but often bears repeating to reinforce the concept. We will first describe the elements of a software architecture. Then we will discuss how to describe it.

12.1.1 Architectural Elements

All of the above definitions focus on components and connectors. As we will see, this is the common thread that runs through the concept of software architectures. These ideas are depicted in Figure 12-1.

The consensus seems to be that two (or more) components interact through a connector. A set of attributes describes each of the components and a different set of attributes describes the connector. Taken together, the diagram represents a particular configuration of components and connectors.

Components   *Components* are the basic building blocks and the active, computational entities in a system. We take "computational" to encompass all forms of processing, including user interfaces, data storage and retrieval, and communications. Components accomplish tasks through internal computation and external communication.

A component communicates with its environment (which includes other components) through one or more *ports* or *interfaces*. A port may be a user interface, a shared variable, a procedure name that can be called by another component, a set of events that can be emitted, or some other mechanism.

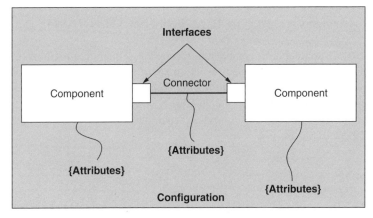

Figure 12-1. Software architecture concept.

Attributes (or properties) of the component specify information for analysis and development of the software, such as protocols, real-time constraints, and behavioral constraints.

Connectors   *Connectors* define the interaction between components and describe the rules that govern those interactions. A connector links the *ports* of two or more components. *Roles* attached to the connectors (as attributes) define the behavior of the attached components. For example, in a unidirectional communication scheme, one component would be the source, while the other component would be the receiver.

We treat connectors independently of components because connectors provide application-independent connection mechanisms. Through connectors we can both abstract and parameterize interactions among components.

In their own right, connectors can be implemented in multiple ways, including shared variables, remote procedure calls, and message passing. The information exchange protocols can vary from the simple, such as Unix byte streams, to the complex, such as client–server protocols or asynchronous multicast protocols.

Attributes are also associated with connectors. For example, attributes may specify the rates, capacities, and latencies of individual connectors. And we can specify different types of interactions, such as:

- Binary versus *n*-ary.
- Asymmetric versus symmetric.
- Information exchange protocols.

Interfaces   A component defines an *interface* through which a connector links one component with another. A component may have multiple interfaces. (*Note:* This use of "interface" is different from that used in OOP or some component technologies.)

A connector relates two interfaces one to the other. A connector may link a component to itself, such as when one component method uses another method in the same component.

An interface is associated with one and only one component. One interface may connect to multiple interfaces in other components. For example, in a bus-oriented software architecture, the interface of each component links to a bus connector, which attaches to multiple interfaces of other components as depicted in Figure 12-2. With the bus connector, a component sends a message to itself over the bus and it is reflected back to the component at the interface to the bus.

Attributes are also associated with ports or interfaces. Attributes may specify the direction of communication, the buffering capacity (if any), and the protocols accepted or emitted, among other characteristics.

Configuration   A *configuration* (sometimes called a *topology*) is a connected graph of components and connectors that describes architectural structure. The configuration must:

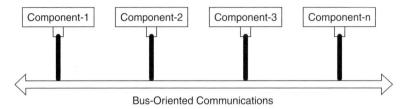

Figure 12-2. A bus-oriented software architecture.

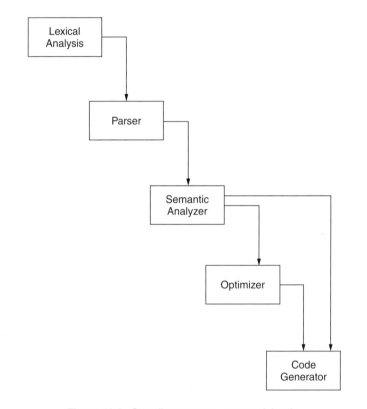

Figure 12-3. Compiler structure—sequential style.

- Adhere to the rules for proper connectivity.
- Satisfy concurrent and distributed properties.
- Adhere to design heuristics and style rules.

Design heuristics and style rules represent constraints on the architecting process. As an example, Figure 12-3 shows one configuration for a compiler. In this configuration, a compiler is implemented as a set of stages that occur in sequential order. Note that the optimizing stage may be skipped entirely.

We can analyze configurations to determine emergent system properties such as end-to-end performance, locations of computational bottlenecks, opportunities for concurrency, and system reliability and security.

12.1.2 Architectural Styles

Garlan and Shaw (1994) use the term *architectural style* to refer to a recurring pattern or idiom for expressing a software architecture to solve a problem. Styles include pipes-and-filters, blackboard systems, and client–server systems. An architectural style is composed of a set of components and connectors, a set of configuration rules, a specification of the behavior of the style, and analysis and examples of systems built in the style. (Note how this mirrors some of the descriptive elements of a design pattern.)

The set of components and connectors enumerates the different types of components and connectors, the specifications of each type, and the behaviors of each type. For example, a connector that implements a procedure call protocol would have a description of its behavior suitable for a user to understand how it should be implemented.

The configuration rules specify what connectors may connect which components, the number of components connected using a connector, and any topological constraints on the configuration. For example, we might specify that the end-to-end connectivity may be no longer than five components.

The behavioral specification provides a conceptual description of how the system will operate, for example, a semantic interpretation of what the system will do. Finally, the examples and analyses would describe some sample systems built using this style to give the user an idea of how to build such a system.

12.1.3 Architectural Description

There are many ways to describe software architectures—both formal and informal. Early eVorts, such as PSL/PSA (Teichroew and Hershey 1977), focused on high-level descriptions of behavior. PSL/PSA was a CASE tool developed at the University of Michigan to support the computer-based development and analysis of a statement of requirements and structure during the design phase. Other eVorts, such as IDEF0 and IDEF1X (http://www.idef.com), focused on structural decomposition. Several of the IDEF reports were initially issued as Federal Information Processing Standards (FIPS) in the late 1970s, but later withdrawn as they were superseded by modern methodologies. In the mid-1980s, DARPA sponsored the development of a number of architecture description languages (ADLs). These are discussed brieXy in Section 19.1.1.

ADLs represent a formal approach to describing software architectures. However, these are often focused on being manipulable by programs rather than people. But we also need a way to describe software architectures that people can readily grasp—a user's manual and a programmer's manual, if you will. Most SDKs come with both of these manuals today, albeit in electronic rather than hardcopy format.

One approach might be to adapt the design pattern description format (Section 3.5) to software architectures. But the design pattern format does not tell us how we could adapt the architecture to create different applications. Extensions to the design pattern format suitable for describing software architectures are the subject of an exercise.

An architectural description must describe the domain-specific architecture that the framework implements so that we can determine how to use it. There may be many design patterns comprising the software architecture(s) of an application framework. Some will be more important to the architecture than others because (1) some patterns are more architectural than others since they describe infrastructure that integrates or connects entities (much as the MVC pattern does for GUIs) and (2) some patterns are more granular than others (such as those embedded in components) and are invisible at the architectural level. Buschmann et al. (1996) draw the distinction between architectural patterns and general patterns.

12.2 WHY DO WE NEED A SOFTWARE ARCHITECTURE?

A software architecture, used as a descriptive mechanism, provides information for both technical and organizational purposes. But a software architecture is also part of a system architecture, which encompasses hardware, software, and telecommunications (including networking).

12.2.1 Motivation for Software Architecture

The motivation for software architecture is that good architecture is like good design. As the size and complexity of a software system increase (hundreds of modules/classes), the global structure of the system becomes more important than the selection of specific algorithms and data structures. Good design can beget good function and good behavior.

Bad design can overcome the best performing algorithms. And poorly designed algorithms and data structures can hobble the performance of a good architecture. A good software architecture helps us to identify points of computational and data flow bottlenecks, so that we can describe the characteristics of algorithms and data structures required for good performance.

Brooks (1987) has identified the problem as one of *software invisibility*:

> In spite of progress in restricting and simplifying the structure of software, they remain inherently unvisualizable, and thus do not permit us to use some of the most powerful conceptual tools.

The lack of a good roadmap to the software architecture of a large, complex software system both impedes the design process and hinders communication during and after the design has been implemented. Rechtin (1991) put it somewhat succinctly: *If you don't know where you are going, any road will get you there!* Without this insight into the overall structure of the system, decisions are made that often impact subsets of the design during implementation. As has been noted in requirements engineering texts, it is easier to fix a problem if it is detected during the requirements elicitation and documentation process than during system development. Arguably, without an overall conceptual view of the system as embodied in a software architecture, problems that could be detected early are missed completely, leading to much rework at later stages of the software development life cycle.

A good software architecture is the result of a well-defined set of principles and practices that are applied throughout the project's lifetime. It is resilient as the inevitable changes occur in requirements, business functions, and technology. And it provides guidance throughout the system life cycle.

12.2.2 Technical Use

From a technical standpoint, the software architecture describes the solution to a class of problems. In doing so, it describes the set of components, the set of connectors, their respective sets of attributes, the configuration of components and connectors, and the semantics of the interactions between components as mediated by the connectors. The software architecture is instantiated in an information system or software application.

Functional and behavioral requirements can be mapped to the software architecture to ensure that mandatory requirements are met and to evaluate and make trade-offs among desirable requirements. Moreover, requirements can be prioritized across multiple "builds" if the software architecture is to evolve over a period of time (such as following Boehm's Spiral Model). Behavioral requirements need to be addressed early in the design cycle or they are often overlooked. Assessing the quality attributes of a software architecture throughout the design process can ensure that they will not be overlooked.

A software architecture allows the system architect flexibility in distributing functional subsystems to hardware, software, and network components without requiring a redesign as elements of subsystems are reassigned. This flexibility helps to minimize costs and supports maintaining and evolving a given application over its entire lifetime by anticipating the kinds of changes that will occur in the system, ensuring that the system's overall design will facilitate such changes, and localizing as far as possible the effects of such changes. It also promotes the reuse of certain existing components, class libraries, legacy or third-party applications, and so on.

A software architecture also provides information that helps to ensure that subsystems are developed in conformance with the best practices associated with systems engineering, software development, and program management.

12.2.3 Organizational Use

A software architecture provides a high-level description of the subsystems that comprise the system architecture from a software perspective. This helps IT/IRM personnel to understand where major information technology assets are deployed and what business operations they support. At the same time, it helps key stakeholders, including senior executives, to understand how the major business operations are supported. Communication among stakeholders in the development of an application is crucial to its success. They must be able to communicate their needs and how they expect those needs to be met.

For individual project managers and their staffs, it provides a context for them to see where their efforts fit into the overall picture and how they relate to other systems. Understanding the interdependencies at a high level helps project managers to identify other projects with which they need to coordinate. And this understanding helps to promote global optimization of the system rather than local optimizations, which can lead to an overall suboptimal system.

A software architecture provides a description that is decomposed into substructures that are relatively independent, have clear responsibilities, and communicate with each other through a limited number of well-defined interfaces. This assists in resource planning and allocation because development work can be partitioned across the subsystems and individual development efforts can proceed in parallel. Integration occurs at specific milestones and specific interfaces. When development teams are geographically dispersed, this can minimize the number of interactions required and foster the development of skill sets for specific functions at particular locales.

12.3 SOFTWARE ARCHITECTING VERSUS SOFTWARE ENGINEERING

There are two ways to attack the solution to any problem. One is to begin with the known facts and formulas and proceed to construct a solution that explains those facts—and, by the way, with some manipulation can solve other problems as well. Or one can begin with a general vision and high-level constructs to develop a general solution, then specialize that solution for the specific problem.

We can make the analogy between a software architecture and a building architecture. A building has a single, physical structure that must provide room for all the elements that make up a building, like the steel skeleton, its walls, the plumbing, the air conditioning ducts and units, the places to store cleaning supplies, the places to put the telephone wiring, and so on. In addition, the building must look good, not blow down in the storm of the century, be pleasing to its occupants, and allow them to do what they're supposed to do.

In designing a building, we note that separate people handle the separate views. Architects talk to owners and design the building to meet the needs of all the parties that have an interest in the building. Structural engineers design the steel; mechanical engineers design the plumbing, heating, and air conditioning; and electrical engineers design the heating/cooling and power systems. The beauty of this is that the structure described by the architect provides for all of the requirements of all the views of the building.

The idea that there is one structure that accommodates all of the views of the building has only recently begun to take hold in the software industry. This lack of a single physical representation for a software system is probably responsible for the perception that software is more complex than other products.

12.3.1 Software Architecting

We usually do not build a building by assembling a pile of bricks, pipes, electrical wiring, wood, and so forth, and then proceed to construct the building. Usually, we draw out some plans that capture some vision of what the building will look like, how it will operate, and what it will support (in the way of usage).

In the software development life cycle, software architecting is that stage when we describe our vision for the application and what it will do at a high level. We will also describe a conceptual structure in terms of some high-level components.

Attempting to understand an application based on reading its source code is difficult for moderately sized systems and impossible for very large systems. The ability to reason about an application based on its architectural description can greatly improve system understanding.

Software architecting is a twofold process:

- The decomposition of a system into its constituent elements.
- The composition of existing elements into a system.

12.3.2 Software Programming and Software Engineering

Software programming usually, but not always, refers to single person (or small team) program design and, perhaps, implementation. Software engineering, on the other hand, almost always carries the connotation of a multiperson design and development effort of a complex system.

How does software architecture relate to these software development efforts? As mentioned previously, every system has a software architecture whether it is made explicit (e.g., properly documented) or not. Whether software programming or software engineering, the challenge is how to make explicitly apparent what the software architecture is. Put another way, both approaches need a software architecture. They may differ in how much of a software architecture is required and how detailed and comprehensive its description.

For example, a software programming team may need a single diagram—perhaps sketched on the back of a napkin over drinks. Some multimillion dollar companies have been launched with less conceptual detail. This single diagram may be sufficient for a tightly knit small team doing software development. On the other hand, a large software engineering team may require a multivolume document to describe a software architecture. Parts of one of the IRS's numerous attempts at describing software systems in its Tax Systems Modernization (TSM) program filled several thousand pages.

12.3.3 Architecture Is Not Design

Software architecting subsumes both analysis and design. So what makes it different? Why is it different than, say, object-oriented analysis and design? Well, in many ways it is the same, but we feel it is a matter of scope. Architecting is related to high-level design. Indeed, one can think of it as replacing the process that we use to call high-level design or functional description.

Why maintain the separation? Principally, because we want architecting to focus on the structural issues and not on the details. Architecture deals with components rather than procedures, with interactions between components rather than interfaces. How the component gets broken down into procedures is beyond the scope of architecture.

In software architecting, we consider a different set of characteristics than when we are programming. Table 12-1 depicts some of these differences.

12.4 DOMAIN-SPECIFIC SOFTWARE ARCHITECTURES

In the late 1980s, DARPA tackled a pervasive problem in developing large, defense-oriented software systems with an approach called Domain-Specific Software Architecture (DSSA) (Tracz 1994). The motivation and rationale for this program was based on the following assumptions:

- Development in specific domains can be optimized.
- Reuse of software modules is more likely if they are taken from other applications within the same domain.

The objective was to "maximize method theft" as one individual put it or, more appropriately, to reuse as many objects as possible. But it was also to minimize intuition by trying to solve a class of problems once—the right way—rather than trying to reinvent a solution for each new problem.

12.4.1 What Is a Domain?

A domain is an area of interest, usually representing a problem space that is a subset of one or more disciplines. For example, DNA research is a domain. When we construct an application, we are developing software for a problem space—a set of

Table 12-1. Different characteristics: architecting versus programming

Software Architecting	Software Programming
Interactions among parts	Implementation of parts
Structural properties	Computational properties
Declarative	Operational
Static description	Dynamic description
System-level performance (end-to-end)	Algorithmic performance
Composition	Integration

problems to be solved within the domain. Usually, the problem space is a subset of all the problems and their accompanying information within the discipline. Sometimes, a domain may represent an intersection of a number of disciplines, hence we speak of interdisciplinary problems.

A domain that is amenable to software architectures that promote successful reuse must meet the following criteria (Biggerstaff 1993):

- Is well understood.
- Is changing slowly.
- Has intercomponent standards.
- Provides economies of scale.
- Fits existing infrastructure.

12.4.2   DSSA Approach

The basic idea of the DSSA program was to make software reuse practical by focusing on specific software problem domains and developing component-based solutions for these problem domains. These components are generic and need to be customized at the time an actual application is implemented. DARPA defined four key steps to the DSSA approach:

1. A *domain model* is developed to establish standard terminology and common semantics for the problem domain.
2. A set of *reference requirements* for all applications within the problem domain is developed.
3. A *reference architecture* is defined for a component-based, standardized, generic system solution to anticipated customer requirements.
4. New applications are developed by determining application-specific requirements, selecting or generating particular components, and assembling the components according to the reference architecture.

The reference architecture, which may include concrete components that must be embedded in every derived application, is adapted to each customer's particular requirements. The DSSA development process occurred in two steps. First, customer-specific requirements for an application were developed and changes from the reference requirements were identified. Specific implementation components were selected to meet the specific requirements. Figure 12-4 depicts the elements of the DSSA development method.

The key activity is to tailor the reference architecture using the application requirements to produce the application architecture. Second, the application design selects specific components to implement the generic components. The components may be stored in a repository, which assists in managing them. The Test Systems assist in analyzing the application to determine if it meets the functional and behavioral requirements.

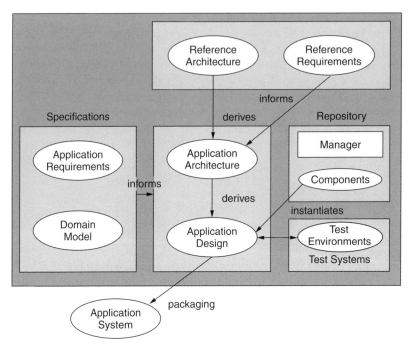

Figure 12-4. DSSA development method.

12.4.3 DSSA Structure

A Domain-Specific Software Architecture (DSSA) is a process and infrastructure that supports the development of a *domain model*, *reference requirements*, and *reference architecture* for a family of applications within a particular problem domain, as depicted in Figure 12-5. A *domain* is defined by a set of "common" problems or functions that applications in that domain can solve/do. It is typically characterized by a common jargon or ontology for describing problems or issues that applications in it address.

Domain Model   A *domain model* is a representation of what happens in the domain (e.g., the domain's "business operations"). Specifically, it describes the functions to be performed, the entities that perform them, and the data that flows between them and is used or produced by the functions. The objective of the domain model is to standardize the terminology and semantics of the problem space (e.g., the set of problems within the domain that a set of applications will support). These, in turn, provide the basis for standardized descriptions of the problem to be solved within the domain.

The elements of a domain model include:

- A customer needs statement, expressed in the customer's words, which specifies a high-level set of functional requirements but is often incomplete and ambiguous.

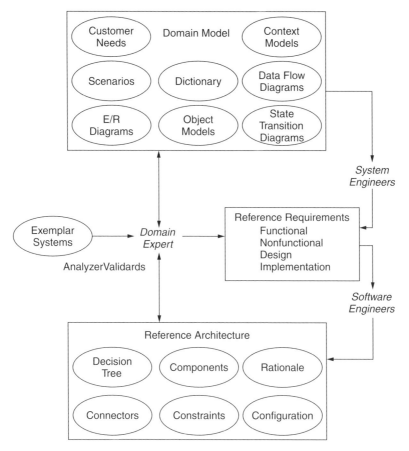

Figure 12-5. DSSA structure.

- A set of scenarios that describe the functional sequences, data flows, and user interactions.
- A domain dictionary that defines the terms used in the domain and which is extracted from the previous elements.
- A context block diagram that shows the high-level of interaction between major elements of the system.
- Entity-relationship diagrams describing the aggregation and composition of data entities within the domain.
- Data flow models that show data transfers between active entities.
- State transition models that show how operations change the state of an attribute.
- Object models that capture the attributes and operations of an entity in the domain.

Object models can often be programmed directly in an object-oriented programming language.

Reference Requirements *Reference requirements* are standard requirements that arise from different functional areas for all of the applications to be built in a domain. Reference requirements define the general functional structure of the problem space (e.g., the functional requirements). They also specify the constraints (e.g., the nonfunctional requirements) on the design and resulting applications. These may include performance, security, user interface styles, and hardware/software platform and programming language requirements. Some requirements may be parameterized so that specific applications will supply the parameters. Some requirements may be allocated directly to components in the reference architecture. For example, the capacity of a database may apply to all applications within the domain.

Application requirements are drawn from particular customer requirements for each specific application. Sometimes, these requirements are refinements of generic reference requirements. However, these requirements may really be design decisions mandated by the customer.

Reference Architecture A *reference architecture* is a standard, generic architecture describing all systems in the domain. It may specify both hardware and software platforms and components. Typically, it is represented in a hierarchical, compositional form but may contain multiple trees if it is representing a distributed set of systems for a complex domain. The functional requirements are allocated to the components. The constraints are used to specify some of the characteristics of the platforms and the components. For example, a performance requirement may, upon detailed analysis, require that the hardware platform speed be at least 2 GHz. The reference architecture is instantiated.

A reference architecture contains the following elements:

- A reference architecture model that describes a configuration of the hardware and software components based on an architectural style.
- An architectural schema that describes the high-level structure and constraints of each of the components, including the major data entities.
- A component dependency diagram describing the interactions among the major components.
- A set of component interface descriptions describing the API of each component.
- A set of constraints organized by parameters, value ranges, default values, and effect on the architecture.
- A rationale (prose description) for the particular description.

12.4.4 Domain Analysis

A domain model is the result of a process of domain analysis, which is an essential aspect of designing high-quality software systems. *Domain analysis* is the process of analyzing and understanding the environment of the end-user community, for example, what business operations the user performs and in what context. Within the software engineering community, domain analysis refers to studying the background knowledge necessary to solve the software design problem. As we proceed to software development, domain analysis encompasses the hardware and software solutions to the problem. If carried out properly, domain analysis can help designers to understand the requirements, identify the fundamental abstractions, verify the design, and drive the implementation.

Domain analysis involves:

- Identifying, capturing, organizing, and understanding objects and operations within the domain.
- A description of these objects and operations using a standardized vocabulary.
- Identifying similar systems or problems within the domain.
- Determining what is reusable across the similar systems.

12.4.5   Domain Environments

There are three environments that domain analysts must be concerned about in defining and developing an application. These are depicted in Figure 12-6.

The first environment is the domain itself, where requirements analysis and architecture definition takes place. The reference architecture provides the skeleton for individual applications developed for the domain. The second environment is the

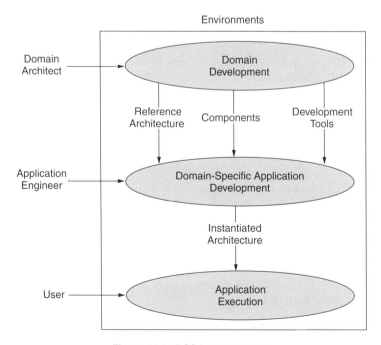

Figure 12-6. DSSA environments.

application development environment in which application-specific requirements are elicited and used to develop individual applications. Finally, the application execution environment is where the application is used to solve problems.

12.4.6 Lessons Learned

The DSSA project provided a number of significant lessons learned and yielded some good engineering processes, but with mixed results. One lesson learned was that the "domain" is not equivalent to the "marketplace" or "industry segment." In fact, the domain to be considered has to be well-bounded in order to prevent scope creep. DSSA does not provide a general solution for a large, market-oriented application.

A second lesson learned was that the canonical architecture for a domain is not consistent over time. Domains for which it is worth expending the time to design a software architecture are ones that are probably dynamic. As a result, the domain's character changes even as one attempts to define the domain software architecture. Thus, there is a constant tension between domain evolution and software architecture (and corresponding software application) correlation.

A third lesson learned was the need for good tools to support the requirements analysis, architecture definition and development, and system development of an information system. The DSSA project developed and demonstrated several sets of tools. It is unclear how these tools have influenced the commercial marketplace. Figure 12-7 depicts how types of tools would support the DSSA process.

Specifically, requirements analysis tools and architecture definition tools remain critical problems yet to be solved. Many such tools look too much like pseudo programming languages (many based on C) to be usable by people who are nontechnical or not trained in programming.

Section 12.8 provides additional references for the DSSA methodology. These papers are all available through NEC's Citeseer project: `http://citeseer.nj.nec.com/cs`.

12.5 ROLES AND BENEFITS

Software architectures play an important role in various stages of the system development life cycle (SDLC) (Garlan 2000). These roles lead to tangible benefits for a variety of stakeholders.

12.5.1 Software Architecture Roles

As Garlan (2000) notes, software architecture can provide assistance in completing the stages of the SDLC:

- *Understanding:* Software architecture aids our understanding and comprehension of large, complex software systems by presenting their high-level design

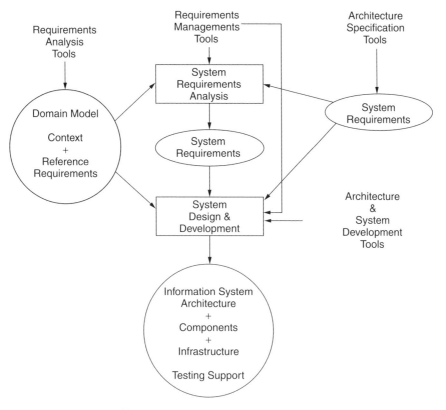

Figure 12-7. Role of domain analysis tools.

and constraints in a way that makes them easier to understand and by capturing and preserving the design rationale.

- *Reuse:* Software architecture promotes reuse of components and partial designs through description and identification of common functions, features, and data usage.

- *Construction:* Software architecture provides the high-level blueprint for module development and integration by indicating the major components, their interactions, and their dependencies.

- *Evolution:* Software architecture explicitly identifies where systems can be modified and expanded, the "load-bearing walls" to which Garlan refers. This assists in assessing the ramifications of changes and preparing resource estimates for these changes. And the separation of component functionality from component connectivity facilitates a plug-and-play implementation.

- *Analysis:* Software architecture provides a basis for more detailed analysis of software designs, although this has not yet substantially materialized in commercial products. Such analysis includes consistency checking, conformance to constraints, and dependency analysis.

- *Management:* Software architecture contributes to overall project management because it enables various stakeholders to see how various pieces fall into place and become available as a system is constructed. By identifying the dependencies between components, it assists in assessing where delays can occur and the impact of such delays due to schedule slippages.

12.5.2 Software Architecture Benefits

There are four major benefits that accrue from producing and documenting a software architecture design.

1. *Analytical Capability:* Once an application is built and deployed, the intended architecture is often lost, as design and implementation documents are often discarded. Without a software architecture description, it is often hard to communicate the complete set of specifications for the application or assess its global properties. With an appropriate set of analysis tools, system designers are able to estimate global properties and capabilities of the system early in the system development life cycle. Additionally, they may be able to determine likely problem areas and possible remediations for them. The analysis tools must be integrated with an effective representation system (such as a UML-based tool) in order to capture and manipulate pertinent information.

2. *Structural Visibility:* A well-defined and commented software architecture helps convey the "big picture" to executive decisionmakers as well as provide the overall context for application developers. These developers can see how their activities contribute to and fit into the overall system, understand how to integrate their components with other (possibly independently developed) components, and use the architecture to assist in making implementation decisions. As maintenance and/or enhancement begins, a software architecture provides a roadmap for making decisions about modifications to the system. During maintenance, often half the effort is focused on figuring out what the structure of the application is and what the pieces do.

3. *Establish Systems Discipline:* The process of developing a software architecture forces the designers to look at the system as a whole rather than as a set of parts. As a whole they must understand how the application's parts interact and how data and control flow through the system in order to assess the services provided by the system. And good engineering design practices such as performance prediction and resource utilization can be assessed.

4. *Maintain Conceptual Integrity:* A software architecture provides the basis for assessing and making subsequent decisions related to enhancements or modifications, including correcting errors, of components and services. During maintenance and/or enhancement, design changes such as changes in algorithm selection, data representation, or functionality can be assessed for their overall impact on the structure and performance of the application.

12.5.3 Realizing Software Architecture Benefits

The benefits of software architectures can be realized through several activities related to development of information systems.

Open Systems The definition of an *open system* is in the eye of the beholder. The DoD's Open Systems Joint Task Force (OSJTF) defines it as:

> A system that implements sufficient open specifications for interfaces, services, and supporting formats to enable properly engineered components to be utilized across a wide range of systems with minimal changes, to interoperate with other components on local and remote systems, and to interact with users in a style that facilitates portability.

The Software Engineering Institute (SEI) asserts that an open system is characterized by the following (SEI 2004):

- well defined, widely used, and non-proprietary interfaces/protocols
- use of standards which are developed/adopted by industrially recognized standards bodies
- definition of all aspects of system interfaces to facilitate new or additional systems capabilities for a wide range of applications
- explicit provision for expansion or upgrading through the incorporation of additional or higher performance elements with minimal impact on the system

They operationalize this definition as the following: An open system is a collection of interacting software, hardware, and human components (SEI 2004):

- designed to satisfy stated needs
- with interface specifications of its components that are
  fully deWned
  available to the public
  maintained according to group consensus
- in which the implementations of the components conform to the interface specifications

An open software architecture allows custom and commercial off-the-shelf (COTS) components to be integrated into the system. Two books in the SEI Series on Software Engineering, by Wallnau et al. (2001) and Meyer and Oberndorf (2001) provide more detailed information.

Reusable Conceptual Frameworks Architectural design and analysis tools can capture and encode a conceptual framework applicable to many types of problems. This framework provides a vocabulary of building blocks, rules for composing and integrating those building blocks, semantic information about their interactions and required interoperability, and information for analyzing the properties of the systems built from the framework. Much of the difficulty in producing complex software systems arises from building the supporting scaffolding required to make decisions to implement the system. Capturing design decisions and parameters allows the creation of variants of existing systems more easily the next time around.

Separability of Implementation A software architecture is distinct from an implementation. One software architecture may lead to many different implementations. Because the software architecture provides specifications, components may be implemented independently of one another but still be integrated into the whole system. This enables "buy or make" decisions on a component-by-component basis.

Reliability Off-the-shelf components that have been carefully designed, implemented, and verified can be leveraged to increase a system's reliability. Current systems implementation approaches often treat each system as a "one-of-a-kind" system that is built from scratch. Such systems have a tendency to be brittle (fragile) and difficult to evolve. Using a framework derived from a software architecture, lessons learned are rolled back into the design and experience is reinvested in improving the framework rather than designing an entirely new one.

Cost The cost of multiple implementations is reduced by having a software architecture that describes the components that are common to all implementations. Component reuse can significantly reduce cost. System generation facilities that ease the creation of implementations from software architectures can also reduce cost.

As noted earlier, developing a complex software system requires considerable tool-building expertise to develop and document the scaffolding to support the design and development of the system. Scaffolding reuse, even as modified to reflect new functionality in subsequent systems, can lead to more robust systems that are quicker to market with potential savings in labor and resources.

12.6 SOFTWARE ARCHITECTURE MODELS

As with design patterns, we have begun to realize that certain software architectures are basic to designing large computer applications. One classification, developed by Garlan and Shaw (1994), and the one we will use, is depicted in Table 12-2.

These architectural idioms are discussed in Chapters 13 through 18.

12.7 WHAT TO LOOK FOR

As you read through the next five chapters, there are several key points that you should look for and also take away from the discussion. Rather than pose these as an exercise, I assert them here so that you don't miss them.

Table 12-2. Classification of architectural styles

Architectural Style	Architectural Idiom
Data flow systems	Batch sequential
	Pipes and filters
Call-and-return systems	Main program and subroutines
	Client–server systems
	Object-oriented systems
	Hierarchical layers
Virtual machines	Interpreters
	Rule-based systems
Independent components	Communicating processes
	Event-based systems
Data-centered systems	Database systems
	Blackboards

Interactions Matter   It is critical to the success of your application to understand how components will interact (e.g., communicate), not just what they compute. The protocol for information exchange among components is essential to getting the right information at the right time to the right place. [*Note:* This is the essential thesis of Wegner's Paradigm Shift (Wegner 1996b).]

Interoperability Matters   The components of an architecture must both integrate and interoperate. Integration means they are syntactically compatible and that functionality can be invoked in one component from another. More important, however, is interoperation in which the functionality of two components complements each other in solving the problem or providing the service.

Differentiation Matters   There are different types of components that perform different functions and services. They interact differently and are packaged differently. One key to successful software architecting is to understand the catalog of components you have to work with, how they interact and interoperate, and how they are packaged. Successful applications arise form choosing the right components.

Decisions Matter   By now, you should realize that different problems have different solutions. There are many different architectures for providing a solution to a problem. Each architecture and each implementation of an architecture (e.g., choice of components, choice of data structures, or choice of communication mechanisms) affects the efficiency and performance of the architecture.

Agility Matters   Components should not make too many assumptions about the context in which they are used and the environments in which they run. Components often need to be deployed to heterogeneous hardware and software platforms. Components must integrate with legacy systems and other peer systems.

12.8 FURTHER READING

DSSA Methodology

Coglianese, L. 1993. *Architecture Component Relationships for the DSSA ADAGE Project.* IBM Federal Systems Co., Oswego, NY.

Hayes-Roth, B. 1994. *A Domain-Specific Software Architecture for a Class of Intelligent Patient Monitoring Agents.* Computer Science Department, Stanford University, Stanford, CA.

Hayes-Roth, B., K. Pfleger, et al. 1995. "A Domain-Specific Software Architecture for Adaptive Intelligent Systems." *IEEE Transactions on Software Engineering*, 21(4): 288–301.

Tracz, W. and L. Coglianese. 1993. *A Domain-Specific Software Architecture Engineering Process Outline.* IBM Federal Systems Co., Oswego, NY.

Tracz, W. and L. Coglianese. 1994. *DOMAIN: A DSSA Domain Analysis Tool.* ADAGE-LOR-94-13. Loral Federal Systems Inc., Oswego, NY.

Tracz, W., S. Shafer, and L. Coglianese. 1993. *DSSSA-ADAGE Design Records.* ADAGE-IBM-93-05A. IBM Federal Systems Co., Oswego, NY.

12.9 EXERCISES

12.1. Discuss the relationship between domain modeling and architectural modeling.

12.2. How would you predict architectural evolution based on domain analysis? What information must you elicit during domain analysis to assist in evolving an architecture?

12.3. Should there be predefined architectural views or should the architectural views depend on the problem domain? [Research Problem]

12.4. Consider the problem of describing a software architecture. How would you extend and/or modify the descriptive framework for design patterns to support describing software architectures?

12.5. From the perspective of the software application developer, describe the software architecture that you would like to receive to begin your detailed design. For example, what structure and qualities should the software architecture document have?

12.6. Describe a set of properties and features that you believe should be included in (a) a requirements analysis tool and (b) an architecture definition tool.

13

DATA FLOW SYSTEMS

A *data flow system* is one in which the availability of data controls the computational process. The basic data flow conceptual elements are the process, the file, and the data flow. Data flows from one process to the next, through a series of processes—usually from the *source* to the *sink*, which are privileged processes that operate at the extreme boundaries of the system. Each process performs one or more operations on the data.

Typically, each process performs one of three operations on the source data:

- Enriches data by adding information to the input data set.
- Refines data by aggregating or extracting information.
- Transforms data by changing its structure and/or representation.

A key focus of the data flow model is the pattern in which data flows. Generally, we are interested in either linear data flows or constrained, cyclic patterns. But data may flow in arbitrary patterns as well.

13.1 THE DATA FLOW MODEL

In computer architectures, data flow programming is a radical departure from the traditional approach based on the von Neumann or control-driven computation model. In the von Neumann model, a processor sequentially fetches instructions and data from memory for execution. In the data flow execution model, a program is simply

Software Paradigms, By Stephen H. Kaisler
ISBN 0-471-48347-8   Copyright © 2005 John Wiley & Sons, Inc.

represented as a graph, where nodes identify computations and arcs identify data paths between producer nodes and consumer nodes. Computation is triggered by the availability of data, which is consumed from inputs and produced at outputs. In effect, the data "flows" through a sequence of locations, each of which performs some operation on it. Data is represented by tokens that flow along arcs. A computation fires when there are tokens on all incoming arcs to that node.

In the data flow model, a piece of data is not represented as a static entity (memory) whose value can be updated time after time. Instead, it is a dynamic entity that is produced once and consumed by another instruction (fine-grained data flow) or by a set of instructions, that is, by a program entity (coarse-grained data flow).

Data-driven computation is an important capability because it enables program designs to be more declarative and less procedural, emphasizing *what* to compute rather than how or when to compute. With rules, it is possible to design and program parts of an application at a higher level of abstraction, with less concern about flow of control.

13.1.1   Data Flow Characteristics

There are two types of data flow systems:

- Transform flow
- Transaction flow

In *transform flow*, incoming input data is transformed within the system into an internal form. While the information is in the system, it may be subject to further transformations while in its internal form. Finally, outgoing data is transformed within the system from an internal form to its external form.

Transaction flow is a special form of transform flow where a single input item triggers data flow along several action paths. Many interactive systems and query/response systems fit this model. Each element along the data flow path usually has multiple outputs. Some elements are incorporated solely as junctions to recombine separate paths.

In both cases, data flow can be modeled as mathematical composition. Let two modules be labeled $f(x)$ and $g(y)$—the simplest case, in which each takes one input and produces one output for every input. Following standard mathematical practice, the combined result of these two modules is $h(x) = g(f(x))$, where the output of f is the input to g.

Data flow architectures are deterministic. The basic idea is that any token read in a downstream module is a token that was written in an upstream module. Tokens are read in the order in which they were written. Basically, any data flow module is only affected by the sequence of tokens on its input ports. It can't tell whether they arrive early, late, or on time (since it has no knowledge of the upstream modules). It will perform the same computation no matter what the token. Thus, its sequence of outputs is the same regardless of the frequency of token arrival on its inputs.

13.1.2   Applications of Data Flow

A data flow architecture is particularly useful when the processing of an application must change dynamically in response to either the properties of the data, changing external conditions, the need for different processing routines, or combinations of these. Manolescu (1997) has identified some applications for which data flow architectures are particularly suitable:

- A high-performance toolkit that is applicable for a wide range of problems from a specific domain.
- Where an application's behavior might need to change dynamically or adapt to different requirements at runtime.
- For complex applications, it may not be possible to construct a set of components that cover all potential combinations, but where components must be dynamically configurable.
- In the black-box paradigm, loose coupling may lead to performance impacts. Being able to choose different algorithms and their implementations based on end-to-end performance metrics is necessary.
- Software modules could have different, incompatible interfaces; share states; or need global variables.
- Some applications require bidirectional data flow or feedback loops.

Data flow architectures are not a good fit for word processors or presentation programs such as Powerpoint. But, surprisingly, they can be used effectively in Excel spreadsheets, which incorporate complex models where recomputation is performed as data values are changed in individual cells. They are also very good for signal processing and image processing applications that perform repetitive computations on multiple data elements.

13.1.3   Data Flow Implementation

A data flow architecture is usually implemented as a number of components that communicate by passing messages through unidirectional ports. A port either accepts or emits a message. Components may have one or more input ports and one or more output ports. The number of ports is determined by the implementation of the transformation function within the component. Any component is dependent only on the upstream components for data, so the connections at the output ports to other components can be changed dynamically at runtime.

In some data flow implementations, each component is isolated from downstream components by a buffer. For maximum flexibility, one thinks of the buffers as having unlimited capacity. This isolates individual components from the performance of upstream components. If an upstream component computes twice as fast as its downstream neighbor, the results just accumulate in the buffer until used. Practically, of course, physical hardware or software limitations impose a finite size on the buffers.

The transformation function implemented in the component should have the following properties:

- The transformation function should not model the domain or depend on a particular solution.
- The components should be designed independently of their use.
- The functions should not have side effects and should be able to cooperate only by using the output of one as the input to another.

Components that do not maintain an internal state are called "memoryless" components. Such components can be dynamically replaced at runtime. This is an important feature of a data flow architecture, which allows behavior to change at runtime in order to adapt to changing requirements.

Now let's return to our model based on mathematical composition. Suppose that $f_1(x)$ and $f_2(x)$ are two different algorithms for processing x, each with its own advantages and disadvantages. At runtime, the processing flow could begin with $h(x) = g(f_1(x))$ but switch to $h(x) = g(f_2(x))$.

13.1.4   Fine-Grained Data Flow

A data flow model can be applied at a fine-grained instruction level in which the basic execution unit is a machine instruction. A fine-grained data flow requires the support of a programming language and machine architecture for problem representation, efficient program mapping, implementation, and execution.

In a fine-grained data flow model, a program is represented as a control flow graph (CFG) consisting of a set of nodes (N) representing operators and a set of edges (E) representing flow between the operators. There is a distinguished start node n_0 and a distinguished termination node n_f. We can define sets corresponding to the predecessors of a node and the successors of a node.

Consider a simple example. The CFG is represented as a directed acyclic graph (DAG). The CFG is constructed from nodes representing operators connected by edges carrying tokens bearing data to and from an operator. When tokens are present on an input edge and no tokens are present on an output edge, the operator is fired, consuming its input tokens and emitting an output token. Figure 13-1 depicts a simple example.

In the data flow model shown in Figure 13-1, a program fragment is represented as a directed acyclic graph in which nodes represent instructions and edges represent the data dependency relationship between the connected nodes. A data element produced by a node flows on the outgoing edge(s) to the connected node(s) for consumption. Node executability is determined by the firing rule, which says that a node can be scheduled for execution if and only if its input data becomes valid for consumption. In this model, every node is purely functional in that it causes no side effects. Also, computation is inherently parallel and asynchronous, since any number of nodes can be executed as long as their input data becomes valid.

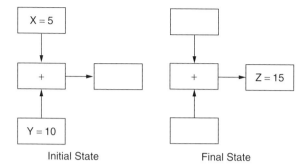

Figure 13-1. Simple data flow graph.

13.1.5   Coarse-Grained Data Flow

A data flow model can also be used as a unique and simple programming concept at the coarse-grained level in which the basic execution unit is a program component; the message-passing among distributed program components is restricted in a data-driven semantics. In the coarse-grained data flow execution model, a distributed application consists of a graph of components. Each component may run on a different or the same physical processor and the message-passing between any two components is through the edges. The execution of any component in the graph depends solely on the availability of the input operands.

13.1.6   Systolic Arrays

A *systolic array*, first conceived by H. T. Kung and Charles Leiserson, is a computer architecture composed of multiple processors usually arranged in a linear or mesh-like fashion. Data flows synchronously across the array between neighbors but may flow in different directions. Each processor at each (time) step takes data from one or more processors to the West (if linear) or the North and West (if mesh-like), performs some computation, and sends it to processors that are South and East.

As an example, consider matrix multiplication. One matrix has its rows fed in from the top of the array and flows down the array while the other matrix has its columns fed into the array from the side and flows across the array. At each time step, the rows and columns advance until the end of the array is reached, once the computation is completed. During each time step, dummy values are fed into the array until each processor has seen one whole row and one whole column.

One well-known systolic array implementation is the iWarp processor developed by H. T. Kung and others at CMU. The iWarp was manufactured by Intel. It extends the systolic array concept of the PC Warp, which was funded by DARPA under the Strategic Computing Program. A graphical depiction of this processor is shown in Figure 13-2.

Systolic arrays are particularly useful for computations that have a regular linear or rectangular structure, such as fast Fourier transforms (FFTs), image processing

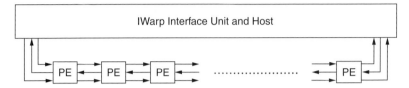

Figure 13-2. iWarp architecture.

algorithms, or sonar and radar processing algorithms, all of which involve substantial matrix multiplication and certain types of search algorithms.

13.1.7 Summary of Data Flow Architecture

The major advantage of a data flow model as a general parallel programming paradigm lies in the following features:

1. Data dependencies among programs are represented as data channels that connect programs. Message-passing between programs is only via data channels. Each program consists of two distinct and relatively separated components: computation and communication. They can be encapsulated and object-oriented for both computation and communication parts. A data flow-based parallel program is close to a sequential program.

2. The execution of a program is activated only by the availability of the data object on which it depends. Thus, the overall computation is inherently parallel and asynchronous.

3. Mapping of a program to a processor is determined solely at runtime by system software. It is also only at runtime that a channel between programs is established to represent the logical relationships among the programs of an application. The overall programming can be much closer to the problem representation and frees the programmer from knowing the underlying machine architecture and implementation details. It is the system software's job to organize and optimize tasks that are closer to the machine implementation, such as program-to-processor mapping, task scheduling, and coordination.

4. Because there is almost no dependency of one program on another, except for the data objects and data types that flow in and out of a program, software modularity and reusability is highly preserved in the system.

Explicit message-passing is the major way in which most current parallel programming systems produce efficient interprogram communications, synchronization, task scheduling, and representation of data dependency among parallel programs. We can view data flow programming as a restricted message-passing system.

In a data flow model, message-passing between two programs is via the flow channel connecting the output ports of an upstream program (A) to the input ports of a downstream program (B). Those ports are predefined so that only data of the same type can be passed. To program A, the message-passing of one instance of a data object out of the program is asynchronized so that the computation part of program A can be resumed soon after it puts data on its output ports. To program B, the communication can be viewed as blocked, as it must wait on its input ports for incoming data before it can start a new computation. The data flow model that requires message-passing flows only through the channels based on the firing rule.

13.2   BATCH SEQUENTIAL SYSTEMS

A *batch sequential system* is a collection of programs that are arranged more or less linearly. The problem is decomposed into a number of stages. Each stage is implemented as a separate program. Typically, the programs are executed in sequential order, although some control may be exercised by using a scripting language such as that provided by the operating system command language processor or the Unix shell.

Each program usually runs to completion. Data is transmitted between the programs via files stored on external storage. A program reads data from one or more files, processes it, and writes one or more files before exiting. Then the next program, if there is one, is initiated.

This architecture arose because of main memory limitations. Limited memory on the order of 32K–128K bytes in the early 1970s was not enough to handle large problems. So the problem was divided into several programs, each of which could fit into the available memory. Data was stored in tape-resident files. The cost associated with this was the extensive I/O required as data was passed between stages because the data had to be read and written from tape drives as each program was executed. Figure 13-3 depicts a simple batch sequential architecture from the early 1970s.

In this example, the job stream consists of N programs labeled "Program 1" through "Program N." The first program is initiated by dropping a card deck into the card reader or kicking off a script that loads and executes the first program. While

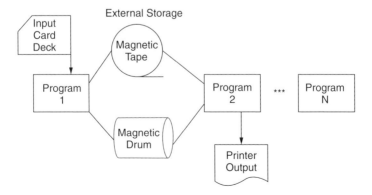

Figure 13-3. Simple batch sequential software architecture.

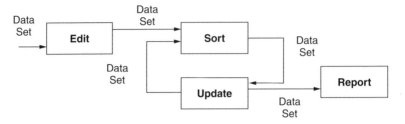

Figure 13-4. Typical batch sequential program.

not shown here, the first program may also read data from magnetic tape or drum as well as using them for intermediate storage.

When Program 1 has completed, after writing its results to tape or drum, Program 2 is initiated. It reads the intermediate results from tape or drum, performs its assigned tasks, and also writes intermediate results to tape or drum. It may also produce output on a printer. This sequence continues until the last program is completed.

A typical program structure might have looked like the diagram in Figure 13-4 (after Shaw and Garlan 1996):

- Edit program, which accepts and validates input transactions.
- Sort program, which organizes the transaction in the same order as the master file.
- Update program, which adds or modifies records in the master file from the transactions.
- Report program, which produces periodic reports.

Up until the mid-1990s, the Internal Revenue Service's Master File Processing was organized in this architectural style. All of the taxpayers in the United States were represented in over a thousand tape reels. Every week, the IRS started reading those tapes reels—one at a time—and updating them with that week's tax transactions. Not every record on each tape was modified, but every record had to be read and written to a new tape in order to insert updates in the proper position in the tape file.

The major limitations of the batch sequential architecture were the high latency for I/O, the limited opportunity for concurrency, and the inability to support interactive systems. The latter limitation directly influenced the invention of time-sharing.

We should note that a batch sequential architecture is a degenerate version of the pipe and filter architecture, which is described in the following section. The degeneracy occurs because a program processes all of its input as one data set.

13.3 PIPE AND FILTER ARCHITECTURE

A *pipe and filter* architecture is one in which one or more data sets are processed in discrete, separable stages. Each stage operates on the entire data set and passes its

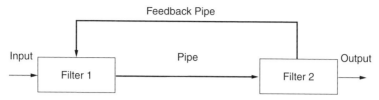

Figure 13-5. Simple pipe and filter architecture.

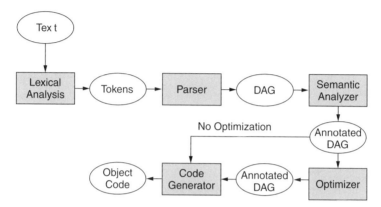

Figure 13-6. Modern compiler: example of a pipe and filter architecture.

results along to the next stage. Concretely, each stage is represented by a component. Each component reads data from one or more data streams at its inputs and writes one or more data streams at its outputs. Pipes may be implemented in multiple ways: shared variables or files, messages, or via remote procedure call. A simple depiction of a pipe and filter architecture is shown in Figure 13-5.

Data enter Filter 1 from some input stream, are processed, and are then transferred to Filter 2 via the Pipe. After processing in Filter 2, the data are emitted via the output stream. The only communication between the two filters is the data stream. So Filter 2 must understand the format of the data stream emitted from Filter 1.

13.3.1 Pipeline Examples

Perhaps the most common usage that computer science students are familiar with is a compiler architecture, which is depicted in Figure 13-6.

The input to a compiler is source code for a particular programming language, say, Fortran. The first filter, Lexical Analysis, scans the source code and extracts the tokens representing the variables, keywords, and operators. It builds a symbol table of these tokens and their locations and properties in the source code.

The second filter, Parser, applies the parsing algorithm to the source code to determine if the source code unit (main routine, subroutine, or function) is a legal programmatic unit. Recursively, the parsing algorithm determines if each statement comprising the source code unit is a legal statement according to the grammatical rules of the programming language. It generates an intermediate representation of the source code unit, such as the DAG (directed acyclic graph) used by the GNU compilers. It also updates the symbol table with additional information determined during the parsing.

The next filter, Semantic Analyzer, applies analysis rules to the intermediate form to ensure that the program's semantics are statically correct. Among other processes, it may transform the DAG through the application of various transformation rules, including the annotation of elements of the DAG. It will produce an annotated DAG whose annotations assist the Optimizer and the Code Generator.

The next filter, Optimizer, rearranges the DAG by applying optimization rules and heuristics. These optimizations may eliminate subtrees of the DAG. The result of optimization is a DAG. Note that optimization is an optional stage in many compilers.

The last filter, Code Generator, transforms the DAG into an object module suitable for binding and loading into an executable module. The Code Generator "walks" the DAG generating code for each leaf.

Another example is a web browser. The primary job of a browser is to convert a stream of bytes into a visual display of text and graphics. A series of processing elements may be involved in this transformation. A network interface reads data from the communication channel and passes it onto a document interpreter. The document interpreter adds structure to the stream of bytes, the result of which is an HTML tree; it passes the HTML tree onto a document formatter. The document formatter creates a display tree by interpreting the HTML (or, more recently, XML), which is passed onto the document displayer for display on the output device, usually a computer display monitor.

Some web browsers use a streaming pipeline, similar to this, to incrementally process data as it comes across the network or from the disk. As soon as information is available anywhere in the pipeline, it is processed and passed on to the next element. This allows the user to start reading the document before it is fully transmitted, resulting in a quicker response time.

13.3.2   A Pipeline Model

In a pipeline, we must differentiate between the control flow and the data flow. A web browser pipeline topology may be constructed in many different ways, depending on the control flow policy selected. However, data flow remains constant, because the information flowing from one filter to another remains the same. In a graphics application, data undergoes multiple transformations to render the final image. However, once a particular display scheme has been selected, the control flow remains constant.

In a pipeline, each processing element may be active or passive, and it may be either a reader (receives a message) or a writer (generates a message). Elements at

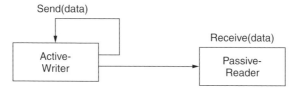

Figure 13-7. Active-writer to passive-reader topology.

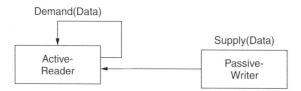

Figure 13-8. Active-reader to passive-writer topology.

the ends of the pipeline usually have one interface, while interior elements may have two or more. When two elements are connected in a pipeline, one element must be a writer and one must be a reader. The side that initiates the message transfer is designated the *active side*. This leads to two topologies: an active-writer connected to a passive-reader or an active-reader connected to a passive-writer.

In the first topology, depicted in Figure 13-7, an *active-writer* initiates the transfer of data by calling the receive method on the passive-reader. The data are passed as a method parameter. This is called a *push flow* with the flow of data from left to right (downstream).

An *active-reader* transfers data by demanding data from a passive-writer by invoking a supply method. The data are passed back to the reader as a return value. This is called a *pull flow*. This topology is depicted in Figure 13-8.

13.3.3 Types of Pipelines

The pipeline model allows us to construct different configurations from components in a safe and pluggable manner (as long as the individual components are guaranteed to be safe). By pluggable, we draw an analogy to two electric cords, where we plug the male end into the female end to form, effectively, one electric cord.

There are several types of pipe and filter architectures that can be developed. Table 13-1 depicts a few categories.

13.3.4 Pipe and Filter Examples

The following sections present a few examples of how pipes and filters have been applied in various domains.

Table 13-1. Types of pipe and filter architectures

Type	Characteristic
Linear pipes	One input, one output per filter
Bounded pipes	Data volume through the pipe is limited (perhaps at each stage)
Typed pipes	Data flowing through pipe has specified data types

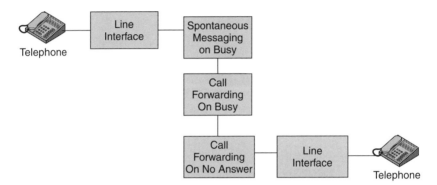

Figure 13-9. A linear example of feature composition (adapted from Zave and Jackson 1998).

Distributed Feature Composition Zave and Jackson (1998) have developed a component-based approach using the pipe and filter architectural model for describing and implementing telecommunications services called Distributed Feature Composition (DFC). They recognized that the feature set of telecommunications systems continues to grow and evolve incrementally. But these features are seldom orthogonal; the documents that describe them rely on earlier documents and often contain internal inconsistencies.

Zave and Jackson set out to develop a mechanism for handling features using dynamically assembled components. In this way, as new features were added, new components (called "feature boxes") were added as well. Feature boxes are akin to filters while two-party voice calls are akin to pipes. Two-party calls are the universal connector in most telephony systems. Because the feature boxes implement features independently, they can be dynamically assembled, making feature composition a modular process.

Figure 13-9 depicts a linear composition of features. A line interface (LI) connects to a telephone line. When a call is initiated, the LI sends a setup message to a box representing the callee port. If it ends successfully, a two-way voice path is created between the caller and the callee. It may end unsuccessfully for reasons such as the intended callee's line is busy. A sequence of features can be configured to respond to different situations. In Figure 13-9, if the call does not succeed, several responses can occur. For example, the Spontaneous Messaging On Busy box plays a message requesting the caller to leave a voicemail for the intended recipient or Call Forwarding

On Busy can send the call to another number to attempt connection. If Call Forwarding is not activated by the subscriber, the box is inactive and transparent to the call.

Since a subscriber may enable or disable different features from the telephone line, the sequence of features responding to a call cannot be static. The DFC approach allows the telephone system to detect which features are enabled and assemble the feature boxes to respond to a call on a per call basis. Features can be added or removed from a subscriber line because of the modularity and independence of the feature boxes.

Although DFC is specific to telecommunications software, the basic idea is applicable to many other disciplines such as telemetry processing, image processing, or data set analysis.

The Unix Shell   As Garlan and Shaw (1994) note, the Unix shell pipe mechanism is an early example of a pipe and filter architecture. Unix uses pipes to connect Unix processes to support one-way (e.g., downstream) communication. Pipes may be created dynamically through an operator implemented by the Unix shell or through Unix system calls.

Automobile Assembly Lines   Another example is drawn from automobile assembly lines. Consider a few of the major tasks required to assemble a car from its component parts:

- Install frame and power chain.
- Bolt the body on the frame.
- Mount the engine.
- Attach the seats and the wheels.

Based on this description of tasks, an assembly line is simply a pipeline of tasks. These tasks can be overlapped in time. While one car is receiving its engine, another car is almost completed, so it receives its seats and wheels. The genius of Henry Ford in creating the Model T assembly line was in task decomposition and concurrent processing (multiple vehicles in different stages of assembly at the same time).

Another example is rendering in computer graphics scenes. Rendering is a collection of operations that is performed to project a view of an object on a surface or a scene. Most rendering engines, which incorporate the set of operations, treat each object as an independent coordinate space in which one or more operations can be performed. For example, the input to a polygonal rendering is a list of input polygons, while the output is a list of colors—one for each pixel on the screen. One flow for building a three-dimensional scene is depicted in Figure 13-10.

13.3.5   The CMU Warp Processor

Carnegie-Mellon University developed a hardware implementation of a systolic array processor (Annaratone 1986) called Warp (because it was fast!) under the aegis of

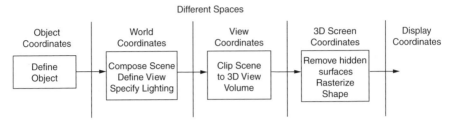

Figure 13-10. Rendering engine workflow.

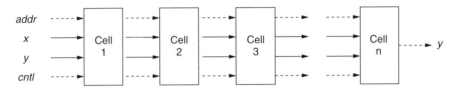

Figure 13-11. The Warp processor (after Annaratone 1986).

DARPA's Strategic Computing Program. The Warp processor takes inputs at one end of the array and produces outputs at the other end as depicted in Figure 13-11.

Each cell was relatively simple. It consisted of a multiplication unit and an addition unit, based on Weitek chips; register files for these units; a data memory for buffering; and two I/O ports (x,y) and one address port (addr). The multiplication and addition units could operate concurrently—each at a peak performance of 5 MFLOPs. Register files on the input and output ports were used to ensure synchronization. The components of the Warp cell were linked by a crossbar. An n-cell Warp processor could perform $O(n)$ computations for each I/O operation. A linear array can be synchronized by a simple, global clock.

The Warp processor was implemented as a seven-layer printed circuit board by General Electric Corp. of Syracuse, NY. A ten-cell Warp processor with a Sun3/80 front-end processor cost about $100,000 and delivered approximately 100 MFLOPs peak performance (nearly equivalent to a Cray-1S). Sustainable performance depended on the particular problem but averaged around 38–50 MFLOPs.

One-Dimensional Convolution A one-dimensional convolution problem is defined as:

Given a sequence of weights $w_1, w_2, \ldots, w_k$ and an input sequence $x_1, x_2, \ldots, x_n$, compute the output sequence $y_1, y_2, \ldots, y_{n-k+1}$ given by

$$y_i = w_1 x_i + w_2 x_{i+1} + \cdots + w_k x_{i+k-1}.$$

The weights were preloaded into the systolic array. The x_i and partial results y_i flowed into the leftmost cell as inputs, and then left to right. However, the x_i moved

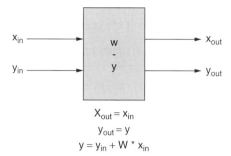

Figure 13-12. Warp cell computations for one-dimensional convolution.

twice as fast as the y_i, so that each y_i met all k consecutive x_i on which it depended. Figure 13-12 depicts the computation at each cell.

In this application the multiplier and adder were fully utilized at 5 MFLOPs each, so in the ten-cell Warp processor, the aggregate computation delivered about 100 MFLOPs. The Warp processor is highly modular so the number of cells can expand indefinitely. In fact, the performance gain is limited by the scalability of the problem. The Warp processor was used for a variety of problems, including image processing, two-dimensional fast Fourier transforms, signal processing applications, and complex matrix multiplications.

The iWarp Chip   The successor processor was developed by CMU and Intel and called the iWarp chip (CMU 1998, Gross and O'Halloran 1998) The basic building block of the iWarp system is a full custom VSLI component integrating a LIW microprocessor, a network interface, and a switching node into a single chip of 1.2 cm by 1.2 cm silicon. The processor could perform both 32-bit IEEE (20 MFLOPs) and 64-bit IEEE (10 MFLOPs) floating point arithmetic. Each cell had four communication channels running at 40 MB/s full duplex. Each cell also contained from 500 KB to 4 MB of static RAM. A typical system consisted of 64 cells in an 8×8 torus delivering up to 1.2 GFLOPs peak performance.

Intel delivered several 64-cell machines to CMU for assessment. However, Intel eventually folded the iWarp technology into the Intel Supercomputing Systems Division and the iPSC product line. Some of this technology found its way into Intel's Delta series of machines that it builds for the Department of Energy.

13.3.6   Issues for the Pipe and Filter Model

A number of issues arise in considering the pipe and filter model that can lead to complicated software architectures.

Ordering of Filters   The ordering of the filters in a pipe and filter architecture can yield different results. Consider a simple application that consists of two filters: one that calculates the square of its input and the other that outputs a number only if it is less than 10000. These two filters can be connected as depicted in Figure 13-13.

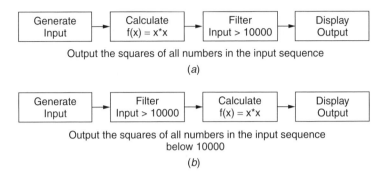

Output the squares of all numbers in the input sequence

(a)

Output the squares of all numbers in the input sequence
below 10000

(b)

Figure 13-13. Importance of filter ordering.

In Figure 13-13(a), an input number is generated. Its square is calculated and passed to the second filter. An output is displayed only if the result is less than 10000. So only input numbers less than 100 will have their squares displayed. In Figure 13-13(b), the squares of all numbers less than 10000 in the input sequence are displayed.

Multiple Inputs/Multiple Outputs   The simplest pipe and filter model assumes a single input and a single output from each filter. Data flows in at some rate, is processed by the filter, and flows out at some rate. The overall performance of the system can be calculated based on a summation of the processing rates of each of the filters mediated by the data flow rates between filters.

Filters may have multiple input and output streams. The number of streams is dependent on the processing algorithm implemented by the filter (Figure 13-14).

When the processing for a given filter requires multiple inputs, the possible difference in arrival rates of the data can impose a performance bottleneck in the system. Similarly, multiple outputs may drain the filter faster than the input streams can supply data. The filter then *stalls* awaiting more data.

Cyclic Configurations   Many pipe and filter models are linear. However, some problems require iterative solutions such as convergence and recurrence problems or systems requiring feedback. A pipe and filter model supporting these types of computations would feed the output(s) from a downstream filter back as the input(s) to one or more upstream filters. Figure 13-15 depicts a simple pipe and filter architecture with feedback. More complex configurations can be designed extending over several filter stages.

Flow Control   Flow control can be exercised as either a push or pull operation. In a data push operation, the upstream filter pushes the data down to the next filter. When data is pushed, it is usually inserted into a buffering mechanism as soon as it is ready. The downstream filter retrieves data from the buffer at its own rate. In a data

Input(s)

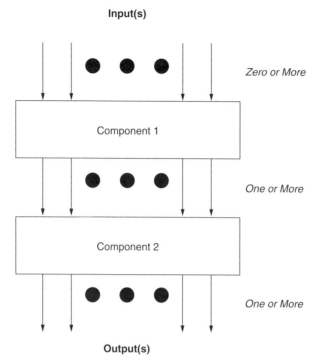

Figure 13-14. Pipe and filter architecture with multiple data streams.

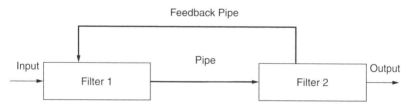

Figure 13-15. Pipe and filter architecture with feedback.

pull operation, the downstream filter requests data from the upstream filter until the request comes through or pulls data from a common buffer. Of course, hybrid combinations are also possible.

13.3.7 Assessment

Pipe and filter architectures have several properties that make them adaptable to many different problem spaces. First, the performance of a pipe and filter architecture can be determined from the composition of the performances of its individual components. For example, in a linear pipeline, the end-to-end performance is just the sum of the performances of the individual filters, assuming negligible transmission times through the pipes. Feedback and multiple inputs and outputs complicate the computations. But these can be modeled using methods analogous to electrical network analysis methods.

Second, pipe and filter architectures support component reusability. A basic assumption is that every filter is independent of every other filter, that is, they do not share any state information. Another assumption is that filters do not know the identity or characteristics of the upstream or downstream filters. Thus, two filters can be connected together provided they agree on the format and content of the data that is being transmitted between them.

Third, they are easily maintainable and extensible. Because of the assumptions above, new filters can be added into a pipeline or at either end or as a branch of the main pipeline. Filters can be updated individually as long as they preserve the ability to process input data sent to them and emit output data expected of them.

Finally, they support concurrent execution. Each filter operates independently of other filters. A filter begins computation when it has data on which to work. Moreover, there is no requirement for a filter to process all of its data before it emits results. So a filter can emit results as they are completed.

However, there are several disadvantages to using a pipe and filter architecture for a problem space. First, as noted above, their degenerate form is the batch sequential architecture. This often results from the belief that a data set must be processed in its entirety rather than as individual items.

Second, pipe and filter architectures do not provide adequate response in interactive systems. Because each stage must fully process its input, end-to-end processing may vary.

Finally, because each filter is independent of other filters, the format of data transmitted between them is often forced to the lowest common denominator. Each filter is forced to parse the incoming data to determine its structure. Alternatively, each data file must carry with it metadata regarding its structure, which must be interpreted by each stage.

13.4   FURTHER READING

Ackerman, W. B. 1982. "Data Flow Languages." *IEEE Computer* 15(2):15–25.

Francois, A. 2003. Software Architecture for Computer Vision: Beyond Pipes and Filters. University of Southern California. Available at http://iris.usc.edu/~afrancoi/pdf/sacv-tr.pdf.

Posnak, E. J., R. G. Lavendar, and H. M. Vin. 1996. Adaptive Pipeline an Object Structural Pattern for Adaptive Applications. Department of Computer Science, University of Texas. Available at http://www.cs.utexas.edu/users/vin/pub/pdf/plop96.pdf.

Preiss, B. 1984. Design and Simulation of a Data Flow Multiprocessor. MS Thesis. Department of Electrical Engineering, University of Toronto. Available at http://www.brpreiss.com/theses/masc/thesis.pdf.

13.5 EXERCISES

13.1. How would you introduce an element of nondeterminism into a data flow architecture?

13.2. Research neural network architectures. Can you use a data flow architecture to implement a neural network? Describe your design.

13.3. If finite buffers are used to mediate the flow of tokens between data flow modules, develop a scheme for handling buffer overflow. What is the impact of allowing data flow modules to be able to query buffers to determine their status?

13.4. Research Petri nets. Can you use a Petri net to define a data flow architecture?

13.5. Develop the code for both the active-writer and active-reader topologies. Then develop algorithms to convert one to the other.

14

CALL-AND-RETURN
SYSTEMS

A *call-and-return system* is a synchronous software architecture in which the client ceases execution while the service provider performs the service. Upon completing the service, the service provider may return a value to the client. Figure 14-1 depicts this concept from a control flow perspective.

A call-and-return architecture may be nested to multiple levels as depicted in Figure 14-2. This model exemplified most early software applications consisting of a large number of subroutines or procedures. The calling trees often had substantial depth.

The call-and-return architectural style is used when the order of computation is fixed. The components make no useful progress while awaiting the results of the request to other components.

14.1 MAIN PROGRAM AND SUBROUTINES

The *main program and subroutines* architecture consists of a main program that acts as a controller (or executive) and one or more subroutines that perform specific functions when called by the main program. This architecture is based on the definition–use relationship, which imposes a single thread of control. The correct operation of the main program and any subroutine is directly dependent on the correct operation of the subroutines it calls. It is supported by sequential imperative, functional, and object-oriented programming languages.

Software Paradigms, By Stephen H. Kaisler
ISBN 0-471-48347-8   Copyright © 2005 John Wiley & Sons, Inc.

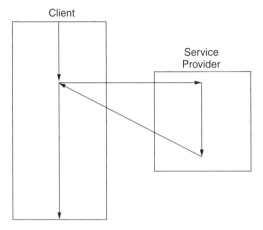

Figure 14-1. Call-and-return control flow.

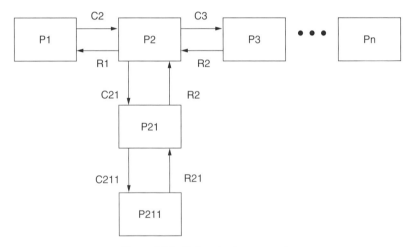

Figure 14-2. Call-and-return example.

Figure 14-3 depicts an example of a main program and subroutines architecture. Here, the main program calls several subroutines, some of which, in turn, call other subroutines. The main routine may call a subroutine several times from different locations in its code. Also, subroutines may call other subroutines.

Garlan and Shaw (1994) call this the classical functional decomposition for software programs. It is the first programming model taught to every student in an introductory programming course, which uses an imperative or functional programming language.

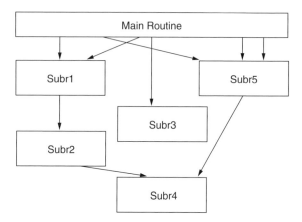

Figure 14-3. Main routine and subroutines architecture.

14.1.1   Master–Slave Architecture

The master–slave(s) paradigm, which is a concurrent variant of the *main program and subroutines* architecture, assumes a coordinating process that distributes the work to one or more slave processes. When a slave process finishes its work, it asks the master process for more work. It requires an appropriate routing system by which the master knows where the slaves reside, their configuration, and their properties. The master–slave model can be implemented on an arbitrary network of processors; it is not dependent on the network topology.

The master–slave model is appropriate for compute-intensive problems in which the slave processes have little or no interaction. Each slave process is given a distinct task to perform; it communicates its results to the master process when it's done. It is most efficient when communication with the slaves can be overlapped with computation by the slave processes.

The master–slave model differs from the data parallel model (see Section 18.3) in the following respect. The data parallel model distributes data to all processes in a static manner, while the master–slave model distributes data to processes a portion at a time. This reflects the fact that processes may advance at different rates.

14.1.2   Advantages and Disadvantages

There are several advantages and disadvantages to the main program and subroutines architecture. A primary advantage is that it is simple to visualize and easy to learn. A single thread of control works its way through the various subroutines. This model is the basis for all imperative, functional, and object-oriented programming languages.

This architecture is easy to reason about from a correctness standpoint. The correctness of any subroutine depends on the subroutines it calls. This is reinforced when global variables are prohibited in the code.

There are several disadvantages to this architecture as well. First, there is the tendency to devolve into spaghetti code. This results from adding subroutines as new requirements arise, or enhancements are made to the system without first remapping all of the requirements to a hierarchical structure. So two subroutines may do almost the same thing but arise from either different requirements or similar requirements added at different times in the application's lifetime. It is usually impossible to draw a diagram of the logical flow from the physical code.

A second disadvantage is scalability. Decomposing large complex systems may yield hundreds or thousands of subroutines. Configuration management becomes difficult. One can lose visibility of the flow of control over several tens or hundreds of subroutines when the calling path reaches tens of procedure calls.

14.2 CLIENT–SERVER SYSTEMS

Client–server systems can be thought of as a special case of the main program and subroutines architecture. The primary difference is the assumption that the client and server are located on different computer systems, although nothing prevents them from being resident on the same computer system. The *client* is an entity that makes a request for a service. The *server* is an entity that can provide that service upon request. The service may yield a result, which is returned to the client. This simple arrangement is depicted in Figure 14-4.

The simplest form of a client–server (C-S) architecture has the client send commands to the server, await their execution, and receive a result from the server. The result may be data or a simple acknowledgment that the command has been completed. More sophisticated implementations impose protocols between the client and the server that restrict the flexibility of the interaction between the two systems but enhance the "ilities" of the total system. These protocols are implemented at layers above the basic communication protocols, such as TCP/IP.

Most servers will serve multiple clients. The frequency and complexity of client requests may or may not be anticipated. In a transaction-oriented system, such as a ticket sales system, the number and type of transactions are fixed, their complexity and duration are known, and the processing and memory requirements are stable.

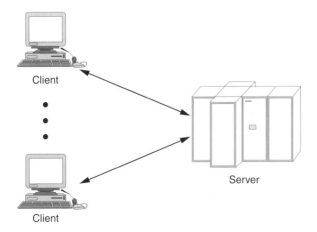

Figure 14-4. A simple client–server architecture.

Servers can be sized to handle a known volume of transactions under specific conditions. On the other hand, general-purpose timesharing systems, which admit many different types of commands, must be sized to provide a specified level and quality of service. But the level and quality of service must degrade gracefully if the number of transactions exceeds the design specifications.

A good example of a client–server system is a simple automated teller machine (ATM) network used by banks. Users typically use ATMs as clients to interface with a small regional application server, which collaborates with a larger server that manages all of the smaller application servers. The application servers are servers to the ATMs and clients to the master server, which usually hosts the consolidated database. ATMs provide the user interface and can be customized (for multilingual support, as an example, at the Bank of America) as required, while the intermediate servers provide the application logic, such as checking on account balances and transferring money between accounts. The application servers allow the system to be scaled since adding servers allows an increased number of ATMs to be supported. However, the application logic can be provided only with the help of the centralized server. The results of these services are communicated to the user through the ATMs. The centralized server ensures that concurrent transactions are handled correctly. It also serves as a central repository for all account information so that users can access their accounts from any ATM worldwide.

14.2.1   Client and Server Design

Although clients and servers both play important roles in a client–server system, most systems are flexible with regard to the distribution of authority, responsibility, and intelligence. Clients are termed "fat" or "thin." Fat clients typically have substantial portions of the application logic along with the presentation logic. Thin clients are programs that contain, usually, only presentation logic, although today the term is used synonymously with "web browser." Shifting application processing from the client to the server or vice versa shifts the capabilities and strengths of the system. For example, if a fat server is being used, it is easy to update the application logic once and the clients may not need to be touched. However, if fat clients are used, the server may not need to be updated, but distributing updates across multiple clients becomes difficult.

A server usually requires two types of software. The *master process* is the single point of access for requesting a service by the clients. A *slave* or *child* process is created to handle each request as it is accepted by the master process. The basic steps are:

- Server opens a well-known (e.g., publicized) port.
- Server listens on the port for requests from clients.
- Server assigns a request to a local port for (possible) communication between client and child process.
- Server spawns a new concurrent child process to service the client over the assigned local port.
- Server awaits further requests while the child process services the client request.

Fat servers, which encompass the above functionality, have been the preferred orientation of implementers for some time, because it is easier to encapsulate data and provide abstract services while hiding the raw data. Fat servers are easier to deploy and update because the data and application logic reside in a centralized repository. Fat servers reduce the problem of limited bandwidth by carrying out more of the work where the data resides, reducing the need for costly data transfers over the network. Mission-critical applications requiring the highest degree of fault tolerance and stability use fat servers for ease of maintenance.

A delicate balance must often be struck between the server design and the client design. Robust web browsers, such as those based on HTML 4, perform substantially more computation and thus move farther along the continuum toward fat clients.

14.2.2   Two-Tier to N-Tier

Client–server systems occur in a number of different architectures. Early versions were implemented as two-tier systems, where the server contained the data repository. The application logic could reside on the client, on the server, or be shared between the two. Two-tier systems have been used extensively in non-time-critical environments. An early implementation is the X Window system (Scheifler and Gettys 1986). Figure 14-5 depicts a basic two-tier system.

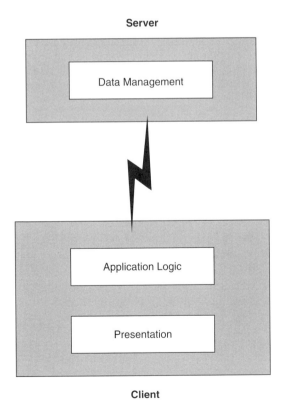

Figure 14-5. Basic two-tier client–server architecture.

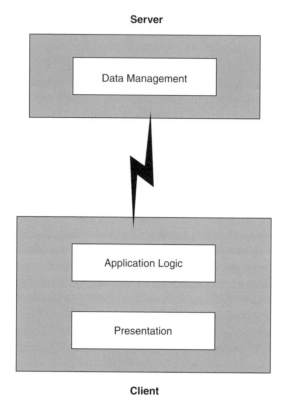

Figure 14-6. Alternate two-tier client–server architecture.

Figure 14-6 depicts an alternate view of a two-tier system where the application logic resides on the client's workstation rather than on the server. If the application(s) send large amounts of data, better performance often arises by placing the application logic at the workstation.

In some cases, the application logic may be distributed across both the client's workstation and the server. This may be required when some software sends large amounts of data or requires direct access to the workstation environment. Figure 14-7 depicts a distributed two-tier architecture.

A three-tier system arises from the two-tier system by installing the application logic on its own server. This separation gives application logic processes more autonomy. The processes become more robust since they can operate independently of the clients and servers. Furthermore, decoupling the application logic from the data allows data from multiple sources to be used in a single transaction without a breakdown in the client–server model. Figure 14-8 depicts a three-tier system.

Many applications benefit from more than three tiers. For example, a Senate application for storing and serving photos uses four tiers: domain controller, web

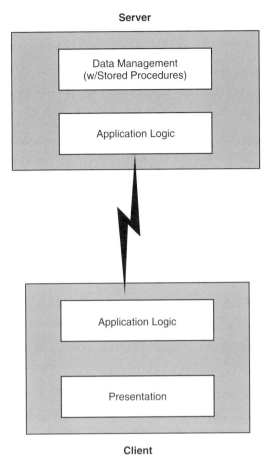

Figure 14-7. Distributed two-tier client–server architecture.

server, application server with photo repository, and database server. It is built on Windows 2000/2003 and operates in its own domain. N-tier systems are becoming more frequent as application systems become more complex.

14.2.3 Connection Versus Connection-Oriented Service

Clients and servers can communicate in two ways, depending on the reliability of communication required by the application.

Connectionless communication, usually via UDP—User Datagram Protocol, implements unreliable delivery of messages. Clients should use connectionless communication when the application service handles errors and participates in broadcast or multicast service, or performance requirements cannot tolerate virtual circuit overhead delays.

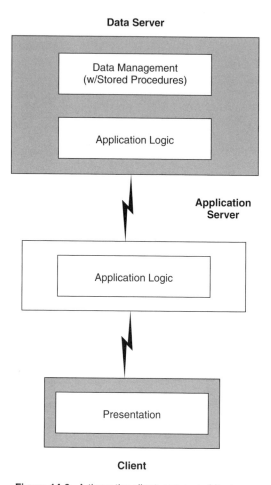

Figure 14-8. A three-tier client–server architecture.

Connection-oriented communication, usually via TCP/IP—Transfer Control Protocol/Internet Protocol, implements reliable delivery of messages. Connection-oriented communication makes programming easier because the protocol includes mechanisms for detecting and handling errors and an acknowledgment mechanism between client and service.

14.2.4 Stateless Versus Stateful Servers

A server may or may not retain information about the clients it services. The information a server maintains about its clients is called *state information*. State information is required if the information exchange between the client and the application consists of multiple messages. The state information may reduce the size of succeeding messages beyond the initial request and may allow the server to respond more quickly to succeeding requests. But state information can become useless if messages are lost, duplicated, or delivered out-of-order, or if the server crashes and must be rebooted.

Stateless servers rely on the application protocol to assume the responsibility for reliability of delivery and service. Thus, the application gives the same response no matter how many times a request arrives [subject to the type of command/request and its effects on the server database(s)]. Stateful designs can lead to complex application protocols and error handling mechanisms.

14.2.5 Variations on Client–Server Systems

There are two variations on the traditional client–server architecture. The *shared writing* variation occurs when both processes may modify the same object at the same time. It extends the client–server architecture by allowing the consumer to also modify the object. The *server–mediator–client* variation introduces a third process that is requested to connect the client with the server, which may be unknown to the client. This variation corresponds to one mechanism that CORBA-based systems can be used to establish client–server connections.

14.2.6 Issues Affecting Client–Server Systems

While client–server architectures are the most widely used software architectures today, they are not a panacea for all complex, interactive systems. A number of issues must be considered in choosing to use the client–server architecture and in designing a client–server architecture.

Designing Servers In designing servers for complex environments, the designer must consider the following issues:

- *Authentication:* Verifying the identity of the client and its rights/privileges. Clients may be restricted to the systems they can access when multiple servers are available.
- *Authorization:* Verifying the rights/privileges of the client. Clients may be restricted in the kinds of commands they may issue, the applications they can run, or the data they can retrieve.
- *Data Security:* Protecting the data stored on the server. Servers must provide protection to prevent unauthorized release or modification of the data stored on them.
- *Protection:* Protecting the system itself from errant applications. Servers must provide mechanisms for trapping errant applications and preventing them from damaging the system and its resources.

Middleware Mechanisms Middleware is used to glue components together. Middleware supports the workflow of integrated business processes and provides connectivity to databases and legacy applications. Most three-tier (or N-tier) systems will include middleware code as an integral part of their implementation. Common middleware products include CORBA and COM. The problem is that middleware is subject to change and adaptation and is used in unforeseen (by the designer) contexts. Dealing with this problem will affect every designer of N-tier architectures at one time or another.

Why is it a problem? Well, let's review the requirements for distributed applications in summary form:

- Transparent, platform-neutral communication.
- Ability to invoke and activate remote components.
- Nonfunctional properties such as performance and scalability.
- Mechanism to find and create remote components.
- Maintaining persistent and consistent states.
- Security issues.
- Data transformation.
- Deployment and configuration support.

Both CORBA and DCOM provide an object-oriented RPC mechanism. But developers must integrate a number of critical services, such as security, transaction processing, and naming themselves. Such integration may require more than 50% of the effort to completely develop the application.

In an N-tier application, we need to connect not only individual components, but the tiers themselves. Remote components should appear to be the same as local components—the property of transparency. One way to achieve this is using the Proxy design pattern (Gamma et al. 1995), which hides the communication mechanism from the client and the server. Different proxies can be emplaced to provide different levels of service. However, the basic Proxy design pattern is not enough. We need a mechanism for locating remote components and for establishing communications.

These services can be provided by the Broker and Bridge design patterns. The Broker connects two Proxy implementations to provide the lookup and communications establishment functions. The Bridge handles the conversion and message buffering functions between the client and the server. This approach provides dynamic reconfigurability, interoperability with other brokers, and location transparency. The downside is that the overall system becomes more complex and is much harder to debug.

14.3   OBJECT-ORIENTED SYSTEMS

Object-oriented systems can also be thought of as a special case of the main program and subroutines architecture. However, whether the objects are collocated or distributed, a key difference is that objects are totally encapsulated so that communication occurs through a message-passing or procedure call mechanism. Object-oriented

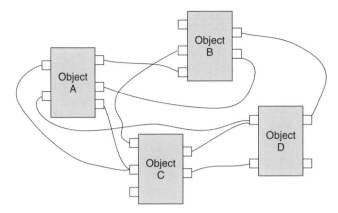

Figure 14-9. An object-oriented system.

systems also support inheritance and/or delegation mechanisms that require dynamic binding at runtime in order to determine the appropriate method to execute. Figure 14-9 depicts a small object-oriented system.

The main problem with object-oriented systems is that an object must know the identity of the other objects with which it wishes to communicate. These identities can be bound statically or dynamically. One way around this is to use an object broker such as CORBA.

There is voluminous literature available on object-oriented systems, O-O programming, and O-O programming languages. We will not attempt to repeat even a small fraction of the technical details here; we merely summarize some of the key ideas.

14.3.1   Core Concepts

Snyder (1993) has identified 11 core concepts that characterize object-oriented systems, which are depicted in Table 14-1 along with the associated benefits.

14.3.2   Inheritance Versus Delegation

Inheritance is a property of object-oriented programming languages in which a subclass has all of the attributes and methods of a parent class. In addition, the subclass can be extended by adding more attributes, more methods, or both. When a subclass adds new attributes, it must override one or more of the methods it inherits in order to make use of that new attribute(s).

When a method is invoked in a subclass, it is redirected to the parent class if the subclass has not defined that method. This may be expensive as the runtime environment may have to search up the class hierarchy to locate the superclass in which the method is actually defined.

In delegation, a method in one object calls a method in another object. In effect, it hands off processing to the other object's method—possibly with specialized

Table 14-1. Object-oriented core concepts and benefits

Core Concept	Benefit(s)
All objects embody abstraction.	Clients access meaningful entities within the domain but are not responsible for inter-preting data.
Objects provide services.	Complex services can be designed to preserve and enforce integrity constraints. Providing only simple services means clients must compose complex services for themselves—leading to duplication and the potential for error.
Clients issue requests for service.	Clients do not have to know what code to execute to perform a service.
	By isolating clients from the services' implementation, it can easily be changed without having to modify the client.
Objects are encapsulated.	(Total) Encapsulation guarantees integrity constraints (see Kaisler 1997). Changes to implementation that do not affect behavior can be transparent to the clients.
Requests identify operations.	Error handling can be provided if an object does not implement a request.
	Requests can be implemented in different ways.
Requests can identify objects.	Handles can be used to pass objects as first-class arguments.
New objects can be created.	Objects with time-varying behavior or new characteristics can be created dynamically.
	System extensibility is supported.
Operations can be generic.	Multiple implementations of a service can be provided with varying arguments or other features, such as security and performance. Each implementation, however, must produce the observably equivalent effects.
	Code can be more general and, therefore, more reusable.
	This leads to a standard conceptual model for the entity represented.
Objects can be classified in terms of their services.	Objects can be logically grouped for easier understanding.
	An interface hierarchy can be established that allows a client to operate on multiple kinds of objects.
Objects can have common implementation.	Sharing one implementation among many clients (and applications) reduces source code duplication, eases maintenance, and reduces executable code size.
Objects can share partial implementation.	Sharing part of an implementation yields the same benefits as a common implementation and makes reuse easier as long as modifications are performed through inheritance.

parameters. This works well when the receiving object provides a common service to many objects in the application. Rather than implementing the service in every class and having it inherited in multiple class hierarchies, it is implemented in a single class.

14.3.3   Advantages and Disadvantages

A key advantage of object-oriented systems is data hiding. Because the data representation is hidden from the clients, the internal representation can be changed without affecting those clients. Formally, this is termed *encapsulation* and leads directly to the next advantage.

Another advantage is that object-oriented systems naturally support concurrent execution. Because the access methods are combined with the data, object-oriented systems can be viewed as collections of interactive agents. Each object can be both a client and a server to other objects. Although many O-O systems have all objects residing on the same machine, there is no reason why they can't be distributed to multiple machines provided the middleware support is available to support remote method invocation between objects.

For one object to communicate with another, it must know the identity and the interface of the other object. If the called object changes its identity or interface, then all other objects that might communicate with it must be changed. CORBA overcomes this problem by supplying services that handle locating objects by certain criteria and providing a generic interface.

14.3.4   Distributed Object Systems

Because of object encapsulation, objects are a good mechanism for implementing distributed systems. Objects can be distributed to different processors; communication occurs through remote invocation methods (point to point) or an object request broker (ORB).

In most cases, no distinction is made between client and server objects. Each distributable object is an entity that can both provide and use services. So designing applications becomes an exercise in determining how to provide services and combinations of services.

Figure 14-10 depicts a distributed object system. In this simplified depiction, each object is running on its own server processor. The objects communicate through software mechanisms of the operating systems to a software bus (such as a CORBA ORB).

This architecture allows the designer to defer decisions on where and how services would be provided until objects actually were distributed. Because objects can be dynamically distributed, this architecture is scalable as new resources can be added at any time as long as they register with the software bus. Moreover, dynamic reconfiguration is possible if objects can migrate across the network from processor to processor.

There is a wealth of literature on object-oriented systems. Section 14.5 provides additional references for further reading on object-oriented systems.

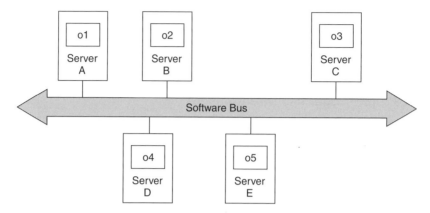

Figure 14-10. A distributed object system.

14.4 HIERARCHICALLY LAYERED SYSTEMS

A *hierarchically layered system* consists of a large software application that is partitioned into layers. Each layer acts as a virtual machine for the layers above it, providing services to those layers. In turn, it acts as a client to the layers below it. Typically, a layer communicates with the layers below it—usually, most directly with the layer immediately below it. A layer does *not* communicate with the layers above it; for example, it does not call procedures or access data there, but only responds to service requests from those layers (Figure 14-11). This approach promotes information hiding because communication between layers occurs only through well-defined APIs. And it promotes reusability since a layer may be replaced in its entirety as long as it preserves its public API.

Many software applications exhibit this structure: operating system kernels, the ISO Open System Interconnection model, and the NIST/ECMA Application Portability Profile, among others. In the ISO model, lower levels describe hardware functions, while the upper levels describe software functions. Similarly, the NIST/ECMA model describes a layered approach to providing software services for complex applications. Kaisler (1982) describes an operating system that is implemented in a hierarchically layered manner.

14.4.1 Hierarchical Abstraction

The hierarchical layer model is based on classical software design using decomposition. Each layer in a hierarchically layered system that knows about one or more layers below it but does not know about the layers above it. An individual layer can reach down into one or more layers below it for services. A general rule of thumb is that no layer should reach more than two layers below it. Otherwise, the ability to replace layers may be compromised.

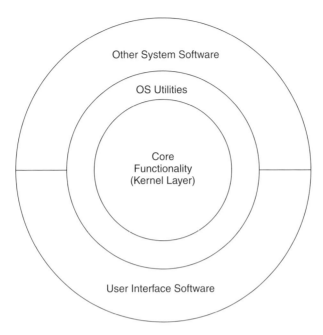

Figure 14-11. Hierarchically layered software architecture.

Each layer above the hardware and above the operating system provides, in effect, a virtual machine to the layers above it. Each layer can be replaced as long as it maintains the APIs required by layers above. It may add new APIs and these will eventually be used, if applicable, as the layers above it are replaced.

14.4.2   Advantages and Disadvantages

Hierarchically layered systems have multiple advantages and a few disadvantages. The primary advantage of layered systems is support for problem spaces whose requirements are well known because they can be partitioned into discrete components that can be incrementally developed. Since the domain is well known, decomposition of functionality is relatively easy. Layered systems support maintainability and extensibility because each layer interacts with the layers above and below it. So changes to one layer affect at most two other layers. Layered systems can support software reusability from the standpoint that since each layer and those below it represent a virtual machine, they become the foundation for a new software architecture for, possibly, a different problem space. Table 14-2 provides more detail on these advantages.

Hierarchically layered systems have some disadvantages as well. Perhaps the biggest disadvantage is that not all systems can be decomposed into hierarchical layers. Certainly, systems exhibiting asynchronous behavior are difficult to implement with this model. Table 14-3 describes some other disadvantages.

Table 14-2 Advantages of a hierarchically layered system

Advantage	Explanation
Divide and conquer	Individual layers can be independently designed once you have partitioned functionality across multiple layers.
Increase cohesion	Well-designed layers have greater cohesion.
Reduce coupling	Well-designed lower layers do not know about upper layers; upper layers invoke functions in lower layers only through their API.
Increase abstraction	Implementation details of lower layers are hidden by their API.
Increase reuse	Layers developed by others can be reused if well-defined partitioning rules are used to decompose problems.
Increase flexibility	New facilities can be added that are built on lower-layer functionality; higher layers can be replaced without affecting lower layers.
Anticipate obsolescence	Tendency toward obsolescence is reduced because individual layers can be replaced once they fail to fulfill the overall needs of the system.
Design for portability	Platform dependencies can be isolated in the lower layers, thus increasing portability (e.g., the Java Virtual Machine).

Table 14-3. Some disadvantages of hierarchically layered systems

Disadvantage	Explanation
Difficult to change behavior	Changing behavior of a layer can become a complex task. While it is easy to add functionality to a layer and slowly evolve the layers above it to use that new functionality, it is difficult to subtract functionality from a layer or split a layer into two layers. As you add functionality to a layer, it can become too complex. This can lead to inefficiencies if functions within the layer share data structures or start to duplicate lower-level functions within the layer.
Level of granularity	It may be difficult to determine the right level of granularity for individual layers. Because layers perform different services, they cannot be of equal weight or complexity. We must avoid the tendency to duplicate services at a lower level within a layer for reasons of efficiency.
Limited visibility may limit efficiency	Since lower-layer functions can be called from any layer above it, it is a good idea to discour-age "long calls", such as procedure calls from layers more than two layers away. This restriction helps to preserve the ability to replace a layer by limiting its visibility. But it means that some services may not be directly accessible or that intermediate processing that is not needed must be performed.

14.5 FURTHER READING

Object-Oriented Systems

Ambler, S. 1997. *Building Object Applications That Work*. Cambridge University Press, Cambridge, UK.

Binder, R. V. 1999. *Testing Object-Oriented Systems: Models, Patterns, and Tools*. Addison Wesley, Reading, MA.

Budd, T. 2001. *Introduction to Object-Oriented Programming*, 3rd Ed. Addison Wesley, Reading, MA.

Fayad, M. and M. Laitenin. 1998. *Transition to Object-Oriented Software Development*. John Wiley & Sons, Hoboken, NJ.

Jones, M. P. 1995. *What Every Programmer Should Know About Object-Oriented Design*. Dorset House Publishing, Dorset, England.

Riel, A. 1996. *Object-Oriented Design Through Heuristics*. Addison Wesley Professional, Reading, MA.

Call-and-Return Systems

Berson, A. 1996. *Client–Server Architecture*. McGraw-Hill, New York.

Goldman, J., P. T. Rawles, and J. R. Mariga. 1998. *Client–Server Information Systems: A Business-Oriented Approach*. John Wiley & Sons, Hoboken, NJ.

Goodyear, M. 1999. *Enterprise System Architectures: Building Client Server and Web Based Systems*. Auerbach Publishers, Philadelphia, PA.

Orfali, R. and D. Harkey. 1998. *Client/Server Programming with Java and CORBA,* 2nd Ed. John Wiley & Sons, Hoboken, NJ.

14.6 EXERCISES

14.1. Describe a problem that cannot be implemented using the hierarchical layer software architecture.

14.2. The main program and subroutines architecture allows any number of subroutines to be used. However, this may lead to spaghetti code. Discuss the maintenance issues associated with this architecture.

14.3. The object-oriented system architecture appears to have unlimited scalability (e.g., supporting an unlimited number of interacting objects). Identify several problems that may affect this view. (*Hint:* Consider the problem of storing handles of objects in other objects.)

14.4. Develop an argument for an upper limit on N in the term N-tier. Describe briefly the functionality you would assign to each tier.

15

VIRTUAL MACHINES

A *virtual machine* (VM) is an emulator that executes on top of a hardware or software platform. Such a machine provides the familiar functions and services expected by computer programs but does so using software rather than hardware. It may provide the same interface as the underlying hardware or software platform (implementing the Wrapper pattern) or an entirely different interface (implementing the Adapter pattern).

15.1 INTERPRETERS

We use the virtual machine concept extensively in computer science. The operating system implements a virtual machine by providing a set of operations layered on top of the hardware machine that enable us to more easily write and execute programs. Each application that runs on top of the operating system is an interpreter in its own right because it insulates us from the underlying hardware and software by giving us a new set of commands and operations to execute.

15.1.1 Command Language Processors

Our early interaction with operating systems occurred through text-based command language processors (Kaisler 1975). We entered statements written in the syntax of an operating system control language. On the IBM 360/370 series machines running OS/3x0, this was a batch-oriented command processor that accepted Job Control

Software Paradigms, By Stephen H. Kaisler
ISBN 0-471-48347-8 Copyright © 2005 John Wiley & Sons, Inc.

Language (JCL). With the advent of the Unix system (Bourne 1978), this processor became known as the *shell*. For microcomputers, Microsoft's DOS became the defining command language processor.

As operating systems became GUI-based, such as the Macintosh OS and Microsoft's Windows, the command processor was embedded in the Window Manager and responded to mouse clicks or other input device signals rather than typed commands.

15.1.2   Programming Language Runtime Environments

A programming language runtime environment provides a set of services for implementing the semantics of the programming language. The runtime environment is bound with the user's application code to form the complete application that runs on top of the operating system. In effect, the runtime environment is a virtual machine, although that term has been more narrowly defined, as we will see below.

The runtime environment manages the data structures that represent and handle the data used by the application. Today, most programming languages are stack- and heap-based, while also providing some form of additional memory allocation and garbage collection. In addition, the runtime environment acts as a mediator between the application and the operating system for obtaining operating system services relating to file and directory management and input/output operation.

15.2   VIRTUAL MACHINE EXAMPLES

Many examples of virtual machines abound. Three virtual machines have been exceptionally successful in the computer industry: the IBM VM System, the Smalltalk VM, and the Java Virtual Machine.

15.2.1   Early VM Systems

A number of early VM systems were distributed through academic circles. One of these was the Pascal-P compiler, which was implemented on over 60 different systems. Pascal-P was designed to operate on a simple machine-independent VM called the Stack Computer (SC) (Nori et al. 1981). The Pascal-P Distribution Kit included an implementation of the compiler on a SC implemented on a PDP-11. To port the Pascal-P system to another machine, one merely had to implement the SC on top of the operating system for that machine.

The SC provides facilities similar to those of a conventional microprocessor operating in user mode. The instruction set includes separate operations for each of the basic Pascal data types such as characters, pointers, integers, and booleans. A SC implementation can use appropriate representations for each data type. At runtime, the memory of the SC is divided into separate regions containing the code, stack, and heap of the runtime environment.

15.2.2 IBM's VM/SP

IBM's VM/SP (Virtual Machine/System Product) is an operating system hypervisor that runs on the IBM 370, 390, and zSeries architectures. It consists of two products: the Control Program (CP) and the Conversational Monitor System (CMS) (IBM 1979). It evolved from an experimental system called CP/67 developed at IBM's Cambridge Scientific Center (Watson 1970, Parmalee et al. 1972). CP/67 was developed as an alternative to the Time Sharing Option (TSO) available for the IBM 360/370 operating system. At the time VM was developed, TSO was a difficult-to-use, slow environment layered on top of the OS/360 (later MVS) batch-oriented operating system. TSO had some severe limitations that flowed through from the underlying operating system, including exclusive use of certain devices. VM allowed a single machine to be efficiently shared among many users. It provided users with virtual devices that were mapped to the actual physical devices attached to the machine. But it also allowed new system configurations to be simulated and tested before implementation.

The CP provided a multiprogramming environment on top of the physical hardware. It intercepted hardware operations from the virtual machines supporting individual users and translated them to actual physical device commands. It captured the results of these operations, translated them appropriately, and passed them back to the virtual machines.

Data was stored in a simple, easy-to-use file system built on top of "minidisks." Minidisks were partitions of a physical disk that were assigned to a single user. To the user, a minidisk appeared to be a disk subsystem attached to a mainframe computer.

The power of VM was expressly demonstrated in its ability to run any IBM operating system under the control of the CP. As Figure 15-1 depicts, a large enough

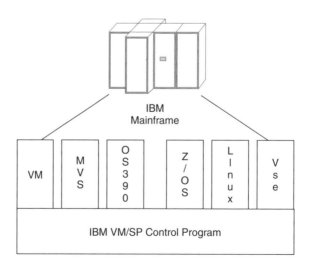

Figure 15-1. The VM/SP environment.

mainframe could execute a mix of IBM operating systems. Indeed, many large organizations used VM/SP to run new versions of their standard operating systems in order to debug them before placing them into production.

Virtual Machine Storage The early versions of VM/SP did not support virtual storage; but once this option became available on the IBM 370 family of machines, VM/SP was enhanced to provide virtual storage support. VM storage could be mapped to virtual storage (V-to-V) or real storage (V-to-R). The difference was based on the amount of real storage available and the translation time for virtual addresses. In V-to-R mode, the amount of virtual storage was limited to some subset of the real storage, but memory access time was faster. In V-to-V mode, the amount of virtual storage could be set equal to the virtual storage supported by the machine hardware, but with an accompanying increase in memory access time due to two levels of virtual address translation.

System Configuration VM/SP emulated all of the devices normally attached to an IBM mainframe configuration. Individual virtual machines could be configured with a mix of devices based on the needs of the individual user. Certain real devices were dedicated to individual users, such as keyboards, monitors, and minidisks. Other devices were attached to a user's virtual machine as needed, such as printers, card readers, and tape drives.

Communication between virtual machines could be accomplished through several mechanisms. One was vCTCA—a virtual Channel-to-Channel Adapter capability. Essentially, the virtual channels associated with two virtual machines were coupled so that data could be passed between them. Another capability was RSCS, the Resource Sharing Communications System, which allowed two virtual machines to communicate across a shared virtual communications link.

User Interface CMS provided a single-user programming and operating environment that gave each user the impression that he was in complete control of an IBM 360/370 computer system. This single-user orientation simplified life for most users because they did not have to worry about interacting with other users.

Users communicated with CMS through an English-like language. This command language was easily extensible. A user could produce a MODULE using a compiler, bind modules using the LOAD and GENMOD commands, and then execute as if it were a base command.

Using CMS, users could run a variety of compilers and other programs. Almost all the compilers available for the IBM batch-oriented operating systems were available under VM/SP. In addition, program editors and debuggers, maintenance and utility programs, and other interactive support programs were available.

Current Capabilities The current version of the product is called z/VM (IBM 2003). The base product includes the following elements: the Control Program (CP), the Conversational Monitor System (CMS), Data Facility Storage Management

System, Hardware Configuration Manager, Language Environment, REXX/VM, and a large set of utilities. It supports the following services, among others:

- *Run Multiple Linux Images:* Linux is supported as an operating system under z/VM. Multiple copies can be run at the same time.
- *Test Programs that Could Abnormally Terminate on a Real Machine:* The isolation provided by a virtual machine allows you to test programs that might crash without actually bringing down the entire machine.
- *Test a New Operating System Release:* A new release of the primary operating system or z/Vm itself can be tested at the same time that production work is also going on.
- *Perform OS Maintenance Concurrently with Production Work:* Program temporary fixes can be applied at the same time that production work is going on.
- *Simulate New System Configurations Before Installation:* You can assess the relative load on the machine and its I/O and disk channels under z/VM before cutting over to the new configuration.
- *Perform Operator Training on New Releases:* You can train operators on new releases or new operating systems prior to deploying them.

15.2.3 The Smalltalk-80 Virtual Machine

Smalltalk was developed in the early 1970s as a way that people might enjoy using computers (Goldberg and Robson 1983). Smalltalk-80 was the first pure class-based object-oriented programming language. All computation is performed by message send operations, which dynamically invoke methods in objects. Even integers and characters are treated as objects although most implementations use more primitive representations.

Smalltalk has traditionally been implemented on a stack-based machine supplemented by a suite of standard libraries. These libraries implemented a variety of data structures as well as common interfaces to peripheral devices. About 100 primitive routines were implemented directly within the virtual machine. These primitives implement simple arithmetic operations, object allocation, process control, and input/output functions. The bytecode operations themselves were focused on manipulating the runtime stack and performing message sends. The initial state of the virtual machine was obtained from a *virtual image* (a precompiled executable module), which described the contents of the heap and the initial programs and tools available within the system.

Smalltalk-80 supported portability at two levels. First, any Smalltalk program could be executed unmodified on any hardware platform supporting a conforming implementation of the VM. Second, existing Smalltalk virtual images may be loaded by different implementations of the virtual machine and primitive routines.

15.2.4 The Java Virtual Machine

One of the holy grails of computing is portability—the ability to move programs from one machine to another and have them run without modification. This had been accomplished by the third generation of programming languages at the source program level. One could reasonably move Fortran or COBOL or Basic programs, among other languages, from machine to machine—even heterogeneous ones—by just recompiling and relinking in order to execute them, as long as there were no machine-dependent features embedded in the programs. At the binary or object level, this was much harder to achieve. The advent of Java, while not a panacea, has made distribution of applets, servlets, and Java programs easy to accomplish through the specification of the Java Virtual Machine (JVM).

15.3 RULE-BASED SYSTEMS

A *rule-based system* (or production system) represents knowledge and reasoning logic as a set of rules rather than a set of imperative statements as is typically found in traditional programming languages. A typical rule-based system (RBS) consists of a set of rules, a database of facts, and an interpreter for executing those rules. Given a data set, the interpreter executes rules that use the data to (possibly) reach a conclusion(s), which is the solution to the problem embedded in the rules. Figure 15-2 depicts the basic architecture of a rule-based system.

Typically, the user interacts with the system through a user interface. Queries are entered based on some predefined syntax. The inference engine parses the query, determines how to evaluate it, and accesses the knowledge base for both rules and data. The knowledge base holds two types of data: (1) specific facts about the problem domain and (2) a set of rules particular to the problem domain for analyzing data and deducing results. The inference engine executes the rules retrieved from the knowledge base until a result is achieved, which is passed back to the user. The working memory serves as a transient storage for temporary computations during the inferencing process.

The inference engine is separated from the knowledge base for two reasons. First, the inference can be used with many different knowledge bases. Second, the knowledge base can grow in an evolutionary fashion as the problem domain is better understood. That means that the overall RBS may become more proficient at solving problems.

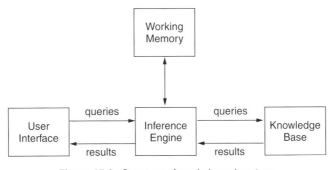

Figure 15-2. Structure of a rule-based system.

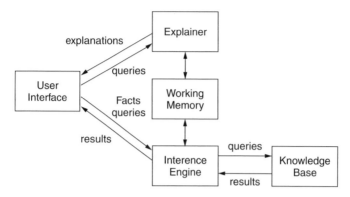

Figure 15-3. RBS with an explanation subsystem.

An enhanced version the RBS architecture is depicted in Figure 15-3. Here, an explainer has been added to the system. Any practical RBS needs an explanatory subsystem to explain its reasoning, because (1) it gives the user confidence that the system has arrived at the right answer, and (2) it makes it easier to debug the system's rules.

15.3.1 RBS Operation

A rule consists of two parts: an if-part and a then-part. The *if-part* (also called the antecedent or conditional part) describes some pattern in the available data that you observe. If the *if-part* (also called the consequent or action part) matches some subset of the data, then the *then-part* is executed. Usually, the then-part prescribes some actions, such a creating new data (in working memory or the knowledge base) or performing a computation.

The basic operation of a RBS is, given a query, to repeatedly execute rules until there is no rule left to execute. The results of executing the set of rules are then presented to the user. In the simplest case, the results of the last rule either contain the answer the user seeks or an explanation of why the query cannot be answered (e.g., lack of sufficient information in the knowledge base).

In each cycle, the inference engine seeks to pick the best rule based on those that match the data in working memory or the knowledge base. Some type of selection criterion is required when multiple rules match the available data. At each cycle, a rule may produce new data in working memory which takes the reasoning process a step further. This is just like a human being following a chain of logical steps to solve a problem. Indeed, RBSs were initially created with the intent to mimic human thought processes.

15.3.2 RBS Types

There are two types of rule-based systems: forward chaining and backward chaining. In a *forward chaining system*, you start with the initial facts and keep using the rules to draw new conclusions (or take certain actions) given those facts. In a *backward chaining system*, you start with some hypothesis (or goal) you are trying to prove and keep looking for rules that would allow you to conclude that hypothesis, perhaps setting new subgoals to prove as you go. Forward chaining systems are primarily data-driven, while backward chaining systems are goal-driven.

Forward Chaining System   In a forward chaining system, the facts in the system are represented in a *working memory*, which is continually updated. Rules, sometimes called condition–action rules, in the system represent possible actions to take when specified conditions hold on items in the working memory. The conditions are usually *patterns* that must *match* items in the working memory, while the actions usually involve *adding* or *deleting* items from the working memory.

The interpreter controls the application of the rules, given the working memory, thus controlling the system's activity. It is based on a cycle of activity sometimes known as a *recognize-act* cycle. The system first checks to find all the rules whose conditions hold, given the current state of working memory. It then selects one and performs the actions in the action part of the rule. (The selection of a rule to fire is based on fixed strategies, known as *conflict resolution* strategies.) The actions will result in a new working memory, and the cycle begins again. This cycle will be repeated until either no rules fire or some specified goal state is satisfied. This process is depicted in Figure 15-4.

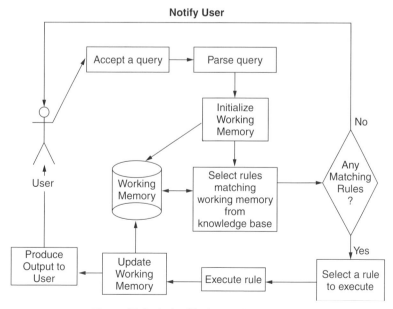

Figure 15-4. A simplified recognize-act cycle.

A number of conflict resolution strategies are typically used to decide which rule to fire. These include:

- Don't fire a rule twice on the same data.
- Fire rules on more recent working memory elements before older ones. This allows the system to follow through a single chain of reasoning, rather than drawing new conclusions from old data.
- Fire rules with more specific preconditions before ones with more general preconditions. This allows the system to deal with nonstandard cases.

You will need to select the conflict resolution strategy that best matches the problem domain. Because a conflict resolution strategy prefers one rule over others when multiple rules are eligible to be executed, rules interact and the order of rules in the knowledge base can be significant. The domain expert must consider when rules apply and in what order they might be executed. Thus, one cannot understand a rule merely by reading it: one must understand its relation to other rules and under what circumstances it will be selected by the conflict resolution strategy. Thus, simply adding rules to a knowledge base to expand its domain coverage can be fraught with danger, as it may cause the entire RBS to cease operating or to operate incorrectly.

This approach is most useful when you know all the initial facts but don't have much idea what the conclusion might be.

Backward Chaining System   A backward chaining system works backward (deduces) from a given goal to a set of facts that support that goal. Given a goal state, the system will try and prove the goal can be reached from the known facts. If it can, then that goal succeeds. If it doesn't, the system will look for rules whose conclusions (previously referred to as *actions*) match the goal. One such rule will be chosen, and the system will then try to prove any facts in the preconditions of the rule using the same procedure, setting these as new goals to prove. Note that a backward chaining system does *not* need to update a working memory. Instead, it needs to keep track of what goals it needs to prove its main hypothesis. Figure 15-5 depicts the backward chaining mechanism.

Forward Chaining Versus Backward Chaining   Whether you use forward or backward reasoning to solve a problem depends on the properties of your rule set and initial facts. Sometimes, if you have some particular goal (to test some hypothesis), then backward chaining will be much more efficient, as you avoid drawing conclusions from irrelevant facts. However, sometimes backward chaining can be very wasteful: there may be many possible ways of trying to prove something, and you may have to try almost all of them before you find one that works. Forward chaining may be better if you have lots of things you want to prove (or if you just want to find out in general what new facts are true); when you have a small set of initial facts; and when there tends to be lots of different rules that allow you to draw the same conclusion. Backward chaining may be better if you are trying to prove

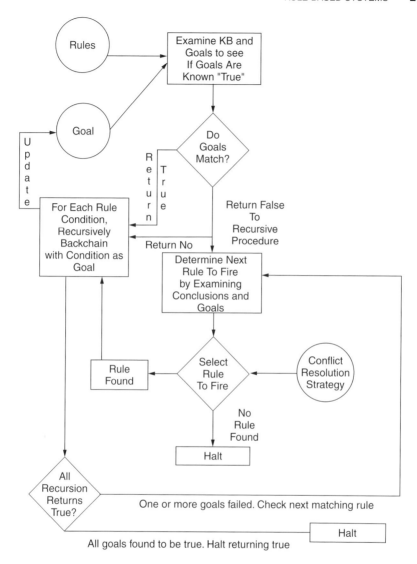

Figure 15-5. A backward chaining mechanism.

a single fact, given a large set of initial facts, whereas, if you used forward chaining, lots of rules would be eligible to fire in any cycle.

In principle, we can use the same set of rules for both forward and backward chaining. However, in practice, we may choose to write the rules slightly differently if we are going to be using them for backward chaining. In backward chaining, we are concerned with matching the conclusion of a rule against some goal that we are trying to prove. So the "then" part of the rule is usually not expressed as an action to take (e.g., add/delete), but as a state that will be true if the premises are true.

15.3.3 RBS Issues

Rules are a convenient way of capturing general knowledge that can apply to a number of different situations. Multiple rules with slight variations can be defined for individual aspects of a problem. To expand the knowledge, we just need to add more rules that either cover more of the problem domain or analyze the problem domain in more depth. The trade-off is that as more rules must be considered at each cycle, the overall performance of the RBS degrades; for example, it takes longer to achieve a result.

In a basic RBS, rules are limited to declarative creation of new knowledge. However, since this leads to weak applications, most RBSs allow computations to be performed through function calls in either the then-part or both parts of a rule. This additional expressive power allows RBSs to solve any problem that other architectures can solve albeit more slowly. This disadvantage is balanced by the powerful explanatory behavior that many RBSs now possess.

15.4 ADVANTAGES AND DISADVANTAGES

There are several advantages and disadvantages to the virtual machine architecture. Some of the advantages include:

- The virtual machine concept provides complete protection of system resources since each virtual machine is isolated from all other virtual machines. This isolation, however, permits no direct sharing of resources.
- A virtual machine is an ideal platform for research and development of new software concepts because it insulates the R&D environment from the operational environment and does not disrupt normal operation.

Some disadvantages include:

- The virtual machine concept is difficult to implement due to the effort required to provide an *exact* duplicate of the underlying machine (when emulating the underlying hardware).

15.5 FURTHER READING

Alpern, B. et al. 2000. "The Jalapeno Virtual Machine." *IBM Systems Journal* 39(1):211–238. Available at http://www.research.ibm.com/journal/sj/391/alpern.pdf.

Blunden, B. 2002. *Virtual Machine Design and Implementation in C/C++*. Wordware Publishing, Plano, TX.

Cheriton, D. R. 1984. "The V Kernel." *IEEE Software* 1(2):19–42.

Creasy, R. J. 1981. "The Origin of the VM/370 Time-Sharing System." *IBM Journal of Research and Development* 25(5):483–490.

Hayes-Roth, F. 1984. "Rule-Based Systems." *Communications of the ACM* 28(9):921–932.

IGDA. 2003. Working Group on Rule-Based Systems. Available at `http://www.igda. org/ai/report-2003/aiisc_rule_based_systems_report_2003. html`.

Lammel, R. 2003. Evolution of Rule-Based Systems. Free University, Amsterdam, The Netherlands. Available at `http://homepages.cwi.nl/~ralf/erbs/paper. pdf`.

Sun Microsystems. 2002. *The Java Virtual Machine Specification,* 2nd Ed. Addison Wesley, Reading, MA.

Van Vleck, T. A Short History of IBM's Virtual machines. Available at `http:// www.cap-lore.com/CP.html`.

15.6 EXERCISES

15.1. Consider a transportable interpreted language that is designed to work on a variety of machines (but not Java!). Users must be able to make some calls to platform-specific, custom functions. How can this be supported in the transportable language without compromising its transportability? (*Hint:* Think about data structure representations, embedded references to objects, and the operating system API.) Describe what capabilities the runtime environment or virtual machine requires. [Requires some knowledge of compilers.]

15.2. Design and implement a virtual machine to support Fortran (or a subset thereof) on a particular architecture. (*Hint*: Examine closely the Java virtual machine.)

15.3. Rule-based systems have been used primarily in artificial intelligence applications. Design the components for a generic rule-based system. [Research Problem].

16

INDEPENDENT COMPONENT SYSTEMS

In the systems we have examined so far, communication is through explicit invocation of some method or subprogram. This means that the calling entity must know both the identity and the signature of the called entity in order to communicate with it. An alternative form of communication relies on implicit invocation, where the information communicated is a data structure that causes the receiving entities to react in some way.

16.1   COMMUNICATING SEQUENTIAL PROCESSES

The most general architecture is just to have a set of communicating sequential processes (CSP) that send messages to each other or invoke each other (such as using the Ada rendezvous mechanism). The CSP model was originated by C. A. R Hoare (1978, 1985) to model concurrent systems. It is not important whether the processes run on one processor or many processors. The important difference to a single sequential process is that the programmer never know how much time a process will need to finish another process. Each process is independent of and distinct from every other process.

16.1.1   CSP Concepts

The basic idea of CSP is that multiple concurrent processes can synchronize with each other most easily by synchronizing their I/O. Hoare proposed that the way to

Software Paradigms, By Stephen H. Kaisler
ISBN 0-471-48347-8   Copyright © 2005 John Wiley & Sons, Inc.

do this is to allow I/O to occur only when (1) process A states that it is ready to out-put to process B specifically, and (2) process B states that it is ready to input from process A specifically. If one of these conditions exists without the other condition being true, the process is put on a wait queue until the other process is ready.

Hoare considered two major problems in concurrent programming: (1) how to communicate among two or more processes and (2) how to synchronize certain actions among two or more processes. In Hoare's view, communication was the passing of a set of parameters from one process to another. To do so, the sending process had to know the signature of the receiving process at a particular point (although this could be generalized to be a single parameter having internal structure).

For synchronization, Hoare wanted to model the occurrence of certain conditions in the receiving process. Since the input command controlled the initiation of communication (e.g., the receiving process had to issue one), Hoare extended the input command to have guard or conditional expressions—all of which had to evaluate to true for the input command to be executed. Moreover, a process could have multiple input commands each accompanied by its own guards. Hoare specified that all input commands be evaluated under certain conditions (e.g., a multiway case statement). This could lead to several input commands, all of whose guards were true and thus capable of being executed. As a result, he also specified that in such a case one and only one of the input commands would be selected for execution. This enabled Hoare to also model nondeterminism in process execution.

16.1.2 Problems with CSP

Before discussing the problems, it is important to realize that Hoare intended CSP to be a modeling tool for describing concurrent processes as opposed to an actual implementation. It was an algebraic approach to describing the behaviors of a set of processes such that complex behaviors could be built up from simple behaviors using a set of well-defined operators. Using this algebra, one could reason about the behavior of a set of processes representing an application under particular conditions. Indeed, CSP was the first approach to formal methods for reasoning about concurrent systems.

That said, there have been several implementations of CSP to support empirical research in processes. Ada 95's task features and rendezvous mechanism is one example.

As originally specified, CSP had a number of problems in modeling concurrent systems. First, it required explicit naming. That meant that every process had to know the name or handle of every process that it wanted to communicate with and specify that name or handle in any message transmission.

Second, it did not include message buffering in the model. Thus, the sending process had to be ready to send, but could not until the receiving process was ready to receive a message. A programmer could provide buffering between two processes, but this often required inserting another process whose sole function was buffering.

Third, the programmer had to be cautious. There was no mechanism for detecting or preventing deadlocks.

Section 16.5 contains additional information regarding CSP and its utilization.

16.2 EVENT-BASED SYSTEMS

Event-driven means that processing only occurs when something, the *event*, happens. That "something" may be a data point changing, an alarm going off, a timer timing out, or a user clicking on an icon or a graphic object. In Java, for example, an event is defined as something that happens that you might want to know about. When a Java component gains the input focus, an event occurs because it might be important for an applet to know about the focus change. Event-based systems are differentiated from a set of communicating processes in that unknown participants (to the event originator or detector) may actually handle the processing of the event.

Event-based systems represent a loose integration of components, which have little or no knowledge of each other and which interact by announcing and responding to occurrences called events. The components of event-based systems are the event handlers, while the connectors are the procedure bindings associated with events. An event handler does not get invoked unless it has previously registered itself with an event.

In an event-based software architecture, components communicate by generating and receiving *event notifications*. A component generates an event when it wants to let the other components know that some significant event occurred either in its internal state or in the state of other components with which it interacts. When event notifications are generated, they are usually propagated to any component that has declared an interest in receiving it. Typically, the generation of an event notification and its subsequent propagation occur asynchronously. Usually, an *event dispatcher* is responsible for the propagation of event notifications to interested components, called *event handlers*. Propagation is usually hidden from the component that generated the event notification; for example, it generally does not know which other components will receive the event notification. In essence, event-based systems operate as multicast systems that decouple the event generators from the event receivers. Figure 16-1 depicts this concept from a control flow perspective.

Event-based software architectures allow programs to respond to inputs from their environment that occur stochastically or on a fixed schedule. Event-based software architectures were originally driven by the needs of real-time systems, particularly for industrial process control, but more recently by graphical user interfaces.

Event-driven systems have some resemblance to simulation systems. In simulation systems, there is a list of jobs (events) to be performed (handled). The central executive or dispatcher retrieves the first job from the list and executes the code associated with the job. The code must eventually return so that succeeding jobs in the list can be executed. If it was not possible to finish an operation, the code for that job would add a new job to the end of the list of jobs such that the operation could be completed at a later time. In event-driven systems, however, the dispatcher must check all event sources to see if a new event has occurred during the time that it was processing the previous event.

Event-based systems differ from other systems that we will examine in this book. There is typically no flow of control. As events happen, they are responded to. This

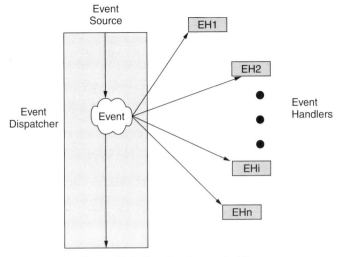

Figure 16-1. Event system control flow.

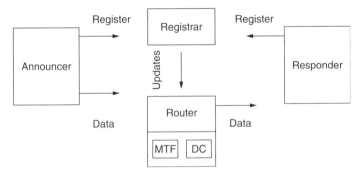

Figure 16-2. An event-based system framework (after Barrett et al. 1996).

means that we can't really "read" the program code. This is because we can't count on the events occurring in a particular order.

In summary, an event-based system is driven by external (sometimes, internal) events. Such systems react continuously to and with their environment and experience bursts of activity in response to the occurrence of events initiated from the external environment.

16.2.1   Event System Design

A general model for an event-based system is depicted in Figure 16-2 (adapted from Barrett et al. 1996). This model depicts participants in an event-based system—announcers and responders. Announcers generate events, while responders handle events. There may be any number of announcers and responders in a system. When an event occurs, the announcer sends a message saying the event has occurred with the appropriate information attached. The *router* (event dispatcher) receives this message and sends it to the set of responders who have registered an interest in that event.

Registration Mechanism

Entities in an event-driven system register their interest or ability to process certain kinds of events. When an event is announced, the run time system invokes the methods or subprograms in each entity having an interest in that event. Thus, the event announcement implicitly causes the execution of subprograms in other entities.

In the most general model, each component must register itself with the event dispatcher regarding the event notifications it wishes to receive and the event notifications that it generates. Registration is the process of obtaining permission to communicate.

A centralized registration mechanism allows greater efficiency because one copy of the message announcing the event can be sent to all responders. The performance of the event dispatcher is related directly to the number of responders who have registered to respond to the event.

The registrar may be simple or complex. A simple registrar just records each announcer that can send a message and each responder that has an interest in a particular event. The registrar can also perform unregistration, which allows dynamic event handling to be implemented.

The registrar informs the router of the messages it may receive about certain events and the names of responders having an interest in those events.

Routing Mechanism

Event notification occurs through a routing mechanism that decouples the announcer from the responders. The announcer sends a message announcing the event to the router. The router looks up the list of responders who have an interest in the event and sends the message to each of them. This approach has been used in various simulation systems [e.g., see Oresky et al. (1990) and Kaisler (1991)]. Messages sent from the router to the responders may be subject to message transforming functions and delivery constraints.

In some systems the function of the registrar and the router is encompassed by one software module. This is the case with the Object Request Broker (ORB) of the CORBA framework (see Section 10.1). Suppose we have three components X1, X2, and X3. X1 sends different event notifications to X2 and X3 (Figure 16-3). Using CORBA, we need two channels—X1 to X2 and X1 to X3. X1 needs to determine which channel to use. If X1 sends an event notification on the wrong channel, it will be rejected or ignored.

The structure of event notifications defines a communication protocol between the announcer and the responders. If the notification contains minimal information, then the announcer and responders may have to engage in a lengthy conversation using other communication protocols in order for the responders to understand the current state.

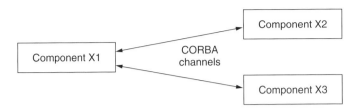

Figure 16-3. Event-based systems using CORBA channels.

Consider the case of a component X attempting to deploy a new software release. Each receiver deploys the software upon receiving the event notification. Suppose the event notification consists merely of "Product A version 2.2 released on June 5th." Receivers would have to communicate with X to find where the software is located, download it, and deploy it to their systems. This could require extensive conversation to obtain the necessary information. An alternative might be to send the software with the event notification or a document containing the necessary information.

Message Transformation Function   Barrett et al. (1996) allow a message to be dynamically altered by the router to correspond to specific characteristics or requirements of the responders. For example, additional content might be added to the message (such as the announcer's identification) or some data may be stripped from the message for certain responders. These modifications are performed by *message transforming functions* (MTFs), of which there may be any number incorporated in the router. A simple MTF might be a filter that selects only certain incoming messages and passes them on to the responders. Another is an aggregator that only sends forward a message when a certain sequence of messages has been received by the router.

Delivery Constraints   Additionally, Barrett et al. (1996) define delivery constraints (DCs) as rules that can be imposed on how messages are delivered to responders. For example, a rule might state that messages must be delivered in the order in which they are received from announcers. DCs may be defined for certain types of messages. While not explicitly shown, MTFs and DCs can be provided by either announcers or responders or both.

16.2.2   Mediating Events

Object-oriented and concurrent programming design encourage the distribution of functionality among different objects and/or processes. But this distribution can often yield objects or processes with a large number of connections to other objects. In the worst case with static binding, every object or process must know about every other object or process.

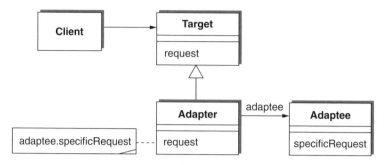

Figure 16-4. The Adapter design pattern.

Although partitioning a system into many objects will generally enhance reusability, the proliferation of interconnections tends to reduce it again. Lots of interconnections make it less likely that an object can work without the support of others—the system acts as though it were monolithic. Moreover, it can be difficult to change the system's behavior in any significant way, since behavior is distributed among many objects. As a result, you may be forced to define many different objects to customize the system's behavior.

So how do we decouple objects, but allow them to interact? The answer is through events that allow one object to signal another. Two design patterns provide mechanisms for this decoupling: Adapter and Mediator.

The Adapter The Adapter design pattern (Figure 16-4) converts the interface of one class to an interface that other clients expect. This lets classes work together that otherwise could not. The Adapter is a variation of the Wrapper pattern that was described in Section 4.2.

The Mediator pattern promotes loose coupling by keeping objects from referring to each other explicitly, and it lets you vary their interaction independently (Gamma et al. 1995).

The Mediator The Mediator pattern provides a mechanism for removing the filtering function from the event handler. The event handler is dedicated to handling events within any time constraints specified, and event notification can occur independently. Figure 16-5 depicts the use of this pattern.

Consider an active badge sensor that tracks an individual as they move around a building. Throughout the building are sensors that receive emissions from active badges. Each individual has an active badge, which they wear while in the building. When an individual moves from one room to the next, the sensor in the room entered notes the presence of the specific badge and notifies a central database of the presence of the individual. Then clients either may be notified of the location of the individual continuously or may query the database for the location of an individual when needed.

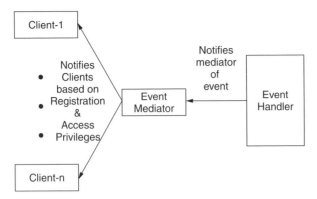

Figure 16-5. Event mediation.

A Mediator may also serve as a buffer. For example, mobile phone customers who have their phones shut off at times may miss important calls. But routing those calls to voice mail from which they can be retrieved as the client desires is a form of mediation that prevents the client from missing those calls. Similar to the active badge concept, when the mobile service detects the client's phone is again active, it can notify him that he has messages awaiting in voice mail.

16.2.3 CORBA Event Service

CORBA's Event Service defines a set of interfaces that provide a way for objects to synchronously communicate event messages to each other. The interfaces support a *pull* style of communication (in which the *responder* requests event messages from the *announcer* of the message) and a *push* style of communication (in which the announcer initiates the communication). Additional interfaces define *channels*, which act as buffers and multicast distribution points between suppliers and consumers.

The Event Service is not a sophisticated event notification system. An event is simply a message that one object communicates to another object. The specification of the CORBA Event Service does not define the content of an event message, so objects must be programmed with "knowledge" about the particular event message structure that is to be shared between communicating suppliers and consumers. Being a message, an event is its own notification. Messages are not subject to transformation because there is no intermediate entity, and any attempt to enforce message delivery is solely the responsibility of the responder.

An application programmer wanting to use this service is faced with several problems: how to locate events of interest, how to advertise new kinds of events, how to match patterns of events, and how to create and maintain networks of event channels to perform matching. Thus, the CORBA Event Service provides only a small subset of the capabilities needed in event observation and notification facility corresponding to the framework presented in Section 16.2.1.

16.2.4   Characterizing Event Systems

Event systems can be characterized according to a number of dimensions:

- *Synchronicity:* The control flow may be synchronous or asynchronous. A synchronous event system would process one event at a time. When an event handler has completed processing its event, it returns to the event dispatcher. In an asynchronous system, once the event handler has accepted the event, control is split between the event dispatcher and the event handler, each of which is implemented as a process.
- *Distribution:* Events may be handled in the same process or distributed to other processes.
- *Registration:* Registration may be static or dynamic. A deregistering function must also be supported.
- *Dispatch and Handling Times:* Dispatch time is that required to recognize the event, determine its type, and pass it to the event handler. Handling time is that required to actually interpret the event, take any action resulting from it, and dismiss the event.
- *Exception Handling:* This is how the event system will handle events that it does not recognize. Two options are to either ignore them or to alert some client that unanticipated events are taking place.

16.2.5   The Cambridge Event Architecture

The Computer Laboratory at Cambridge University has developed the Cambridge Event Architecture (CEA) to support asynchronous operation by means of events, event classes, and event occurrences as object instances (Bacon et al. 2000). CEA uses a publish-register-notify paradigm with event object classes and source-side filtering based on parameter templates. Figure 16-6 depicts the general model of this paradigm.

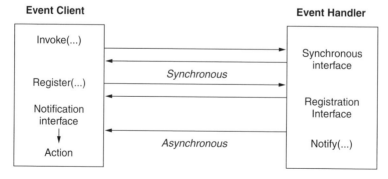

Figure 16-6. The publish-notify event architecture.

Synchronously, the client registers itself with the Event Handler. It may also invoke other routines and services associated with the event handler through the synchronous interface. Whenever an event occurs, the client is notified of the event asynchronously through the notification interface. A similar mechanism is used in JavaBeans, whereby a listener registers interest with any object that can raise an event.

Registration   Each object that can handle an event has a Register(. . .) method in its interface. Any component may register with the object via this method to be notified when the event occurs. Alternatively, an object may be able to handle multiple events and the client can specify a wild card parameter that allows it to be notified of any events of certain types.

Access control for security operations can be enforced by not allowing a client to register for events that it does not have authority to see.

Notification   Each client has a Notify(. . .) method in its interface that allows it to be notified when events have occurred for which it has expressed interest by registering for them with the proper event handler. When an event occurs, the event handler matches the event with a template associated with each registration. Subject to access restrictions, each client that has registered for the event will be notified of its occurrence.

Mediation   CEA uses a mediation mechanism as discussed in Section 16.2.2. CEA performs source-side filtering, meaning that events are analyzed and filtered before clients are notified. This has the advantage of scalability but may slow notification as more templates have to be analyzed. Other schemes multicast event notification to all clients and perform filtering at the client. While this may ensure quick notification of events, it may make the clients unnecessarily complex, allow them to become aware of events that they may not need to know about, and may overload the communications infrastructure.

Composite Events   Bacon notes that an extension of this basic mechanism leads to the ability to filter composite events. A *composite event* is a collection of events from different sources. The mediation mechanism can receive notification of a set of events and only notify selected clients when specified events have occurred, possibly in order or within a certain time interval. Considering the active badge sensor again, a supervisor may want to be notified when several individuals from her group have congregated in a particular room or around the water cooler.

Another application of composite events can assist in failure detection in telecommunication networks. Each node in the network uses a variation of the heartbeat protocol to notify other nodes that it is alive and operational. A mediator can be configured to receive notification of these heartbeats, count them, and after a predetermined number of absences to take corrective action. In this case, mediation might be located at each node to allow each node to implement its own policy regarding the failed node. Moreover, as Bacon suggests, varying the heartbeat rate allows a priority structure to be overlaid on the network so that critical nodes that fail can be detected sooner.

16.2.6   Advantages and Disadvantages

The primary advantage of an event-based system is that a component can operate without being aware of the existence of other software components. It must know the structure of event notifications of interest to it and be able to register that interest with the event dispatcher.

Event-based systems provide strong support for software reusability. New components can be introduced into the system merely by executing the registration procedures that declare their interest in and ability to respond to events. Similarly, components already registered can be updated in place by changing their processing mechanisms as long as they continue to respond properly to the events for which they have registered interest. Or they can be replaced by other components by reregistering without affecting other components in the system.

These two features provide a high degree of composition and reconfigurability of software architectures.

The primary disadvantage of event-based systems is that a central monitor must handle all event announcements and dispatch those events to all components that have registered an interest in them. This can lead to conflict in two ways. First, any component does not know how many, if any, other components will respond to a particular event or how they will respond to it. Second, even if it knows other components that may/will respond to the event, it does not know in what order they will respond or when they will finish responding. This may cause conflict in shared data structures and require synchronization and mutual exclusion, which defeats some of the advantages for event-based systems.

A third problem has to do with the information communicated with the event. In Unix, a signal is basically a one-bit event that indicates a particular condition has occurred. The process receiving the signal must determine the cause and what response to make. Complex events may require additional data to be passed with the name of the event to the receiving component. However, all of the data may not be readily available in a form that can be passed with the event. In that case, receiving components must rely on a shared database of information to support their processing of the event.

16.3   EVENT SYSTEM ISSUES

When designing event-based systems, the architect must address several issues, including scalability, exception handling, security, event buffering, and quality of service.

16.3.1   Scalability

The internal architecture of the event service affects the scalability. Intuitively, we want the event service to scale in terms of the number of participating components and the number of events that can be handled in variety and quantity. If an event service is implemented as a centralized service, it may quickly become a bottleneck as the number of components grows. As the number of different events grows, the registration and dispatching mechanisms become more complex. On the other hand, distributed event services may have to repropagate events from one event service to another in order to ensure that every interested component receives the notification.

16.3.2 Exception Handling

The event service must be able to handle exceptions that occur during event recognition and processing. The primary exception that occurs during event recognition is an unknown event. The event dispatcher may ignore it or send a notification event to one of the handlers (perhaps a special handler) to alert the clients of the system. Unknown events often occur with the physical failure of external devices. During event processing, the structure of the event may contain faulty data that leads to a processing failure. The event handler can discard the event or notify a special handler to alert the clients.

16.3.3 Security

Events may be seen by all processes in the most general case. But there are applications where it is required that events only be seen by or delivered to authorized customers. Event-based access control requires that access control can be carried out against each event occurrence.

The event handler is responsible for checking if an event can be delivered to the interested consumers. However, the servers must have the right to notify the consumers. The event handler should support secure method invocation, such as that specified by the OMG CORBA Security Standard.

16.3.4 Event Buffering

In certain systems, generally non-real-time, an event may happen before a client has expressed interest in that event. Or a client cannot handle all of the events that are being supplied, especially when variable time is required to process each event. Buffering can alleviate the problem of forcing too many events on a client. Using a time-to-live parameter, events beyond a certain age in the buffer can be discarded. While a client may still miss events, the number of missed events can be reduced and event processing smoothed out over time.

16.3.5 Quality of Service

In many systems, multiple types of events may need to be processed, and processing time may vary with event type as well as among events of a given type. Events may or may not be given priorities. Often, there are certain events that need to be delivered quickly, such as fault events in a telecommunication system, where we want to identify and repair the problem quickly. On the other hand, performance events can tolerate some delay since they are usually just logged and analyzed off-line at a later time. Sometimes, we want to specify the priority of an event and its method of handling, for example, expedited delivery. And sometimes, events must be guaranteed delivery within a specified time, a specified order, or just once. All of these require a reliable transport protocol.

16.4   BROKER SYSTEMS

A broker system communicates between distributed software systems in order to enable remote use of services. The objects reside in separate address spaces and their methods are invoked by remote method calls. The goal of the broker system is to make transparent the separation between the client and the server. A broker system implements a broker design pattern.

Classic broker systems include CORBA, Microsoft's OLE and COM/DCOM, IBM's SOM/DSOM, the World Wide Web model using HTTP, and the Java Remote Method Invocation (RMI) mechanism.

16.4.1   Remote Method Calls

A *remote method call* (RMC) is usually delivered over some sort of network communication infrastructure (the characteristics of which do not concern us here except for some consideration of performance and reliability). We can liken a RMC to a RPC and, in most cases, the two are almost indistinguishable.

A RMC is divided into a request and a response. The request asks for a service from the server and the response delivers the result, if any, to the client. As a side effect, the service is performed at the server. RMCs may be either synchronous or asynchronous. A synchronous RMC requires that the client cease execution until the server returns the response. On the other hand, an asynchronous RMC allows the client to proceed with its own execution while the server is performing the service; but the server must "call back" the client with the response.

The RMC must identify the data to be sent to the server and the server node on which the target object resides. Representation of a remote reference must span the differences in hardware architectures, so it is specified by an architecture-neutral IDL. The IDL generates the object wrappers, including the marshalling and unmarshalling code, via the Proxy pattern to bridge the conceptual gap between the local client and the remote server.

16.4.2   Broker System Design

As noted above, a Broker System implements a broker design pattern. The design pattern depicted in Figure 16-7, which describes a broker system, specifies some of the functions needed to implement a distributed broker system. The client and the server each require a proxy, which performs the marshalling and unmarshalling of data and implements the basic communication mechanism. The Broker pattern

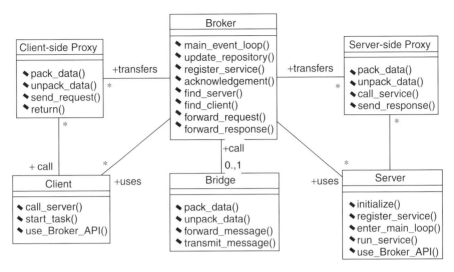

Figure 16-7. Broker System design pattern.

Table 16-1. Some advantages of a Broker System

Advantage	Explanation
Divide and conquer	Dividing a system into separate processes allows each to be developed independently and forces partitioning of functionality among the processes, such as a client–server system.
Increase cohesion	A server can provide stronger cohesion with multiple clients.
Reduce coupling	There is usually only one communication channel among the communicating processes.
Increase abstraction	Each process can be implemented using a different abstraction.
Increase reuse	Different frameworks exist for building distributed systems. Servers can be designed to be used in multiple systems.
Increase flexibility	Distributed systems can be redesigned to add more clients, more servers, or both. Brokers can be enhanced with new functionality to service additional clients.
Design for portability	Clients can be written for new platforms but still access brokers and remote objects on other platforms.

handles the communication between the two proxies. Note that the broker provides functions for locating both the client and the server objects. The Bridge pattern is used to mediate the protocol between the two proxies.

16.4.3   Advantages and Disadvantages

Broker Systems have several advantages and disadvantages; see Table 16-1 and 16-2.

Table 16-2. Some disadvantages of a Broker System

Disadvantage	Explanation
Restricted efficiency	Interfaces to services must be constructed to handle uncertainty of the nature of clients that will invoke the service. Thus, additional error checking must be performed routinely on every invocation, and steps must be taken to ensure that permanent changes are not made until successful execution is assured.
Performance	Location transparency means less urgency in topologically locating services for efficient access, such as shortest communications path or fastest connection between client and service.
Lower fault tolerance	In many large systems, just one instance of a service will be activated. Access to that service and potential disruption of the overall system functionality can occur if network access is lost or the hardware/software platform fails.

16.5 FURTHER READING

CSP and Its Utilization

Bredereke, J. 1999. Modular, Changeable Requirements for Telephone Switching in CSP-Oz. http://citeseer.nj.nec.com/cache/papers/cs/13698.

Cheng, M. H. M. Communicating Sequential Processes—A Synopses. http://citeseer.nj.nec.com/cache/papers/cs/11924.

Roscoe, A. W. 1997. *Theory and Practice of Concurrency*, Prentice Hall, Englewood Cliffs, NJ.

Roscoe, A. W., M. Reed, and J. Foster. 2001. The Successes and Failures of Behavioral Models. http://citeseer.nj.nec.com/481410.htm.

Schneider, S. 1999. *Concurrent and Real-Time Systems: The CSP Approach*, John Wiley & Sons, Hoboken, NJ.

Event-Based Systems

Bass, L., P. Clements, and R. Kazman. 1998. *Software Architecture in Practice*. Addison Wesley, Reading, MA.

Grundy, J. C., J. G. Hosking, and W. B. Mugridge. 1997. "Visualizing Event-Based Systems: Issues and Experiences." In *Proceedings of the 1997 Software Visualization Workshop*, Adelaide, Australia, December 11–12, 1997, pp. 77–86.

Krishnamurthy, B. and D. S. Rosenblum. 1995. "Yeast: A General Purpose Event-Action System." *IEEE Transactions on Software Engineering* 21(10):845–857.

Luders, F. 2003. Use of Component-Based Software Architectures in Industrial Control Systems. Department of Computer Science and Engineering, Malardalen University, Sweden.

Tombros, D. 1999. An Event- and Repository-Based Component Framework for Workflow System Architecture. Ph.D. Dissertation, University of Zurich, Switzerland.

16.6 EXERCISES

16.1. Consider the design of an operating system. (If you have not studied this, find a good book on operating systems such as Tanenbaum (2002)). Design a minimal operating system using an event-based model. [*Hint:* See Kaisler (1982) for some design ideas and hints.]

16.2. There are many examples of broker systems used in the financial domain: for example, mortgage bond sales, eBay auctions, and commodities markets. Research one of these domains and describe how a broker-based system supports the domain. [Research Problem]

17

DATA-CENTRIC SYSTEMS

Data-centric systems use a central database to store all problem-related information. The single database provides convenient access to information, simplifying the process of extracting data in a variety of formats. For example, the information about a pipeline in a gas transmission facility can be displayed as graphic images or printed as a materials list. Figure 17-1 depicts the general structure of this architecture.

The primary benefits of a data-centric architecture include:

- *Data Integrity:* Data is entered once, at any time; erroneous, duplicated data is not possible.
- *Design Reuse:* Accurate, reliable data are available when needed.
- *View-Generation:* Alternate views of the data are facilitated by a single source of data, which means the same data is always displayed.
- *Process Flexibility:* The data management process is not constrained to application usage or sequence.
- *Data Interaction Independent of Application:* Data can be accessed by the user through multiple applications.
- *Scalability:* The database can grow with application and domain needs.

Software Paradigms, By Stephen H. Kaisler
ISBN 0-471-48347-8   Copyright © 2005 John Wiley & Sons, Inc.

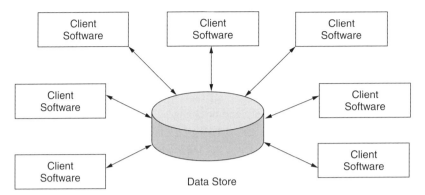

Figure 17-1. Data-centric general structure.

17.1 DATABASE SYSTEMS

A *database* is a collection of related data, that is, known facts that can be recorded and have an implicit meaning. A database has the following properties (Elmasri and Navathe 2003):

- It is a logically coherent collection of data with some inherent meaning.
- It is designed, built, and populated with data for a specific purpose. It has an intended group of users and some preconceived applications in which these users are interested.
- It represents some aspects of the real world called the *miniworld*.
- Changes to the miniworld are reflected in the database.

17.1.1 Database Management Systems

Database management systems (DBMSs) provide repositories for storing and managing data. A DBMS usually implements a data structure paradigm. A central assumption is the separation of the logical definition of data from the underlying physical implementation. Underlying the logical structure of a database is the concept of a *logical data model*. The most common are flat files, indexed sequential files, network structures (e.g., the CODASYL model), and relational systems. Object databases have slowly emerged as a powerful model, but the lack of standards for representation and implementation and concerns over scalability and performance have limited their general acceptance.

Database management systems are general purpose software systems designed to manage large quantities of data. They support the definition of storage structures and provide data manipulation mechanisms. The main functional areas of a DBMS include the following (Abiteboul et al. 1995):

- *Persistence:* Data managed in DBMS should be persistent; that is, its life span should extend beyond that of a particular application so that it may be reused later.

- *Concurrency Control:* The DBMS must support simultaneous access to shared information in an environment presenting a coherent database state to each database user.

- *Data Protection:* The DBMS should provide integrity control mechanisms to prevent inconsistencies in the stored data, recovery and backup mechanisms to guard against hardware failures, and security mechanisms to prevent an unauthorized user from accessing and/or changing sensitive information.

- *Secondary Storage Management:* A DBMS manages amounts of data that are too large to fit in main memory. Thus, the DBMS has to use various techniques to manage secondary storage such as indexing, clustering, and resource allocation.

- *Compilation and Optimization:* The DBMS must provide translation mechanisms between the applications and the external and logical levels.

- *Interfaces:* The DBMS should provide interfaces to define the structure of stored data (data definition languages—DDLs) and to manipulate the stored data (data manipulation languages—DMLs).

- *Distribution:* The DBMS must provide transparent access to multiple locally separated and heterogeneous information sources.

Data entry and retrieval is performed through transactions. The order of update to the database—in the simple case—is determined by the order of the transactions. Modern DBMSs such as DB2, Oracle, Sybase, and SQL Server 2000 all support concurrent transaction processing. As a result, a transaction monitor is usually built into the DBMS to enforce the ACID properties.

Database management systems have been thoroughly discussed in technical papers and books. There is not sufficient room here to fully explore them. So see Section 17.4 for references for further exploration.

17.1.2   Object-Oriented Database Systems

Object-oriented database systems (OODBSs) were developed in order to effectively support the database functionality needed by several classes of applications (e.g., engineering design), which requires more advanced data structuring concepts than those provided by relational database systems. Research in OODBSs started at the beginning of the 1980s and led to the development of systems like O2 (Babaoglou and Marzullo 1993). OODBSs support a data model that is based on a collection of objects. Objects are units of instantiation with a unique identity and a state. In addition to conventional database system's functionality, an OODBS must provide a set of object-related features (Atkinson et al. 1992):

- *Complex Objects:* The OODBS must support the construction of complex objects from simpler ones by applying the appropriate constructors. Basic operators such as retrieve, copy, and delete must be able to deal with complex objects.

- *Object Identity:* The data model must support object identity so that objects exist independent of the value of their state. Two objects can be identical (they are the same object) or equal (the value of their state is equal).

- *Object Encapsulation:* An object encapsulates both program and data. An object in an OODBS thus has both a data part and an operation part.
- *Types and Classes:* Depending on the chosen approach, an OODBS should support either the notion of a type or that of a class. A *type* summarizes the common features of a set of objects. It consists of a type interface and a type implementation. A *class* is a runtime concept that contains two aspects: an object factory used to create new objects and an object warehouse that refers to the set of objects that are instances of the class.
- *Type or Class Hierarchies:* An OODBS must support inheritance. Inheritance allows the factoring out of common specifications and implementations of objects.
- *Overriding, Overloading, and Late Binding:* An OODBS must allow the redefinition of operation implementation for specialized types (*overriding*), the use of identical names for different implementations (*overloading*), and the choice of the appropriate implementation at runtime (*late binding*).
- *Computational Completeness:* The Data Manipulation Language (DML) of an OODBS must allow the expression of any computable function.
- *Extensibility:* The OODBS must allow the definition of new types based on predefined types and must make no distinction between system-defined and user-defined types.

Additional extensions specific to OODBSs include type checking and inference facilities, extended transactions, and version mechanisms.

17.1.3   Active Database Systems

Conventional relational and object-oriented database systems are passive because they only execute actions when explicitly requested to do so through queries or update operations. A database system is called *active* (Dittrich et al. 1995, Widom and Ceri 1996) when, in addition to the "normal" database functionality, it is capable of reacting autonomously to user-defined situations and then executing user-defined actions. The central concept of *active database systems* (ADBSs) is that of *event-condition-action rules* (ECA rules), also called *triggers*, through which the reactive behavior is specified. In general, an ECA rule has the following operational semantics:

- when the defined event occurs,
- if the defined condition is valid, then
- execute the defined action.

The main extensions to the functionality of conventional database systems include event and rule definition, as well as rule execution. This functionality is briefly discussed below.

Rules in Active Database Systems   An ADBS extends a passive DBMS by providing support for *reactive behavior*. This reactive behavior is specified by means of rules, which the data definition language incorporates in operations to define rules. In their most general form, ADBS rules consist of three parts:

- *Event*—which causes the rule to be triggered.
- *Condition(s)*—which are checked when the rule is triggered.
- *Action(s)*—which are performed when the rule is triggered and the condition evaluates to true.

The *rulebase* of an ADBS consists of the set of defined rules. Once the rulebase is defined, the ADBS monitors the relevant events. For each rule, when its event occurs, the ADBS evaluates the condition of the rule; if the condition is true, it executes the rule's action. Multiple rules may be executed for a single event. ADBS features that are related to ECA rules include operations to create, modify, and delete rules, commands to deactivate rules (which are then not triggered by events until the corresponding activation command is executed), and mechanisms to define relative or absolute rule priorities.

Events in Active Database Systems   *Events* in an ADBS denote the occurrence of situations of interest on which a predefined reaction must be performed. An ADBS event can be conceived as a pair (*<event type>*, *<occurrence time>*), where *<event type>* denotes the description of the situation of interest and *<occurrence time>* represents the point in time when the situation actually occurs (Dittrich et al. 1995). The designer of an ECA rule event specifies only the event type. At runtime, multiple events of this type may occur. Event types may refer to occurrences in the database system or its environment. Although no standard presently exists for the supported event types, most ADBSs support the types of events included in Table 17-1.

Event types in an ADBS can either be primitive or composite. *Primitive event types* correspond to basic occurrences and can be directly mapped to a point in time determined by the occurrence type. *Composite event types* are constructed by combination operators or *event constructors*:

- *Logical operators* such as conjunction, disjunction, and negation.
- *Sequence operator* denoting a particular occurrence order for two or more events.
- *Temporal operators* denoting event types defined in relation to another event type.

Composite events are mapped to a point in time based on information about their component events. *Event restrictions* may be defined for composite events to specify conditions that the component events must fulfill in order to form a legal composition. Restrictions may refer to *event parameters* or other properties of the composite event (e.g., that all its components occurred within the same transaction).

Rule Conditions   *Conditions* in ECA rules specify the conditions that have to be satisfied after the event has occurred in order for the action to be executed. Conditions are evaluated once the rule fires, but their exact evaluation time depends

Table 17-1. ADBS event types

Operation	Description
Data modification	These event types are specified based on the modification operations provided by the database system. In a relational ADBS supporting SQL, these can be insert, delete, or update operations on a particular table. In case of an object-oriented ADBS and depending on the provided ML, it may refer to constructor or destructor methods defined for a stored object type.
Data retrieval	These event types are specified based on retrieval operations, for example, a select operation in an active OODBS suporting OQL.
Transactional	These event types are specified based on transaction operations in the ADBS, such as begin or commit of a named transaction program.
Temporal	These event types, which refer to temporal occurrences, include: • *Absolute temporal* event types specified as a specific point in time, for example, 10:00 on September 11, 2001. • *Periodic temporal* event types, as, for example, "every Monday at 12:00" or "every hour."
Application-defined	These event types are specified by allowing the ADBS application to declare an event type, which is then used in ECA rules. The application notifies the ADBS of the occurrence of events of this type.

on the rule execution model of the ADBS (see below). Table 17-2 specifies the types of conditions that can be distinguished.

Rule Actions *Actions* in ECA rules are executed when the rule is triggered and the condition evaluates to true. Table 17-3 presents types of operations that can comprise an ADBS rule action.

If the rule language allows the definition of event parameters, then the action can reference values bound to event parameters. Many ADBSs allow action sequences to be defined in ECA rule actions. Actions may cause the occurrence of further events, leading to cascaded rule triggering.

Rule Execution Model The rule execution model prescribes how an ADBS behaves once a rulebase has been constructed. This behavior includes the semantics of rule processing and the interaction of rule processing with query and transaction processing. As a result, a large number of alternatives with respect to rule execution semantics exist. The dimensions along which a rule execution model is characterized include, for example, rule processing granularity, conflict resolution strategies when multiple rules are triggered, sequential versus concurrent rule processing, and coupling modes. For a detailed discussion of these issues, refer to Widom and Ceri (1996).

Table 17-2. Rule conditions

Condition	Description
Database predicates	These are defined in the formalism for condition expressions supported by the database system, for example, a "where clause" in a relational DBMS.
Database queries	These are defined in the database query language. The meaning is that the condition is true if the query, when executed, produces a nonempty answer.
Calls to procedures/object methods	These are written in an application programming language, which may or may not access the database. If the procedure returns a boolean value, then this is the value of the condition; otherwise, the meaning may be that if the procedure returns data then the condition is true. If the rule language allows the definition of event parameters, then the condition can reference values bound to event parameters.

Table 17-3. Types of RBS actions

Operation	Description
Data modification	*Operations* written in the ADBS DML; for example, object creation or settor method calls in an active OODBS
Data retrieval	*Operations* written in the ADBS DML; for example, accessor method calls in an active OODB
Database commands	Controlling operations, such as transaction control operations (e.g., commit, rollback)
Application procedures and methods	Application-specific procedures, which may or may not access the database

In general, events occur within transaction boundaries and rules are executed within transactions. The transaction in which the event occurs is called the *triggering transaction*. If the rule executes in one or more transactions, then these are called *triggered transactions*. The *coupling modes* (McCarthy and Dayal 1989) determine the relation between rule processing and database transactions. They refer to the transactional relationship between the pairs (*<event triggering>*, *<condition evaluation>*) and (*<condition evaluation>*, *<action execution>*). Possible coupling modes include—but are not limited to—the following:

- *Immediate:* Further rule processing takes place immediately in the same transaction.
- *Deferred:* Further rule processing takes place at the commit point of the current transaction. This mode is useful for enforcing integrity constraints.
- *Decoupled:* Further processing takes place in a separate transaction.

17.2 BLACKBOARD SYSTEMS

A *blackboard architecture* emulates the chalk and blackboard that many of us (and we know who we are!) were used to as kids during our early years of school. Basically, a blackboard is a database into which a process can insert, retrieve, or remove data. It was developed in the AI community as a repository for knowledge to deal with partially defined, complex problems where multiple processes could focus on solving a problem one piece at a time.

Consider the aforementioned chalkboard surrounded by a group of human specialists and experts. The specialists work cooperatively and collaboratively to solve a problem that has been written on the blackboard. Each specialist observes the blackboard and the data written on it. As they see opportunities to apply their expertise, they write additional information on the blackboard. Some are able to contribute immediately, while others must wait until someone else has contributed something toward the problem solution. Each contribution may or may not enable other specialists to apply their expertise and, so, advance the problem toward solution. This process continues until all those assembled agree that a solution to the problem has been achieved.

Now, let us replace the human experts by software processes. Each process can read the blackboard and see what information is there. If sufficient information is available for the process to perform a computation, it does so and places the result back on the blackboard. One or more processes continually test the contents of the blackboard to see if a solution has been achieved. Note that this approach bears some resemblance to the data flow approach discussed in Chapter 13. What differs is the control flow that manages the central repository. Figure 17-2 depicts a modern compiler implemented using the blackboard architecture.

In a blackboard system, the components will be the knowledge sources and the connector is just the control mechanism.

Blackboard technology was developed in the early 1970s. One of the first blackboard systems was used to implement the Hearsay-II speech recognition system at

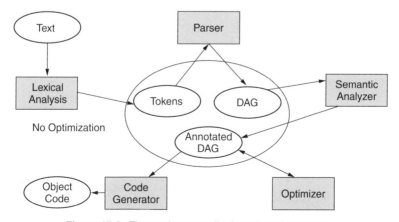

Figure 17-2. The modern compiler in a shared repository.

Carnegie-Mellon University (Erman et al. 1980). Several books have explored other blackboard systems, including those by Engelmore (Englemore and Morgan 1988) and Jagannathan et al. (1989). Nii (1986a, 1986b) describes a detailed architecture for a blackboard system and several applications.

17.2.1   Structure of the Blackboard System

The generic structure of a blackboard system is depicted in Figure 17-3.

Knowledge sources (KSs) are represented by independent processes. They contain computational code and world- and application-specific knowledge. A KS reacts to changes in the content on the blackboard.

The blackboard is a shared memory structure that contains the entire representation of the problem or application state. KSs communicate through the blackboard by posting new data or information to it and retrieving information from it. Whenever data is changed on the blackboard, a control component notices that change. It determines which KSs are interested in that data and builds a queue of KSs that will be activated to interact with the blackboard. A scheduler activates each KS on the pending KS queue with a message that describes the data that has been changed. When a KS is activated, it processes the message. It then decides whether to read the data, perform some computation, and, possibly, write some data back to the blackboard.

17.2.2   Problem-Solving Models

Three problem-solving models can be used in a blackboard system:

- *Backward (or Deductive) Reasoning:* Knowing a given solution, the application works backward to determine what data support that solution.

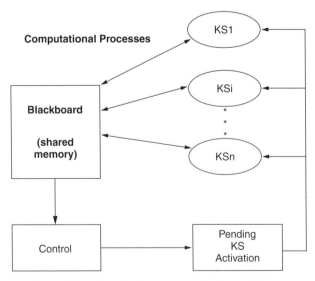

Figure 17-3. Generic Structure of a Blackboard System.

- *Forward (or Inferential) Reasoning:* Knowing a given set of input data, the application works forward toward a solution using appropriate criteria or metrics to determine when a solution has been found.

- *Opportunistic Reasoning:* One or both of the above methods may be used depending on the availability of initial information.

17.2.3   Role of Knowledge Sources

In the human metaphor given in the opening paragraphs of this section, the human specialists possess different areas and degrees of expertise. Each specialist is a self-contained expert on some aspects of the problem and can contribute independently of the other specialists in the room.

The knowledge sources in a blackboard system also possess this functional modularization of expertise. Each KS can solve certain aspects of the problem. No KS requires any other KS to make its contribution. However, it is assumed that no KS can solve the problem entirely on its own.

This independence provides the blackboard system designer some powerful capabilities. Just like data flow systems, KSs can be replaced, enhanced, added, or subtracted from the blackboard system at any time.

Like object-oriented systems, the KSs encapsulate their local knowledge and problem-solving expertise from external viewers. It does not matter how each KS works as long as it contributes to the problem solution.

17.2.4   Advantages and Disadvantages of Using a Blackboard

Typically, a blackboard system is used when there is no deterministic way to solve a problem. Rather, the problem is solved—to the extent it can be—through opportunistic and incremental changes in knowledge about the problem state. Each KS incorporates some expertise that contributes to the solution. Each KS may be dependent on raw data (e.g., external events) or processed information from other KSs. The key to solving such problems is that at each step there may be many options for decision-making leading to the next step in the problem solution. Some or all of these options must be explored; it is often best to explore them in parallel and exchange information, which helps to eliminate choices that do not lead to satisfactory or optimal solutions.

The blackboard model is useful when diverse approaches are needed to solve a problem. This is especially true of problems for which there are no deterministic solutions or problems whose nature changes with time. Different computational methods, embodied in the KSs, can be used to attack the problem from several different perspectives. For example, if the problem involves both diagnosis of a problem and planning and executing corrective actions, multiple diagnostic techniques may be required to identify the problem and its causes. Equally so, multiple corrective actions may need to be taken requiring different planning tools.

One of the disadvantages of the blackboard system (as with many other systems) is that its problem solving is only as good as the input data, the fidelity of the computational processes, and the initial world knowledge. Errors in both the input data and the world knowledge can have a significant compounding effect.

Another disadvantage is scalability. Substantial effort is required to develop a blackboard system. So it does not scale down to simple problems. Each KS is typically a complex program in its own right because it embodies a substantial amount of expertise. Developing each of these KSs may require considerable effort.

17.3 THE LINDA MODEL AND LANGUAGE

Linda is not an independent programming language, but a set of constructs that are embedded into an existing programming language as an extension that facilitates distributed and parallel programming. Linda was developed by David Gelerntner (Ahuja 1986, Carriero and Gelerntner 1990). In effect, Linda implements a primitive blackboard facility where the control resides in the application. More information on Linda can be found at the Linda Group's website at Yale University: http://www.cs.yale.edu/Linda/linda.html.

17.3.1 Linda Objects

Linda utilizes two fundamental objects: tuples and tuple spaces. A *tuple* is a collection of any number of *fields*. Each field has a fixed data type associated with it, which is drawn from the underlying language. A field can be either "formal" or "actual." Formal fields are place holders with types but no values. Formal fields are created by adding a "?" in front of a variable of the language. An "actual" field has a value of the associated type. The definition of Linda places no constraints on the use of types of the underlying language.

A *tuple space* is simply a collection of tuples. The tuple space is a bag and not a set, so it may contain several copies of the same tuple. The tuple space is the fundamental medium of communication in Linda. Linda processes communicate through the tuple space—the sender interacts with the tuple space and the receiver interacts with the tuple space. Figure 17-4 depicts a simple tuple space.

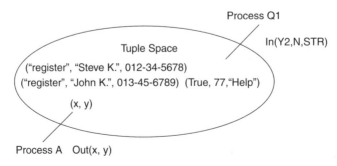

Figure 17-4. Linda tuple space.

17.3.2   Linda Operators

Linda consists of six operators:

- The OUT operator inserts a tuple into the tuple space.
- The IN operator extracts a tuple from the tuple space. It finds a tuple that "matches" its arguments.
- The RD operator is similar to IN, except that it does not remove the matched tuple from the tuple space—it leaves it unchanged in the tuple space.
- INP is a nonblocking predicate that acts like IN.
- RDP is a nonblocking predicate that acts like RD.
- The EVAL operator allows the insertion of a tuple into the tuple space and can be evaluated at a later time.

These are the basic Linda operators. Other implementations have defined additional operators. Indeed, an implementer can extend the Linda operator set as desired as long as the basic six operators are included.

17.3.3   Tuple Matching

The IN and RD operators work by tuple matching, for example, comparing a template against the tuples stored in the tuple space.

A template M and a tuple T match if:

1. M and T have the same number of fields.
2. Corresponding fields have the same types.
3. Each pair of corresponding fields FM and FT (in M and T, respectively) match. Two fields match only if:

   - Both FM and FT are actuals with "equal" values.
   - FM is a formal and FT is an actual.
   - FT is a formal and FM is an actual.

If a template matches a tuple, then any formals in the template are assigned values from the tuple.

If no matching tuple can be found for a template of an RD or IN operation, then these operations block and the process awaits for a tuple to appear. This permits synchronization among different processes. INP and RDP attempt to locate a matching tuple and return 0 if they fail and 1 if they succeed. If they succeed, then any formals in the template of the INP or RDP are assigned values from the tuple that matched the template.

The OUT operator inserts the tuple into the tuple space after the evaluation of all fields contained in its arguments. For example,

```
r = in("sphere-1", ?r);
out("VOL =", compute_sphere_volume(r)) ;
```

will result in calling the function `compute_compute_sphere_volume(r)` first and then depositing the tuple with the value returned by that function in the second field. It is equivalent to

```
r = in("sphere-1", ?r);
v = compute_sphere_volume(r);
out("VOL =", v) ;
```

The EVAL operator allows the insertion of a tuple that is not completely evaluated into the tuple space with the implication that it will be evaluated at some future time. For example, consider the following:

```
r = in("sphere-1", ?r);
eval("VOL =", compute_sphere_volume(r)) ;
```

Here, the tuple inserted into the tuple space is `("VOL=", compute_sphere_volume(r))`. In fact, a process is created that executes the function invocation `compute_sphere_volume(r)` and places the value in the tuple. For lengthy computations, rather than wait for the computation to complete when the OUT operator is used, the EVAL operator allows the computation to proceed concurrently with other program or tuple space activity.

17.3.4   Linda Issues

Linda is nearly close to the minimal information repository system that one can implement. On the other hand, with some analysis, Linda can evolve into a powerful capability.

Linda has been implemented in concurrent and distributed environments. In distributed environments, however, Linda makes no provision for processor failure, for example, assuming that they will not fail. Linda must be extended to specify the processor ID of the tuple space in which data are to be stored. If a processor should fail, the application must attempt to recover from the failure. Linda has no recovery mechanisms built into its code.

17.4   FURTHER READING

Database Management Systems

Connolly, T. and C. Begg. 2001. *Database Systems: A Practical Approach to Design, Implementation, and Management*. Addison Wesley, Reading, MA.

Date, C. J. 2003. *An Introduction to Database Systems*, 8th Ed. Addison Wesley, Reading, MA.

Kimball, R., L. Reeves, M. Ross, and W. Thornwaite. 1998. *The Data Warehouse Lifecycle Toolkit*. John Wiley & Sons, Hoboken, NJ.

Rob, P. and C. Coronel. 2001. *Database Systems: Design, Implementation, and Management*, 5th Ed. Course Technology, Boston, MA.

Data-Centric Systems

Bancilhon, F., C. Delobel, and Paris C. Kanellakis. 1992. *Building an Object-Oriented Database System, The Story of O2*. Morgan Kaufmann, Los Altos, CA.

Corkill, D. 1991. "Blackboard Systems." *AI Expert* 6(9):40–47. Available at `http://www.bbtech.com/bibli.html`.

Craig, I. 1995. *Blackboard Systems*. International Specialized Book Services, Bristol, UK.

Embley, D. 1998. *Object Database Development: Concepts and Principles*. Addison Wesley, Reading, MA.

Gelernter, D. and Nicholas Carriero. 1992. "Coordination Languages and their Significance". *Communications of the ACM* 35(2):97–107.

Harrington, J. 1999. *Object-Oriented Database Design Clearly Explained*. Morgan Kaufmann, Los Altos, CA.

17.5 EXERCISES

17.1. Figure 17-2 depicts a modern compiler implemented as a shared repository or blackboard architecture. Using Linda develop a small compiler for arithmetic expressions.

17.2. Design an error recovery mechanism for Linda. [Research Problem]

17.3. Discuss the similarities and differences between active data-base systems and blackboard systems.

18

CONCURRENT SOFTWARE ARCHITECTURES

The term "concurrent programming" has often been reserved for the type of programming activities and mechanisms that support simultaneous activities in a software application. Feldman (1990) has defined concurrent programming as "an approach to achieving a more faithful representation of objects in the world being modeled by a program."

Decomposing an application into multiple processes is important in single-user applications since it allows these processes to execute simultaneously on a multiprocessor system. This same application can still be run on a uniprocessor, but the concurrency is apparent rather than real (Kaisler 1997). Apparent concurrency occurs because—from the viewpoint of any process—there are other processes with whom it communicates but for whom it knows nothing about how fast or when they execute.

Our focus in this chapter is to examine concurrent software architectures. Previous chapters have examined some basic software architectures. Each of these might be implemented as concurrent systems. Certainly, pipe and filter stages and client–server modules can be distributed across multiple machines.

18.1 BASIC CONCEPTS

A *concurrent system* typically has many parts (processes) running at the same time. The *degree of concurrency* is the number of parallel operations that can occur simultaneously. It is based on the unit of granularity. In real concurrency, it is limited by the number of physical processors.

Software Paradigms, By Stephen H. Kaisler
ISBN 0-471-48347-8   Copyright © 2005 John Wiley & Sons, Inc.

$$
\begin{array}{ll}
X := 2; & : P \\
\\
Y := A = B; & : Q \\
\\
Z := \sin(30.0); & : R
\end{array}
$$

Figure 18-1. Simple concurrency example.

18.1.1   Fine-Grained Versus Coarse-Grained Concurrency

Consider the sequence of statements in Figure 18-1. The statements are independent of each other; that is, the execution of any statement does not depend on the execution of any of the preceding statements. If we had three processors, we could execute the statements P, Q, and R in parallel—assigning one statement to each processor. We often denote that statements can be executed in parallel by the notation:

$$P \parallel Q \parallel R$$

This means that P, Q, and R could be executed in parallel, but do not *have* to be executed in parallel.

If there is one execution of the programming containing the three statements in which the execution of P, Q, and R overlaps in time, then we say they are *concurrent* with respect to each other. At the statement level, we call this *fine-grained parallelism*.

From this example, we can extend the notion of concurrency to processes executing under the control of an operating system. This is sometimes referred to as *coarse-grained parallelism* because the concurrency takes place between processes composed of multiple statements.

18.1.2   Coarse-Grained Systems

A *process* is an artifact of the operating system (OS). A process consists of an allocation of memory, protected from all other memory and processes running at the same time. Each time you start an application under the OS you launch a new process.

A given process may have one or more threads of execution. Typically, these threads share some resources, such as memory and access to open files. Threads are often called "lightweight processes," with little overhead but less protection from one another.

Threads are the mechanism by which your application can appear to do more than one thing at a time. A typical multithreaded application may be writing to the disk while it is reading from the database, at the same time that it is updating its display. Another very important use of threads is in server applications that support multiple users. Each new user is given a separate thread of execution for their data.

A *multiprogramming system* is one that allows two or more programs to run at the same time. On Unix, each program is executed as a process. A *multithreaded system* is one that allows a single program to do more than one thing at a time. In Ada 95, tasks are actually implemented as threads because they share the program's address space. The difference is the context in which the concurrent activities can occur. Multiprogramming systems schedule and manage many processes at once. Multi-threaded systems may have one process with many threads sharing a common address space. A multiprogramming system may have many processes running, each with many threads running.

Threading, done well, can greatly increase the performance of an application. If the system would otherwise be waiting to print or to read data from the disk, the ability to continue working can be a great benefit.

However, there can be adverse effects on performance by using threads. Many applications are actually slowed down by the addition of threads. If two tasks are going to execute in parallel, in memory and without human intervention, multi-threading can make them both go slower than they otherwise would, as the operating system must switch back and forth between the two threads. Each thread switch brings a bit of overhead due to saving and restoring the necessary data in memory.

This said, however, we believe that the best way to build large systems successfully is to provide an environment in which each user (human or thread) feels that the resources of the entire computer system are available to him.

We'll not explore the mechanisms for concurrent programming here because there are many excellent books that provide a detailed description and analysis of these mechanisms; see Section 18.6.

18.1.3   Process Interaction

Multiple processes in an application cooperate through communication. Communication may be either synchronous or asynchronous. The simplest form of interaction is synchronized message passing along *channels*. Simple channels can be either point-to-point or buffered. Figure 18-2 depicts a simple point-to-point channel.

A can write on Channel c at any time but must wait for a read operation by B to retrieve the value. Similarly, B can read from Channel c at any time but must wait for a write. Only when both A and B are ready to communicate, can the communication proceed over Channel c. This models the basic Ada 95 rendezvous.

We can decouple the communication between A and B so that they can proceed independently, by buffering the channel between them, as depicted in Figure 18-3.

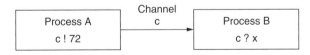

Figure 18-2. A Simple Point-To-Point Channel.

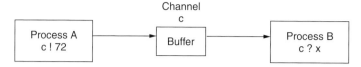

Figure 18-3. Buffered channel.

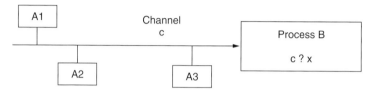

Figure 18-4. An any-to-1 channel.

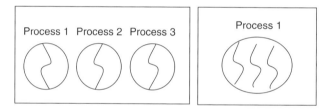

Figure 18-5. Threads model.

We can implement the buffer as either a shared storage location or another process that mediates between Processes A and B. The buffer provides temporary storage for the value passed along Channel c. So A can write to the buffer and continue to execute; then, later, B can read from the buffer.

However, more complex channel structures can also be implemented. Occam, for example, supports any-to-1, 1-to-any, and any-to-any channels. An any-to-1 channel is depicted in Figure 18-4. Here, Processes A1, A2, or A3 can communicate with Process B. This model emulates multiple clients communicating with a database server, for example.

18.1.4   Threads

A *thread* is a locus of control through a process' instructions. Unlike a process, all threads share the address space of the program. As a result, synchronization and mutual exclusion mechanisms are required to prevent threads from conflicting with one another. Threads are sometimes referred to as "lightweight processes." Multiple threads may execute within a single process as depicted in Figure 18-5.

Threads exhibit *apparent concurrency* (Kaisler 1997) or psuedoparallelism. From the perspective of the individual thread, each thread seems to be running in parallel. But viewed from a system perspective, threads run one at a time.

Processes Versus Threads

A *process* is a group of resources:

- An address space (e.g., memory allocation)
- A program image (e.g., an executable image)
- File handles, child process ids, accounting data, etc...
- A unit of resource ownership

A *thread* is:

- A program counter (whose range is over the address space)
- Registers and CPU state
- Stack/heap of called procedures and data
- A unit of dispatching (execution path through program)

Threads provide a useful programming model for asynchronous behavior because they can encapsulate units of work that can then be scheduled for execution at run-time, based on the dynamic state of a system.

Threads Models There are two basic models for threads: the POSIX model and the Microsoft model. POSIX threads (Pthreads), originally developed for Unix-based systems, have been implemented for many other operating systems as well. These are described in POSIX 1003.1-2001 (IEEE 2001, Butenhof 1997). Microsoft developed its own model for threads for Windows NT/2000. These are often called Win32 threads (Lewis and Berg 1996). Java has its own version of threads, which are managed within the JVM. This makes Java threads portable and enables the JVM to support concurrency on any machine on which it is implemented.

Threads models are often differentiated by the level of operating system support. Modern operating systems support multiple threads per process, but with different support mechanisms. Table 18-1 describes the type of support for several modern operating systems.

Threads can be further differentiated by whether they are user-level threads, kernel-level threads, or both. Kernel space threads are implemented at the very basic foundations of the operating system itself. User space threads avoid the kernel but are limited to a single user process and perform "cooperative multitasking" within the process. Table 18-2 differentiates these implementations further.

Advantages and Disadvantages Threads are thought to be cheaper and easier to use than multiple processes for several reasons. Running multiple threads over

Table 18-1. Operating system support for threads

Operating System/ Environment	Support
Solaris	Multiple thread support within OS
Windows 2000	Multiple thread support within OS
Linux	Multiple thread support within OS
Java	Multiple thread support within JVM
Macintosh OS X	Multiple thread support within OS

Table 18-2. Description of thread types

User-level threads

- The OS kernel is not aware of the existence of threads.
- Thread management is performed by a thread library that is an extension to the OS or implemented by a programming language (such as Java).
- Thread switching does not require kernel mode privileges.
- Scheduling is application specific; different scheduling algorithms may be used for each application.
- Thread states are independent of process states.
- Most system calls are blocking calls.
- Two threads in a process cannot run on two different processors.

Kernel-level threads

- All thread management is done by the kernel using the vendor model.
- Programmers use API for the kernel thread facility (embedded in kernel).
- Kernel maintains context information for processes and their threads.
- Switching between threads requires kernel intervention.
- Processor scheduling is performed on a thread basis; threads can be scheduled to multiple processors (if available).
- Blocking is done on a thread level.
- Kernel routines may be multithreaded.

Hybrid user and kernel threads

- Thread creation is done in user address space, as are scheduling and synchronization.
- Processes are managed in kernel address space.
- Mapping is between kernel threads and user threads.
- These are good for user-level parallelism when logical parallelism does not need to be supported by physical parallelism.

the same address space is thought to be cheaper than running multiple copies of the same program as individual processes because the interprocess communication mechanism can be time-consuming.

A context switch between two threads is also thought to be cheaper than a context switch between two processes because less information needs to be saved at each context switch, and the OS does not need to change the memory mapping. Multiple threads share the I/O ports of the program (process) in which they are running.

Shared memory programming with threads is a natural programming model for shared memory machines. A single program text initially starts executing on one processor. This program may execute a statement like `spawn(aProcess,0)`, which will cause some other processor to execute the code associated with `aProcess` with argument 0 as a separate process. Subroutine `aProcess` can "see" all the variables it can normally see according to the scoping rules of the serial language. The main program that spawned `aProcess` can later wait for `aProcess` to finish with a barrier statement, go on to spawn other parallel subroutine calls, and so on.

However, user space threads cannot take advantage of symmetric multiprocessors (SMPs), because a single user address space is assigned to a single processor, each with its own memory.

However, there are also some disadvantages to using threads. Threads are difficult to program, particularly if the implementing programming language does not provide first class support for mutual exclusion and synchronization mechanisms. Because threads arose from the Unix operating system and the C programming language, they have a distinctly C flavor. C and C++ do not provide first class support for threads, but rely on the underlying operating system. This requires that the programmer develop extra code to use them properly within their programs. We contrast this with the implementation of tasks in Ada 95 and Java threads.

18.2 PARALLEL PROGRAMMING

The fundamental premise of parallel processing is that running a program in parallel on multiple processors is faster than running the same program on a single processor. To achieve this desired speed-up, the program must be decomposed so that different data or instructions can be parceled out among the processors, allowing simultaneous execution. When it works, you get the combined speed and memory of multiple computers working together to solve your problem. This can only work if your problem contains concurrency, that is, multiple activities or tasks that can take place at the same time.

Parallel programming, then, is the process of writing a program that can be run on multiple processors. The job of the parallel programmer is to find this concurrency, develop algorithms for it, and implement programs that can use it. This concurrency is often called *exploitable concurrency*. In some cases, the source of concurrency is obvious. In other cases, you will need to dig deeply into the problem to understand where the concurrency lies. Sometimes, you will need to completely recast the problem and rethink about its solution structure in order to find the exploitable concurrency.

In general, the performance gain of parallel operations should be proportionate to the number of processors participating in the computation. In some cases, the gain may be greater, for example, two processors have twice as much memory as one processor. But the gain is dependent on the particular architecture and how the software architecture maps to the hardware architecture. In most cases, however, the gain is somewhat less, because parallel processing inevitably requires a certain amount of communication and synchronization overhead. Communicating even a small amount of data can be more time-consuming than any single computation. Minimizing communications costs and idle time among processors is key to achieving optimized parallel performance.

A parallel program reduces overall runtime by sharing the work to be done among many processors. To achieve such a reduction in runtime, several threads—independent units of computation—are executed on different processors. Introducing the concept of threads means that mechanisms for generating threads, synchronizing threads, communicating data between threads, and terminating threads have to be established. These aspects of program execution constitute the dynamic behavior of a parallel program. Clearly, the dynamic behavior of a parallel program is significantly more complex than that of a sequential program.

Parallel programming arises from the availability of multiple processors. The standard classification of machines, which is largely due to Flynn (1972), is depicted in Figure 18-6.

SIMD and MIMD are the focus of much parallel programming effort. SIMD is often divided into Vector SIMD and Parallel SIMD. Examples of Vector SIMD machines are the Cray-1/XMP/YMP families, the NEC SX-2, and the Fujitsu VP2

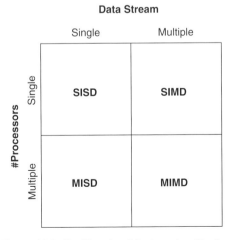

Figure 18-6. Traditional architecture classification.

machines. Examples of Parallel SIMD machines are the Connection Machine CM-1/CM-2 and the MasPar MP-1/MP-2. Examples of MIMD machines include the Cray J90 family, the Connection Machine CM-5, the Kendall Square KSR-1, and the IBM SP1/SP2.

Many existing parallel programming languages require the programmer to explicitly specify these aspects of parallel program execution. Objects specific to parallel execution, like semaphores and monitors, are used to describe synchronization between threads. Managing these new objects, however, adds a new dimension of complexity to program development. For example, the results of the parallel program might become nondeterministic. The design of robust, large-scale parallel systems becomes a daunting challenge.

18.2.1   Embarrassingly Parallel

An *embarrassingly parallel* problem is one in which we have concurrent execution by a collection of independent tasks. Once the tasks have been defined, the potential for concurrency is (almost) obvious. While the source of the concurrency is often obvious, taking advantage of it in a way that makes for efficient execution can be difficult. The challenge in implementing embarrassingly parallel algorithms is to allocate tasks so that they all finish their work at about the same time and, thus, balance the computational load among the available processors. *Near embarrassingly parallel* problems have two added steps in that the initial data is distributed to independent processors and the final results must be aggregated for presentation or further analysis.

The general problem structure underlying an embarrassingly parallel problem is depicted in Figure 18-7. Here, we assume that for i and j two different values of the loop index, subsolution(P, i), does not depend on subsolution(P, j). Thus, the original problem can be decomposed into N independent subproblems such that we can solve the whole problem by solving all of the subproblems and then combining the results.

If the function compute_P modifies only local variables, then we can partition this loop across the available number of processors without affecting the outcome, as long as each is executed exactly once. All the subproblems are defined before

```
Problem P;
Solution problemSolution;
Solution subsolutions[N];
for (i = 0; i < N; i++)
   {
   subsolutions[i] = compute_subsolution(P, i);
   }
problemSolution = compute_P(subsolutions);
```

Figure 18-7. Embarrassingly parallel problem.

computation begins. Each subsolution is saved in a distinct variable (array element), so the computation of the subsolutions is completely independent.

Image processing and manipulation is a rich domain for problems of this sort. So are many 3-D modeling problems involving dynamical solutions that are mapped to a grid architecture. For example, given a large image, groups of pixels, usually square or rectangular, are distributed to multiple processors. Geometrical transformations such as shifting, scaling, clipping, and rotation can be applied to each group.

Here is an extract of a program to perform this kind of computation:

```
/* for each process */
for (i = 0, row = 0 ; i < MRows ; i++, row = row+10)
  {
  send(row, Pi);
  } /* send row number */

for (i = 0 ; i < M ; i++) /* initialize temporary map */
  for (j = 0 ; j < M ; j++)
    {
    temporary_map[i][j] = 0;
    }

/* for each pixel */
for (i = 0 ; i < (M*N) ; i++)
  {
  /*accept new coords */
  recv(oldrow,oldcol,newrow,newcol, Pany)
  if !((newrow<0)||(newrow>=M)||(newcol<0)||(newcol>=N))
    {
    temporary_map[newrow][newcol]=map[oldrow][oldcol];
    }
  }

/* update bitmap */
for (i = 0 ; i < M ; i++)
  for (j = 0 ; j < N ; j++)
    {
    map[i][j] = temporary_map[i][j];
    }

Slave:

/* receive row number */
recv(row, Pmaster);
for (oldrow = row ; oldrow < (row+10) ; oldrow++)
  for (oldcol = 0 ; oldcol < N ; oldcol++)
    {
    /* transform coords */
```

```
newrow = oldrow + delta_x; /* shift in x direction */
newcol = oldcol + delta_y; /* shift in y direction */
/* send result to master */
send(oldrow,oldcol,newrow,newcol, Pmaster);
}
```

Another formulation of an embarrassingly parallel problem is to execute multiple copies of a sequential program with each copy using different parameters—an SPMD approach. We do this to explore a solution space in which we know the solutions are independent.

Grid computing, a recent approach to implementing parallel architectures inexpensively, provides a means of supporting distributed, large-scale computations. Foster and Kesselman (1999) describe it as "computing power from a plug in the wall." The basic idea is that one shouldn't need to care about the location where data is being processed. What is important are speed, safety, and reproducibility of results. This is an obvious analogy with the electrical power grid: you do not need to know where electrical power is being produced. All that is important to you is that it is delivered to your home in a reliable way.

18.2.2   Variations on a Theme

Massengill, Mattson, and Sanders (1999) describe some common variations of the embarrassingly parallel architecture.

Accumulation Via Shared Data Structure   Some computations accumulate subsolutions in a shared data structure because other processes need access to partial or whole subsets of the subsolution data. The computations are no longer independent since access to the shared data structure must be synchronized. However, concurrency can be obtained if the order in which data is added to the subsolutions does not affect the result.

Transaction processing is a good example of this variation. Individual transactions are processed independently. However, the transactions are all directed toward a single database. Consider a bank ATM transaction as a concrete example. In general, transactions should not interfere with each other since a person can only process one ATM transaction at a time. But suppose both husband and wife use the same account and perform ATM transactions at two different machines. Thus, there is a need for synchronization on the shared data structure—at both the database and the individual account level.

Other Than a Complete Solution   The normal termination criterion is for all tasks to be complete in order for the problem to be regarded as solved. For some problems, it may be possible to obtain a solution without completing all tasks. For others, it may not be possible to determine if a complete solution exists, and so it is necessary to determine when a partial solution is enough. For example, if we are searching for an item in a large search space and we know it exists, then the search can stop as soon as the subspace in which the item resides is found. In the worst case, the whole space must be searched to find the item.

Partial Subproblem Definition   In some cases, not all subproblems are known initially. Some subproblems are generated during the solution to the problem. Each subproblem may be assigned to a task, but new tasks are created dynamically as new subproblems are generated. This makes the computational time and effort associated with finding the solution difficult to determine. It may also be difficult to ensure that the termination condition will be met.

18.2.3   Motivation for Parallel Programming

There are many reasons for engaging in parallel programming, but all have to do with speed. About fifteen years ago, a set of "Grand Challenges" was proposed for driving the development of parallel processors. Such processors would satisfy the 3T metaphor—teraFLOPs, terabytes, and terabits—equation to computational speed, computational storage, and communication speed. The idea was that such problems could not be solved with current computer technology but might be solvable with the next generation of technology or the one beyond that. Some examples of Grand Challenge problems included modeling of large DNA structures, global weather forecasting, modeling of multiple (more than three) astronomical bodies, and complete 3-D aerodynamical modeling of an airframe.

Sufficient parallel hardware exists to begin attacking these problems, although the processors individually and in the aggregate to fully solve them are not ready. The major challenge of the Grand Challenges is not the hardware, but how to set up the problem, represent the data, distribute the computations and data to different processors, coordinate the individual computations, and aggregate the results. There are no general methods known for accomplishing this task, but there are lots of specialized approaches.

The task is eased somewhat by parallel programming libraries that provide, in effect, virtual machines on which to build parallel programs. We address two of these—PVM and MPI—in section 18.4.3.

18.3   DATA PARALLEL SYSTEMS

Data parallelism means applying the same operation, or set of operations, to all the elements of a data structure. This model evolved historically from SIMD architectures. One of the earliest computer architectures to exhibit data parallelism was the Illiac IV. The simplest examples are operations on arrays such as $C = A + B$, where A, B, and C are arrays, and each entry may be added in parallel. Data parallelism generalizes to more complex operations like global sums, and to more complex data structure like linked lists.

Communication in data parallelism is implicit. If a statement like $C = A + B$ requires communication, because elements of the arrays A, B, and C are stored on different processors, this is done invisibly for the user. Synchronization is also implicit, since each statement completes execution before the next one begins.

18.3.1   A Data Parallel Example

Consider the following example:

$$C = A \times B$$

where, A, B, and C are all matrices of equal rank. Mathematically, this can be expressed as

$$C_{i,j} = \sum_k A_{i,k} B_{k,j}$$

All of the computations can be done in parallel. So some Fortran code for this computation might look like

```
do i = 1,n
   do j = 1,n
      do k = 1,n
         C(i,j) = C(i,j) + A(i,k)*B(k,j)
      continue
   continue
continue
```

Let's assume that we have matrices of the size $bn \times bn$ and a parallel processor having a configuration of $n \times n$ processors, for $b = 2$ and $n = 3$. Processor $P_{i,j}$ computes the (i, j)th block of C. (See Figure 18-8.)

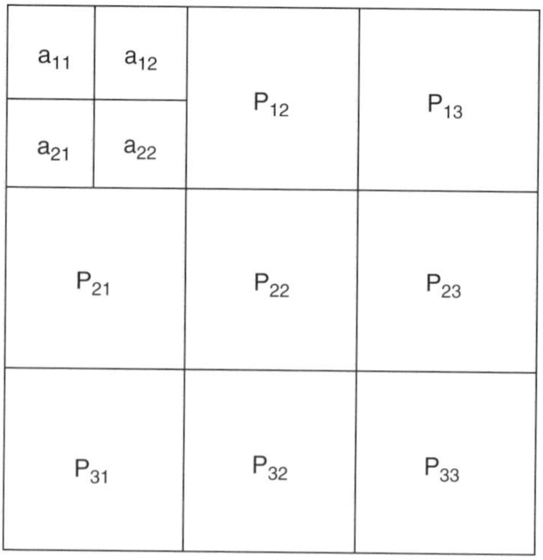

Figure 18-8. Matrix multiplication allocation to physical processors.

The data parallel model is suitable for applications that perform operations on large, regular data sets such as arrays. By partitioning the data set and distributing it to different processors, better performance can be achieved by executing the same operations in parallel on subsets of the original data set.

The data parallel model can be characterized as follows. All processors execute the same program. All data structures are assigned to a rectangular grid of virtual processors. These virtual processors are ultimately mapped to a physical configuration. One or more virtual processors may be mapped to a single physical processor depending on the number of virtual and physical processors.

The physical processor to which the virtual processors have been assigned will compute the values for all data elements assigned to it. Global communication primitives affect communication among the virtual and physical processors. There is an implicit global barrier after each communication, so computation proceeds as a series of communicate–compute pairs of events.

18.3.2 Data Parallel Languages

Data parallel languages have two distinguishing features: a syntax for describing the distribution of data across processors and a method for making clear the parallel nature of calculations.

Fortran 95 and High Performance Fortran (HPF) (`http://www.crpc.rice.edu/HPFF/`) are two variations of the venerable Fortran programming language that support data parallel constructs. Compiler directives allow programmer speciWcation of data distribution and alignment. New compiler constructs and intrinsics allow the programmer to do computations and manipulations on data with diVerent distributions.

High Performance Fortran is a set of extensions to the Fortran 90 standard that permits programmers to specify how data is to be distributed across multiple processors in a parallel programming environment. HPF allows programmers to specify potential parallelism without specifying the low-level details of message passing and synchronization. The HPF compiler assumes the responsibility for scheduling the parallel operations on the physical machines.

The X3J11 ANSI C Committee accepted the Data Parallel C Extensions (DPC) as a technical report in 1994. DPC has "shape" declarations that allow it to describe the distribution of data. Here's a simple example:

```
/* defines a shape, 2 dimensional, 10 x 10 */
shape [20][20] S;
main()
{

   /* defines a parallel variable int of shape S */
   /* parallel variable "a" has a rank of 2 and is 20x20 */
   int sum;
   int:S a;
```

```
/* assigns all 400 elements of parallel variable "a" to 1 */
a = 1;

/* performs summation reduction of parallel variable "a"
into scalar variable "sum" */
sum += a;

printf(" sum %d \n",sum); /* value of sum is 400 */
}
```

A "shape," just like HPF's "template" directive, is a specification for parallel data. In a shape, you must have the following:

• *Rank:* How many dimensions the shape has.
• *Dimensions:* The number of positions in each of its dimensions.
• *Layout:* How a parallel object is distributed.

There are three types of shapes:

• *Fully Specified:* One in which the rank and dimensions are known when the shape is declared, for example, shape [20][20] S;.
• *Partially Specified:* One in which only the rank is defined, for example, shape [ ] [ ] Q;.
• *Unspecified:* One in which there is no rank information, for example, shape X;.

Any standard C variable can be specified as a parallel variable under DPC.

Both HPF and DPC have an array syntax that allows entire arrays to be manipulated with a single statement.

Other than Fortran 90/HPF and DPC, most data parallel programming languages are immature and still in a research mode. HPF and DPC are the only data parallel standard programming languages.

18.3.3   Use of Data Parallel Model

The main feature of the data parallel model is its relative ease when compared to message passing. Data distribution is simple, because it is achieved by compiler directives. All interprocess communication and synchronization are invisible to the developer because they are performed by the underlying runtime system.

The data parallel model scales automatically. It provides data padding to ensure a program will run on any size platform. The trick is to match the program to the right size platform.

Performance depends on how well the compilers and runtime systems handle all interprocess communication and synchronization. The data parallel model is most efficient with minimal, but regular, interprocessor data dependencies.

It is difficult to write data parallel programs because the programmer must visualize the layout and the communications that occur between the virtual processors. At the same time, it is easy to debug data parallel programs because of the single thread. After each communication, each processor can be examined to determine its state.

18.4   MESSAGE PASSING SYSTEMS

The main alternative to data parallel programming on symmetric multiprocessors (SMPs) or scalable parallel processors (SPPs) is a *message passing* model. The message passing model usually involves running some number of sequential programs, possibly independent, which communicate by calling subroutines like send(data, destination_proc) and receive(data,source_proc) to send data from one processor (source_proc) to another (destination_proc). In addition to sending and receiving data, there are usually subroutines for computing global sums, barrier synchronization, and so on.

It is often inconvenient to maintain n independent programs. So message programs usually consist of a single program replicated n times. A program decides what to do by knowing its logical processor number (e.g., id = 1, 2, 3, etc.). Thus, programs on different processors can run more or less independently. This is called SPMD programming (single program, multiple data).

The message passing model is defined as:

- A set of processes uses only local memory.
- Processes communicate by sending and receiving messages.
- Data transfer requires cooperative operations to be performed by each process (a send operation must have a matching receive).

There are many versions of message passing systems. Two that have achieved significant development and usage are Message Passing Interface (MPI) and Parallel Virtual Machine (PVM), because they do not require modification to the host programming language. We'll briefly review these two systems in the following sections.

18.4.1   Synchronous Versus Asynchronous Messages

When messages are transmitted and received between two processes, the nature of the transmission and reception process determines how the two processes will operate.

Synchronous message passing essentially implies that the sender of the message waits until the message is actually accepted by the recipient. Unless and until the recipient reads the message, the sender remains blocked. Figure 18-9 depicts this mechanism.

This is an effective technique to synchronize two processes. Once the message has been read, both processes can proceed. In short, the first one to get to the message

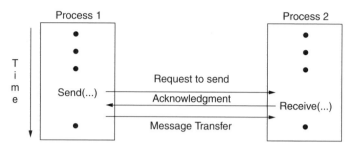

Figure 18-9. Synchronous message passing mechanism.

reading point waits for the other one to catch up. *Rendezvous* is a mechanism in Ada that uses a similar principle, but at the language level. Sending synchronized messages is not very common in most programming languages. But there are many variants of it at the language level, the most famous being *RPC* (remote procedure call). RPC essentially allows one process to invoke a procedure in another process. The caller waits for the call to finish and gets the reply before proceeding. Here, synchronization is implicit but need not be implemented using synchronized messaging primitives.

Asynchronous messages are those where the sender continues immediately, or at least after making sure that the message has reached the other process' message buffer (but the message may not necessarily be read). This allows a program to use network bandwidth more effectively and also overlap computation with message transmission. On the other hand, if any replies are involved, the sender now has to code additionally for collecting replies from all its clients.

Asynchronous messages can also be limited by the number and/or size of the buffers. A sender can't send too many messages to a client that hasn't read anything yet. A quenching mechanism acts to block the sender when it attempts to send. This is how transport protocols like TCP/IP usually work.

18.4.2 Message Passing Interface

The Message Passing Interface (MPI 1994) is a standard, portable message passing library definition developed in 1993 by a group of parallel computer vendors, software writers, and application scientists. The initial version was rather conservative. For example, dynamic tasking was not supported, nor were C++ bindings. In 1997, the standard was revised to the version known as MPI-2 with several enhancements. It encompasses over 100 routines affecting data layout and communication.

MPI, strictly speaking, is a specification, rather than a product. However, a public domain implementation has been provided in C to help implementers understand the nuances of the specification. The design of MPI is intended to hide the operating system specifics from the application program in order to provide the greatest portability in a distributed and heterogeneous environment. Some things are assumed: threads, TCP/IP, a file system, and C, but none of this is required.

A MPI application can be viewed as a collection of concurrent communicating programs. Each program calls functions in the MPI function library. Programs may run on the same processor or distributed processors, whether homogeneous or heterogeneous. Each program has a task identifier or rank.

Specifically, the MPI standard defines the following elements:

- Point to point (P2P) communication.
- Collective operations.
- Process groups.
- Communication domains.
- Process topologies.
- Profiling interface.
- F77 and C bindings.

Versions are available for Fortran, C, and Ada 95 programs. Implementations are available on a wide variety of parallel machines. The current version 1.2.5 is available from `http://www-unix.mcs.anl.gov/mpi/mpich/`. More detailed information can be found in Pacheco (1997) and Snir et al. (1997).

MPI Program Structure   A MPI-based program is a program written in a traditional programming language, such as Fortran or C, but augmented with additional statements that define the program's execution environment and specify and conduct communication.

Every MPI-based program requires three statements:

```
/* the mpi include file */
#include <mpi.h>

/* Initialize MPI */
ierr=MPI_Init(&argc, &argv);

/* How many total PEs are there */
ierr=MPI_Finalize();
```

These statements incorporate accesses to the MPI library, initialize the MPI system, and terminate the MPI system. All other statements are optional but provide considerable flexibility in specifying how the program is to be executed.

Communication   Tasks belong to named task groups. A group allows a set of tasks to perform a restricted set of operations or to receive a broadcast message intended only for members of the group. To isolate messages intended for one group from another, MPI uses the concept of a *communicator*, which establishes a channel for communication among or between groups of tasks. An *intracommunicator* is used for communication among the tasks of a single group. A default intracommunicator,

MPI_COMM_WORLD, includes all available tasks at runtime. An *intercommunicator* is used for communication between tasks in two or more disjoint groups.

Communication is based on sending and receiving messages, which are identified by the sender's ID, the receiver's ID, the message tag or ID, and the communicator. Messages may be sent in four ways: standard, buffered, synchronous, or ready. Both standard and buffered are asynchronous sends. Ready send acts like an interactive chat session. Messages may be broadcast to all members of a task's group. Receiving messages default to a blocking operation, but a nonblocking receive is available as well.

All MPI messages are typed. Each send or receive—blocking or nonblocking, point-to-point or broadcast—must specify a MPI datatype. Primitive data types correspond to the standard C data types, such as MPI_REAL and MPI_INTEGER, but must be mapped to the data types supported by the target machine's compiler. Aggregate data types can be constructed through a record mechanism similar to C's struct operator.

Some combinations of send and receive calls can lead to deadlock. Thus, the user must understand the semantics of these calls. Successive messages sent by one task to another task in the same domain are received in the order in which they are sent.

Performance can be improved by overlapping communication and computation, so a nonblocking send will post the message and return immediately. Similarly, a nonblocking receive accepts the message and returns immediately. Collective communications transmit data among all tasks in a given group. A barrier operation provides a synchronization point for all tasks associated with a communicator.

Topologies   A *virtual topology* is a logical task arrangement that maps the tasks to the underlying problem geometry and the algorithm used to solve the problem. For example, in many numerical problems a 2-D or 3-D grid arrangement is used. But a general topology might be configured according to a graph.

The virtual topology can be used to assign tasks to physical processors in order to improve the performance of communication between given machines and particular tasks. Topology creation functions—either graph-like or Cartesian-like—take a communicator for a set of tasks and create a new communicator that maps the topology over the set of processes.

A Simple Example   Let us examine the classic "Hello, World" program written in MPI:

```
#include <stdio.h>
#include "mpi.h"
main(int argc, char **argv)
   {
   int myrank;        //rank of process
   int np;       //number of processes
```

```
   int source;         //rank of sender
   int destination;    //rank of receiver
   int tag=50;         //tag for messages
   char message[100;

   MPI_Status status;

   MPI_Init(&argc, &argv);
   MPI_Comm_rank(MPI_COMM_WORLD,&myrank);
   MPI_Comm_size(MPI_COMM_WORLD,&np);

if(myrank!=0
   {
   sprintf(message,"Hello from %d!",myrank);
   dest=0;
   MPI_Send(message,strlen(message)+1,
     MPI_CHAR,destination,
     tag,MPI_COMM_WORLD);
   }
else
   {
   for(source=1;source<p;source++)
     {
     MPI_Recv(message,100,MPI_CHAR,source,tag,MPI_COMM
     _WORLD,&status);
     printf("%s\n",message);
     }
   }
MPI_Finalize();
}
```

Setting this up on an appropriate multiprocessor and executing the statement

```
mpirun -np 4 ./helloworld
```

produces the following output:

```
Hello from 1!
Hello from 2!
Hello from 3!
```

18.4.3 Parallel Virtual Machine

Parallel Virtual Machine (PVM) (Sandarac 1990) is a message passing programming system for the development and execution of large concurrent or parallel applications that consist of many interacting, but relatively independent, components. Originally designed to enable a network of heterogeneous Unix computers to emulate a parallel system based on message passing, it has been ported to clusters of workstations, SMPs, and MPPs. PVM was developed by the Heterogeneous Networking Project in 1989 at Oak Ridge National Laboratory, University of Tennessee, and Emory University.

PVM provides a virtual machine implemented as a dynamic set of networked heterogeneous systems, which are managed as a single computer from the application's point of view. It consists of two components: a library of functions that resides on each host computer and a daemon (pvmd).

A PVM application consists of a number of sequential programs, each corresponding to one or more processes in a concurrent program. Each program is compiled for its own machine. One program must be manually initiated on one host; it has the responsibility for activating the rest of the programs, which are known as *tasks*. The programs can be identical but work on different ranges of data, as in the SPMD model, or independent entities, such as in the blackboard model. The number of tasks and their creation and termination are not fixed at program initiation. Each program is identified by a task identifier that is assigned when the task is created. The task ID is used when communicating with other tasks.

Task Communication   Tasks communicate by sending messages to one another. Each message is identified by a task ID and a message tag or identifier. Sending is asynchronous, while receiving messages can be blocking, nonblocking, or timed. At the lowest level, PVM uses pvmd to access TCP/IP for intersystem communication. Messages may be sent to a single task or to multiple tasks through a broadcast function.

Consider the following simple PVM tasks:

P:

```
      . . .
      pvm_spawn(..., &child)
      p1();
      pvm_send(child, waittag);
      pvm_recv(child, gotag);
      p2();
      . . .
```

Q:

```
      dad = pvm_parent();
      q1();
      pvm_recv(dad, waittag);
      q2();
      pvm_send(dad, gotag);
      . . .
```

After the spawn, the two processes run asynchronously on their respective machines. P performs the computation p1, while Q performs the computation q1. Eventually,

P sends a message to Q with tag = waittag. The block receive (pvm_recv) forces Q to synchronize with P. Q performs q2, then sends a message to P with tag = gotag. P is forced to wait for Q because of its blocking receive.

Q could be a server waiting for requests from any number of tasks. The server logic for Q might look like the following:

```
QServer:

    dad = pvm_parent();
    while (1)
      {
      pvm_recv(dad, -1,..., tag);
      switch (tag)
        {
        1: p1(); break;
        2: p2(); break;
        ...
        default:...
      }
      pvm_send(dad, readyforwork,...);
      }
```

18.4.4 Message Passing Status

MPI and PVM are both very mature; other message passing libraries vary in maturity. Research and industry scientists have been working with message passing for many years. The functionality of these libraries is relatively simple and easy to implement. These libraries are critical to all distributed memory parallel computing. Vendors must provide a robust set of libraries to make their products competitive.

In message passing, the development of anything but simple programs is difficult. The programmer must explicitly implement a data distribution scheme and all interprocess communication. It is the programmer's responsibility to resolve data dependencies and avoid deadlock and race conditions. Since the user is required to explicitly implement a data distribution scheme and all interprocess communication, the performance depends on the ability of the developer. Scalability depends on the programmer's design of the application and decomposition of the tasks.

18.4.5 Fortran D Tools

Many people will scoff and say: "Programming in Fortran...that's so ancient." Well, Fortran is still a widely used and widely useful programming language. It is also one that has driven much of the parallel programming system design. Over twenty years ago, George Michael (1980) suggested that he couldn't tell me what the syntax or semantics of programming languages would be in the year 2000, but at least one of them would still be called Fortran. And how right he was!

The Fortran D system grew out of a research effort at Rice University (1997) to develop a suite of tools for Fortran D, an abstract, machine-independent parallel programming language. The D system's philosophy was based on two approaches:

1. Aggressive parallelizing compilers with advanced program analysis and code generation capabilities.
2. Tools that enable a programmer to develop and tune programs at the source language level, without having to understand the complex, machine-dependent code generated by a parallelizing compiler.

The Fortran D tools assisted a user in analyzing a program, instrumenting it, and then displaying and analyzing the collected performance data. Data known or deducible at compile-time was recorded for later integration with performance data that only became available at runtime.

The D system tools were focused on four areas: an editor, automatic data distribution, performance analysis, and a program analysis repository.

See Section 18.6 for additional reading on the D system.

The D Editor   The D Editor was a structured editor for Fortran that provided users feedback about the parallelism and communication in a program. Using multiple windows, the Editor displayed the source code, highlighted nonlocal array references, and displayed loop dependencies in colors indicating the degree of parallelism possible. Another feature was to display the computation and communication cost of the individual procedures and loops, relative to the full program, based on data collected by instrumentation inserted by the compiler.

The dPablo Performance Browser   This browser allowed the user to display and manipulate performance data collected from an instrumented Fortran D program. Performance data and array reference patterns could be correlated with selected code regions within the user's program. Users could review the absolute time spent in executing a procedure. By displaying array reference patterns, users could discern how specific communication events affected array access and see unnecessary data movement due to poor data layout. Performance metrics could be tied to source code lines. So clicking on a source code line would bring up the associated performance data. Users could also examine detailed performance data by processor.

18.5   A PARALLEL PROGRAMMING METHODOLOGY

Parallel hardware architectures have been available since the early 1960s (e.g., the CDC machines). But software that takes advantage of these machines is much less available due to several factors. One is the widespread belief that such software is difficult to write. Another is that the parallel programming systems that are available are difficult to use. And, finally, when we teach parallel or concurrent programming, we focus more on how the parallelism is implemented rather than on finding and exploiting the parallelism in any problem. Much of the experience in parallel or concurrent programming gained by students is minimal and an afterthought to a regular programming or concepts course or taught from a theoretical viewpoint with little pragmatics.

Rather than trying to fix the existing parallel programming environments, the focus should be on how to exploit parallelism. Programmers need tools that enable them to understand and express the concurrency in an algorithm. In other words, we need to solve this problem at the level of algorithm design.

There is a significant body of theoretical work on parallel and concurrent programming. Making these concepts available to algorithm designers and programmers in a usable way is a major challenge.

18.5.1 Motivation

Ideally, we would like to have our parallel programming mechanisms be independent of a particular computer architecture or even a particular programming language. This would allow us to develop programs once but be able to run them on many different machines while choosing the level of performance that we desire.

However, since the motivation for parallel programming is to achieve high performance for specific classes of problems, programming languages and machines are often chosen for a perceived level of performance. Programs are then adapted and customized to the idiosyncrasies of the particular language/machine combination.

When designing parallel programs, it is unclear (at present) whether or not the specification of parallel algorithms can transcend the differences between the architectures on which they will be implemented and the application domains from which problems are drawn. Certain algorithms will perform better on certain architectures. This is addressed in more detail in Section 18.5.5.

At present, obtaining the best performance for a particular algorithm requires that the architectural model for the underlying machine must be reflected through to the programmer. One goal of parallel programming design and language research is whether or not we will ever be able to write a machine-independent program that would perform well on different architectures.

Parallel programming language design is still in its infancy although parallel programming has been conducted for over forty years. It is unclear what kinds of syntactic and semantic constructs should be provided to the programmer by the programming language to help in constructing efficient yet understandable programs that can run either on a particular architecture or on parallel machines in general.

However, one approach is based on the notion of design patterns. If we can find patterns of parallelism and concurrency, we can describe them in a language-independent manner that will allow programmers to understand them but will also identify some of the constraints that will affect their translation into specific programming languages. Much of the work on patterns, as described in Part III, was focused on object-oriented sequential patterns. Only recently has substantial effort been directed to identifying parallel and concurrent patterns (Schmidt 1993, 1995a, 1995b; Massengill and Chandy 1996; Massengill 1999).

In the following sections, we present some of the work of Massengill, Mattson, and Sanders on designing parallel programs.

18.5.2   Choosing a Parallel Programming Model

Choosing a parallel programming model to implement the algorithm for your problem solution requires mapping the units of concurrency in your problem to the units of execution on the computer system that will run the resulting program. Most designers choose one of nine basic parallel programming models to begin their program design and implementation.

The target platform or computer system often constrains the choice of the programming model. The interconnection of the processors, the memory model, the type of processor, and many other factors can eliminate some programming models from consideration.

A good parallel algorithm must strike a balance between two opposing forces. On the one hand, we'd like the algorithm to be abstract, but efficient, so that we can map it to any parallel platform. On the other hand, the algorithm must be adaptable to the target platform architecture in a way that yields satisfactory performance.

18.5.3   Problem Decomposition

To find the exploitable concurrency, you need to break your problem down into parts that can execute simultaneously. The goal of this exercise is to determine the problem's *decomposition*. Decomposition has two aspects. First, you need to determine the stream of instructions that the program executes. You will need to divide this stream into chunks (e.g., threads, processes, or tasks) that can execute simultaneously. Efficient parallel programming is obtained when the tasks execute with minimal need to interact. As the overhead of interaction among processes or tasks increases and even approaches the individual task execution time, the efficiency decreases.

Second, you must consider how the data is used within the program, by which tasks or processes, how and when modified, and how best to divide it among the tasks or processes. When data must be modified by multiple tasks, you need to set up global protection structures to ensure mutually exclusive updates. For shared data, the goal is to design the algorithm so that tasks don't get in each other's way as they work with the data.

In general, it is not clear which should be done first: the task decomposition or the data decomposition. What is clear is that these two dimensions of the decomposition heavily depend on each other and to some extent must be considered together.

Task Decomposition   Task decomposition focuses on grouping together operations that can be performed within concurrently executing entities—which are usually called processes or tasks. These operations should be largely independent of those occurring in other concurrent entities.

Task decomposition is useful if you can visualize the computation as a set of mutually occurring actions that require little interaction. Functions that are repeated on a fixed schedule and are largely self-contained are good candidates for this approach. Massengill et al. (1999) note that this is currently not feasible using automatic means, because it requires an in-depth knowledge of what the solution structure is for the problem.

The best way to start is to specify everything as a task that logically seems so. Don't worry about generating too many task descriptions, because the goal is to identify where the possible concurrency might lie in the program.

At most, you could have one task for each function in your program. However, in most cases, the communication among tasks overwhelms the computation done in tasks. Thus, you need to coalesce subsets of tasks into single tasks. Some experimentation may be required to decide which tasks get collapsed. Usually, this is dependent on how much data must be transferred between tasks. Collapse tasks to eliminate large data transfers through the interprocess communication mechanism.

On the other hand, have enough tasks to keep all of the units of execution busy. This means distributing the work across the tasks so that most of the units of execution are busy all of the time during the main part of the program.

Data Decomposition Data decomposition focuses on examining the data structures and the patterns of data usage in a program. There are several common data structures that can be divided into subsets, such that they can be operated on concurrently. Array manipulation, recursive data structures, and iterations over data structures are specific examples. For example, many large physical problems manipulate large matrices of floating point numbers.

As you examine the data structures, try to determine if there are logical boundaries among subsets, such as the rows or columns in matrices or subsets of a list of data.

As with task decomposition, consider "chunking" the data to minimize the dependencies between the chunks. For example, some algorithms cross rows, columns, or subarrays in a matrix. Allocating rows to different tasks or processors requires communication. The size of the row, column, or subarray and its computational time should greatly exceed the interprocess communication time. So you should scale the data chunk size and the associated computational effort to offset the overheads associated with data dependencies.

18.5.4 Implementing a Parallel Algorithm

To implement a parallel algorithm, we need three pieces of information:

1. The number of tasks or processes.
2. A description of how the problem's data is decomposed onto and shared between the tasks.
3. An ordering among the tasks to express temporal or other constraints.

Implementation involves mapping the abstract tasks to the concrete units of execution of the target platform.

You must understand the constraints that the target platform and its programming environment imposes on your algorithm implementation. One primary constraint is how many units of execution (UEs) your target platform will support. An algorithm that works well for ten UEs may not scale to hundreds of UEs. While you should avoid choosing an absolute number of UEs, you should determine an order of magnitude in order to determine their distribution across physical processors.

Another constraint concerns the interaction among UEs. For example, how will they exchange information? How efficient is the information exchange between processes? What effect on performance will it have? There may be hardware support for information sharing that makes frequent data exchange possible and effective. On the other hand, the processors may be connected by a slow network, meaning information sharing can be inefficient, and so you need to avoid communication whenever possible. These features (and others) have an effect on how you structure your algorithm.

You must also consider the programming environment that you will use. Some programming environments do not support the full flexibility offered by a particular target platform. Understanding the programming environments and what programming models they support is essential to a good implementation.

18.5.5 Select an Algorithm Structure

Given our three pieces of information—the number of tasks, how data is to be shared, and the ordering of the tasks—we need to find an algorithm structure that provides an efficient problem solution. There are three main structures for algorithms:

1. *Organization by Ordering:* There may be well-defined interaction structures among groups of tasks. The key issue is how these groups are ordered with respect to one another. The MVC model for GUIs is an example.
2. *Organization by Tasks:* Some algorithms consist of groups of tasks, where only one group is active at a time and the interactions are among the tasks in a group.
3. *Organization by Data:* The structure and decomposition of the data determine the structure of the algorithm and the interactions among the tasks.

Table 18-3. Algorithm structures

Organizing Principle	Algorithm Structures
Ordering	Pipeline processing
	Asynchronous composition
Tasks	Embarrassingly parallel
	Separable dependencies
	Protected dependencies
	Divide and conquer
Data	Geometric decomposition
	Recursive data

Table 18-3 depicts some of the algorithm structures based on the organizing principle (Massengill et al. 1999).

18.6 FURTHER READING

Concurrent Programming

Bacon, J. 1992. *Concurrent Systems: An Integrated Approach to Operating Systems, Database and Distributed Systems.* Addison Wesley, Wokingham, UK.

Ben-Ari, M. 1990. *Principles of Concurrent and Distributed Programming.* Prentice Hall, Hertfordshire, UK.

Kann, C. W. 2003. *Creating Components: Object Oriented, Concurrent, & Distributed Computing in Java.* Auerbach Publishers, New York.

Schneider, Fred B. 1997. *On Concurrent Programming.* Springer-Verlag, New York.

Schneider, S. 1999. *Concurrent & Real Time Systems: The CSP Approach.* John Wiley & Sons, Hoboken, NJ.

The D System

Adve, V., A. Carle, E. Granston, et al. 1994. "Requirements for Data-Parallel Programming Environments." *IEEE Transactions on Parallel and Distributed Technology* 2(3):48–58.

Hiranandani, S., K. Kennedy, C-W. Teng, and S. K. Warren. 1994. "The D Editor: A New Interactive Parallel Programming Tool." In *Proceedings of Supercomputing '94*, Washington, DC, November 1994.

Kremer, U. 1993. Automatic Data Layout for Distributed-Memory Machines. *Technical Report CRPC-TR93299-S.* Center for Research on Parallel Computation, Rice University. Available at `http://www.cs.rice.edu/~dsystem/techPapers.html`.

18.7 EXERCISES

18.1. Is there a problem that cannot be implemented as a concurrent algorithm? Describe it. What are its characteristics?

18.2. Critics suggest that Fortran is outmoded and that better programs can be written in more modern programming languages (whatever "better" means). Pick a reasonably complex parallel programming problem and demonstrate why it cannot be written in either Fortran D or High Performance Fortran, if you believe it cannot.

18.3. Pick a sequential program. Develop a concurrent version and measure its performance.

18.4. Many multiplayer games are implemented using concurrent systems. Discuss the design problems inherenrt in this approach.

19

SOFTWARE ARCHITECTURE CHALLENGES

Although software architecture has been a nascent discipline for almost ten years, most effort has been focused on modeling and description and little on evaluation and assessment. Additionally, as we begin to use software architectures to drive the system development, we realize that some problems arise due to size and complexity. In this chapter, I try to identify and describe some of these problems and how to resolve them, at least partially.

19.1 SOFTWARE ARCHITECTURE DESCRIPTION

Early software description used "box-and-line" descriptions that depicted the components and their interconnections. Such description captured the syntactic structure, but none of the semantic structure of an architecture. As Garlan (2000) notes, "these informal diagrams cannot be formally analyzed for consistency, completeness, or correctness."

Many languages for describing high-level system designs have been developed and used over the past three decades. Examples include PSL/PSA and SADT. Research in software architectures indicated the need for a new generation of languages referred to as architecture description languages (ADLs). They capture the high-level structure of a software system and provide a basis for a coarse-grained static analysis of the characteristics of these applications. Most support some form of formal analysis. Several systems, particularly those in the defense community, have been described in these languages, but, to date, they have not been widely used in the commercial sector.

Software Paradigms, By Stephen H. Kaisler
ISBN 0-471-48347-8   Copyright © 2005 John Wiley & Sons, Inc.

Another approach is to extend the Unified Modeling Language (UML), which is used to describe software, to support architectural concepts. Armour et al. (2003) describe some modifications to the UML along with a case study. Other authors have also described extensions to the UML, but there has been no standardized approach that combines all of these activities into a single extension.

19.1.1 Architecture Description Languages

DARPA funded multiple efforts to develop ADLs that would capture both syntax and semantics. They provide a conceptual framework, a concrete syntax, and a model for semantics specification. ADLs allow one to reason about the correctness of software systems at a correspondingly high level of abstraction. Accompanying tools help software architects and designers to specify, present, assess, and simulate software architectures. Table 19-1 lists some ADLs, their developers, and their use (`http://www-2.cs.cmu.edu/~acme/adltk/adls.html`).

Table 19-1. Sample ADLs

ADL	Developer	Use
Acme	Carnegie-Mellon University	Supports the integration of multiple models written in different ADLs.
C2	USC ISI (Taylor et al. 1996)	Developed specifically to represent command and control software architectures. Supports an implementation framework and runtime modification of the system.
MetaH	Honeywell (Honeywell 1994)	Specifies real-time aspects of hardware and software; provides support for functional and behavioral characteristics of a system.
ArTek	Teknowledge Corp.	Describes the architecture of large-scale systems as a means of supporting communication and coordination in multicontractor projects, and to document the architecture of the resulting system.
Darwin	Magee (Magee et al. 1995)	Used for the specification, construction, and management of software applications; it is focused on dynamic, concurrent, and distributed systems.
Rapide	Stanford University (Rapide Design Team 1994)	Provides an executable ADL based on a rule–event model for prototyping, simulating, and analyzing software applications.
SADL	SRI	Provides support for describing the structure and semantics of a software application through explicit mappings.
UniCon	Carnegie-Mellon University (Shaw et al. 1995)	Supports architecture construction by interconnecting predefined or user-defined architectural components.
Wright	Carnegie-Mellon University (Allen 1997)	Provides a formal modeling system focusing on connector types and analyses associated with architectural interconnections.

Medvidovic (1997) offers a scheme for classifying and analyzing ADLs based on the support they offer for the three elements of a software architecture: components, connectors, and configurations. He also assesses them with respect to tool support for each language.

All of these languages and systems support architectural design, but each does it with a distinctive approach. However, many of the ADLs bear a strong resemblance to a diminished C/C++; for example, they look more like programming languages than specification languages. As a result, there is no standardization and no way to combine results from one system into another or to verify a representation in one system by recasting it in another system. Some effort has been focused on integrating results, such as the Acme system (Garlan et al. 1997). Actually, Acme is both an architectural interchange language and a system for supporting descriptions written in the language.

19.1.2   An ADL Example

Let's look at an ADL example based on Rapide (Figure 19-1) (Luckham and Veral 1995). Two components are depicted: a Server and a Client. Each component is

```
type Server is interface
action       in Initialize();
             in Compute(Value: Float);
    out Result(Value: Float);

constraint
    match Start -> Initialize'Call -> (Compute'Call *);

behavior
    NewValue : var Float;
begin
    (?x in Float) Compute(?x) => Result($NewValue);;

end Server;

type Client is interface
action       in Result(Value: Float);

    out Initialize();

    out Calculate(Value: Float);
behavior
    InitialValue : var Float := 0.0;
begin

    Start => Initialize;
    Calculate($InitialValue);;

end Client;
```

Figure 19-1. A client–server architecture in Rapide.

```
architecture ClientServer() return root is
C : Client;
S : Server;
connect

    (?x in Float) C.Calculate(?x) => S.Compute(?x);
    (?y in Float) S.Result(?y) => C.Result(?y);

end ClientServer;
```

Figure 19-1. (*Continued*)

modeled with an interface that specifies both the functionality that is provided by the component and the functionality that the component expects to be provided by other components. In Rapide, these functionalities are specified using events. The Server component can receive and process two events: Initialize and Compute. In turn, it generates one event, Result. These events are used at the architectural level to connect components. In this client–server system, the Calculate functionality that is required by the Client component is attached to the function Compute that is provided by the Server component. Thus, whenever the Client component generates a Calculate event, it is received by the Server component as a Compute event.

Most ADLs model the interactions between components as well as describing those components. In Rapide, we specify the relationship between the events that a component receives and the events that it generates. The behavior of the Server component is to produce a single event, Result, for each Compute event that it receives. Also, from the specification we see that the Initialize event is simply consumed by the Server component; no events are produced by the Server component as a direct result of receiving an Initialize event.

Many ADLs also allow the specification of constraints on the behavior of the components and their interactions. The Server component requires that it receive a single Initialize event before it can process any number of Compute events. Such constraints can be used by analyzers to verify the consistency of a system by determining whether any of the constraints are violated.

19.1.3 Architectural Analysis

Software architecture descriptions allow us to reason about some of the properties of the software design at a high level. The quality of a software system is a function of how its features interact in predictable ways. Features arise from the functionality provided by its components. Some properties, such as reliability, performance, and safety, are emergent properties arising from the interaction patterns among a set of components.

If we know the features of two individual components, call them c1 and c2, then reasoning from composition suggests that a function f, such that f(c1, c2), can describe a feature arising from the composition of c1 and c2.

19.1.4 Documenting Software Architectures

The Software Engineering Institute (SEI) has developed guidelines for documenting software architectures (Bachmann et al. 2001, 2002a, 2002b). Good documentation helps to ensure communication between stakeholders and designers.

19.2 DESIGN ISSUES

There are many design issues associated with software architectures. Some of these have to do with the "ilities"—those properties that result from a good software architecture. Others have to do with representation, such as the use of architecture design languages.

19.2.1 Scalability

A critical issue with software architectures is how well they scale. Software architectures should be scalable from small to large applications and from uniprocessors to distributed systems.

Table 19-2 presents my assessment of the scalability of the different software architecture models.

19.2.2 Transparency

Transparency arises from the need to facilitate distributed system construction. The details of behavior and the differences in interoperation mechanisms should be hidden from the users and the applications. Transparency enables the interfacing system to be shielded from certain actions of the interfaced system by encapsulating the activities of the interfaced system and by providing global system information about its use. It minimizes the amount of knowledge required to interact with the target system. And, in turn, this minimizes the structure of the interface required to enable communication between the two systems.

Transparency, however, is a multidimensional issue. Putnam (1997) identifies eight different types of transparency that the system architect must consider (Table 19-3).

Table 19-2. Assessment of software architecture scalability

Software Architecture	Assessment
Call-and-return systems	Limited
Data flow systems	Readily expandable
Virtual machines	Requires coding
Independent component systems	Requires coding; individual components can scale
Data-centric systems	Limited; depends on repository server(s)

Table 19-3. Types of transparency

Type	Definition
Access	Masks differences in data representation and invocation mechanisms to enable interoperability between components
Location	Masks the use of information about location in space when identifying interfaces
Migration	Masks, from an element, the ability of a system to change the location of that element, that is, to achieve load balancing or fault tolerance
Failure	Masks, from an element, its failure and possible recovery, to ensure fault tolerance
Relocation	Masks the use of an interface from other interfaces bound to it
Replication	Masks the use of a group of compatible components exhibiting mutual behavior to support an interface in order to enhance performance or provide reliability
Persistence	Masks, from an element, variations in the ability of a system to provide processing, storage, and communication functions to that element
Transaction	Masks coordination of activities among a configuration of components, to achieve consistency

Table 19-4. Assessment of software architecture transparency

Software Architecture	Assessment
Call-and-return systems	Requires explicit knowledge of server(s) by clients
Data flow systems	Good beyond immediate neighbors
Virtual machines	Good
Independent component systems	Depends on communication mechanism and middleware
Data-centric systems	Requires explicit knowledge of server(s)

Transparency requires consideration of heterogeneity of supporting software and hardware, the location and mobility of components, and the mechanisms required to achieve a given level of performance in the event of failures and the existence of heterogeneous hardware and software components (Table 19-4).

19.2.3   Integrating Components

The components of a software architecture must be integrated into a unifying whole and they must interoperate. Integration means the pieces fit together well. Interoperability means that they work together effectively to produce an answer (Table 19-5).

When building an application from components, the components rarely integrate with each other "out of the box."

Table 19-5. Assessment of software architecture integratability

Software Architecture	Assessment
Call-and-return systems	Easy to integrate with coding
Data flow systems	Easy to integrate since only upstream/ downstream connectivity involved
Virtual machines	Easy to integrate
Independent component systems	Depends on adherence to APIs
Data-centric systems	Easy to add new clients, especially if transaction mechanism available

19.2.4   Extensibility

Another critical problem for software architectures is extensibility. A software architecture specifies a solution to a class of problems. The characteristics of the class of problems define the boundary of the software architecture. If the nature of the problems changes, the boundary of the software architecture must be extended through the addition of new functionality to encompass the new characteristics (Table 19-6).

Extensibility can be engineered at compile-time or at runtime. For example, Van Der Hoek et al. (1999) cite the example of a software that can provide multiple alternative ways of achieving the same functionality. They consider a numerical optimization system that can operate slow, but very precise, or fast, but very approximate. This system can be configured for the desired operational mode by appropriate selection of source files. A different approach is to include multiple software modules that can be selected at runtime to obtain the desired result with the desired time.

One way to extend software systems is to plug in components. Apple supports this concept through extensions to the Macintosh Operating System. Netscape pioneered the idea of plug-ins to provide the ability to display different images encoded in different graphics formats.

19.2.5   Flexibility

Software architecture implementations may be modified before and during implementation. The ease with which this modification can be accomplished determines the flexibility of the software architecture (Table 19-7). For example, components may be replaced as part of the configuration of a specific implementation. During execution, components may be dynamically loaded to overwrite existing components (such as allowed by Common Lisp).

19.2.6   Monolithic Middleware

At one time, we faced the problem of applications becoming large, bloated collections of code. This was due, in part, to the poor performance of communication networks. So applications had to do almost everything for themselves. As communication networks become more reliable and more powerful, applications were decomposed and distributed across multiple machines. Client–server architectures are an exemplar of this trend.

Table 19-6. Assessment of software architecture extensibility

Software Architecture	Assessment
Call-and-return systems	Easily extensible by adding new clients or new servers
Data flow systems	Easily extensible by adding new elements
Virtual machines	Moderately extensible but requires coding
Independent component systems	Moderately extensible but requires coding
Data-centric systems	Easily extensible for clients; more difficult for servers

Table 19-7. Assessment of software architecture flexibility

Software Architecture	Assessment
Call-and-return systems	Difficult to modify during runtime
Data flow systems	Difficult to modify during runtime
Virtual machines	Moderately difficult to modify during runtime
Independent component systems	Ease depends on availability of middleware, such as an ORB
Data-centric systems	Difficult to modify

Table 19-8. Assessment of software architecture need for middleware

Software Architecture	Assessment
Call-and-return systems	Buffering; translation of data types; and transformation of arguments and call structures
Data flow systems	Not required
Virtual machines	Not required
Independent component systems	Required to support dynamic lookup, access, and modification
Data-centric systems	Usually requires transaction processing mechanism

As we distributed applications, we found that developing one-for-one interfaces became tedious and made it difficult to add new components into an application. Middleware partially alleviated the integration and communication problem among components. But, as more functionality has been pushed into middleware, middleware itself has become a bloated application, often on par in complexity with the original applications (Table 19-8).

19.2.7 Reflective Architectures

A reflective program is one that can reason about its own structure and behavior. To enable reflections, the elements that comprise a program must themselves be manipulable. This means that the elements must be "first class." While this idea

Table 19-9. Assessment of software architecture reflection

Software Architecture	Assessment
Call-and-return systems	Not required
Data flow systems	Not required
Virtual machines	Required for dynamic extensibility
Independent component systems	Required for dynamic extensibility
Data-centric systems	Not required

originated with AI systems, it is being applied to frameworks built using traditional languages (Table 19-9).

A metalevel architecture that supports reflection would provide a programming system that would allow users to construct new language-level objects that would stand on an equal footing with previously existing features. A language built of such programmable objects would be arbitrarily extensible and would permit language as well as application-level objects to be utilized to help the system adapt and evolve as requirements change. An interesting consequence is that the metaobjects themselves might be subject to change as well.

Foote (1992) has identified some principles that underlie the design and development of metalevel architectures.

Reflective metalevel architectures should be designed with message passing at the bottom, malleable self-representations, extensionality, abstract inheritance, first-class representation, abstract dispatching, and abstract scope.

All significant elements of a language's programming model ought themselves to be reflected in first-class elements of that language's metalevel architecture. For instance, if the programming model makes extensive use of a notion like "class," then Class objects should be explicit, first-class elements of the metaarchitecture that coexist with ordinary application objects at runtime.

Hence, a framework for object-oriented reflective metalevel architectures might draw from a rich palette of potential metaobjects, including variables, selectors, messages, interpreters, script sets, handles, environments, continuations, contexts, message queues, stores, closures, classes, types, prototypes, signatures, methods, code, threads, and instances.

19.3 ANALYSIS OF SOFTWARE ARCHITECTURES

All design involves trade-offs. The problem is what means we should use for making informed decisions about alternatives. Design decisions are often made for nontechnical reasons, such as business needs, cost and schedule, or availability of skilled personnel. To support the decision-making process, we need to know what questions to ask and to ask them early enough to affect the design process.

One of the benefits of software architectures that we cited in Chapter 12 was the support for analysis of the properties—both static and emergent—of an application.

There are several kinds of analysis we can perform on software architectures, including:

- Structural
- Systems engineering
- Performance

19.3.1 Structural Analysis

A system's functionality specifies what it does (or should do given the right inputs). This functionality is usually comprised of a set of smaller functions, which individually are simpler and easier to conceptualize. Various techniques can be used to decompose a system's functionality. For some domains, the system functionality is well-understood and has been well-described in canonical terms. In the DSSA methodology, this would yield the reference architecture.

A system's structure, as we have noted previously, is a collection of parts and connections between those parts. The allocation of functions to structural parts is essential to understanding how the system will achieve the desired functionality. There are many ways to allocate function to structural alternatives. System architects choose allocations based on system requirements and constraints, which are not directly implied by the system's functional description.

Structural analysis focuses mostly on the static properties of the application by reviewing the software architecture description. For example, we can assess architectural consistency by asking whether the parts fit together properly. To do so, we examine the descriptions of components and their interfaces to ensure that each side of a connector specifies only information that matches the other side. One can view consistency checking as the analog to type checking in programming languages. How much checking you can do depends on how much you say about the components and the connectors. For example, does the proposed behavior of the component conform to the protocols of the connector(s) to which it is attached.

Consistency checking often requires that you make some assertions about the architectural description. For example, in a client–server architecture, you should assert that "all clients must be attachable to one server." To perform consistency checking, you test the truthfulness of these assertions. Note that the converse assertion may be acceptable within your application configuration. As an exercise, consider the truthfulness of this assertion in a mobile communications system.

An associated property is completeness, in which we ask whether every function in the requirements document is assigned to a component, whether every component implements at least one function, and whether every component interacts with at least one other component. The same questions can be asked for connectors, interfaces, and roles. Additionally, we want to ask if there is any missing functionality, for example, functionality implied by the description that does not seem to be specified in the requirements document.

19.3.2 Systems Engineering Properties

I refer to system engineering properties as the "ilities" because most of these properties are described by nouns ending in "-ly" or "-y", such as reliability, affordability, verifiability, maintainability, and security. There are a plethora of these; good systems engineering books address these in considerable detail.

When we design software architectures, we must consider design choices from both a static and a dynamic perspective. The static perspective views topology (configura-tion), whereas the dynamic perspective views the behavior of the resulting application.

Topological Quality Attributes   A software architecture can be evaluated using a number of quality attributes based on its static description, including modifiability, portability, integratability, testability, and reusability.

One "ility" is verifiability, which assesses how well the actual implementation matches the software architecture description.

Behavioral Quality Attributes   An information system built according to a software architecture can be evaluated using a number of quality attributes by observing its execution, including performance, security, availability, usability, and functionality.

- Performance refers to the responsiveness of the system. It is a function of how much communication and interaction there is between the components of the system. Since communication takes longer than computation, it can have a significant impact on design choices.
- Security refers to the ability of a system to protect itself against corruption of data and/or release of data. Security must be embedded into the system from the initial design. Specific security components need to be identified in the software architecture.
- Availability refers to the ability of a system to continually process, possibly in a degraded mode without loss of significant functionality, in the event of partial component failure. Redundancy and/or recovery mechanisms must be specified in the software architecture.
- Usability refers to the ability to use the system to accomplish useful work on the part of the user(s). It is more than just the quality of the user interface, although that is a significant factor. Navigation through the functionality of the system is also important.
- Functionality refers to the ability of the system to provide the right tools, processing, data structures that are relevant to the problem domain. Ability to add new functionality to enhance usability is a highly desirable feature of the software architecture as it leads to the implementation of the system.

Properties of a System Versus Properties of Its Parts   We can assess the properties of the elements of a software architecture on an individual basis. The hard part, and one for which there is no general algorithm, is how to combine the individual element properties to arrive at an overall evaluation of those same properties applied to the system. For certain properties, this is doable by specific algorithms for specific architectures, but in general this is not possible today. For example, you can use queuing theory to assess the end-to-end performance of a system using an asynchronous message passing communication method. Similarly, there are well-known techniques for assessing and combining reliability measures.

19.3.3 Performance Analysis

An open research problem in software architecting is how to evaluate the performance of a software architecture. There are two aspects to this:

1. To validate design choices with respect to performance indices.
2. To compare alternative architectural designs.

We are concerned with the end-to-end performance of the application as well as performance of individual components or subsystems.

19.3.4 Analytical Techniques

There are many analytical techniques that we can apply to software architectures—too numerous to give more than passing mention here. Many of them are the subjects of books in their own right.

An early technique, and one that is still often applied, is the back of the envelope/napkin approach, in which the designer scribbles some diagrams on a napkin, visually inspects them, perhaps writes a few calculations, and pronounces the design both workable and acceptable. This technique works well if one is recognized as a preeminent expert in the field, but it is remarkably inaccurate in every other respect.

More formal modeling techniques include both descriptive and mathematically based approaches. For example, UML-based tools, CSP (Communicating Sequential Processes), Petri Nets, and Queuing Theory are well understood but may not fully capture the dynamics and nuances of the interactions among system components.

Newer tools such as the architectural definition languages coupled with logic-based representations and simulation systems provide more exact information but require (steep) learning curves, extensive mathematical ability, and careful matching of tools and techniques to the domain.

19.3.5 The Architecture Tradeoff Analysis Method

The quality of a large software system is determined by its software architecture. Qualities such as performance, availability, and modifiability depends more on the overall software architecture than on code-level practices such as language choice,

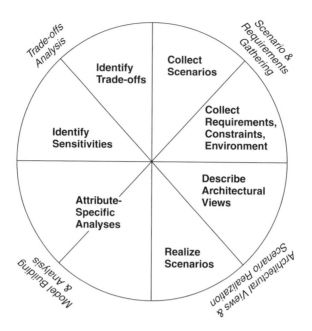

Figure 19-2. ATAM Six Step Approach.

detailed design, algorithms, data structures, and testing. This is because end-to-end processing exceeds local module processing.

Kazman et al. (1998, 2000) have developed a technique called the Architecture Tradeoff Analysis Method (ATAM). Because the attributes of a system interact, the ATAM approach identifies trade-off points—dependencies between attributes and the nature of the relationships that can affect the overall architecture. The ATAM is a spiral model that encompasses six steps as depicted in Figure 19-2.

The general approach for applying this method is to identify the initial constraints, environment, and requirements. Candidate architectures are generated that realize the scenarios. Different architectures may result based on the weight given to different scenario elements. Then, each architectural attribute is analyzed in turn, and in isolation, with respect to the proposed architecture. Then, trade-off points are identified that affect multiple attributes. These trade-offs are used to change the requirements, change the constraints and/or environment, or change the architecture. The designer may reevaluate several times until specific relations between the attributes are satisfied. Table 19-10 describes each step in more detail.

The ATAM approach focuses attention on specific requirements that directly affect the architecture by identifying the trade-off points where candidate architectures vary in their attributes based on the importance of their requirements. In addition, the ATAM approach helps to uncover implicit requirements through the interdependencies that trade-off points exhibit based on the scenarios.

The ATAM is analytically intensive and requires explicit identification of procedures for valuating the attributes within a candidate architecture. However, some

Table 19-10. ATAM step description

Step	Description
Step 1: *Collect scenarios*	Usage scenarios are gathered from a representative set of stakeholders. Use case modeling is an excellent tool to assist in developing scenarios.
Step 2: *Collect requirements, constraints, and environment*	Attribute-based requirements, constraints, and environment are extracted from the scenarios.
Step 3: *Describe architectural views*	Candidate architectures are generated that represent a solution to the problem domain. Each is described in terms of the attribute. Legacy systems and external systems must be incorporated into the designs. Keep the number of alternative architectures small, but consider at least a few alternatives during the design process.
Step 4: *Attribute specific analysis*	Each attribute is analyzed, in isolation, against each candidate architecture. Both valuation and justification are required. The results of this step are statements about system behavior.
Step 5: *Identify sensitivities*	One or more architectural attributes are varied within each candidate architecture. The change in value and behavior is assessed and described based on the change. Values that change significantly, according to some threshold, are deemed to be sensitivity points.
Step 6: *Identify trade-offs*	Trade-off points are determined by identifying attributes that have significant changes in value over multiple candidate architectures. For example, client–server architectures are sensitive to the number of servers. However, security may vary inversely since there are more servers to attack. So the number of servers is a trade-off point.

attributes cannot be objectively assessed, so the designers must recognize and address the subjective assessments.

19.4 FURTHER READING

Albin, S. T. 2003. *The Art of Software Architecting*. John Wiley & Sons, Hoboken, NJ.

Bosch, J. 2000. *Design and Use of Software Architectures: Adopting and Evolving a Product-Line Approach*. Addison Wesley, Reading, MA.

Clements, P., F. Bachmann, L. Bass, et al. 2002. *Documenting Software Architectures: Views and Beyond*. Addison Wesley, Reading, MA.

Dikel, D., D. Kane, and J. Wilson. 2001. *Software Architecture: Organizational Principles and Patterns*. Prentice-Hall, Upper Saddle River, NJ.

Hofmeister, C., R. Nord, and D. Soni. 1999. *Applied Software Architecture*. Addison Wesley, Reading, MA.

Sewell, M. and L. Sewell. 2002. *The Software Architect's Profession: An Introduction*. Prentice-Hall, Upper Saddle River, NJ.

19.5   EXERCISES

19.1. Select an application with which you are familiar and have access to the source code, if not the architectural description. Try to reverse engineer the architectural description from the source code.

19.2. Using the results of Problem 1, select five properties from those discussed in this chapter and analyze your architectural description for those properties.

19.3. Select an appropriate tool, such as a UML-based representation system or a Petri Net tool, and represent an architectural description in that tool.

19.4. You have decided to build your dream software engineering tool. What software architecture(s) would you use and why would you use it (them)?

19.5. Review the ATAM papers by Kazman et al. (1998, 2000). Select a software architecture of some complexity and apply the ATAM to it.

IV

FRAMEWORKS

Important progress has been made toward reusing software through the application of the O-O paradigm and the use of component technology. However, these technologies only provide reuse at the level of individual, often small-scale, components. Design patterns, as discussed in Part I, demonstrate reuse of design structures for building small, complex components focused on single problems. The more complex problem of reuse at the level of large components that can be adapted for individual applications is not addressed by the O-O paradigm itself.

Recently, interest in software reuse has shifted from the reuse of single components to entire system designs or application structures. A software system that may be reused at this level for creating complete applications is called a *framework*. Frameworks are based on the idea that it should be easy to produce a set of specific, but similar, systems within a certain domain starting from a generic structure. Succinctly, frameworks are generic architectures complemented by an extensible set of components.

Frameworks are usually large O-O structures that can be tailored for specific applications, provide infrastructure and flexibility for deploying O-O technology, and enable reuse at a larger granularity. They do not have to be O-O structures, although they are commonly implemented this way. The design of the framework fixes certain roles and responsibilities among the components, as well as specifying standard protocols for the communication and collaboration between them.

A framework describes a collection of object classes and their interactions with one another; that is, it specifies the protocol for information exchange among the set of classes. Loosely defined, a framework is a collection of objects that work together to accomplish a task. In fact, the commonly held view is that the components of a framework are abstract classes that must be instantiated when the framework is used

Software Paradigms, By Stephen H. Kaisler
ISBN 0-471-48347-8   Copyright © 2005 John Wiley & Sons, Inc.

in a design. Frameworks can contain subframeworks, which represent subsets of the components of the larger system.

Unlike toolkits, frameworks emphasize design reuse over code reuse, although the resulting code can still be reused. A framework usually defines the overall structure of all applications derived from it, a partitioning into classes and objects, the key responsibilities of individual classes, how they collaborate, and the thread of control. The developer is responsible for customizing the framework to a particular application. Customization consists mainly of extending the abstract classes from the framework, although this does not exclude the possibility of providing additional concrete classes that can be used directly.

Frameworks invert the role of control between the application and the infrastructure. The infrastructure calls/invokes application routines. In conventional systems, the developer's own program provides all of the structure and controls execution flow and makes calls to function libraries as necessary. By using a framework, the developer has only to prepare those components that are missing in the framework according to the desired application behavior.

20

FRAMEWORK CONCEPTS

A framework comprises classes (or structures) implementing generic application components as well as concrete components that fulfill specialized tasks. To build a complete program, software developers find and instantiate the appropriate components, use them to bind the parameters of application components, and combine them into an executable program.

There is no common definition for frameworks, but most do have a common theme of reuse. A widely accepted definition is given by Johnson and Foote (1988):

> A framework is a set of classes that embodies an abstract design for solutions to a family of related problems....

Some different views include:

> If objects are abstractions that are sometimes difficult to explain, frameworks present an event more intriguing challenge. The key distinction between a framework and an arbitrary collection of classes, however closely related those classes might be functionally, is that a framework describes not only the objects but also their interactions with one another.
>
> —Taligent Corp. (1994)

> An abstract class is a design for a single object. A framework is the design of a set of objects that collaborate to carry out a set of responsibilities. Thus, frameworks are

Software Paradigms, By Stephen H. Kaisler
ISBN 0-471-48347-8   Copyright © 2005 John Wiley & Sons, Inc.

larger scale designs than abstract classes. Frameworks are a way to reuse high-level design.

—Johnson and Russo (1991)

A framework is most valuable when it predefines and preimplements the most difficult parts of the solution within the problem domain. Figure 20-1 depicts this usage. Both Application 1 and Application 2, which are two different applications, can be derived from the framework.

A framework is like a class library but differs from a class library because the flow of control is bidirectional between the application and the library. The library may call user-written code and vice versa. An operation can be defined in a library class but implemented in a subclass in the application. Figure 20-2 helps to visualize this.

The principal difference is where application control resides. In a class library (left side), the application invokes services from various classes that are statically or dynamically bound to it. On the right side, control is exercised by the framework, which calls on application-specific subclasses to provide application-specific computation and data. This has loosely been characterized as the "Hollywood Principle"—Don't call us; we'll call you. Table 20-1 summarizes the differences between frameworks and class libraries.

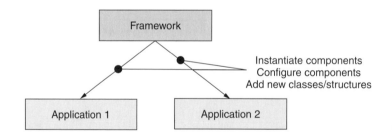

Figure 20-1. Application development from a framework.

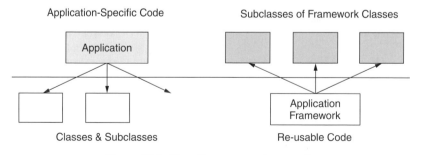

Figure 20-2. Class library versus framework.

Table 20-1. Class libraries versus frameworks

Class Libraries	Frameworks
Classes are instantiated by the client.	Customization occurs through subclassing.
The client calls the functions in the classes.	Calls function in the client code.
There is no predefined flow of control (or embedded in the client).	Framework determines flow of control based on problem solution.
There is no predefined interaction between client and class libraries—decision by client.	Pattern of interaction is based on problem solution.
There is no default behavior.	A default behavior or solution is provided.

20.1   TYPES OF FRAMEWORKS

There are many types of frameworks. They can be simple or complex, low-level or complex domain structures. Fayad and Schmidt (1997) offer two classification schemes for frameworks. Taligent Corp. (1994) offers a different classification scheme.

20.1.1   Structural Frameworks

The first classification due to Fayad and Schmidt (1997) I will call *structural frameworks* because they are oriented toward a particular structural component of a system architecture. These kinds of frameworks are used to build pieces of an enterprise system architecture.

- *System Infrastructure Frameworks:* These frameworks simplify the development of portable and efficient system infrastructure including operating systems, communication frameworks, and frameworks for user interface. Because they are typically used internally within the organization, they are not usually sold to customers directly.
- *Middleware Frameworks:* These frameworks are used to integrate distributed applications and components. They enhance the ability of software to be modularized, reused, and easily extended. Examples of middleware frameworks include ORB frameworks, message-oriented middleware, and transactional databases.
- *Enterprise Application Frameworks:* Their primary use is to support the development of end-user applications and products. They are oriented to domain-specific applications such as telecommunications, avionics, manufacturing, education, and financial engineering. Despite the high cost of development, enterprise frameworks can provide a substantial return on investment since they support the development of end-user applications and products directly.

20.1.2   Classification by Usage

Fayad and Schmidt offer another way to classify frameworks. They consider how the framework can be extended to adapt or customize it to the specific conditions of the application domain. There are two alternatives—white-box versus black-box—and a variety of hybrids, which, collectively, can be called gray-box frameworks.

White-Box Frameworks   A framework is a *white-box framework*, also known as an *architecture-driving framework*, if it is based on inheritance and dynamic binding to create an application skeleton. The framework is extended either by inheriting from the framework base classes or by overriding predefined methods.

A white-box framework defines interfaces for components that can be plugged into it via object composition. However, white-box frameworks are difficult to use because they require in-depth understanding of the classes to be extended. Another limitation, due to subclassing, is the dependence among methods: for example, overriding one operation might require overriding another and so on. Subclassing can lead in this case to an explosion of classes, because even a simple extension may affect many classes that have to be extended or changed.

Because white-box frameworks emphasize reuse through inheritance, every application requires the creation of many new subclasses. While the classes are mostly simple, their number for larger applications makes it difficult to learn the design of an application when it is to be changed. The disadvantage is that the programmer must understand the details of how the framework works—sometimes in its entirety. This means that a significant intellectual investment must be made before the programmer can use the framework in a productive fashion. In particular, you will need to know:

- How subclasses work with their parents and other superclasses.
- How to access both public and private code (depending on programming language).
- How to override existing methods.
- How to access the parent's methods.

There are two ways to use white-box frameworks (Shull et al. 1999, Travassos et al. 2002):

1. With a system-wide technique, first find the class in the framework that best matches the functionality that you need to implement. Determine how to parameterize the class, including subclassing, and how to implement it as part of your application.
2. Find the example in the example set, if there is one provided with the framework, that best matches the functionality you need. Determine which piece of the example is relevant to your problem and how to modify it to meet your application needs.

Shull and co-workers noted that the second method is much more amenable to beginners in framework programming than the former. Less intellectual investment is required, but at the expense of failing to understand the depth and breadth of the framework. The success of this approach is based on the quality and completeness of the example set. Shull and co-workers also noted that this approach led to more effective use of the framework than using the hierarchical approach.

Black-Box Frameworks   A black-box framework, also known as a *data-driven framework*, is constructed using component composition and delegation with parameterization rather than inheritance. (Although the component may be comprised of multiple objects, it is represented as one entity.) It emphasizes dynamic relationships rather than static class relationships.

New functionality can be added to a framework by composing existing objects in new ways to reflect the behavior of an application. The user in this case does not have to know the details of framework components, but only how to use existing objects and how to combine them. Black-box frameworks are generally easier to use and extend than white-box frameworks, but they are more difficult to develop since their interfaces and hooks have to anticipate a wider range of potential use cases. Due to their predefined flexibility, black-box frameworks are more rigid in the domain they support. Heavy use of composition can also make the designs harder to understand.

Gray-Box Frameworks   The previous types represent the extremes. Most frameworks represent a hybrid of these two approaches. We call these *gray-box frameworks*, because they combine elements of both extremes. Indeed, for large, very complex applications, a number of white-box frameworks may be embedded within a black-box framework. Figure 20-3 depicts such a case.

In this example, two ways to access database tables are depicted—one through a GUI that displays data in a tabular or spreadsheet format and one that displays it through a database query language. Each of these access modes may use a framework to implement the appropriate functionality (e.g., look at the construction of Oracle's interfaces).

20.1.3   Taligent's Classification

Taligent (now absorbed into IBM) groups frameworks into three categories as shown in Table 20-2.

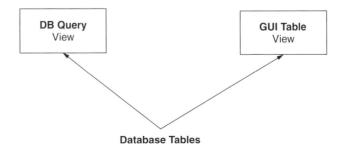

Figure 20-3. Multiple mode access to database tables.

Table 20-2. Taligent framework classifications

Category	Description
Application frameworks	Application frameworks aim to provide a full range of functionality typically needed in an application. This functionality usually involves features such as GUI, documents, and databases. Two examples are the MFC (Microsoft Foundation Classes), which is used to build applications for MS Windows, and the JFC (Java Foundation Classes), a platform-independent development environment.
Domain frameworks	Domain frameworks are used to implement applications for a specific domain, such as banking or aviation control systems. Domain-specific software usually has to be tailored for a particular organization and often must be developed from scratch. Frameworks can help reduce the amount of work that needs to be done to implement such applications. This allows organizations to develop higher quality software for their domain while reducing the time to market.
Support frameworks	Support frameworks typically address very specific, computer-related domains such as memory management or file systems. Support for these kinds of domains is necessary to simplify program development. Support frameworks are typically used in conjunction with domain and/or application frameworks; that is, they are elements of a larger framework.

20.2   FRAMEWORK ELEMENTS

What should a framework provide to the end-user? The answer is a set of services that enable the programmer to design, develop, and implement a complete application. These services are distributed across the layers of a framework and constitute functionality useful to all applications built on top of the framework.

20.2.1   A Framework Architecture

There are many ways to construct a framework—too numerous to explore in detail here. Fayad et al. (1999a, 1999b) delve into many different frameworks and examine their different architectural constructs. Figure 20-4 depicts a possible layered architecture for a framework.

This layered framework architecture defines layers for a generic interactive business application. Table 20-3 describes the functionality of each layer.

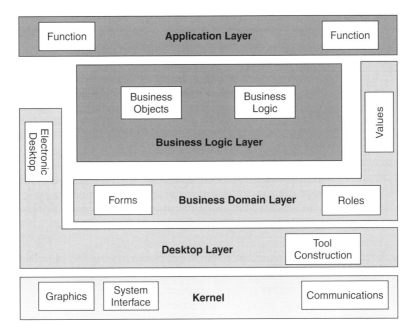

Figure 20-4. Layered framework architecture.

Table 20-3. Generic framework functionality

Layer	Functionality
Kernel	This layer provides basic functionality like a metaobject protocol, object trading, or a container library. It also provides general services like access to the operating system, client–server middleware, and data stores. It may consist of both white-box and black-box frameworks (Johnson and Foote 1988). These frameworks can be widely reused, as they do not incorporate any domain-specific knowledge.
Desktop	This layer specifies the common behavior of applications. It defines both the basic architecture as well as the look and feel of the interactive application. It ensures uniform behavior and technical consistency. It is usually a white-box framework. This layer can be reused by every business domain for which applications with an interactive user interface are designed.
Business Domain	This layer defines and implements the core concepts of the business on top of the Desktop and Kernel layer. It forms the basis for every application in this domain. This layer consists of domain-specific classes and value types that are common to all domain applications. It is usually a white-box framework that typically provides more interfaces than implementations. Final implementation is postponed to the Business Logic layer.

Table 20-3. (*Continued*)

Layer	Functionality
Business Logic	This layer is composed of separate partitions for each business unit. The frameworks in these partitions are based on the Business Domain, the Kernel, and the Desktop layer. They are implemented by subclassing the Business Domain and Desktop layer classes. Usually, each subclass only implements the abstract methods defined in the respective superclass. In these layers, we find classes and tools for specific tasks within the business domain.
Application	This layer defines concrete applications. Its separation from the Business Logic layer is motivated by the need to configure application systems for different workplaces. Applications that meet the requirements of an individual organization are found in this layer.

The architecture of each framework will differ. Some frameworks correlate their architectures to the structure of the problem domain, while others take a more general approach.

20.2.2   Framework Services

The services that a framework offers an application developer vary with the types of applications that the framework designer perceives will be built on top of the framework. Figure 20-5 depicts a set of possible framework services that might be used to implement interactive applications accessible by web browsers or PDA clients.

20.2.3   Framework Design Elements

Mattson (1996) suggests that four design elements are essential for implementing object-oriented application frameworks: abstract classes, design patterns, dynamic binding, and contracts.

Abstract Classes   Abstract classes are distinct from concrete classes because they cannot be instantiated. Mattson cites Hursch's (1994) rule that all superclasses should be abstract (known as the ASC rule). The implications of this rule are straightforward:

- If the class is to serve for instantiation only, provide a concrete class.
- If the class is to serve for subclassing only, provide an abstract class.

An abstract class captures a general concept that can later be specialized. Abstract classes help to prevent later restructuring of the class hierarchy as the framework evolves. Thus, all instantiation occurs at the leaves of the framework class hierarchy.

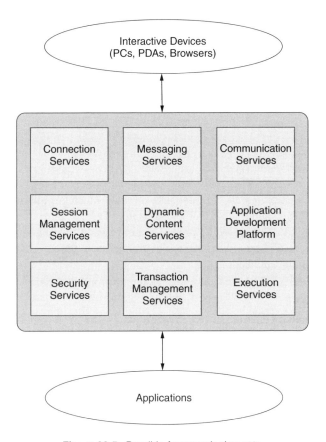

Figure 20-5. Possible framework elements.

Design Patterns   As we saw in Part I, design patterns specify the components that make up a framework. At a higher level, domain design patterns represent subsets (or subsolutions) of the overall solution set. As noted, design patterns become elements of a software architecture and are instantiated as components, which become elements of a framework.

Dynamic Binding   Dynamic binding allows the framework to be extended at runtime and also allows components of the framework to select the best component to provide a service at a specified time. This is essential in large systems, where many variants may be available; dynamic binding protects each component against changes in other components.

Contracts   Contracts have been proposed at several levels of abstraction (Meyer 1992, 1997). Specifying a module's functionality doesn't ensure that it will do what it is supposed to do. But the corollary seems to be obviously true: if we don't state what a module is supposed to do, there is little likelihood that it will do it. The design by contract approach suggests that every element has an associated specification. Where elements are instantiated as components, this ensures the components will provide the necessary services. Where elements are abstract and user-defined, it provides detailed guidance to the user for the functionality to be provided by the components.

20.3   USING FRAMEWORKS

To use a framework, we must choose one that (nearly) matches the type of application we are going to build. Note that I say "nearly" because all frameworks require some customization. The matching process requires that we have good requirements for the application and a good description of the candidate frameworks that might be used to develop the application.

It is not always easy to determine if a framework is compatible with the intended application. One reason is that the requirements may be stated in a way that cannot be mapped to the framework description. Another is that the description of the framework is not complete enough to determine if we can meet all (or most) of the requirements of the application.

Once we have selected a framework, we must *learn* how to use it before we can *use* it. Often, this is best accomplished with a detailed example that accompanies the framework and shows how to implement (at least) a simple application. The MacApp framework provided several shells that a programmer could extend and customize to develop an application. However, tutorials and comprehensive descriptions of the framework are also useful and, in some cases, necessary to be able to understand the framework.

It is important to note that to understand how a complex framework works may take significant amounts of time. Sometimes, it is best to build a toy application to get the basics of the framework, throw it away, then delve deeper into understanding the framework. Many times, trying to jump into designing the final application with a poorly understood framework will lead to delays or disaster (e.g., a failed application).

Application design is based on the defined requirements. The application design should conform to the structure and services provided by the framework. The application will be built by extending the framework with specific code for the application's desired functionality plus any additional structural extensions to the framework that are required to implement the application.

Simple applications may use just one framework, but large, complex applications, particularly those that are distributed across multiple computer systems, may use multiple frameworks for their implementation. For example, there may be one framework used for implementing the business logic and another framework used to implement the user interface.

20.3.1   Roles for Framework Use

There are several roles that people can play in using frameworks.

- *Framework Selector:* This person is responsible for choosing the tools and methodology for developing the application(s). He uses information that describes the purpose and the domain of the application to select a framework from among the available candidates. He may or may not also be the framework user.
- *Framework User:* This person customizes the framework to produce the desired application. His primary requirement is to know how to do something in or to the framework, but not necessarily to understand why it is done that way. Customization occurs at hot spots. The framework user needs to know which classes can be or should be subclassed, what methods to override, and where he needs to provide additional code.
- *Framework Maintainer:* This person must understand the architecture and design rationale of the framework in order to modify and enhance it. This requires knowledge of the application domain that the framework is intended to support. He must understand the internal architectural details and update the framework documentation as modifications are made in order to make it useful to application developers.
- *Framework Developer:* This person develops new or alternative frameworks for application domains. He often seeks ideas from other frameworks, even if they were developed for other domains. This is because high-level constructs such as design patterns and software architectures are often transferable from one domain to the next. He is interested in both abstract concepts and concrete detail. Framework development is often the most time-consuming phase in a framework's life cycle.

20.3.2   Implementing Frameworks

Frameworks can be implemented in several ways, but two models seem to be prevalent: contracts and hot spots (Demeyer et al. 1997).

- *Contracts:* The common functionality of a specific domain is captured in a framework contract. A contract specifies which parts of the framework are to be reused and imposes a common structure for all the applications that use the same framework. The implementation and functionality of a contract is usually hidden from the user. Because the framework forms the skeleton of all applications, the contract details have a direct impact on the performance of an application. As a result, performance and correctness are the two main driving forces when designing the framework contracts.
- *Hot Spots:* A variable aspect of an application domain is called a hot spot (Schmid 1997). Applications will differ from each other with regard to at least

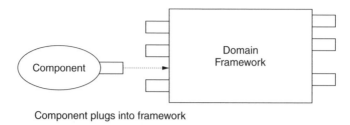

Component plugs into framework

Figure 20-6. Component integrates with framework.

one hot spot. A framework is tailored for a specific application by implementing its hot spots accordingly. A hot spot allows a user to "plug in" an application-specific class or subsystem, either by selecting from a set of those supplied with a black-box framework or by programming a class or subsystem in a white-box framework (*Note:* Areas of immutability within a framework have been referred to as "frozen spots.")

In either case, a component is integrated with the framework. The component interface must match the framework specification because the framework invokes the component's procedures or methods to provide a service (Figure 20-6).

The OMG has formalized this approach with its Business Object Component Architecture (BOCA). Business Object Components are encapsulated with a protocol that enables communication with other components within the framework.

Consider a client–server application like an order entry system. This system accepts a purchase order as input and produces a validated order as output. The order entry system is treated as a black box: that is, its internal operations are hidden from other components. The validated order becomes input to another system, such as the order shipping system. Alternatively, if the purchase order is incomplete or has an error, an exception is raised and the order is sent to yet another system to communicate with the client.

Within this client–server component may be encapsulated other components as well as glue code to integrate these components. For example, the processing and validation of a purchase order might be decomposed into the following operations, each implemented as a component in its own right: checking the purchase order, looking up customer information, checking inventory availability, verifying catalog pricing, and generating the shipping order. Each of these components may communicate with external data sources as well, such as the catalog component, which implements and maintains the product catalog.

The order entry system must have multiple interfaces, perhaps each implemented as a different subsystem. For example, orders may be taken by a clerk over the phone, or be submitted via email, or be entered through a web-enabled interface, or come in over the transom as hardcopy mail, which must be entered manually through an interface. Each of these has different characteristics, although all must basically accept the same information. Because user interfaces are expensive and time-consuming to build, developing componentized versions can minimize the cost of building new systems. The customization occurs in the actual data that must be collected while the functionality remains the same from system to system.

20.3.3   Advantages and Disadvantages of a Framework

There are many benefits that derive from using a framework to develop applications. Table 20-4 presents some of these benefits.

But there are also some disadvantages to using frameworks. The main obstacle to using frameworks is the learning curve. There is often a (steep) learning curve in understanding what the framework describes and how to use it. The learning curve

Table 20-4. Some benefits of a framework

Benefit	Description
Reusability	The main advantage of frameworks is that they capture the programming expertise necessary to solve a particular class of problems. Programmers use frameworks to obtain such problem-solving expertise without having to develop it independently.
Commonality	Frameworks capture a common core of software that will form the foundation for integrated systems.
Standardization	Program development costs can be reduced through adherence to industry or organizational standards, including the use of commercially available software components whenever possible. As more applications are created from the framework, the base code becomes more robust.
Engineering base	Through standardization and an open architecture, establish a large base of trained software/systems engineers.
Training	Reduce training costs and improve productivity through enforcement of a uniform human–machine interface, commonality of documentation, and a consistent "look and feel."
Interoperability	Applications using a framework are more likely to be compatible with each other.
Scalability	Through use of the architectural infrastructure, improve system scalability so that systems will operate with the minimum hardware resources required.
Portability	Increase portability through use of open system concepts and standards and promote vendor independence for both hardware and software.
Security	System security is built into the problem solution rather than added on.
Time	Once a framework is understood, the development time for another application should decrease because the code and the design of the problem solution do not need to be replicated.
Maturity	Frameworks evolve with use and revisions. A framework's maturity depends on the number of times it has been refined.

Table 20-5. Other disadvantages of using frameworks

Disadvantage	Description
Development effort	Developing reusable frameworks for complex application domains is a very difficult task. Very often, only expert developers possess the skills required to produce frameworks successfully.
Learning curve	Learning to use a framework requires considerable effort. The complexity of frameworks often requires an in-depth understanding before a programmer can become productive.
Hidden architecture	The software architecture of a framework is not usually obvious; it is hard to extract it just by reading about the classes. On the other hand, it is often hard to make a specific software architecture explicit in a framework.
Reengineering	It is often difficult to go from a white-box framework to a black-box framework and vice versa. And it is difficult to bridge incompatible frameworks.
Internal architecture	Many frameworks define their own internal event loop, which makes it difficult to combine two frameworks into one application.

gets steeper the more complex the framework and the problem domain that it supports. Table 20-5 describes a few other disadvantages.

20.4 DOCUMENTING FRAMEWORKS

Framework documentation has two aspects. One is to communicate the framework design and the decisions made in building the framework. Another is to specify where it can be customized as applications are built. The latter aspect is especially important because rules and constraints imposed by the developer may make no sense and, hence, the framework will not be used as intended. These rules are often implicitly hidden and difficult to find.

Documenting frameworks is a difficult problem. The framework design fixes certain roles and responsibilities. And it specifies the protocols for collaboration among its elements. Variability across applications that can be built from the framework is factored into hot spots. Customizing is performed by subclassing existing classes and redefining a small number of methods. But sometimes protocols must be maintained, so additional parallel classes need to be developed.

20.4.1 Why Describe Frameworks?

A framework exists to support the development of a family of applications. Reuse involves an application developer or a team of application developers. While the framework developer is likely to be expert in the domain, the application developers may not be. Frameworks are not easy to understand upon first encounter. The design tends to be abstract in order to factor out the commonality and incomplete, thus requiring subclasses to be developed. The large learning curve faced by a first-time user can be a serious impediment to using the framework.

This leads us to consider the reasons for describing a framework in sufficient detail to enable it to be used to create new applications within the domain.

First, the framework developer needs to sell the framework to the application developer. The framework developer needs to provide enough information for the user to determine its utility and applicability to his problem domain. This information should include an overall architecture and the specific points where the framework can be customized or extended.

Second, the application developer is reusing an architecture developed for a particular problem domain. The description must contain enough information to allow the framework to be adapted or modified to fit the target problem domain. From a reuse point of view, we have to document frameworks succinctly, unambiguously, and understandably. The components of the framework should be searchable and their descriptions readable and/or extractable. Butler and Denommee (1996) focus explicitly on documentation oriented toward the application developer.

Third, large, complex systems are likely to be constructed from several frameworks. To permit integration and interoperability of subsystems instantiated from each framework, the architectural assumptions and interfaces for each framework need to be explicitly described.

Finally, large applications evolve, usually through continuous reengineering. The underlying framework must often evolve with the application. An architectural description of the framework allows the developer to assess subsequent versions and to plan changes in a way that minimizes disruption of other parts of the application.

Framework documentation is not a free by-product of the development of the framework. It should be carried out from the very beginning of the framework development process. Otherwise, you might lose important design information. As the framework evolves, it is essential to capture information about the changes, but in a way that preserves earlier design decisions. Because of the often steep learning curve before one can use a framework, this design information is essential to conveying to the user the rationale for the structure of the framework.

20.4.2 Elements of a Framework Description

Just as with software architectures we have different views, so with a framework there will be several different views. The views will help us to gain an understanding of the framework as well as the assumptions made in its construction. The description needs to be more than just the strategy used to solve the primary design problem that the framework addresses. Subordinate issues and policies, once described, may identify hidden assumptions, which can affect integration and interoperability.

At a minimum, a framework description should have the elements depicted in Table 20-6.

Table 20-6. Framework description

Element	Meaning
Overview	This element provides the context for the usage of the framework, including any discussion of domain-specific characteristics and constraints.
Model of the application domain	The model describes the main elements of the problem domain and how they relate to each other, including behavior and interactions. This model results from a detailed domain analysis and is best expressed in the UML.
Domain design space	The framework provides a solution architecture for many problems in the domain. Each problem can be solved using a variety of approaches. The design space describes the recommended approaches and techniques for solving certain problems and the rationale for selecting those approaches over others. Understanding the design space allows the application developer to choose specific approaches for individual problems as well as determining where and how to add new approaches.
Examples	Just as with design patterns, we need examples to help us understand how to use the framework to build applications. Examples help application developers to create applications using the framework. Ideally, a range of examples from simple to advanced should be presented. A hotspot or hooks may need several examples in order to present the full flexibility of the framework.
Architectural patterns	As we saw in software architectures (see Chapter 12), there are some distinct architectural patterns that can be used to build applications to solve specific kinds of problems. The framework may incorporate some of these architectural patterns as well as implement new ones.
Scenarios	Scenarios help us to understand how applications built from the framework will be used by end-users. They are invaluable because they give concrete examples of the relationships of framework components to one another, including their behaviors. Scenarios also show how the solution to a particular problem flows through the framework and the application components.

20.4.3 Heuristics for Framework Documentation

Several authors describe how to document frameworks. Chen and Xu (1999) offer the following heuristics for documenting frameworks:

1. The documentation should be tailored to the scope and level of the application domain of the framework.
2. Multiple views of the framework should be provided for different audiences.

3. An overview of the framework should be prepared, both as a live presentation and as the first recipe in the cookbook.

4. A set of example applications that have been specifically designed as documentation tools is required. The examples should be graduated from simple to advanced and should incrementally introduce one hot spot at a time. A hot spot that is very flexible may need several examples to illustrate its range of variability, from straightforward customization through to elaborate customization. One of the simpler examples should be used in the overview presentation. The cookbook recipes will use sample source code from the example applications.

5. A cookbook of recipes should be written, and organized by pattern languages. The recipes should use the example applications to make their discussion concrete. Cross-references to any other available documentation should be provided.

6. Documenting frameworks costs a lot of time and money, and the money spent on documentation should be appropriate to the whole product.

7. Documenting frameworks should be done from the very beginning of framework development.

8. The documentation should include both low-level, method-oriented documentation and high-level descriptions of frameworks.

9. The documentation should have both static views and dynamic views of the framework.

10. The framework should be documented accurately.

11. Avoid information redundancy, and document frameworks simply and effectively. Encapsulate information not useful to application developers.

12. Changes to the documentation should be easy to make in case the framework is modified.

13. Use as much advanced software technology as possible to make the documentation easy to understand and customize.

14. Design patterns and interobject behavioral composition are useful techniques to document black-box frameworks.

20.5 DESIGNING FRAMEWORKS

Frameworks are a relatively recent design structure for application domains. Because a comprehensive body of knowledge about framework design does not yet exist, numerous methodological issues remain to be resolved about how to use frameworks to effectively implement application programs.

Designing a framework is an iterative process that requires both domain knowledge and software engineering expertise. A framework must be simple enough to be learned easily and quickly by the application developer. It must incorporate a theory of the problem domain and a solution for a set of problems within that domain. The key problem is to determine how much of the problem solution should be hardwired and how much should be customizable through hot spots.

We should note that lessons learned from "programming in the small" do not easily translate or scale to "programming in the large." As the number and complexity of components increase, the number of interactions between components becomes much more complex. As a result, framework development and implementation require enhanced skills for success. Previous sections have focused on some of the ideal aspects of components and frameworks.

Designing frameworks is still much of an art rather than a science. Indeed, it appears to be an iterative process, which requires both domain and design expertise. There is a contention between making the framework easy to learn and use, and making it rich enough to apply to many different problems within the domain. It must embody substantial domain knowledge in order to be applicable to many problems within the domain.

Initially, frameworks were monolithic and solved an entire problem. For larger problems, the framework became too complex and was not easily understandable. The recent trend is to develop smaller frameworks for small problems and "glue" them together. Large applications become systems of frameworks.

Experience has shown that frameworks cannot be developed in a top–down fashion. Johnson and Foote (1988) note that "useful abstractions are usually designed from the bottom up, i.e., they are discovered, not invented." This suggests that a set of implementations of several solutions to a problem is necessary to force the understanding and evolution of the abstract classes that form the framework.

20.5.1   Flexible Framework Design

First and foremost, we should design frameworks to be *flexible*. This means that the abstract components can be used in many different contexts within the problem domain. Finding the balance between what should be abstract and what should be concrete when implementing a framework is still a trial-and-error process.

Second, the framework should be *complete*. Wherever possible, it should provide default implementations and built-in functionality. The default application should allow the developer to implement a simple application with little effort and should enable users of the framework to understand how instantiation should proceed.

Third, it should be *extensible*. Obviously, a framework that is extensible allows the user to adapt it to specific problem characteristics within the domain. There is a balance that must be struck between built-in functionality that cannot be changed because it is essential to overall framework operation and that which can be customized to yield problem-specific behavior.

Finally, we need to document our frameworks in order to make them *understandable* to the users who will use them to implement applications. Documentation includes following standard design and coding guidelines and providing graduated examples of the framework.

20.5.2 Identifying Entities

In designing an application program, one of the first tasks is to identify the entities that exist in the application domain. Most object-oriented analysis methods focus on real-world objects, but this technique is neither straightforward nor sufficient. Actual objects can serve as units of modularization, but often it is the cooperation between objects that is more important than the objects themselves. Moreover, when entities are composite objects, determining the proper level of abstraction may be difficult.

In frameworks, we focus more on services that are to be provided by components than on the actual objects themselves. While a framework may implement some components, it generally leaves component implementation to the user who is building an application from the framework.

20.5.3 Determining Behavior

In considering the entities of a framework, it is essential to determine how they are activated and how they contribute to the overall behavior of the system. When an application is organized as a group of cooperating objects, individual objects must make assumptions about the objects that they interact with that often go well beyond the constraints that we place upon the fidelity of input parameters. As a consequence, the behavior of one object is determined—in some part—by the behavior of other objects around it (e.g., with which it interfaces). This seems to contradict a fundamental tenet of object-oriented programming regarding isolation (namely, that objects must know at least the handles of other objects in order to send them messages or invoke methods). However, it is this circularity of behavioral definition that makes it difficult to define the overall behavior of the system.

Another aspect of behavior that can cause significant problems is the fact that the behavior of objects is parameterizable. Different behaviors can be exhibited based on input parameters and the current state of the object (based on its history).

In frameworks, the behavior of components should be independent of the components they interact with, for example, a component should provide the same service to any client that requests it. This assumes that components are "stateless." In fact, it is difficult for a component to be stateless, because this would require a large transfer of information at each service request in order to provide all the information necessary to be able to provide a service.

20.5.4 Aggregation

Complex applications are often built from complex entities that are implemented as composite objects. Object-oriented design provides a basic mechanism for modeling and implementing composition but offers little support for aggregate or collaborative behavior.

Composite objects require some form of "glue" that binds the parts of the aggregates together. It must be based on the behavior of the individual objects because composite objects result from cooperative relationships among multiple objects.

Thus, the topology of the composite object is an important factor in determining its behavior.

Once objects can be composed in specified ways, these aggregates form new abstractions with a different granularity and behavioral model.

20.5.5 Instantiation

Unlike object-oriented programming, an inherent part of framework programming is a specification for a particular structure, including its constituent components and the procedures for constructing it.

A framework enables application development through the instantiation of standard objects, which are integrated according to predefined patterns. Ideally, we would like to be able to create applications without any programming merely by picking the right objects, choosing the right instantiating parameters and topology, and letting them generate the executable program from object libraries.

20.5.6 Concurrency

An interesting problem in frameworks is concerned with concurrency. If individual objects are independently executable in a concurrent manner, how does one characterize the concurrent behavior of a composite object? The notion of active objects needs further development to ensure that concurrency is supported as a first-class feature.

20.5.7 Integration and Interoperability

The reuse of existing object libraries and frameworks as well as the integration of legacy systems and standard "shrink-wrapped" software packages is an open problem. Another aspect is the combination of several applications that are instantiated from the same framework. Since every application is itself a tightly coupled, self-contained entity, it is difficult to take advantage of the behavior between individual objects when such interaction might be beneficially useful to the integration process.

20.5.8 Framework Design Guidelines

Numerous guidelines for how to define frameworks have been proposed in the literature (Taligent Corp. 1994, Johnson 1992, Johnson and Russo 1991). Here, we capture a few of these to demonstrate the issues that must be considered in designing frameworks.

Design Frameworks for Replaceability Rather than Reuse Reuse is a poor design goal because frameworks that have been designed for reuse tend to attempt to handle all possible cases rather than imposing strict constraints. It is better to design a framework that can be removed entirely and replaced with another framework while preserving the externally visible protocols.

As an example, consider a GUI framework. If one designs an application framework to work with a particular GUI framework, then the eventual system implementation is locked into using that GUI framework for its lifetime. However, if one designs an application framework so that the GUI framework can easily be replaced by another, this will allow the application to be ported to another framework.

Frameworks that result from following a reuse design goal tend to be monolithic and try to handle every operation required: printing, event handling, database access, graphics, and interapplication communication. Replaceability implies developing separate frameworks to handle different categories of operations.

A Framework Without a Test Suite Is an Incomplete Framework   A framework should have a clearly defined boundary between it and its clients and servers. Thus, it should be possible to simulate the inputs and responses of those clients and servers. Also, test programs can be written to test each framework in isolation. When documenting a framework, its test suite should be used to demonstrate how it works with a reasonably complex example.

Don't Build a Framework If You Don't Thoroughly Understand the Domain   Because frameworks represent distilled knowledge about a domain, you should have previously built several applications within the domain—with the attendant successes and mistakes—in order to understand what is essential to the domain and how problems are solved within the domain. Without this distilled knowledge, it is likely that you will build a monolithic framework that is not easily extensible.

Make the Framework Easy To Use   Taligent suggests that a framework is easy to use if the framework provides useful functions with no extra work. This means the framework must be extended with a small amount of user code (but may support/require extensive configuration). Moreover, its approach to solving the problem occurs in incremental steps from simple problems to sophisticated problems. This allows the user to see how the problem solution evolves along the way.

One approach to making frameworks more usable is to build a general, flexible framework and then specialize it for subproblems within the domain. Specialization occurs through making concrete more of the components that were abstract in the more general framework. While this requires extra effort and yields multiple derivative frameworks that solve specific problems, it also can ensure that a common base exists for all of the problem-specific frameworks.

20.6   PROBLEMS WITH FRAMEWORKS

Problems with frameworks fall into two areas: composition and evolution. When developing a framework, the designers often assume that the framework will be the only framework present when applications are going to be created with it. Complex applications may require the use of more than one framework in an application. This may lead to composition problems that have to be solved when two or more frameworks are combined. Frameworks are usually designed and developed through an iterative process (Mattsson 1996). The framework may then be used to create many applications. As applications are developed, lessons are learned and new insights are gathered into the processes within the framework's domain, such that it becomes necessary to change the framework. This process is called framework evolution. Framework evolution has consequences for applications that have been created with the framework. If APIs in the framework change, the applications that use them may have to be changed too.

20.6.1 Domain Scope

The framework developer must determine the size of the framework, which is dictated by how much of the problem domain is to be encompassed by the framework. Large domains require considerable investment to analyze and more time to develop the framework. It may be difficult to justify such expenditures when the potential applications are assessed.

A smaller domain scope may yield smaller frameworks. But such frameworks may be generally less applicable to domain problems. These frameworks are also more sensitive to domain changes. So the framework needs to be revised and, perhaps, expanded as do the applications derived from it. Early savings by limiting scope may be offset or exceeded by the costs associated with rework later in the framework's life cycle.

Smaller frameworks eventually get larger due to the natural human tendency to increase the size of the framework as the developer realizes they can solve just one more problem if they just include one more useful aspect.

20.6.2 Composition

Composition problems arise from the basis for frameworks: a framework is meant to be the foundation for applications in a particular domain. The generic properties of a framework emphasize individual applications rather than composite applications.

Components within frameworks are focused on domain-relevant behavior of the real-world entities that they represent. Most components incorporate cohesive behavior to support component interaction. When two frameworks are composed, a component must provide both domain behavior and cohesive behavior within the context of both frameworks—something most components are not designed to do.

Frameworks generally do not cover the complete domain. Most frameworks focus on the most common functionality required to implement a large number of applications within the domain. During composition, users must assess the degree of overlap and develop an approach for dealing with it. Where little overlap occurs, the user may have to develop a substantial number of components to provide the required functionality. However, as frameworks evolve over time, previously missing coverage may be provided and may conflict with user-provided extensions. Considerable redesign of a framework is then required to be repeated for subsequent versions of the application, if the application is to benefit from the improvements of later framework versions.

The solution to this problem is standards. Standard definitions and descriptions of a domain, including its ontology, are required. Different frameworks can be developed for the standard. As the standard evolves, so do the frameworks. And framework designers can take into account that frameworks might be composed with other frameworks. However, domain definition and specification is extremely difficult to do and is an open research area as of this writing.

Framework composition can occur in two ways: horizontally or vertically. Horizontal integration is required when the two frameworks that are to be composed can be found on the same layer in a software system. Vertical integration occurs when one framework must depend on the services of another framework, that is, a layered system. Another issue is whether communication between the frameworks is one-way or bidirectional. Two-way communication may require changes to both frameworks and increases the complexity of any glue code written to compose them.

The biggest issue, of course, with frameworks is whether or not the user has access to the source code. Coupled with inadequate documentation, this issue mitigates against the use of frameworks because substantial time and effort, even trial and error, have to be invested to use the framework. Research in software reuse has identified that the perceived effort required for reusing a component should be less than the perceived effort of developing the component from scratch. Access to the source code is important since framework composition may require editing of the framework code to add behavior necessary for other frameworks. If no access to the source code is available, the only way to achieve the additional behavior required from the framework is through wrappers encapsulating the framework.

20.6.3 Composition Issues

As the usage of frameworks becomes more common, application designers are starting to compose frameworks to assist in developing complex, distributed applications much the way they composed components. Traditional framework-based application development assumes that the application is based on a single framework that is extended with application-specific code. Most frameworks are developed for reuse by extension with newly written application-specific code and not for composition with other software components. This focus on reuse through extension causes a number of problems when software engineers try to compose frameworks. If we want to integrate two or more frameworks into a superframework, we need to understand the assumptions each framework makes about its environment, what infrastructure it requires to support it, and how it connects to that infrastructure.

Mattsson and Bosch (1998) have identified a number of problems that affect the composition of frameworks. This section is largely drawn from their work.

Framework Control   Application control is embedded in the framework components. When necessary, these components call the application components provided by the user that have been used to customize the framework. To do this, most frameworks make use of dynamic binding.

Sparks et al. (1996) differentiate between "called" and "calling" frameworks. *Called frameworks* are passive entities whose components are invoked by other parts of the application. *Calling frameworks* are active entities that control the application and call the customized components supplied by the user.

When composing frameworks, difficulties arise when both frameworks expect to be in control of the application. The control loops of the respective frameworks can collide with each other—each trying to control interactions with the user or external devices. To remedy this situation, frameworks need to be developed to allow them to assume either a calling or called mode of operation.

Alternatively, each framework can be provided its own thread of control. Adaptation occurs through coupling the threads through interprocess communication. However, all components that can be accessed by both frameworks need to be extended with synchronization code to ensure mutually exclusive access. Coupling of the control loops must be tighter because events can occur that have application-wide relevance (e.g., must be made known to both frameworks). When one frameworks detects an event, it must notify the other framework as well.

Modifying a framework to adapt its mode of operation or to couple its control loop with that of another framework becomes more difficult if the control loop is distributed across multiple components.

Framework Gap A *framework gap* occurs when two frameworks are composed to support an application, but do not completely cover all of the application's control and computational requirements (Sparks et al. 1996).

If the framework is a called framework as shown in Figure 20-7, the framework gap problem may be solved with an additional framework interface including both

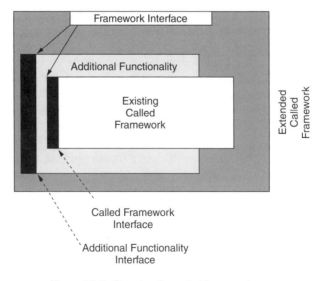

Figure 20-7. Covering the called framework gap.

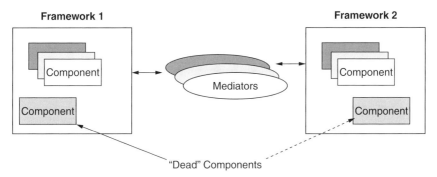

Figure 20-8. Integrating calling frameworks.

the existing and additionally required functionality. Here, the called framework is extended to a new framework with additional functionality. The extended called framework interface must call methods either in the existing framework or in the added functionality.

When the framework is a calling framework, mediating components are required [see Figure 20-8 (Gamma et al. 1995)] because framework 1 must be informed of events and actions occurring in framework 2 that are of application-wide importance. This communication from one framework to another must occur in terms under-standable to the receiving framework—hence the need for mediators. Sometimes the mediators will replace existing framework code functionality (although the code is usually left within the framework).

One problem with this approach is that the mediators become dependent on the current versions of the frameworks. Changing the frameworks may invalidate the mediator components or require additional mediator components.

Composite Entity Functionality One of the reasons for composing frame-works is to represent complex entities that may not be entirely supported by either framework. Consider the Model-View-Controller (MVC) software architecture, whose software architecture is depicted in Figure 20-9.

Each of the three layers can be implemented using a framework (such as ET++ or Garnet for the user interface, a domain-specific framework for the middle layer, and a persistence framework for the Controller). Some real-world entities must be rep-resented in all three frameworks.

Straight composition, as discussed above, may lead to complex mediators and/or glue code that does not result in the desired behavior or consistent representation. For example, changes of the state caused by messages to the application domain-spe-cific part of the resulting object will not automatically affect the user interface and persistence functionality of the objects.

One approach is to extend the application functionality by using an Observer (Gamma et al. 1995) that interacts with each of the three frameworks in a specific way. The Observer code will be dependent on the implementation of the three frameworks.

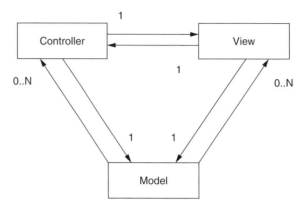

Figure 20-9. Model-View-Controller software architecture.

Component Overlap During Composition   When two frameworks are composed, they may contain representations of the same real-world entity. Each component is used within its own framework. The two components must be integrated, but typically one cannot replace the other. If the two representations contain mutually exclusive property sets, then they can be integrated directly. However, when there is overlap between the property sets, the integration problem becomes more difficult. Mattson and Bosch (1998) have identified three cases that must be considered.

1. Both components represent the same property, but with different representations; for example, different data types or structures. In this case, a mediator must be used to effect conversion between the two representations. Moreover, every time the component is updated in one framework, the mediator must effect the update in the other framework. For example, a sensor value may have to be converted from integer to floating point.

2. Both frameworks represent a property p, but one represents it as a state variable while the other represents it as a method that dynamically calculates the value as needed. For example, an actuator's state (e.g., open or closed) may be stored as a state variable, through indirect deduction from other state variables or through direct measurement.

3. Situations occur as the result of composition where execution of an operation in one framework will require changes to the state of components in the other framework. Using the example from the case above, a command to the actuator to "open" will require that the other framework's representation have its state changed to "open." Identifying such occurrences requires a component-by-component inspection of the two frameworks and the provision of glue code where such interactions must occur.

Composition with Legacy System Components   Frameworks are designed to solve problems in a particular domain. A specific application is constructed by extending and/or customizing the framework. Most frameworks will be implemented within an existing domain consisting of legacy applications. Thus, the framework will have to be integrated with legacy system components. This is not a trivial exercise, as most legacy components are usually not object-oriented while most frameworks are implemented using the object-oriented model. However, legacy components can be integrated using wrappers or adapters (Gamma et al. 1995).

To demonstrate this, we adapt an example from Mattsson and Bosch (1998). Suppose we have a process control system constructed before the advent of object-oriented programming. This system is composed of numerous components for sensors, gauges, and actuators as well as code modules that linked together provide the control and computation elements of the application. This process control system is to be replaced—in part—by a new system built using an object-oriented framework because new equipment has been installed. However, some old equipment is being retained and the legacy components interact with that equipment. So the legacy components must be integrated into the new process control system (Figure 20-10).

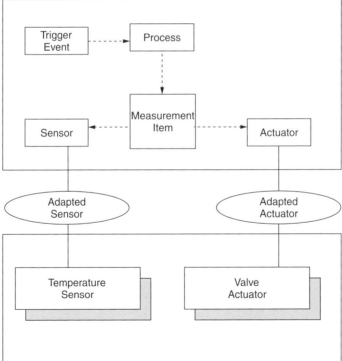

Figure 20-10. Integration of legacy components into a framework.

We have temperature sensors associated with particular pieces of legacy equipment. We must be able to read the values of those sensors and display them within the new process control framework. To do so, we create a component that wraps or adapts the legacy temperature sensor with code compatible with the framework (interface, data types, etc). We can use this component anywhere in the framework. When we finally replace the legacy equipment, we need to modify only one component to incorporate the new equipment. The disadvantage is that every piece of legacy equipment needs its own component with multiple methods to handle the specific features and characteristics of that equipment.

20.6.4   Framework Breakage

When a framework evolves, all applications developed using that framework are affected if they choose to update to the new framework version.

The framework developer may not know all of the applications that are built from the framework. He may evolve the framework based on feedback from some developers, including his own usage. But these modifications to the framework may cause the phenomenon of *framework breakage* in which an application built using the framework is updated to a new version and then ceases to work or does not work properly.

Framework breakage presents a major research problem in both framework design and the use of frameworks. On the one hand, frameworks cannot remain static if they are to have a significantly long useful lifetime. On the other hand, they cannot evolve so radically that they cause many applications to break when the framework version underlying an application is updated.

20.7   FRAMEWORK DOMAINS

We have left until now the question: What can frameworks be used for? Put another way, what applications are (most) amenable to development using frameworks? Alternatively, we can state this as: What applications do people really want? This question really has two answers.

First, frameworks can be applied to any application domain. Among the more recent popular domains for frameworks are industry-specific frameworks for eCommerce, workflow and office automation systems, portals and community websites, and, on a larger scale, intranet/Internet distributed applications.

Second, frameworks are most useful for developing medium to large complex applications because of the learning curve, the customization and extension effort, and the maintenance effort.

Frameworks have been defined for a large variety of domains such as multimedia (Posnak et al. 1997), operating systems within computer science and financial systems (Baumer et al. 1997), and many others (Fayad et al. 1999a, 1999b; Fayad and Johnson 2000).

20.8 FURTHER READING

Carey, J. and B. Carlson. 2002. *Framework Process Patterns: Lessons Learned Developing Application Frameworks*. Addison Wesley, Reading, MA.

Lewis, T. et al. 1995. *Object Oriented Application Frameworks*. Manning Publications, Greenwich, CT.

Mozilla.org. 2003. Creating Applications with Mozilla. Available at `http://books.mozdev.org/html/index.html`.

Sunsted, T. 2001. The Practice of Peer-to-Peer Computing: The P2P Application Framework. Available at `http://www.106.ibm.com/developerworks/java/library/jp2papp/`.

20.9 EXERCISES

20.1. Pick a non-object-oriented programming language. Describe how you would implement both a white-box and a black-box framework in this programming language.

20.2. The Java `Observer` and `Observable` classes allow you to implement black-box frameworks. Investigate the details of these classes and describe a black-box framework for an event-based software architecture. [Research Problem]

20.3. An application framework for Web-enabled, eBusiness applications must invoke legacy business logic. Identify five design patterns that are good methods for maintaining separation between Web application logic and business logic. Justify your answer.

20.4. Pick a domain with which you are familiar. Develop the requirements for the domain and decompose its structure. Describe the conceptual model of an application framework for applications within that domain.

20.5. It has been suggested that an operating system (e.g., Windows, MacOS X, Linux) is an application framework. Identify 10 requirements for an application framework, pick an operating system with which you are familiar, and argue convincingly why this might be so.

20.6. Frameworks can be very complex and difficult to understand. What mechanisms would you use to minimize complexity and ease the understanding of an application framework?

20.7. Do you think it would be harder to build an application framework in a programming language paradigm other than object-oriented programming? Why or why not? Argue convincingly with supporting references.

21

GUI FRAMEWORKS

Early frameworks were oriented toward programming environments and applications development using GUIs. Exemplars include Interviews (Linton et al. 1989), ET++ (Weinand et al. 1988), Smalltalk-80 (Goldberg and Robson 1983), and MacApp (Pugh and Leung 1988, Wilson et al. 1990). We'll briefly survey the Smalltalk, MacApp, and Taligent commercial frameworks in this chapter.

Gamma and colleagues developed ET++ (Weinand and Gamma 1994) because making computers easier to use through graphics and pictures rather than just text and numbers made them easier to learn and more fun to use. However, they knew that it required considerable effort because the developer had to provide both the application functionality as well as the graphical functionality that presented and manipulated information and interacted with the user. It is not uncommon for 50–80% of the code in a GUI-based application to be devoted to the user interface.

Toolboxes had been developed in the late 1970s and early 1980s, for example, the Motif toolbox from the X Windows Consortium and the Macintosh Toolbox. But toolboxes are just collections of library functions that implement the low-level functions of the user interface. Generally, toolboxes are not extensible without modifying the source code. Much of the application program's code was used to glue together the toolbox routines that provided the basic GUI functionality. Toolboxes did not provide an architectural framework for constructing applications and user interface consistency was only enforceable at the level of individual widgets.

This led Gamma, Weinand, and others to develop GUI development frameworks that prescribed an architectural solution for implementing a GUI-based application.

Software Paradigms, By Stephen H. Kaisler
ISBN 0-471-48347-8   Copyright © 2005 John Wiley & Sons, Inc.

21.1 SMALLTALK-80 PROGRAMMING ENVIRONMENT

The Smalltalk-80 programming environment (Goldberg and Robson 1983, Winston 1998) is a multiwindowed, interactive environment for programming and computing. It is one of the earliest exemplars of an integrated framework that allows programs to be designed, developed, debugged, and deployed within a single computational environment. Smalltalk influenced the Xerox Star 8010, the Apple Macintosh operating system, and the Windows 9x/NT/2000 operating systems.

Smalltalk was originally conceived as part of Alan Kay's Dynabook project at Xerox PARC. The Dynabook was based on a vision of inexpensive notebook-sized personal computers for both adults and children, with the power to handle all their information-related needs. It was based on the assumption of ample memory and processing power, as well as a flat-screen display sensitive to the touch of a finger. He envisioned a multitude of uses for such devices, in areas as diverse as the drawing of pictures, storage of information, instrumentation of music, the dynamic simulation and graphical animation of models, the representation of objects in three-dimensional space, or the computation of inventories and cash flows within a company. Note that his vision has been achieved in modern day personal digital assistants (PDAs).

Kay felt that existing languages did not meet the needs of this diverse community of users. Thus, development of a new programming language was given a high priority. Seymour Papert at MIT had developed a language called Logo that features ease of use because it was developed for children to use. Kay adopted many of its core concepts but focused on a building block approach that supported the dynamic environment of programming that he had in mind. Smalltalk is the result; it is the first language based on the notions of objects and using messages to communicate between them.

Smalltalk is so named because it was intended for use by children without any prior programming experience. The first usable version was called Smalltalk-72 and became available in 1972. It is the subject of a very famous *Byte* magazine cover. It evolved through several revisions to Smalltalk-76, which added the mechanism of inheritance, until Smalltalk-80 became the first publicly released version. Although Smalltalk has continued to evolve with support from IBM and others, and Xerox spun off the Smalltalk group as ParcPlace Systems, the basic concepts have largely been adhered to.

21.1.1 Smalltalk's Central Concept

The central concept behind the Smalltalk-80 environment is the Model-View-Controller (MVC) paradigm. In the MVC paradigm, three basic activities are separated into three separate subsystems. The *view* activity manages the graphical and/or textual output to the portion of the bitmapped display that is allocated to its application. The *controller* activity interprets the mouse and keyboard inputs from the user, directing the model and/or the view activities to change as appropriate. The *model* activity manages the processing and data of the application domain, responds to

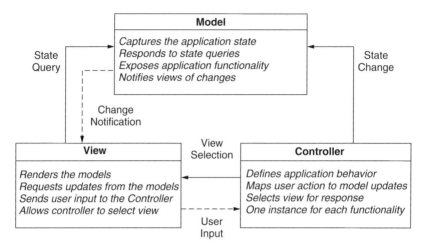

Figure 21-1. The MVC paradigm flow of control.

requests for information about its state from the view, and responds to instructions to change state from the controller.

The flow of control can be depicted succinctly as in Figure 21-1.

Because Smalltalk-80 is an object-oriented programming environment, these activities are encapsulated in objects that are inherited in order to create an application. The application is embedded within the Smalltalk-80 environment.

The MVC objects define an application environment. These objects communicate with each other in order to provide a coherent interaction with the user and a consistent set of operations to facilitate. Two objects, *View* and *Controller*, are predefined in the Smalltalk-80 environment. Application-specific functionality is defined through inheritance and specialization from these generic objects. The model is application-dependent as it represents the application's behavior. A generic object, *Object*, defines a standard set of methods for all entities within the Smalltalk-80 programming environment. Every model inherits from and specializes the methods of *Object*.

The following sections describe the MVC objects in greater detail (Burbeck 1992).

Views   A *view* is a screen representation for presenting information from a model to the user. Every application has at least one view. In the Smalltalk-80 programming environment, windows represent views on a bitmapped display. Windows require two views with one nested inside the other. The outermost view, known as the topView, is an instance of *StandardSystemView* or one of its subclasses. It handles the window's title bar, which gives access to the standard window operations that are performed by the associated controller, which is an instance of *StandardSystemController*. Within the topView are one or more application-dependent subViews. The standard Smalltalk-80 workspace, in which you can type text, has as its subView an instance of

Table 21-1. Some Smalltalk-80 subViews

View	Description
BinaryChoiceView	The thumbs up/down prompter
SwitchView	Used as tool buttons in BitEditor and FormEditor
BooleanView	Used for browser instance/class switch
DisplayTextView	Used for message in the upper subView of a yes/no prompter
CodeView	Used for browser subView, which shows code
StringHolderView	Used by workspaces
FillInTheBlankView	The familiar question prompter with a text answer
FormMenuView	Used for buttons by BitEditor and FormEditor
FormHolderView	Used by BitEditor and FormEditor for edited form
ListView	Used for browser list subviews
StandardSystemView	Provides topView functions
BrowserView	An application for browsing code
InspectorView	An application for viewing an execution stack

StringHolderView. SubViews may have subViews of their own based on the needs of the application.

A view makes itself visible on the screen by sending itself the message *self display*. Specifically, the *update*: method in *View* sends *self display*. *View display* in turn sends *self displayBorder. self displayView. self displaySubviews.* Each application inherits from View and specializes these methods in order to achieve the type of display required by the application. The Smalltalk-80 programming environment includes many subclasses of View that provide predefined behavior for different kinds of data structures. Table 21-1 briefly describes some of these views; consult Goldberg and Robson (1983) for more details.

Controllers   In most Smalltalk-80 environments, the primary interaction device is the mouse. As you move and click the mouse, the objects on the Smalltalk-80 screen respond based on directions from their associated controllers. There is no single authority, however. Each view has its own *controller*. The controller provides the mechanism for controlling the user's interactions with the model. The controllers coordinate their actions since only one controller can have control at any time.

All the controllers for all the views are arranged in a hierarchical ordering. The first-level subViews under topView have their controllers ordered based on the ordering of the subViews on the screen. Within each subview, its subview's controllers are also hierarchically arranged. When an interrupt occurs due to a mouse button click, control is passed down the ordered list of controllers. Each controller refuses control if it determines the cursor is not within the immediate boundaries of its view. If a subview has subviews, it must poll the controllers of each of those subviews to determine if the cursor is within any of their immediate boundaries. This cooperation among controllers usually ensures that the right controller responds to the mouse click.

The most visible consequence of control moving from view to view is the movement of the scroll bars from window to window. As the cursor crosses boundaries of subViews within the browser, the scroll bar of the just exited subView disappears and the scroll bar for the entered subView appears.

Most applications use the mouse for pointing and menu options. Most controllers are therefore subclasses from *MouseMenuController*, which provides the basic instance variables and methods. On the Xerox PARC machines (the Dolphin, Dorado, and Dandelion), the three buttons of the mouse were labeled red, yellow, and blue, so the messages that were sent were *redButtonMessages*, *yellowButtonMessages*, and *BlueButtonMessages*.

The *Controller controlLoop* method, as its name implies, is the main control loop. Each time through this loop, it sends *self controlActivity*. This method is reimplemented in *MouseMenuController* to check each of the mouse buttons. For example, it sends *self redButtonActivity* if the red button is pressed and its view has the cursor. The xxxButtonActivity checks for a non nil xxxButtonMenu and, if found, sends the message *self menuMessageReceiver perform: (redButtonMessages at: index)*.

The *StandardSystemController* is a subclass of *MouseMenuController*, which is specialized to operate at the top level of a window's controller hierarchy. It manages the *blueButtonMenu*—the frame, close, collapse,... behaviors of windows that apply to the topView. Each subview controller should be a subclass of *MouseMenuController*.

Models   The *model* represents the application's data and the business rules that govern access to and updates of this data. Often the model serves as a software approximation to a real-world process, so simple real-world modeling techniques apply when defining the model.

Model objects are the data-bearing objects of your application. A well-designed MVC application has all its important data encapsulated in model objects. Any data that is part of the persistent state of the application should reside in the model objects once the data is loaded into the application.

Ideally, a model object has no connection to the user interface used to present and edit it. However, performance considerations sometimes mandate an alternative approach and there is flexibility in how this is actually implemented. But, in general, a model object should not be concerned with interface and presentation issues.

21.1.2   Brief Language Overview

Smalltalk is (in my opinion) the only pure object-oriented language that cleanly supports the notion of classes, methods, messages, and inheritance. A Smalltalk program is composed of a collection of objects and their instances. Objects communicate by exchanging messages. The programming environment itself is a collection of specialized objects for software development, testing, and management (Goldberg and Robson 1983, LaLonde and Pugh 1990). A large number of predefined classes are provided in the Smalltalk programming environment for all sorts of things that give the language its flexibility. Most of these classes are defined in Smalltalk itself. A few primitives exist, defined in the machine language of the host computer system

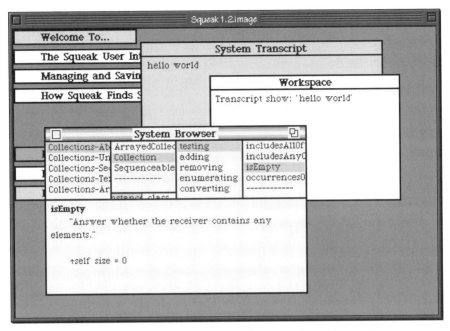

Figure 21-2. Squeak screen image of programming environment.

on which the virtual machine is implemented, but these are largely for efficiency reasons.

The user opens Smalltalk in the programming environment. A screen shot of the Squeak programming environment (http://www.squeak.org) is shown in Figure 21-2.

The *System Browser* allows the user to inspect the class hierarchy, to open the class to inspect its methods, and to edit and modify the code of a class. In the *Workspace*, the user types Smalltalk expressions that are evaluated. The Transcript records the history of the user's interactions and system actions, including any output generated by the user's evaluation of Smalltalk expressions in the Workspace.

21.1.3   The Virtual Machine

Smalltalk is implemented on a *virtual machine* (VM), which masks the characteristics and idiosyncrasies of the underlying hardware and operating system. The VM provides a set of byte codes in which Smalltalk classes are encoded. The VM interprets these byte codes in order to execute Smalltalk, including the programming environment.

The programming environment is distributed as a virtual image (VI), for example, a collection of compiled Smalltalk classes–Smalltalk source code translated into the byte codes. The VI is machine-independent, while the VM is machine-dependent. Porting Smalltalk to another platform requires that one develop an implementation of the VM to run on that platform's operating system. The success of this approach led to Sun Microsystems adopting the same approach for the Java programming language.

Numerous implementations of Smalltalk have appeared over the past two decades, but today the key survivors are PARCPlace's VisualWorks, which resulted from its merger with DigiTalk; IBM's Visual Age Smalltalk; and Squeak, a public domain version.

21.1.4 MVC uses Design Patterns

Johnson (1992) (`http://c2.com/cgi/wiki?ModelViewControllerAsAnAgg regate DesignPattern`) notes that MVC is made up of several smaller design patterns. The views form a tree using the Composite pattern. The relationship between views and models is based on the Observer pattern. The controllers are implemented as Strategies of the views. A view may use an Adapter pattern to convert the model to a standard interface usable (and expected) by the view. Views create controllers through the use of a Factory pattern.

Furthermore, the model is often implemented using the Mediator pattern, such as the Smalltalk browser. And views are often extended through the addition of properties using the Decorator pattern.

HotDraw HotDraw is a 2-D graphics drawing program developed by John Vlissides (1990) for his Ph.D. thesis. It is a framework written entirely in Smalltalk. A HotDraw application edits drawings made up of figures. Figures are composed of lines, ellipses, text, and other objects. A drawing editor built from HotDraw contains a set of tools that create new figures and manipulate the drawing. Only one tool can be active at a time and this tool accepts input from the user via either keyboard or mouse. When a figure in a drawing is selected by the user, it presents a set of handles (e.g., markers on the screen that can be grasped by the mouse). Manipulating a handle changes some property of the figure or performs some action. For example, one might grasp the corner handle of a rectangle and drag it horizontally or vertically to increase its width or length.

MVC Implementation HotDraw is implemented using the MVC architecture embedded in the Smalltalk framework. The Drawing Controller handles input from the user either from the mouse or the keyboard. Because Smalltalk supports a three-button mouse, input from the buttons is treated differently depending on which button is pressed and what the current context is. Pressing the left mouse button selects operations that are tool-dependent, while the middle and right mouse buttons provide behavior associated with the window in which the drawing is depicted. The Drawing Controller is responsible for handling all input from the user based on the current context and so is more complex than the standard controllers included in Smalltalk.

A system with different toolsets can be created by subclassing Drawing Controller so that each application has its own controller and adds new tools and actions for tools to its own controller. The controller decides at runtime which action to perform. To ensure the right action is performed, the mouse clicks or keyboard entries are passed to the tool object to interpret and execute the proper method.

The Drawing View displays the drawing that is to be created and manipulated in a window. The Drawing View handles the buffering necessary to prevent the figure from flashing on the screen as it is being redrawn after a user manipulation.

The Drawing Editor is the model of the system. An application is started by sending an open message to the Drawing Editor. The Editor must know the tools for the tool palette and the type of drawing to create. Most programs redefine the default tools method so that they can add their own tools and redefine the behavior of other tools.

Advantages of the MVC Framework   The MVC framework has the following benefits:

- One model could be viewed in several different ways. The separation of model and view allows multiple views to use the same model. Consequently, an application's model components are easier to implement, test, and maintain, since all access to the model goes through these components.
- New types of clients can easily be added to the framework, each accessing the same model. To support a new type of client, you simply write a view and controller for it and wire them into the existing model.

21.1.5   Smalltalk References

Numerous articles and books have been written about the Smalltalk programming language since its inception in the early 1970s. As one of the first self-contained programming environments, it sets the standard against which other programming environments need to be assessed. Section 21.5 provides some additional information on the Smalltalk programming environment and language.

You might also consult `comp.lang.smalltalk`, a news group that has varying amounts of information regarding Smalltalk.

21.2   MACAPP FRAMEWORK

MacApp is a programming environment for Apple Macintosh OS applications (Pugh and Leung, 1988, Schmucker 1986, Wilson et al. 1990). It differed from previous frameworks in that it was basically a working skeleton application that programmers could easily customize. MacApp was implemented on top of the Macintosh Toolbox, a set of routines that implemented the Macintosh GUI environment. In a sense, MacApp is a virtual machine layered over the Toolbox that made programming new GUI applications much easier.

MacApp has been improved continuously since its first release. As of this writing, Release XV.1, which supports MacOS X, has been released and, effective October 2001, Apple has terminated support for the MacApp framework. Information on MacApp can be found at `http://developer.apple.com/tools/macapp/`.

MacApp sets the standard for an application development framework in the following ways:

- It is a standalone, "clickable" vanilla application that runs under the Macintosh OS. It has menu bars and windows, works with the clipboard, and prints—all functions one normally expects of a Macintosh application.
- It is a vanilla application since all the windows are empty, the menus are blank, and it prints out blank paper.
- It can easily be extended by subclassing and overriding.
- It provides a set of special null methods that enable the framework to access your code. The programmer overrides these methods to do routine customization like enabling menu items or processing mouse clicks.
- It provides a set of standard Macintosh control widgets.

MacApp was originally written in Object Pascal, a hybrid language developed by Apple by grafting object-oriented support onto Pascal. A new data type, object, has been added to the standard Pascal data types. Objects are like record data types in Pascal. However, functions and procedures may also be associated with objects in addition to fields. This enabled Apple to write the original MacOS (pre OS X) as a procedural operating system with object-oriented support. Subsequently, MacApp was ported to C++ to provide support for C++ applications.

21.2.1 Application Structure

Interactive graphics-based applications are event-driven. MacApp incorporates the event-loop model as the basic structure of a Macintosh application. As the user types on the keyboard, clicks the mouse button, or inserts a floppy disk, MacApp receives the interrupt event data from MacOS and passes it to the application.

Macintosh applications are difficult to program because the programmer must learn large parts of the Macintosh Toolbox to support the user interface and interact with the operating system. To avoid this long learning curve, MacApp provides a simple framework that allows a programmer to obtain a working, if simple, application with a few hundred lines of code. The programmer can then evolve the application incrementally to provide all the desired functionality and features. This allows the programmer to get an application running quickly. The feedback associated with seeing a running application soon after working with a development system is both reassuring and energizing to many programmers.

21.2.2 MacApp Contents

MacApp XV consists of over 200 classes and over 2000 methods. The classes of MacApp are meant to map to the Macintosh OS objects, so there are classes named TApplication, TDocument, TWindow, TButton, TClipboardView, and so forth. The interconnections between these classes reflect the standard Macintosh application. So TApplication contains all of the TDocument objects and these, in turn, contain a list of TWindow objects for handling how they display themselves.

The standard Macintosh application contains one TApplication object, one or more TDocument objects, and so on. These objects are instances of subclasses of the MacApp classes. Within a subclass, the programmer overrides the methods to provide the functionality specific to the application. Each method name begins with the word "Do."

MacApp ships in a shrink-wrapped package with ten complete applications of varying degrees of complexity. The programmer chooses the application closest to the desired application and customizes and massages it until it matches the desired appearance and functionality.

21.2.3 MacApp Example

MacApp uses a factory method to instantiate document objects (Onion and Harrison 1996). This method, DoMakeDocument(), exists in its application base class, TApplication. The user-defined application class is expected to override this method to create an instance of the user-defined document type.

```
class TMyApplication : public TApplication
  {
  virtual TDocument*
  DoMakeDocument(CommandNumber cmd, TFile* file)
    {
    return new TMyDocument;
    }
  <other methods>
  };
```

To create a new document, the application calls DoMakeDocument() with the appropriate arguments. If you want to open an existing file, you call TApplication::OpenOld(), which in turn invokes DoMakeDocument() to virtually construct the document:

```
TApplication::OpenOld(CommandNumber cmd, TList* files)
  {
  // Find file descrption via directory
  ...

  // Determine document type
  ...

  // Create new document
  aDocument = DoMakeDocument(docType, file);

  // Prepare internal document view
  ...

  return aDocument;
  }
```

This looks pretty straightforward, but MacApp had an inherent limitation. With just one application object per TApplication, there was only one factory method. It had to be extended for each document type to be opened: thus the argument

CommandNumber, which allows the client to specify the type of document to be opened. Internal to OpenOld, a C++ switch statement is used to select the code pertinent to the document type. The limitation with this approach is that to extend the application to new document types you had to modify and recompile the source code.

21.3 THE TALIGENT FRAMEWORK

Taligent was founded by IBM and Apple in 1992 to develop a completely object-oriented operating system based on the framework concept. Hewlett-Packard joined the founders in 1994. Taligent's idea was to produce an operating system that could enable programs to be built up of small, interchangeable parts. You would build your system in an evolutionary way, so that you could replace obsolete, buggy, or immature parts with new ones, instead of replacing the whole program, and thereby losing its good features.

However, Taligent eventually scrapped the operating system concept and replaced it with an "application framework," the Taligent Application Environment (TAE), that could run on top of any OS, making acceptance easier since you can still run old programs for the OS. In 1995, the framework was renamed CommonPoint as it entered beta testing.

The company delivered a set of tools for rapid application development under the name CommonPoint that consists of more than a hundred object-oriented frameworks. The Taligent approach made a shift in focus to many fine-grained integrated frameworks and away from large monolithic frameworks. Taligent's (1993, 1994) philosophy was that it should be easier and less expensive to build new applications from the framework than designing them from scratch.

Ultimately, HP dropped out and IBM purchased Apple's interest in Taligent. Much of the CommonPoint framework survives today and has been integrated with IBM's SOM technology (Myers 1995).

21.3.1 The Taligent Model

CommonPoint provides an application system with a set of standard services and APIs for various host operating systems. User applications invoke the CommonPoint service APIs, which, in turn, invoke the operating system services of the respective host operating systems. In effect, the CommonPoint application system creates a virtual machine on top of the underlying operating system (Figure 21-3). Applications written to the CommonPoint application system are portable to different hosts with recompilation and binding.

21.3.2 The CommonPoint Frameworks

CommonPoint provides two types of frameworks:

- *Application Frameworks:* These frameworks provide a rich set of features that allow the creation of interactive, easy-to-use applications.

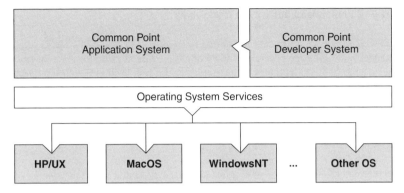

Figure 21-3. The Taligent model.

Figure 21-4. CommonPoint frameworks.

- *System Services:* These frameworks provide a complete set of system-level services on which the CommonPoint application system is built.

These are further subdivided into three categories of frameworks as depicted in Figure 21-4.

Application Frameworks Application frameworks provided features for developing interactive applications. The CommonPoint Application Frameworks are divided into three categories as depicted in Table 21-2 (http://root.cern.ch/).

The Presentation Framework was the generic framework used by most users because it unified a number of document models and user interface mechanisms.

The System Services Framework supports specific problem areas. For example, the Data Access Framework provides mechanisms for accessing, querying, and modifying data on remote or local SQL databases.

21.4 OTHER FRAMEWORKS

Numerous academic frameworks have been developed over the past twenty years, especially those intended to explore the development of user interface management

Table 21-2. CommonPoint application frameworks

Framework Type	Usage	Subframeworks
Embeddable data types	Support viewing and editing of complex data types, with fullsupport for linking and embedding	Graphics Editing Framework Text Editing Framework Document Data Access Framework Time Media User Interface Framework
Desktop frameworks	Provide support for the CommonPoint application model, including its user interface policy, its look and feel, and its compound document architecture	Workspace Frameworks Presentation Framework Document Frameworks User Interface Frameworks
Application services	Support media and data handling services needed to create industrial-strength interactive applications	Interoperability Services Printing Scanning Time Media Localization Services Text Graphics

Source: http://pcroot.cern.ch/TaligentDocs/TaligentOnline/DocumentRoot/1.0/Docs/taxonomy/Application Frameworks.html.

systems (UIMSs). A plethora of GUI toolkits can be found at http://www.free-soft.org/guitool/. Frameworks have also been developed for specific application domains.

21.4.1 ET++ and MET++

One of the most frequently used GUI frameworks was ET++ developed by Gamma and Weinand (Gamma, Weinand, and Marty 1989; Weinand and Gamma 1994). It was later superseded by MET++ (Ackermann 1996), which extended the basic concepts to a multimedia application framework. MET++ supports the development of multimedia applications by providing reusable objects for 2-D graphics, user interface components, 3-D graphics, video, audio, and music.

Collaboration and communication mechanisms between these objects are built into the framework. Thus, using the class library enables a programmer to build a running application where control flow, event dispatching, and message passing are preimplemented. MET++ manages the standard behavior of a multimedia application such as time synchronization and user interaction. A developer customizes the MET++ application framework by composing reusable objects, by building subclasses through inheritance, and by overwriting hook methods to add the specific functionality required by the application.

MET++ is implemented in C++ and runs on Unix workstations. The MET++ architecture is depicted in Figure 21-5 (Universitat Zurich 1994).

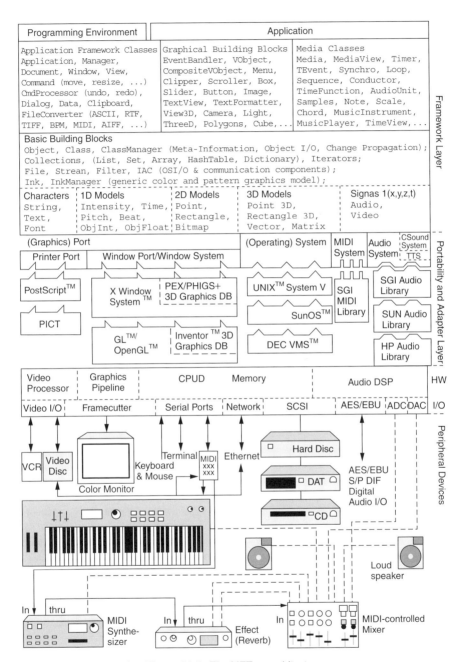

Figure 21-5. The MET++ architecture.

Object: Root of inheritance
    System: Operating system abstraction for portability
        UnixSystem: Unix operating system support
    WindowSystem: Windowing system abstraction for portability
        SunWinSystem: SunWindows support
        XWinSystem: XWindows support
    Port: Drawing device abstraction
        WindowPort: Window abstraction for drawing portability
            SunWindowPort: SunWindow drawing support
            XWindowPort: XWindows drawing support
        PrintPort: Printing abstraction for printer portability
            MacPictPrinter: Macintosh PICT creation support
            Postscript: Postscript printer support
    Command: A command object
        ImageCommand: Abstract command class for iconedit
            BitMover: Moves bitmap section in iconedit
            RectCommand: Draws rectangle in iconedit
    EvtHandler: Event handling code
        VObject: Root of visible object hierarchy
            CompositeVObject: Composite pattern for recursive VObject
                Button: A standard button widget
                Scroller: A widget to scroll a VObject
                Matte: A layout object
                Box: A layout box
                    HBox: A horizontal layout box
                    VBox: A vertical layout box
                    Expander: A layout box to expand bounds
            ImageItem: A bitmap object
            View: A view of a document's data
                IconView: View of icon in iconedit
          Clipper: Rectangular graphical clipping object
            Window: Window object
        Manager: Manages a Window
            Application: An application for managing documents
                iconedit: The iconedit application
            Document: A document containing some data
                IconDocument: Document for iconedit
    Ink: An ink used for drawing
        RGBColor: An RGB-deWned colored ink
        Bitmap: An bitmap-based tiled pattern ink

Figure 21-6. The ET++ inheritance hierarchy (partial).

Figure 21-6 depicts part of the ET++ inheritance hierarchy to give you a feel for its richness.

21.5 FURTHER READING

Kaehler, T. and D. Patterson. 1986. *A Taste of Smalltalk*. Norton & Co., San Francisco, CA.

LaLonde, W. 1994. *Discovering Smalltalk*. Addison Wesley, Reading, MA.

LaLonde, W. and J. R. Pugh. 1991. *Inside Smalltalk*, Vols. I and II. Prentice Hall, Englewood Cliffs, NJ.

Lewis, S. 1995. *The Art and Science of Smalltalk*. Prentice Hall, Englewood Cliffs, NJ.

Pinson, L. J. 1988. *An Introduction to Object-Oriented Programming and Smalltalk*. Addison Wesley, Reading, MA.

Pletzke, J. 1997. *Advanced Smalltalk*. John Wiley & Sons, Hoboken, NJ.

21.6 EXERCISES

21.1. Here's an exercise that I give to my students in CS210 at GWU. Acquire the source code for the text-based adventure game called Colossal Cave. This is available on many websites. This game is at least 30+ years old and was one of the first games to be developed to exploit the time-sharing phenomenon and interactive computing. Pick a GUI development tool, such as Java's AWT or Swing classes, Microsoft Windows SDK, MET++, or some other tool and develop a Windows-based version of Adventure. This project can be done in a semester by two or three people. Usually the source code has to be upgraded or converted.

21.2. Discuss whether it is a good idea to rely on the host operating system for specific services. Of the services mentioned in this chapter, which ones should you implement natively (e.g., within the framework itself) and which should you rely on the operating system to provide?

22

DEVELOPMENT FRAMEWORKS

Application frameworks have continued to evolve since the early frameworks that focused primarily on GUI development.

22.1 JAVA AS A FRAMEWORK

Sun Microsystems started developing Java as a programming language for embedded systems. However, over the past ten years, Java has evolved into a comprehensive set of services that classify it as an application development framework. The most advanced is the Java 2 Platform, Enterprise Edition, also known as J2EE.

J2EE is a set of specifications, each of which dictates how a type of functionality is to be supplied with Java technology. The J2EE platform provides a complete framework for design, development, assembly, and deployment of Java applications built on a multitiered distributed application model. It is primarily oriented to the development and deployment of enterprise-level, Web-oriented applications using the Java language. The J2EE application architecture is depicted in Figure 22-1.

The J2EE application architecture contains four programming environments, called *containers*:

- *EJB Container:* Supports the development, deployment, and runtime management of enterprise beans, which implement the business processes and represent business entities.

Software Paradigms, By Stephen H. Kaisler
ISBN 0-471-48347-8   Copyright © 2005 John Wiley & Sons, Inc.

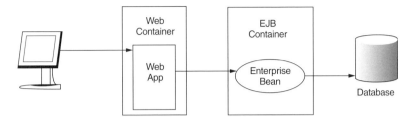

Figure 22-1. J2EE application architecture.

- *Web Container:* Supports the development, deployment, and runtime management of servlets and JavaServer pages, which comprise the Web applications.
- *Client Container:* Supports the execution of J2EE application clients; it is basically J2SE.
- *Applet Container:* Supports the execution of Java applets and is usually embedded in a Web browser.

J2EE contains a CORBA-compliant ORB. EJB containers communicate via CORBA standard protocols such as RMI-over IIOP and the Object Transaction Service. EJB was discussed in Section 10.4.

22.1.1 J2EE Overview

The J2EE platform is designed to provide both server-side and client-side support for developing distributed, multitier applications. The J2EE model defines a client tier, a middle or business logic tier, and a back-end tier. The client tier supports a variety of different client types. The middle tier supports both web services and business logic. There may be multiple middle tiers to meet the business operations needs of the organization. The back-end tier supports enterprise information systems and databases. The J2EE platform does not restrict the location of the tiers, so all three can run on one hardware platform or be distributed across multiple hardware platforms.

The middle tier is implemented using EJB containers. Containers are standardized runtime environments that provide specific services to components. Every EJB container provides support for responding to client requests, processing those requests, and returning the results. To utilize the back-end systems, all containers provide mechanisms for accessing enterprise information systems, including the Java Data Base Connectivity (JDBC) solution to access relational databases. Containers also provide a mechanism for dynamic configuration of application behavior at runtime. Through the use of XML deployment descriptors, components can be configured to a specific container's environment.

Clients Multiple client types are supported including web-enabled clients, stand along Java applications, or Java applets. Clients are assumed to access the middle tier using web services such as HTML, (S)HTTP, and XML. This approach provides a simple programming and development model that can lead to rapid development and deployment of applications.

Complex client components can be developed using JavaBeans. Typically, client JavaBeans components would access the middle tier containers through servlets. The client components would be provided as applets that are dynamically downloaded into the user's browser. Alternatively, the client can be a Java applications, which can be downloaded and installed using Java Web Start technology. In either event, the downloaded application or applets can be trusted if the source site is trusted. Moreover, in the case of applets, the user is always assured of using the current version of the applet. And Java Web Start technology can check to ensure that the latest version of the application has been installed and warn the user if the application needs to be updated.

J2EE supports non-Java clients as long as they access the middle tier through web standard services. In fact, the middle tier can be made client agnostic, although Java-based clients have access to additional services.

Business Logic Components   Business logic components reside in the middle tier (except for those services provided by enterprise-wide information systems in the back-end tier). Business logic components will be built using the Enterprise JavaBeans (EJB) technology. EJB containers support the development and implementation of reliable, robust services.

Enterprise Information Systems   Enterprise information systems reside in the back-end tier. J2EE provides mechanisms for accessing these systems. The basic APIs are the following:

- The J2EE Connector architecture is the infrastructure for interacting with a variety of enterprise information system types, including ERP, CRM, and other legacy systems.
- The JDBC API can be used to access relational data from the Java programming language.
- The Java Transaction API (JTA) can be used to manage and coordinate transactions across heterogeneous enterprise information systems.
- The Java Naming and Directory Interface (JNDI) can be used to access information in enterprise name and directory services.
- The Java Message Service (JMS) can be used to send and receive messages via enterprise messaging systems such as the IBM MQ Series.
- The JavaMail API is used for sending and receiving e-mail.
- Java IDL provides a mechanism for calling CORBA services.
- Java APIs for XML provide support for integration with legacy systems and applications, and for implementing Web services in the J2EE platform.

22.1.2 Advantages of J2EE

A J2EE application is comprised of one or more Enterprise JavaBeans that encapsulate the business logic for an organization. Other elements of the J2EE architecture provide additional functionality and service. J2EE provides the following advantages to application developers:

- *Simplicity:* Because EJB handles many functions such as security, transaction processing, multithreading, and resource allocation, it is easier to develop N-tier client–server applications.
- *Application Portability:* Because EJB components can be deployed on any J2EE-compliant server, they can become the basis for third-party component markets.
- *Component Reusability:* Because each EJB component is a building block of an application, EJB components can be reused in many applications. EJB components deployed on a J2EE server can be called via the CORBA communication protocols.
- *Build Complex Applications:* The J2EE architecture supports the development of complex applications since EJB components can be stubbed out while development proceeds incrementally. Multiple developers can provide EJB components and other glue code for an application.
- *Separation of Business and Presentation Logic:* While business logic is captured in EJB, presentation logic is captured in applets or JavaBeans executing in J2SE on the client's workstation or system.
- *Distributed Deployment:* EJB can be deployed in many different environments as long as it provides a J2EE-compliant server. Applications can be implemented on a single server or distributed across many servers, transparently to the client.
- *Application Interoperability:* EJB makes it easy to integrate applications from many vendors as long as communication occurs between the EJB components.
- *Integration with Non-Java Systems:* Through other Java services, such as the Java Message Service (JMS), non-Java systems can be integrated with EJB-based applications.

J2EE has been heavily documented in articles, white papers, and books. Section 22.5 provides some additional references for digging deeper into this framework.

22.1.3 Java Media Framework

The Java Media Framework (JMF) extends the Java environment with additional classes and JavaBeans to support time-based, multimedia applications. Among the functions supported are 2-D and 3-D imagery, speech, telephony, and sound. JMF was originally developed in 1997 for playback only but was extended to JMF2.0 in

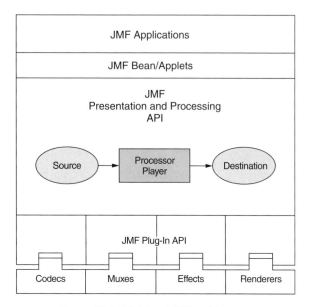

Figure 22-2. High-level JMF architecture.

1999 for capture and playback. JMF 2.0 also supported plug-in components that allowed third-party development. The high-level architecture for JMF 2.0 is depicted in Figure 22-2.

The JMF Presentation and Processing API controls the conversion of the media stream from an analog or digital representation to an digital or analog representation. This may involve capture and store, retrieval and playback, or capture and store and playback. This API, in turn, invokes methods in the JMF Plug-In API that actually manages and controls plug-in components, such as muxes, codecs, effects modules, and renderers.

JMF uses four manager components:

1. *Manager:* This component in the Presentation and Processing API handles the construction of Players, Processors, DataSources, and DataSinks. This level of indirection allows new implementations to be integrated seamlessly with JMF. From the client perspective, these objects are always created the same way whether the requested object is constructed from a default implementation or a custom one.

2. *PackageManager:* This component maintains a registry of custom components that are integrated with JMF.

3. *CaptureDeviceManager:* This component maintains a registry of all capture devices currently integrated.

4. *PlugInManager:* This component maintains a registry of all plug-in modules.

22.1.4   Sun One Application Framework

Sun Microsystems has developed the Sun One Application Framework for delivering web-enabled applications and services using a common foundation. It extends the J2EE environment with specific components oriented to the Service-to-Workers and Model-View-Controller web-based service architectures (Sun Microsystems 2003).

Sun One provides a skeleton based on design patterns that enterprise architects can use to develop Web-based service applications. In particular, it defines Model and View entities and provides a base Controller logic that can be customized to meet the organization's needs. Sun One integrates JSP technology to support servlet definition and implementation.

Additional information on the Sun One application framework can be found at the Sun Microsystems web site: `http://docs.sun.com/db/coll/ S1_appframe20_en`.

22.2   MICROSOFT'S .NET FRAMEWORK

Microsoft has embraced a distributed architectural concept for hosting applications based on Internet technology. It has termed this concept the ".NET" platform. The .NET framework builds on the lessons learned by Microsoft in implementing and deploying the COM/DCOM and ActiveX technologies. As of this writing (June 2003), Microsoft has embedded .NET version 1.1 into Microsoft Windows Advanced Server 2003.

.NET provides both a software development environment and a software support environment built around core Windows concepts and Microsoft programming languages. This combination provides transaction services, message queuing, directory services, and web services in a single entity and eliminates the need for middleware that formerly provided the glue to tie these services to the operating system.

22.2.1   Why .NET?

Over the past ten years, since the advent of technology of the Web, the world of computing has changed considerably, perhaps even radically. Where computing used to be a collection of workstations, minicomputers, and, perhaps, mainframes, coupled together by local area networks, now computing is a distributed activity. With broadband almost an ubiquitous technology, the concept of computing has migrated from a localized phenomenon to a national or even worldwide phenomenon. That doesn't mean a lot of computing isn't done on local workstations; what it means is that today's users reach out more and more through the web to obtain different types of computing services from other locales.

One aspect of this is that as people travel more and more, they expect information that they routinely use in work, play, and their daily lives to be accessible and available wherever they go, on multiple devices—from workstations to PDAs to cellular telephones that are Internet-enabled. Access to information worldwide leads to server-based applications and databases.

The .NET framework is an overlay for the Internet. It can be implemented on any Windows-enabled device. Visual Studio .NET, Microsoft's end-user development environment, allows applications and databases to be developed for any device running .NET. .NET supports XML, which is rapidly becoming the lingua franca of the information exchange world because of its versatility and flexibility.

The .NET architecture was developed based on the following principles (Miller 2001):

- Make Internet-scale distributed computing ubiquitous.
- Exploit inexpensive cycles and bandwidth across the net on different machines.
- Support seamless integration of multiple applications and devices.
- Deliver software as a service.
- Establish next generation user experience.
- Put the user in control of security and privacy for his technology and data needs.

22.2.2 The .NET Framework Architecture

The .NET Framework is depicted in Figure 22-3.

With COM (Section 10.3), components could be integrated, but each component had to provide its own plumbing and objects could not interact directly with other

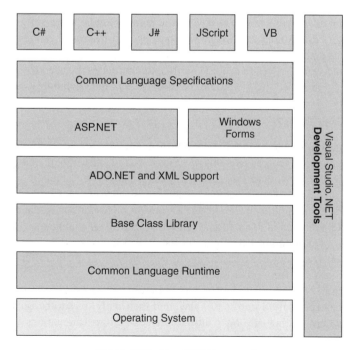

Figure 22-3. The .NET Framework.

objects. Within the .NET Framework, the common runtime library allows any object to interact with any other object because of the common substrate. As a result, duplicative plumbing is eliminated and direct interoperability is introduced.

The .NET Framework also extends the notion of objects. Some programming languages, such as C++ and Java, treat only certain entities as objects, but primitive data types were not implemented as objects. Smalltalk and Common Lisp, however, treat primitive data types as objects. The .NET Framework takes the Smalltalk approach and introduces some new primitive data types such as SQL and decimal datatypes.

The .NET Framework is not a black-box framework. Every .NET class is available for extension through inheritance. However, it is not a white-box framework either in that you don't get to see the source code for all of the .NET classes.

The .NET Framework is language neutral. You can write components in any of the Microsoft-supplied languages and have them interact because of the Common Runtime Library. Microsoft also supports developers of other programming languages in using the Common Runtime Library, which broadens the options available to developers.

Common Language Runtime   The Common Language Runtime (CLR) environment provides key services to support the execution of applications written in the Microsoft-supported programming languages. The Microsoft programming language compilers all compile source code to a common intermediate form from which object code can be generated. This approach allows each programming language to use a single copy of standard runtime environment routines rather than writing individual copies of these routines for each programming language. This approach was pioneered by both the DEC for its VAX compilers and the Free Software Foundation in its Gnu compilers.

Class Libraries   Base classes provide standard functionality that is common to all applications, including such functions as input/output, string manipulation, thread management, network communications, text manipulation, and user interface services. There are four sets of data management classes: ADO.NET classes allow access to data represented as XML through OLE, COM, Oracle, and SQL Server interfaces; XML classes manipulate XML objects; ASP.NET classes are for web services; and Windows Forms classes are for developing desktop clients. All classes work with all Microsoft programming languages to provide a common development and runtime environment.

XML provides a universal data format. All .NET services are defined in XML. XML is the representation standard for interactions among different services, because it can be understood by computers (as well as people) and provides reusable, self-defining descriptions of data. Since the description can be carried with the data and is specified in a standard format, each service component just needs to understand XML. Thus, XML promotes true interoperability among applications.

Supported Programming Languages   The full complement of languages supported by the .NET Framework is depicted in Figure 22-4 (from `http://msdn. microsoft.com/netframework/productinfo/overview/default.asp`).

Supported Programming Languages		
APL	Fortran	Pascal
C++	Haskell	Perl
C#	Java	Python
COBOL	Microsoft Jscript®	RPG
Component Pascal	Mercury	Scheme
Curriculum	Mondrian	SmallTalk
Eiffel	Oberon	Standard ML
Forth	Oz	Microsoft Visual Basic®

Figure 22-4. .NET Framework supported programming languages.

22.3 IBM'S SAN FRANCISCO PROJECT

IBM instituted the San Francisco project (IBM 1998) in the early 1990s as a business operations-oriented framework. The San Francisco project was focused on providing a generic framework for building business management applications. Its goal was to create a reusable, business level, component framework providing processes and services implemented in Java. IBM originally targeted its AS/400 series machines in order to provide its VARs with a foundation on which to build customized solutions. The services originally available include General Ledger, Accounts Receivable, Accounts Payable, Order Management, and Warehouse Management.

At the time (early 1998), IBM was the first company to commit to delivering a business level framework of such scope. But the San Francisco Framework quickly spawned a number of competitors, some of whom offered total solutions rather than a framework. Figure 22-5 depicts how the components would be used.

It has now metamorphosed into a product offering: IBM's Business Components, which operate with WebSphere, IBM's mainframe-based web server.

22.3.1 San Francisco Components

San Francisco consists of three layers of reusable code for use by application developers (Monday et al. 2000):

Foundation Layer The Foundation layer provides the infrastructure and services that are required to build industrial-strength applications in a distributed, managed-object, multiplatform application. It provides a degree of technology insulation from specific object services as well as hardware and operating system platforms. It also provides the underlying infrastructure that is used to support the Common Business Objects and the Core Business Processes. Programmers must inherit from these classes if they want to use the services provided by the Foundation layer. It contains two types of classes, as depicted in Figure 22-6:

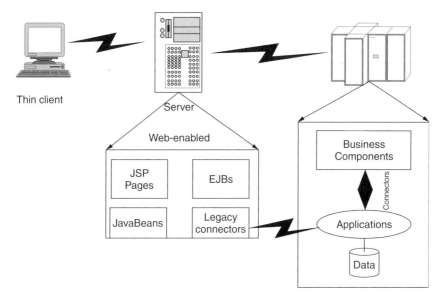

Figure 22-5. IBM San Francisco usage.

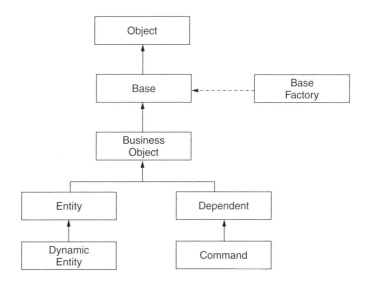

Figure 22-6. San Francisco Foundation classes.

- Object Model Base classes, which provide object services (object transaction service, collections, communication between distributed objects, and persistence management).
- Utilities, such as schema mappers and administrative tools.

In San Francisco, the programmer does not create objects using the Java new operator but instead uses the appropriate Base Factory class, which returns a Java handle to a distinct object. Because transaction processing is embedded in San Francisco, using this handle enables any client to use transaction services to communicate with other objects.

Common Business Objects The Common Business Objects layer provides definitions of commonly used business objects and default business logic that can be used as the foundation for interoperability between applications. These objects include:

- Business objects common across domains:
    Address
    Areas, Projects, Countries
    Business Partner Hierarchy
    Calendar
    Payment Methods
    Company Hierarchy
    Credit Checking
    Currency
    Fiscal Calendar
    Unit of Measure
- Support for design patterns useful in many domains such as lifecycle and extensible items.
- Common financial interfaces that enable an application in one domain to access commonly needed business processing of another application domain.

Core Business Processes The Core Business Processes layer provides generic business processes. For example, San Francisco contains the General Ledger Core Business Process, which includes the architecture, design, and default logic to build a General Ledger application. The developer, instead of building it from scratch, needs only to enhance and extend this layer to build a customized General Ledger application. The initial Core Business Processes are depicted in Figure 22-7.

Accounts Payable and Accounts Receivable include the basic payables and receivables ledgers and "accounts" for individual customers and suppliers. Core transaction types include invoices, credit notes, payments, and adjustments with currency gains/losses. Items can be posted immediately or for approval and can be split

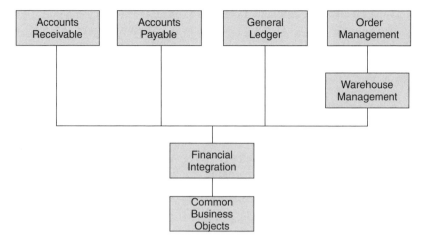

Figure 22-7. San Francisco Core Business Processes.

into installments with associated discounts. Additional links support associated documentation.

General Ledger includes charts of accounts, journals, processes for closing journals, amortizing items across financial periods, balances by specified criteria, revaluation with recognition of currency gains and losses, including the Euro, and external bank interfaces.

Order Management includes pricing and discounts, integration with warehouse management for back orders, picking and shipping, order acknowledgment, and integration with Accounts Receivable invoicing, all supported by a life cycle process for each order.

Warehouse Management includes inventory tracking, with allocated inventory and expected deliveries, reorder and backorder management, stocktaking, costing, picking, and shipping for simple items and mutely-part kits.

These individual subsystems are integrated through a Financial Integration subsystem that provides a common data repository for the data required to support the enterprise.

22.3.2   Benefits and Disadvantages of the San Francisco Approach

Given its goals, several benefits could accrue from using the San Francisco Framework and component suite:

- Because many of the components were pretested, the time to develop and deploy applications could be reduced.
- Applications could be developed that spanned multiple platforms, because San Francisco components were written in Java.
- San Francisco components could be used to extend existing applications and work with existing data.

- San Francisco components could be used to create scalable, flexible applications.

However, by most reviews, San Francisco failed to achieve its goals. In most cases, reviewers found it to be too large an undertaking, leading to unwieldy code, a labor- and knowledge-intensive effort to "get up to speed" to be productive, and difficult to adapt to the requirements of individual organizations. Complexity scales with the number of programmers working on an application. At one point, IBM had over 200 programmers working on the San Francisco product. That equates to 200 different viewpoints of what the software was to do.

San Francisco was a heroic undertaking at a time that the technology wasn't just right. Java was not yet robust enough and the middle-tier infrastructure in a multi-tier system wasn't available. Today, Java has achieved a robustness that makes it a good vehicle for multitier applications, but it is unclear whether it can yet support very large undertakings such as San Francisco was intended to be.

22.3.3 WebSphere Applications

As noted previously, IBM rolled the San Francisco components into its WebSphere Business Components offering. WebSphere Business Components provide a whole product solution offering prebuilt, pretested code, the environment, and roadmaps to assemble components into successful applications.

22.4 POOMA

For a change of pace, consider POOMA. POOMA is a high-performance C++ toolkit for parallel scientific computation. POOMA is a library that provides scientific programmers with high-level abstractions that support high-performance computing. The basic objects in POOMA are fields, meshes, arrays, and layouts—precisely the same objects that scientific programmers use in describing their algorithms. Code is written in C++, but using data parallel constructs similar to those in Fortran 90. (http://www.codesourcery.com/pooma/pooma_overview).

22.5 FURTHER READING

J2EE

Alur, D., J. Crupi, and D. Malks. 2003. *Core J2EE Patterns: Best Practices and Design Strategies*, 2nd Ed. Prentice Hall/Sun Microsystems Press, Englewood Cliffs, NJ.

Eckel, B. 2002. *Thinking In Java*, 3rd Ed. Prentice Hall, Englewood Cliffs, NJ.

Edwards, W. K. 2000. *Core Jini*, 2nd Ed. Prentice Hall, Englewood Cliffs, NJ.

Halter, S. L. and S. J. Munroe. 2000. *Enterprise Java Performance*. Prentice Hall/Sun Microsystems Press, Englewood Cliffs, NJ.

Oaks, S. 2001. *Java Security*, 2nd Ed. O'Reilly and Associates, Sebastopol, CA.

Oaks, S. and H. Wong. 1999. *Java Threads*, 2nd Ed. O'Reilly and Associates, Sebastopol, CA.

Sun Microsystems. 2002. *Designing Enterprise Applications with the J2EE Platform*, 2nd Ed.

Frameworks

Johnson, M., R. Baxter, and T. Dahl. 2000. *San Francisco Life Cycle Programming Techniques*. Addison Wesley, Reading, MA.

Monday, P., J. Carey, and M. Dangler. 2000. *San Francisco Component Framework: An Introduction*. Addison Wesley, Reading, MA.

Sun Microsystems. 2003. *Sun One Application Framework Developer's Guide*.

22.6   EXERCISES

22.1. An eBusiness application framework is to be developed to enable two or more companies to exchange information stored in (possibly) heterogeneous databases. How would you use Enterprise JavaBeans to develop this framework? (You may need to do some more detailed reading.)

22.2. Compare and contrast Microsoft's .NET Framework with JavaSoft's J2EE Framework. Highlight what is unique about each framework. Discuss how you would make them integrate and interoperate.

22.3. Research the requirements for middle-tier infrastructures. Are any of the large development environments (such as Microsoft's .NET, JavaSoft's J2EE, IBM's WebSphere) capable of satisfying these requirements? [Research Problem]

22.4. Review the architecture for Microsoft's .NET Framework. The programming languages are removed five layers from the base operating system. In effect, this means there are up to five virtual machines between the base hardware and the business application logic written in one of the supported programming languages. Argue pro or con whether this is too many layers.

23

CHALLENGES IN FRAMEWORKS

There are many challenges to developing and using frameworks. Developing robust, efficient frameworks that are extensible and reusable for complex application domains is a difficult problem. The skills to successfully produce frameworks are often acquired through experience and mentoring as opposed to coursework. Another challenge is the maintainability of a framework. Because applications often change frequently, the underlying framework must change as well to support the application. Modification may occur on both a functional and a behavioral level. Framework developers and maintainers must ensure that successive modifications to a framework do not invalidate services of earlier versions.

23.1 DEVELOPING FRAMEWORKS

As we have proceeded through this book, we have increased the complexity of the software structures that we have discussed. Frameworks are the most complex, general-purpose software structures that we will examine. However, frameworks are also the most difficult software structures to develop. The GoF (Gamma et al. 1995) assert: "If applications are hard to design, and toolkits are harder, then frameworks are hardest of all."

This difficulty is due in part to the inherent conflict between reusability and tailorability. On the one hand, we try to package software components so that they can be reused in as many application domains as possible. But we also try to design software architectures that are easily adapted to the requirements of the target application

Software Paradigms, By Stephen H. Kaisler
ISBN 0-471-48347-8   Copyright © 2005 John Wiley & Sons, Inc.

domains. As a result, building a framework is essentially an evolutionary process (Johnson and Russo 1991) because frameworks more than any other software product are subject to change and refactoring (Opdyke 1992). Johnson suggests three steps for developing a framework: analysis, design, and test.

23.1.1 Analysis Phase

In the analysis phase, you should analyze the problem domain to understand overall structure, to determine the specific functionality provided, and to identify the well-known abstractions. The latter represent the commonly agreed upon features and characteristics of the domain. Your analysis can be aided by collecting several examples (Johnson suggests at least four or five) to help you assess your design as you define your vision for the framework. A simple assessment is how you would provide a capability from one of the examples in the framework you are designing.

Finding the abstractions is difficult. The goal is to recognize commonalities among all of the elements of the example so that they can be represented just once in your framework. Some examples will be more important or more influential than others. Prioritizing your examples can help you decide which capabilities are most important to your framework.

23.1.2 Design Phase

The next step is to design your framework. This is an iterative process. Start with a skeleton that captures your vision for the framework based on your understanding of the hierarchy of abstractions that describe the domain. Iteratively, enhance the skeleton by adding additional components as you assess your design against the examples previously chosen.

23.1.3 Test Phase

Finally, test your framework by using it to implement each of the chosen examples as a new application. Assess the difficulty of implementing specific domain behaviors required by the example in your framework. Testing will probably lead you to enhance the framework with additional components as you see how it would actually be used.

23.2 APPLICATION DEVELOPMENT USING A FRAMEWORK

The structure of a framework is captured in both its class definitions and in the set of structural and behavioral relationships among its classes. Structural relationships specify the number of instances of a framework class and the interconnection among those instances that must exist when the system is executed. One common way of representing the structural relationships is through an entity-relationship diagram.

Interconnections may be realized in several ways. The principal mechanism is through messages, whereby one instance requests some operation be performed of another instance. Sometimes, instances will store the handles of other instances as the values of attributes.

Three basic activities are required to implement an application from a framework: instantiation, refinement, and extension.

23.2.1 Instantiation

Instantiation is used to produce an application from a framework. This application may be executed in concert with other applications as part of a larger application or in standalone mode. Most frameworks define abstract modules or subsystems that defer some or all of the details of the implementation to the individual application. So an important aspect of instantiation is to complete the implementation of the framework by plugging in implementations of these abstract modules or subsystems.

Figure 23-1 depicts the generic structure of an application framework environment. The application can be thought of as enclosing the application framework because the application framework is the skeleton on which application-specific modules are hung.

During instantiation, the appropriate number of instances must be created and the structural and behavioral relationships must be established.

23.2.2 Refinement

Refinement adapts a framework to a specific domain. Inherent to this operation are the activities of subclassing existing framework classes, adding new classes, extending existing structural and behavioral relationships, and adding new structural and behavioral

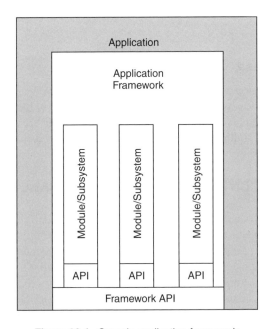

Figure 23-1. Generic application framework.

relationships. Existing relationships can be extended by adding new messages and by specializing the data flows in the original framework. Data passed as arguments in messages may also be refined.

23.2.3 Extension

Extension adapts a framework to be useful in a more general domain. It includes subclassing existing framework classes and adding new structural and behavioral relationships. Figure 23-2 depicts the relationship between a framework and its extension.

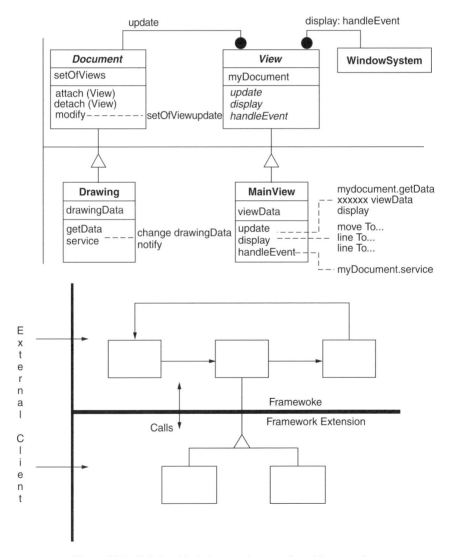

Figure 23-2. Relationship between a framework and its extension.

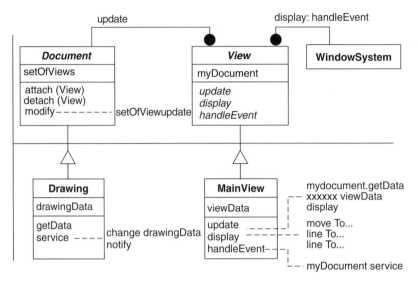

Figure 23-3. Example of framework extension.

The framework's components are depicted above the horizontal, heavy line. In the figure, one of those components has been extended through subclassing and instantiation. The clients [e.g., application-specific code (or other framework components)] can invoke specific functions and behaviors either of concrete framework components or extended framework components.

An example of this extension is depicted in Figure 23-3. Document and View are two components of a GUI framework. Drawing extends Document and MainView extends View. The extensions—Drawing and MainView—define and implement the methods required to support the project.

23.3 TESTING FRAMEWORKS

Testing objects is a difficult problem because the tests must be performed on instances of an object rather than the class specification. Because the behavior of an instance is determined by the values assigned to its attributes, to adequately test a class may require testing many instances of the class. There are specific issues that arise in testing objects:

- Because objects are essentially software black boxes, we can only truly test the external entities (e.g., the methods).
- Individual operations within a class cannot be tested in isolation because they depend on the internal state of an object.
- Because objects collaborate through messages, where messages may be bound to polymorphic operations, testing occurs by sending a test message to an object that is assumed to be in a specific state and analyzing the result.

- Objects are defined by classes that are related via inheritance relationships, so testing often requires knowing the characteristics of the class hierarchy.
- Integration testing must take into account polymorphism, inheritance, collaboration, and aggregation as mediators of the behavior of an object's methods.

This problem is compounded when we consider the problem of how to test a pattern. Both the individual classes and the aggregation of objects must be tested in a pattern.

23.4 ISSUES IN FRAMEWORK USAGE

There are a number of issues in framework usage that can significantly affect the success of a project if not adequately planned and prepared for.

23.4.1 Steep Learning Curve

Learning how to use a framework requires a steep learning curve. Users must understand the architecture, components, and interactions among components in order to use a framework effectively. For large, complex frameworks, it may take months for the user to fully grasp the structure and services and to understand the API of the framework.

To mediate this problem, it is best to begin developing a prototype application—perhaps a scaled down version of the actual application. Plan to throw it away, as Fred Brooks (1987) suggested. You can begin by identifying the high-level services that are provided for key components of the application and provide "stubbed" components. As you gain an understanding of the methods of each component, you can replace the stubs with actual code. Incremental evolution of a prototype application in this manner will teach you a lot about how the framework operates and what is required of you to build a successful application.

23.4.2 Developing Frameworks Is an Iterative Process

An application framework provides services to user-provided components, which encompass the specific domain functionality. Application frameworks are rarely created ab initio. Usually, several versions of an application are created that, upon review, lead to an awareness of some common services. These services are factored out and repackaged as the beginnings of an application framework. Successive applications use this application framework, which is refined each time it is used as users evolve an awareness of additional services that are generally needed. Additionally, since the application framework captures the skeleton of the solution to the problem, the framework's functionality evolves as the user's understanding of how to solve the problem evolves.

Of course, frameworks age, just like the rest of software. Eventually, one has evolved a framework to a point where adding new functionality and services becomes difficult because of the interactions among the framework elements. Additionally, adding new services may lead to conflict with previously included services. The Adapter design pattern can be used to insulate one service from another or to embed one service in another. At some point, it becomes easier to rewrite the framework or pursue a new solution structure for the class of problems.

23.4.3 Hidden Architecture and Assumptions

Unlike other applications, a framework incorporates a control model that ties the parts of the framework together to provide a skeletal solution for a class of problems. The control model for a GUI development framework is the standard event loop, which captures and dispatches events intercepted by the operating system and passed to the framework. Additionally, most GUI development frameworks incorporate some form of the Model-View-Controller architecture.

The framework designer often makes a lot of assumptions about future applications in developing a framework. This can lead to problems when seemingly innocuous changes in the control flow of the application can be difficult to implement with the framework. Many developers who tried to port GUI-based applications to web-based applications discovered that simple tasks, such as consistency among the fields of a form, become very difficult to ensure in a web environment.

One concern is the impedance mismatch between two frameworks. One framework, providing the control flow, may use multiple threads of control, while the other framework, providing services, may assume a single thread of control. Such mismatches may be very difficult to resolve without compromising the performance of the overall application.

The use of two framework control models may also introduce gaps in services and functionality. For example, two frameworks that implement batch sequential and event-driven control models may not be able to respond to requests from each other. Or a framework may implement multiple control models, such as an event-driven framework, that also implements wizards to act on behalf of the user. Web-enabled applications with multiple windows and forms open must be able to support requests from any one of them. This leads to a significant management problem within the application because the richness of the control models leads to a complex state space that must be maintained.

23.4.4 Information Access

Hooks provide information about the way in which a framework is used (e.g., information on its internal state). Because the framework provides the control model, the user-provided components do not need to maintain a control state model, as this is done inside the framework. However, user-defined components often need information on the status of the framework. When two frameworks are used to implement an application, the services of one framework may not match up to the services of the other framework.

Sometimes callbacks are used to provide the information. However, callbacks are difficult to use since it is hard to determine what state the framework is in when the callback is invoked. And when two frameworks are interacting, there may be a mismatch between the requesting and serving frameworks due to conflict between their methods. Adapters and wrappers can mediate this conflict and enable communication.

23.5 EXERCISES

23.1. Select an application domain of interest to you and design and document a framework for that domain.

23.2 Select an existing large application for which comprehensive documentation exists. Reverse engineer the application framework architecture and primary components from the documentation. If you have access to the application for execution, determine the interaction(s) among some of the components. [Requires additional research]

23.3 Develop an M × M matrix in which the rows and columns are labeled by the architectural styles described in Part III of this book. For each cell of the matrix, determine and argue pro and con whether or not two frameworks – each implementing one of the architectural styles (which implies a control model), could be integrated.

BIBLIOGRAPHY

The following abbreviations are used in this bibliography to represent the names of technical journals that are frequently referenced and widely available.

ACM   *Association for Computing Machinery*
IEEE   *Institute of Electrical and Electronic Engineers*
OOPSLA   *Object-Oriented Programming Systems and Languages*

Abiteboul, S., R. Hull, and V. Vianu. 1995. *Foundations of Databases.* Addison Wesley, Reading, MA.

Ackermann, P. 1996. *Developing Object-Oriented Multimedia Software—Based on the MET++ Application Framework.* Springer-Verlag GmbH, Heidelberg, Germany.

Aho, A. V. and J. D. Ullman. 1992. *Foundations of Computer Science.* Computer Science Press, Rockville, MD.

Ahuja, S., N. Carriero, and D. Gelernter. 1986. "Linda and Friends." *IEEE Computer* 19(8): 26–34.

Alexander, C. 1964. *Notes on the Synthesis of Form.* Harvard University Press, Cambridge, MA.

Alexander, C. 1977. *A Pattern Language.* Oxford University Press, Cambridge, UK.

Alexander, C. 1979. *The Timeless Way of Building.* Oxford University Press, Cambridge, UK.

Allen, R. J. 1997. A Formal Approach to Software Architecture. Ph.D. Thesis, Carnegie Mellon University, Technical Report Number: CMU-CS-97-144, May 1997.

Altman, R., Y. Natis, et al. 1999. Middleware: The Glue for Modern Applications. Gartner Group, Strategic Analysis Report, 26 July 1999.

Software Paradigms, By Stephen H. Kaisler
ISBN 0-471-48347-8   Copyright © 2005 John Wiley & Sons, Inc.

Andrews, G. 1991. *Concurrent Programming: Principles and Practices.* Benjamin Cummings, Menlo Park, CA.

Andrews, G. and F. B. Schneider. 1983. "Concepts and Notations for Concurrent Programming." *ACM Computing Surveys* 15(1):3–42.

Annaratone, M., E. A. Arnold, T. R. Gross, et al. 1986. "Warp Architecture and Inplementation." In *Proceedings of 13th International Symposium on Computer Architecture*, Tokyo, Japan, pp. 346–356.

ANSI/IEEE Std 829-1983 (Standard for Software Test Documentation) and ANSI/IEEE Std 1008-1987 (Standard for Software Unit Testing). In *Software Engineering Standards*, SH12534, 3rd Ed. IEEE, New York, 1989.

ANSI. 1994. Data Parallel C Extensions, version 1.6, X3J11 DPCE Subcommittee, December 31, 1994.

Apple Computer, Inc. 1992. *Macintosh Human Interface Guidelines.* Addison Wesley, Reading, MA.

Apple Corp. 1994a. *OpenDoc for Macintosh.* Cupertino, CA.

Apple Corp. 1994b. *OpenDoc Technical Summary.* Cupertino, CA.

Apple Computer Corp. 2001. Apple QuickTime Component Types. `http://developer.apple.com/quicktime/qttutorial/components.html#Types`.

Appleton, B. 1999. Patterns and Software: Essential Concepts and Terminology. `http://www.enteract.com/~bradapp/`.

Armour, F., S. Kaisler, and S. Liu. 1999a. "A Big Picture Look at Enterprise Architectures." *IEEE IT Pro* 1(1):35–42. (Translated into Japanese and reprinted in *Nikkei Computer*, 1999.9.13 issue, Tokyo, Japan.)

Armour, F., S. Kaisler, and S. Liu. 1999b. "Building an Enterprise Architecture Step-by-Step." *IEEE IT Pro* 1(3):49–57.

Astrachan, O. and E. Wallingford. 1998. Loop Patterns, Principles of Programming Languages'98. `http://www.cs.duke.edu/~ola/patterns/plopd/loops.html`.

Atkinson, M., F. Bancilhon, D. DeWitt, et al. 1992. "The Object-Oriented Database System Manifesto." In F. Bancilhon, C. Delobel, and P. Kanellakis (eds.), *Building an Object-Oriented Database System: The Story of O2.* Morgan Kaufmann, Los Altos, CA.

Babaoglou, O. and K. Marzullo. 1993. "Consistent Global States of Distributed Systems: Fundamental Concepts and Mechanisms." In S. Mullender (ed.), *Distributed Systems.* Addison Wesley/ACM Press, Reading, MA.

Bachmann, F., L. Bass, P. Clements, et al. 2001. Documenting Software Architectures: Organization of the Documentation Package, CMU/SEI-2001-TN-010. Carnegie-Mellon University, Pittsburgh, PA.

Bachmann, F., L. Bass, P. Clements, et al. 2002a. Documenting Software Architectures: Documenting Behavior, CMU/SEI-2002-TN-001. Carnegie-Mellon University, Pittsburgh, PA.

Bachmann, F., L. Bass, P. Clements, et al. 2002b. Documenting Software Architectures: Documenting Interfaces, CMU/SEI-2002-TN-015. Carnegie-Mellon University, Pittsburgh, PA.

Bacon, J. 1992. *Concurrent Systems: An Integrated Approach to Operating Systems, Database, and Distributed Systems.* Addison Wesley Ltd., Wokingham, UK.

Bacon, J., K. Moody, J. Bates, et al. 2000. "Generic Support for Distributed Applications." *IEEE Computer*, March 2000.

Baker, H. G. 1991. "CLOStrophobia1: Its Etiology and Treatment." *ACM OOPS Messenger* 2(4):4–15.

Bal, H., J. G. Steiner, and A. S. Tanenbaum. 1989. "Programming Languages for Distributed Computing Systems." *ACM Computing Surveys* 21(3):261–322.

Bar, H., M. Bauer, O. Ciupke, et al. 1999. The FAMOOS Object-Oriented Reengineering Handbook. `http://www.iam.unibe.ch/~scg/Archive/famoos/handbook/`.

Barrett, D., L. A. Clarke, P. L. Tarr, and A. E. Wise. 1996. A Framework for Event-Based Software Integration, UM-CS-1996-068. Computer Science Department, University of Massachusetts, Boston.

Barth, T., G. Flender, B. Freislerben, et al. 2000. CORBA-Based Runtime Support for Load Distribution and Fault Tolerance. Available at `http://citeseer.nj.nec.com/593096.html`.

Basili, V. and H. D. Rombach. 1988. Towards a Comprehensive Framework for Reuse: A Reuse-Enabling Software Evolution Environment, CS-TR-2158. University of Maryland, College Park, MD.

Bass, L., P. Clements, and R. Kazman. 1998. *Software Architecture in Practice*. Addison-Wesley, Reading, MA.

Baumer, D., G. Gryczan, R. Knoll, et al. 1997. "Framework Development for Large Systems." *Communications of the ACM* 40(10): 52–59.

Beck, K. 1997. *Smalltalk Best Practice Patterns.* Prentice Hall, Englewood Cliffs, NJ.

Beizer, B. 1983. *Software Testing Techniques.* Van Nostrand Reinhold, New York.

Ben-Ari, M. 1990. *Principles of Concurrent and Distributed Programming.* Prentice-Hall Ltd., Hertfordshire, England.

Berczuk, S. 1994. "Finding Solutions Through Pattern Languages." *IEEE Computer* 27(12): 75–76. `http://world.std.com/~berczuk/pubs/Dec94ieee.html`.

Berge, C. 1985. *Graphs.* North-Holland, Amsterdam.

Bharat, K. and L. Cardelli. 1996. Migratory Applications. DEC Systems Research Center, Palo Alto, CA.

Biggerstaff, T. 1993. "Directions in Software Development and Maintenance." Keynote Address, *International Conference on Software Maintenance*, Montreal, Quebec, Canada, September 1993.

Birrell, A. D. and B. J. Nelson. 1984. "Implementing Remote Procedure Call." *ACM Transactions on Computer Systems* 2(1):39–59, February.

Bobrow, D. and M. Stefik. 1983. *The Loops Manual.* Intelligent Systems Laboratory, Xerox Corporation, December 1983.

Boehm, B. W. 1986. "Understanding and Controlling Software Costs." *10th IFIP World Congress*, pp. 703–714. North-Holland, Amsterdam.

Bohm, C. and G. Jacopini. 1966. "Flow Diagrams, Turing Machines, and Languages with Only Two Formation Rules." *Communications of the ACM* 9(5):266.

Bohrer, K. A. 1998. "Architecture of the San Francisco Framework." *IBM Systems Journal* 37(2):156–169.

Booch, G. 1987. *Software Components in Ada.* Benjamin Cummings, San Francisco, CA.

Bosch, J. 1998. Specifying Frameworks and Design Patterns as Architectural Fragments. University of Karlskrona/Ronneby, Sweden.

Bosch, J., P. Molin, M. Mattson, and P. Bengtsson. 1999. "Framework Problems and Experiences." In M. E. Fayad, D. C. Schmidt, and R. E. Johnson (eds.), *Building Application Frameworks: Object Oriented Foundations of Framework Design*, pp. 55–82. John Wiley & Sons, Hoboken, NJ.

Bourne, S. R. 1978. "The UNIX Shell." *Bell System Technical Journal* 57(6): 1971–1990.

Brant, J. M. 1992. HotDraw. Masters Thesis, University of Illinois, Urbana.

Brinch-Hansen, P. 1972. "Structured Multiprogramming." *Communications of the ACM* 15(7):574–577.

Brinch-Hansen, P. 1973. *Operating System Principles*. Prentice Hall, Englewood Cliffs, NJ.

Brockschmidt, K. 1994. *Inside OLE 2*. Microsoft Press, Redmond, WA.

Brooks, F. P. 1987. "No Silver Bullet: Essence and Accidents in Software Engineering." *IEEE Computer* 20(4):10–19.

Brooks, F. P. Jr. 1995. *The Mythical Man-Month*, Anniversery Edition. Addison-Wesley, Reading, MA.

Brown, A. W. and J. A. McDermid. 1991. "On Integration and Reuse in a Software Development Environment." In F. Long (ed.), *Software Engineering Environments*, Vol. 3, pp. 171–194. Conference Proceedings, Aberystwyth, Wales. Ellis Horwood, Upper Saddle River, NJ.

Burbeck, S. 1992. Applications Programming in Smalltalk-80: How To Use Model-View-Controller. `http://st-www.cs.uiuc.edu/users/smarch/st-docs/mvc.html`.

Buschmann, F., R. Meunier, R. Rohnert, et al. 1996. *Patterns of Software Architecture—A System of Patterns*. John Wiley & Sons Ltd., London, England.

Butenhof, D. R. 1997. *Programming with POSIX Threads*. Addison Wesley, Reading, MA.

Butler, G. and P. Denommee. 1996. Documenting Frameworks to Assist Application Developers. Department of Computer Science, Concordia University, Quebec, Canada.

CAMPL. 2002. *The CAML Language*. `http://caml.imria.fr`.

Campagnoni, F. R. 1994. "IBM's System Object Model." *Dr. Dobb's Journal* 11(2): 24–28.

Carriero, N. and D. Gelerntner. 1990. *How To Write Parallel Programs*. MIT Press, Cambridge, MA.

Chen, Q. and F. Xu. 1999. Framework Documentation, University of Nevada at Reno, Reno, NV. `http://www.cs.unr.edu/~chen_q/docu.html`.

Clements, P. and P. Kogut. 1995. *Features of Architecture Representation Languages*. `http://www.sei.cmu.edu/activities/architecture/projects.html`.

CMU. 1998. Information on the iWarp Chip. `http://www-2.cs.cmu.edu /afs/cs.cmu.edu/project/iwarp/archive/WWW-pages/iwarp.html`.

Coplien, J. 1996. "Objects and Beyond: Broadening Beyond Objects to Patterns and to Other Paradigms." *Computing Surveys* 28A(4), December. `http://www.acm.org/surveys/1996/ObjectsAndBeyond/`.

Coplien, J. 1997. "The Column without a Name: Patterns, Idioms, Culture, and Languages." *C++ Report* 9(8): 42–47.

Coplien, J. 2000. Multi-paradigm Design. Ph.D. Thesis, Departmenta Informatica, Vrije University, Brussels, Belgium.

Coplien, J. and D. Schmidt (eds.) 1995. *Pattern Languages of Program Design*. Addison-Wesley, Reading, MA.

Demeyer, S., T. D. Meijler, O. Nierstrasz, and P. Steyaert. 1997. "Design Guidelines for 'Tailorable' Frameworks." *Communications of the ACM* 40(10): 60–64.

DeSouza, D. F. and A. C. Wills. 1998. *Objects, Components, and Frameworks with UML: The Catalysis Approach.* Addison Wesley, Reading, MA.

Deutsch, L. P. 1989. *Design Reuse and Frameworks in the Smalltalk-80 System*, Frontier Series, Vol. II, pp. 57–71. Association for Computing Machinery, New York.

Dijkstra, E. W. 1975. "Cooperating Sequential Processes." In F. Genuys (ed.), *Programming Languages.* Academic Press, New York.

Dittrich, K. R., S. Gatziu, and A. Geppert. 1995. "The Active Database Management System Manifesto: A Rulebase of ADBMS Features." In T. Sellis (ed.), *Proceedings 2nd International Workshop on Rules in Databases (Athens, Greece, September 1995).* Springer Verlag, Berlin.

Elmasri, R. and S. B. Navathe. 2003. *Fundamentals of Database System,* 4th Ed. Benjamin Cummings, San Francisco, CA.

Engelmore, R. S. and A. Morgan (eds.) 1988. *Blackboard Systems.* Addison Wesley, Reading, MA.

Erman, L. D., F. Hayes-Roth, V. R. Lesser, and R. Reddy. 1980. "The Hearsay-II Speech-Understanding System: Integrating Knowledge to Resolve Uncertainty." *ACM Computing Surveys* 12(2):213–253.

Even, S. 1979. *Graph Algorithms.* Computer Science Press, Rockville, MD.

Fayad, M. E., and R. E. Johnson. 2000. *Domain-Specific Application Frameworks.* John Wiley & Sons, Hoboken, NJ.

Fayad, M. E. and D. C. Schmidt. 1997. "Object-Oriented Application Frameworks." *Communications of the ACM* 40(10): 32–38.

Fayad, M. E., D. C. Schmidt, and R. E. Johnson. 1999a. *Implementing Application Frameworks.* John Wiley & Sons, Hoboken, NJ.

Fayad, M. E., D. C. Schmidt, and R. E. Johnson. 1999b. *Building Application Frameworks.* John Wiley & Sons, Hoboken, NJ.

Feldman, M. 1990. Support Materials for Language and System Support for Concurrent Programming, SEI-CM-25. Carnegie-Mellon University, Pittsburgh, PA.

Flanagan, D., J. Falrey, W. Crawford, and K. Magnusson. 2002. *Java Enterprise in a Nutshell*, 2nd Ed. O'Reilly & Associates, Sebastopol, CA.

Floyd, R. 1979. "The Paradigms of Programming." *Communications of the ACM* 22(8): 455–460.

Flynn, M. J. 1972. "Some Computer Organizations and their Effectiveness." *IEEE Transactions on Computers*, C21(8): 880–886.

Foote, B. 1992. *Living Languages.* Workshop on Programming Languages: The Next Generation, OOPSLA'92. Vancouver, British Columbia, Canada.

Foster, I. and C. Kesselman. 1999. *The GRID: Blueprint for a New Computing Infrastructure.* Morgan Kaufmann, Los Altos, CA.

Fowler, M. 1997. *Analysis Patterns: Reusable Object Models.* Addison Wesley, Reading, MA.

Gacek, C. 1998. Detecting Architectural Mismatches During System Composition. Ph.D. Dissertation, University of Southern California, Los Angeles.

Gamma, E., A. Weinand, and R. Marty. 1989. Integration of a Programming Environment into ET++: A Case Study. *European Conference on Object-Oriented Programming (ECOOP) 1989*, pp. 283–297.

Gamma, E., R. Helms, R. Johnson, and J. Vlissides. 1995. *Design Patterns, Elements of Reusable Object-Oriented Software.* Addison Wesley, Reading, MA.

Garlan, D. 2000. "Software Architecture: A Roadmap." In A. Finkelstein (ed.), *The Future of Software Engineering.* Association for Computing Machinery, New York.

Garlan, D. and M. Shaw. 1994. An Introduction to Software Architecture. CMU-CS-94-166. School of Computer Science, Carnegie-Mellon University, Pittsburgh, PA.

Garlan, D., R. Allen, and J. Ockerbloom. 1995. "Architectural Mismatch: Why Reuse Is So Hard." *IEEE Software* 12(6):17–26.

Garlan, D., R. T. Monroe, and D. Wile. 1997. "Acme: An Architecture Description Interchange Language." In *Proceedings of CASCON'97*, pp. 169–183, Ontario, Canada.

Geysermans, F. and J. Miller. 2003. Implement the Observer Pattern on the Web Services Realm, IBM Corp. `ftp://www6.software.ibm.com/software/developer/library/ws-dbarch.pdf`.

Goldberg, A. and D. Robson. 1983. *Smalltalk-80: The Language and Its Implementation*. Addison-Wesley, Reading, MA.

Gonnet, G. H. and R. Baeza-Yates. 1991. *Handbook of Algorithms and Data Structures*, 2nd Ed. Addison Wesley, Reading, MA.

Gray, J. and A. Reuter. 1993. *Transaction Processing: Concepts and Techniques*. Morgan Kaufmann, San Francisco, CA.

Gross, T. and D. R. O'Halloran. 1998. *iWarp: Anatomy of a Parallel Computing System*. MIT Press, Cambridge, MA.

Hartigan, J. 1975. *Clustering Algorithms*. John Wiley & Sons, Hoboken, NJ.

Haskell. 2002. `http://www.haskell.org`.

Hauck, E. A. and B. A. Dent. 1968. "Burroughs B6500/6700 Stack Mechanism." *AFIPS Spring Joint Computer Conference* 32: 245–252.

Hayes-Roth, F. 1994. A Domain-Specific Software Architecture for a Class of Intelligent Patient Monitoring Agents. Computer Science Department, Stanford University, Stanford, CA.

Heiler, S. 1995. "Semantic Interoperability." *ACM Computing Surveys* 27(2):271–273.

Henderson-Sellers, B., C. Szyperski, A. Taivalsaari, and A. Wills. 1999. Are Components Objects? In *OOPSLA '99 Companion*, Panel Discussion.

Hetzel, B. 1988. *The Complete Guide to Software Testing*, 2nd Ed. QED Information Sciences, Wellesley.

Hewlett-Packard Laboratories. 1995. Public Domain Implementation of the Standard Template Library. Available from `ftp://butler.hpl.hp.com/stl/`.

Hoare, C. A. R. 1972. "Notes on Data Structuring." In O.-J. Dahl, E. W. Dijkstra, and C. A. R. Hoare (eds.), *Structured Programming*, pp. 83–174. Academic Press, New York.

Hoare, C. A. R. 1974. "Monitors: An Operating System Structuring Concept." *Communications of the ACM* 17(10):549–557.

Hoare, C. A. R. 1978. "Communicating Sequential Processes." *Communications of the ACM* 21(8): 666–677.

Hoare, C. A. R. 1981. "The Emperor's Old Clothes." *Communications of the ACM* 24(2):75–83.

Hoare, C. A. R. 1985. *Communicating Sequential Processes*. Prentice Hall, Englewood Cliffs, NJ.

Honeywell. 1994. Languages and Tools for Embedded Software Architectures. `http://www.htc.honeywell.com/projects/dssa/dssa_tools.html`.

Horstmann, M. and M. Kirtland. 1997. DCOM Architecture, MSDN article, `http://msdn.microsoft.com/library/default.asp?url=/library/en-us/dndcom/html/msdn_dcomarch.asp`.

Howie, C. T., J. T. Kunz, and K. H. Law. 1996. Software Interoperability. Data and Anaysis Center for Software, Rome, NY. `http://www.dacs.dtic.mil/techs/interop/title.shtml`.

Huckle, T. 2003 Collection of Software Bugs. (Updated regularly). `http://wwwzenger.` `informatik.tumuenchen.de/persons/huckle/bugse.html`.

Hunt, J. F. and W. F. Tichy. 1994. Selected Patterns for Software Configuration Management. `citeseer.nj.nec.com/252191.html`.

Hursch, W. L. 1994. "Should Superclasses Be Abstract?" In *Proceedings of the 8th European Conference on Object-Oriented Programming*, Bologna, Italy.

IBM Corp. 1979. Operating Systems in a Virtual Machine. GC20-1821.

IBM Corp. 1998. San Francisco: Concepts and Facilities. SG24-2157-00. Rochester, NY.

IBM Corp. 2003. z/VM General Information: Version 4 release 4.0, White Plains, NY.

IEEE. 2001. The Single Unix Specification, Version 3, IEEE Std 1003.1-2001.

Jagannathan, V., R. Dodhiawala, and L. S. Baum (eds.) 1989. *Blackboard Architectures and Applications*. Academic Press, New York.

James, M. 1985. *Classification Algorithms*. John Wiley & Sons, Hoboken, NJ.

Johnson, R. 1992. "Documenting Frameworks Using Patterns." In *Proceedings of OOPSLA '92*, Vancouver, Canada, pp. 63–76.

Johnson, R. E. and B. Foote. 1988. "Designing Reusable Classes." *Journal of Object-Oriented Programming* 1(2):22–35. `ftp://st.cs.uiuc.edu/pub/papers/frameworks/designing-reusable-classes.ps`.

Johnson, R. E. and V. F. Russo. 1991. Reusing Object-Oriented Designs. University of Illinois Technical Report UIUCDCS 91-1696. `ftp://st.cs.uiuc.edu/pub/papers/frameworks/reusable-oo-design.ps`.

Kaisler, S. 1975. Operating System Command Languages. M.Sc. Thesis, Department of Computer Science, University of Maryland, College Park, MD.

Kaisler, S. 1982. *Design of Operating Systems for Small Computer Systems*. John Wiley & Sons, Hoboken, NJ.

Kaisler, S. 1985. *Interlisp: The Programming Language*. John Wiley & Sons, Hoboken, NJ.

Kaisler, S. 1991. Designing Geopolitical Simulations Using Knowledge-Based Systems, The World Congress on Expert Systems, Orlando, FL, December 16–19.

Kaisler, S. 1997. Making Concurrency Explicit: Converting Object-Oriented to Process-Oriented Systems. D.Sc. Dissertation, George Washington University, Washington, DC (also University Microfilm, Ann Arbor, MI).

Kazman, R. et al. 1998. "The Architecture Tradeoff Analysis Method." In *Proceedings of the ICECCS'98*.

Kazman, R., M. Klein, and P. Clements. 2000. ATAM: Method for Architecture Evaluation, SEI/CMU-20000TR-004. Carnegie-Mellon University, Pittsburgh, PA.

Keller, J., C. W. Kessler, and J. L. Traff. 2001. *Practical PRAM Programming*. John Wiley & Sons, Hoboken, NJ.

Knuth, D. E. 1973. *The Art of Computer Programming, Volume 3: Sorting and Searching*. Addison-Wesley, Reading, MA.

Kogut, P. and P. Clements. 1994. Features of Architecture Representation Languages. Carnegie-Mellon University Technical Report CMU/SEI, Pittsburgh, PA.

Kuhn, T. 1996. *The Structure of Scientific Revolutions*, 3rd Ed. University of Chicago Press, Chicago, IL.

LaLonde, W. R. and J. R. Pugh. 1990. *Inside Smalltalk*, Volumes I and II. Prentice Hall, Englewood Cliffs, NJ.

Lea, D. 1996. *Concurrent Programming in Java: Design Principles and Patterns.* Addison-Wesley, Reading, MA.

Leeb, A. 1996. A Flexible Object Architecture for Component Software. Master's Thesis, MIT, Cambridge, MA.

Lewis, B. and D. J. Berg. 1996. *Threads Primer.* SunSoft Press, Mountain View, CA.

Linton, M. A., J. M. Vlissides, and P. R. Calder. 1989. "Composing User Interfaces with Interviews." *IEEE Computer* 22(2): 8–22.

Luckham, D. C. and J. Vera. 1995. "An Event-Based Architecture Definition Language." *IEEE Transactions on Software Engineering* 21(9):717–734.

McCarthy, D. R. and V. Dayal. 1989. The Architecture of an Active Data Base Management System. ACM SIGMOD, June 1989.

Maclean, S. 1997. On the Singleton Software Design Pattern, TR DSSE-97-4. Department of Electronics and Computer Science, University of Southampton, United Kingdom.

Maes, P. 1987. "Concepts and Experiments in Computational Reflection." In *OOPSLA '87 Proceedings*, Orlando, FL, October 4–8, pp. 147–155.

Magee, J., N. Dulay, S. Eisenbach, and J. Kramer. 1995. "Specifying Distributed Software Architectures." In *5th European Software Engineering Conference (ESEC'95)*, Sitges, Spain, pp. 137–153.

Magee, J., J. Kramer, and D. Giannakopoulou. 1999. "Behaviour Analysis of Software Architectures." In *1st Working IFIP Conference on Software Architecture (WICSA1)*, San Antonio, TX, 22–24 February.

Manolescu, D. 1997. "A Data Flow Pattern Language." In R. Martin, D. Riehle, and F. Buschmann (eds.), *Pattern Languages of Program Design 3.* Addison Wesley, Reading, MA.

Martin, R., D. Riehle, and F. Buschmann. 1997. *Pattern Languages of Program Design 3.* Addison Wesley, Reading, MA.

Massengill, B. 1999. "Experiments with Program Paralleliation Using Archetypes and Stepwise Refinement." *Parallel Processing Letters,* 9(4).

Massengill, B. and K. Mani Chandy. 1996. Parallel Program Archetypes. CS-TR-96-28. California Institute of Technology, Pasadena, CA.

Massengill, B. L., T. G. Mattson, and B. A. Sanders. 1999. "Patterns for Parallel Application Programs." In *Proceedings of the Sixth Pattern Languages of Programs Workshop* (PLoP 1999).

Mattson, M. 1996. Object-Oriented Frameworks—A Survey of Methodological Issues, LU-CS-TR: 96-167. Department of Computer Science, Lund University, Sweden.

Mattson, M. and J. Bosch. 1998. Framework Composition: Problems, Causes, and Solutions. Department of Computer Science and Business Administration, University of Karlskrona/Ronneby, Ronneby, Sweden.

Mattson, M. and J. Busch. 1999. *Characterizing Stability of Evolving Frameworks.* Research Report 8/99, University of Karlskrona/Ronneby, Ronneby, Sweden.

Medvidovic, N. 1997. "A Framework for Comparing and Classifying Architectural Description Languages." In *Proceedings of 6th European Software Engineering Conference*, pp. 60–76, Number 1301 in Lecture Notes in Computer Science. Springer-Verlag, Berlin.

Meijers, M. 1996. Tool Support for Object-Oriented Design Patterns. Masters thesis, INF-SCR-96-28, Utrect University, Utrecht, The Netherlands.

Meusel, M., K. Czarnecki, and W. Köpf. 1997. "A Model for Structuring User Documentation of Object-Oriented Frameworks Using Patterns and Hypertext." In *Proceedings of ECOOP'97—Object-Oriented Programming*, Lecture Notes in Computer Science. Springer-Verlag, Berlin.

Meyer, B. 1992. "Applying Design by Contract." *IEEE Computer* 25(10): 40–51.

Meyer, B. 1993. "Systematic Concurrent Object-Oriented Programming." *Communications of the ACM* 36(9):56–80.

Meyer, B. 1997. *Object-Oriented Software Construction*, 2nd Ed., Series on Computer Science. Prentice Hall, Englewood Cliffs, NJ.

Meyer, B. 1999. "On to Components." *Computer* 32(1):139–140.

Meyer, B. C. and P. Oberndorf. 2001. *Managing Software Acquisition: Open Systems and COTS Products*. Addison Wesley, Reading, MA.

Michael, G. 1980. Personal Communication at Lawrence Livermore Laboratory, Livermore, CA.

Microsoft Corp. 1987. *The Windows Interface: An Application Design Guide*. Microsoft Corporation, Redmond, WA.

Microsoft Corp. 2001. Understanding the Distributed Object Component Model (DCOM) Architecture. `http://www.microsoft.com/ntserver/techresources/appserv/COM/dcom_architecture.asp`.

Miller, J. 2001. Microsoft .NET: The Vision. `http://research.microsoft.com/collaboration/university/europe/events/dotnetcc/version1/20010903-MSRCambridge.ppt`.

Monday, P., J. Carey, and M. Dangler. 2000. *San Francisco Component Framework: An Introduction*. Addison Wesley, Reading, MA.

Mowbray, T. J., W. J. Brown, and H. W. McCornnick III. 1998. *AntiPatterns: Refactoring Software, Architectures, and Projects in Crisis*. John Wiley & Sons, Hoboken, NJ.

Mowbray, T. J. and R. Malveau. 1997. *CORBA Design Patterns*. Wiley Computer Publishing, Hoboken, NJ.

MPI. 1994. MPI: A Message-Passing Interface Standard, May 5, 1994. `http://www.mcs.anl.gov/mpi/mpi-report/mpi-report.html`.

Musser, D. R. and A. Saini. 1996. *STL Tutorial and Reference Guide: C++ Programming with the Standard Template Library*. Addison Wesley, Reading, MA.

Myers, W. 1995. "Taligent's CommonPoint: The Promise of Objects." *IEEE Computer* 28(3):78–83.

NCITS. 2002. ANSI X3. 135–1999 Database Language SQL. New York, NY.

Nelson, B. J. 1981. Remote Procedure Call. Xerox PARC CSL-81-9.

Newell, A. and H. A. Simon. 1972. *Human Problem Solving*. Prentice Hall Englewood Cliffs, NJ.

Nii, H. P. 1986a. "The Blackboard Model of Problem Solving." *The AI Magazine* 7(3):82–106.

Nii, H. P. 1986b. "Blackboard Systems Part Two: Blackboard Application Systems." *The AI Magazine* 7(3):82–106.

Noble, J. 1996a. Found Objects. Macquarie University, Sydney, Australia.

Noble, J. 1996b. Some Patterns for Relationships. Macquarie University, Sydney, Australia.

Noble, J. 1997. Arguments and Results. Macquarie University, Sydney, Australia.

Nori, K. V., U. Ammann, K. Jensen, et al. 1981. *Pascal-P Implementation Notes*. In: *Pascal—The Language and Its Implementation*, pp. 125–170. John Wiley & Sons, Ltd., London, UK.

Norman, D. 1988. *The Psychology of Everyday Things*. Basic Books, New York.

Normark, K. 1996. Hooks and Open Points. Department of Mathematics and Computer Science, Aalborg University, Denmark. `http://cs.auc.dk/~normark/./hooks/hooks.ps`.

OGRI. 1995. Adage System Overview. Open Group Research Institute, Cambridge, MA.

Onion, F. and A. Harrison. 1996. "Framework Class Factories." *C++ Report*, November/December.

Opdyke, W. F. 1992. Refactoring Object-Oriented Frameworks. Ph.D. thesis, University of Illinois at Urbana-Champaign. `ftp://st.cs.uiuc.edu/pub/papers/refactoring/opdyke-thesis.ps.Z`.

Open Management Group. 2000. *CORBAServices Specification*. `http://www.ohttp://www.omg.org/technology/documents/corbaservices_spec_catalog.htmmg.org/technology/documents/corbaservices_spec_catalog.htm`.

Oresky, C., A. Clarkson, S. Kaisler, and D. B. Lenat. 1990. "Strategic Automated Discovery System (STRADS)." In P. Fishwick and D. Modjeski (eds.), *Knowledge Based Simulation: Methodology and Application*. Springer-Verlag, Berlin.

Pacheco, P. S. 1997. *Parallel Programming with MPI*. Morgan Kaufmann, Los Altos, CA.

Papaconstantinou, Y., S. Abiteboul, and H. Garcia-Molina. 1996. Object Fusion in Mediator Systems. Department of Computer Science, Stanford University. `http://www-db.stanford.edu/pub/papers/fusion.ps`.

Parmalee, R. C., et al. 1972. "Virtual Storage and Virtual Machine Concepts." *IBM Systems Journal* 11(2).

Perlis, A. 1982. "Epigrams on Programming." *ACM SIGPLAN Notices* 17(9): 7–13.

Perry, D. and A. L. Wolf. 1992. "Foundations for the Study of Software Architecture." *ACM Software Engineering Notes* 17(4): 40–52.

Posnak, E. J., R. G. Lavender, and H. M. Vin. 1997. "An Adaptive Framework for Developing Multimedia Software Components." *Communications of the ACM* 40(10): 43–47.

Pree, W. 1995. *Design Patterns for Object-Oriented Software Development*. Addison Wesley, Reading, MA.

Prieto-Diaz, R. 1988. "Status Report: Software Reusability." *IEEE Software* 10(3):61–66.

Pugh, J. R. and C. Leung. 1988. "Application Frameworks: Experience with MacApp." In *Proceedings of the 19th SIGCSE Technical Symposium on Computer Science Education*, February 25–26, Atlanta, GA, pp. 142–147.

Putnam, J. R. 1997. Distributed System Interoperability Perspectives Position Paper, 1997 Software Engineering & Economics Conference, MITRE Corporation, Bedford, MA.

Raj, G. S. 2000. The Factory Method Design Pattern. `http://gsraj.tripod.com/design/creational/factory/factory.html`.

Rapide Design Team. 1994. *The Rapide-1 Architectures Reference Manual, Version 1*. Program Analysis and Verification Group, Computer Systems Lab., Stanford University, Stanford, CA.

Rechtin, E. 1991. *Systems Architecting: Creating and Building Complex Systems*. Prentice-Hall, Englewood Cliffs, NJ.

Rice University. 1997. The D System. `http://www.cs.rice.edu/~dsystem/`.

Riehle, D. 1997. "Composite Design Patterns." In *Proceedings of the 1997 Conference on Object-Oriented Programming Systems, Languages and Applications (OOPSLA '97)*, pp. 218–228. Association for Computing Machinery, New York.

Riehle, D. 1997. A Role Based Design Pattern Catalog of Atomic and Composite Patterns Structured by Pattern Purpose. Technical Report 97-1-1, UbiLabs.

Riehle, D. and H. Züllighoven. 1996. "Understanding and Using Patterns in Software Development." *Theory and Practice of Object Systems* 2(1):3–13.

Rising, L. 1998. *Patterns Handbook: Techniques, Strategies, and Applications.* Cambridge University Press, Cambridge, UK.

Sammet, J. 1967. "Formula Manipulation by Computer." *Advances in Computers* 8: 47–102.

Sammet, J. 1969. *Programming Languages: History and Fundamentals.* Prentice-Hall, Upper Saddle River, NJ.

Scheifler, R. W. and J. Gettys. 1986. The X Window System. *ACM Transactions on Graphics* 5(2):79–109.

Schmid, H. A. 1997. "Systematic Framework Design by Generalization." *Communications of the ACM* 40(10): 48–51.

Schmidt, D. 1993. "The ADAPTIVE Communication Environment: An Object-Oriented Network Programming Toolkit for Developing Communication Software." In *Proceedings of 12th Annual Sun Users Group Conference*, San Francisco, CA.

Schmidt, D. 1995a. "Active Object—An Object Behavioral Pattern for Concurrent Programming." In *Proceedings of the Second Pattern Languages of Programs Conference*, Monticello, Illinois, September 6–8.

Schmidt, D. 1995b. "Using Design Patterns to Develop Reusable Object-Oriented Communication Software." *Communications of the ACM* 38(10):65–74.

Schmidt, D. 1996. "Asynchronous Completion Token—An Object Behavioral Pattern for Efficient Asynchronous Event Handling." Presented at the 3rd Annual Pattern Languages of Programming Conference in Allerton Park, Illinois, September 4–6.

Schmidt, D. 1997. "Proactor—An Object Behavioral Pattern for Demultiplexing and Dispatching Handlers for Asynchronous Events." Presented at the 4th Annual Pattern Languages of Programming Conference in Allerton Park, Illinois, September 2–5.

Schmidt, D., M. Fayad, and R. Johnson. 1996. "Software Patterns." Guest editorial for *Communications of the ACM, Special Issue on Patterns and Pattern Languages* 39(10): 36–39.

Schmidt, D. and S. Vinoski. 1997. Object Adapters: Concepts and Terminology. *C++ Report*, October. `http://www.cs.wustl.edu/~schmidt/PDF/C++-report-col11.pdf`.

Schmidt, D. and S. Vinoski. 2002a. Dynamic CORBA, Part 3—The Dynamic Skeleton Interface. *C/C++ Users Journal*, November. `http://www.cuj.com/documents/s=7977/cujcexp2011vinoski/`.

Schmidt, D. and S. Vinoski. 2002b. Dynamic CORBA, Part 1: The Dynamic Invocation Interface. *C/C++ Users Journal*, July. `http://www.cuj.com/documents/s=7981/cujcexp2007vinoski/`.

Schmucker, K. J. 1986. *Object-Oriented Programming for the Macintosh.* Hayden Book Company, San Francsico, CA.

SEI. 2004. Open Systems Defintion. `http://www.sei.cmu.edu/opensystems/faq.html`.

Shaw, M., R. DeLine, and D. Klein. 1995. "Abstractions for Software Architecture and Tools to Support Them." *IEEE Transactions on Software Engineering* 21(4):314–335.

Shaw, M. and D. Garlan. 1996. *Software Architecture: Perspectives on an Emerging Discipline.* Prentice Hall, Upper Saddle River, NJ.

Shull, F., W. L. Melo, and V. Basili. 1996. An Inductive Method for Discovering Design Patterns from Object-Oriented Software Systems. Department of Computer Science, University of Maryland, College Park, MD. Available at `http://citeseer.nj.nec.com/shull96inductive.html`.

Shull, F., G. H. Travassos, and J. Carver. 1999. Evolving a Set of Techniques for OO Inspections, CS-TR-4070. University of Maryland, College Park, MD.

Simon, H. A. 1973. "The Organization of Complex Systems." In H. H. Pattee (ed.), *Hierarchy Theory*, pp. 3–27. G. Braziller, New York.

Smith, J. and D. Stotts. 2003. SPWR: Flexible Automated Design Pattern Extraction from Source Code, TR03-016. Department of Computer Science, University of North Carolina, Chapel Hill, NC. Available at `http://rockfish-cs.cs.unc.edu/pubs/ase03-spqr.pdf`.

SML. 2002. *Standard ML of New Jersey.* `http://www.smlnj.org`.

Snelling, D. and G. K. Egan. 1994. A Comparative Study of Data-Flow Architectures, UMCS-94-4-3. University of Manchester.

Snir, M., S. W. Otto, S. Huss-Lederman, et al. 1997. *MPI: The Complete Reference.* MIT Press, Cambridge, MA.

Snyder, A. 1993. "The Essence of Objects: Concepts and Terms." *IEEE Software* 10(1):31–42.

Sparks, S., K. Benner, and C. Faris. 1996. "Managing Object-Oriented Framework Reuse." *IEEE Computer* 29(9):53–61.

Srinivasan, R. 1995. RPC: Remote Procedure Call Protocol Specification Version 2, RFC 1831. `http://www.faqs.org/rfcs/rfc1831.html`.

Stage, J., K. Normark, and K. G. Larsen. 1996. Quality Software—Concepts and Tools. The Software Engineering Programme, Institute for Electronic Systems, Aalborg University, Denmark.

Steele, G. Jr. 1990. *Common Lisp: The Language*, 2nd Ed. Digital Press, Maynard, MA.

Stefik, M. J., D. G. Bobrow, and K. M. Kahn. 1986. "Integrating Access-Oriented Programming into a Multiparadigm Environment." *IEEE Software* 3(1): 10–18.

St. Pierre, M. 1996. Z39.50 and Semantic Interoperability. Distributed Indexing/Searching Workshop, Cambridge, MA. Available at `http://www.w3.org/Search/9605-Indexing-Workshop/index.html`.

Sunderam, V. 1990. "PVM: A Framework for Parallel Distributed Computing." *Concurrency: Practice and Experience* 2(4): 315–339.

Sun Microsystems. 2003. Sun One Application Framework Overview. `http://docs.sun.com/db/doc/817-0447-10`.

Szyperski, C. 1998. *Component-Based Software: Beyond Object-Oriented Programming.* Addison-Wesley/Pergamon, Essex, England.

Taligent Corp. 1993. Leveraging Object-Oriented Frameworks. Cupertino, CA.

Taligent Corp. 1994. Building Object-Oriented Frameworks. Cupertino, CA.

Tanenbaum, A. S. and A. S. Woodhull. 1997. *Operating Systems: Design and Implementation*, 2nd Ed. Prentice-Hall, Englewood Cliffs, NJ.

Taylor, R. N., N. Medvidovic, K. M. Anderson, et al. 1996. "A Component- and Message-Based Architectural Style for GUI Software." *IEEE Transactions on Software Engineering* 22(6): 390–406.

Teichroew, D. and E. A. Hershey III. 1977. "PSL/PSA: A Computer-Aided Technique for Structure Documentation and Analysis of Information Processing Systems." *IEEE Transactions on Software Engineering* SE3(1):41–48.

Thomas, A. 1998. Enterprise JavaBeans Technology: Server Component Model for the JavaTM Platform. `http://java.sun.com/products/ejb/white_paper.html`.

Thompson, S. 1999. *Haskell: The Craft of Functional Programming*, 2nd Ed. Addison-Wesley, Reading, MA.

Tidwell, J. 1999. Common Ground: A Pattern Language for Human–Computer Interface Design. `http://www.cs.vu.nl/~martijn/patterns/index.html`.

Tracz, W. 1994. "DSSA Frequently Asked Questions." *ACM Software Engineering Notes* 19(2):52–56.

Travassos, G., F. Shull, J. Carver, and V. Basili. 2002. Reading Techniques for OO Design Inspections, CS-TR-4353 and UMIACS-TR-2002-33.

Ungar, D. and R. B. Smith. 1987. "Self: The Power of Simplicity." In *OOPSLA '87 Conference Proceedings*, pp. 227–241, Orlando, FL, October. Published as *ACM SIGPLAN Notices* 22(12): 227–242.

Universitat Zurich. 1994. Source file for the architecture available via FTP: `ftp://ftp.ifi.unizh.ch/pub/projects/met++/papers/MET++Architecture.ps.Z`.

Van Der Hoek, A., D. Heimbigner, and A. L. Wolf. 1999. Capturing Architectural Configurability: Variants, Options, and Evolution, TR-CU-CS-859-99. Department of Computer Science, University of Colorado, Boulder.

Vlissides, J. 1990. Generalized Graphical Object Editing. Ph.D. Thesis, Department of Computer Science, Stanford University, Stanford, CA.

Vlissides, J. 1998. "Composite Design Patterns (They Aren't What You Think)." *C++ Report*, June.

Vlissides, J. and M. A. Linton. 1990. "Unidraw: A Framework for Building Domain-Specific Graphical Editors." *ACM Transactions on Information Systems* 8(3):237–268.

Waldo, J. 2001. "The JINI Architecture for Network-Centric Computing." *Communications of the ACM* 42(7):76–82.

Wallnau, K. C., S. A. Hissam, and R. C. Seacord (2001). *Building Systems from Commercial Components*. Addison Wesley, Reading, MA.

Wallnau, K., J. Stafford, S. Hissam, and M. Klein. 2001. "On the Relationship of Software Architecture to Software Component Technology." In *Proceedings of the 6th International Workshop on Component-Oriented Programming* (WCOP6), Budapest, Hungary.

Warren, H. Jr. 2002. *Hacker's Delight*. Addison Wesley, Reading, MA.

Watson, R. W. 1970. *Timesharing System Design Concepts*. McGraw-Hill, New York.

Wegner, P. 1987. "Dimensions of Object-Based Language Design." In *Proceedings of the OOPSLA '87 Conference*. ACM Press, NY, pp. 168–182.

Wegner, P. 1996a. "Interoperability." *ACM Computing Surveys* 28(1):285–287.

Wegner, P. 1996b. The Paradigm Shift: From Algorithms to Interaction, Brown University, unpublished.

Weinand, A., E. Gamma, and R. Marty. 1988. "ET++—An Object-Oriented Application Framework in C++." In *Proceedings of the OOPSLA '88 Conference. ACM SIGPLAN Notices* 23(1):46–57.

Weinand, A. and E. Gamma. 1994. "ET++—A Portable, Homogenous Class Library and Application Framework." In W. R. Bischofberger and H.-P. Frei (eds.), *Computer Science Research at UBILAB; Proceedings of the UBILAB Conference 94*. UVK Universitaets-Verlag Konstanz.

Welie, M. 2001. Designing Your Site's Navigation. Available at `http://www.welie.com/articles/site-navigation.pdf`.

Widom, J. and S. Ceri. 1996. *Active Database Systems: Triggers and Rules for Advanced Database Processing*. Morgan Kaufmann, Los Altos, CA.

Wilson, D. A., L. S. Rosenstein, and D. Shafer. 1990. *Programming with MacApp*. Addison Wesley, Reading, MA.

Winston, P. H. 1998. *On to Smalltalk*. Addison-Wesley, Reading, MA.

Wirth, N. 1975. *Algorithms + Data Structures = Programs*. Prentice-Hall, Englewood Cliffs, NJ.

Wright, S. 2002. The Ada 95 Booch Components Repository. `http://www.pogner.demon.co.uk/components/bc/`.

Yellin, D. M. and R. E. Strom. 1997. "Protocol Specifications and Components Adaptors." *ACM Transactions on Programming Languages and Systems* 19(2):292–333.

Yourdon, E. (ed.) 1976. *Techniques of Program Structure and Design*. Prentice Hall, Englewood Cliffs, NJ.

Zave, P. and M. Jackson. 1998. "A Component-Based Approach to Telecommunication Software." *IEEE Software* 15(5):70–78.

GLOSSARY

ACM   Association for Computing Machinery

ADL   Architecture Description Language

ADT   Abstract Data Type: A type of data whose internal form is hidden behind a set of access functions. Objects of the type are created and inspected only by calls to the access functions. This allows the implementation of the type to be changed without requiring any changes outside the module in which it is defined.

Algorithm   A detailed sequence of actions to perform to accomplish some task.

API   Application Programming Interface

Architecture   As a term it can refer to several things: a discipline, an instance of a building, a description of an information system, or the intangible structure of the system itself.

ASP   Active Server Page (Microsoft)

Asynchronous   Not synchronized by a shared signal such as clock or semaphore, proceeding independently.

AWT   Advanced Windowing Toolkit

C++   An object-based programming language, descended from the C programming language.

CASE   Computer-Aided Software Engineering

CBSE   Component-Based Software Engineering

CCM   CORBA Component Model

CLOS   Common Lisp Object System

Software Paradigms, By Stephen H. Kaisler
ISBN 0-471-48347-8   Copyright © 2005 John Wiley & Sons, Inc.

COE Common Operating Environment

COM Component Object Model (Microsoft)

Common Lisp An ANSI standard definition of the venerable Lisp language.

Context Switch The process of switching the CPU from executing one process (thread) to executing another.

CORBA Common Object Request Broker Architecture

COTS Commercial Off-the-Shelf

CMU Carnegie-Mellon University

CRUD Create-Retrieve-Update-Destroy, a set of database operations.

DAG Directed Acyclic Graph

DARPA Defense Advanced Research Projects Agency

DBMS Data Base Management System

DCE Distributed Computing Environment (OSF)

DCOM Distributed COM (Microsoft)

DDE Dynamic Data Exchange (Microsoft)

DDL Data Definition Language

DFC Distributed Feature Composition

DLL Dynamically Loadable Library (Microsoft)

DML Data Manipulation Language

DoD Department of Defense

DOS Disk Operating System—various manufacturers

DS Distributed System

DSOM Distributed System Object Model

DSSA Domain-Specific Software Architecture

EBC Event-Based Component

ECLE Edit-Compile-Link-Execute

EJB Enterprise JavaBeans

Embedded Object An embedded object is created by wrapping an existing structure or process—something that is not already an object—with appropriate interface code (Snyder 1993).

Encapsulated Object An object is encapsulated when clients can access it only by issuing requests (Snyder 1993). [Kaisler (1997) calls this *total encapsulation*.]

EXE An executable file under IBM's OS/2 or Microsoft's Windows operating systems.

FPL Functional Programming Language

Generic Operation An operation having different implementations for different objects, with observably different behaviors, but uniformly accessible (Snyder 1993).

GoF Gang of Four (Gamma, Helms, Johnson, and Vlissides)

GUI Graphical User Interface

Handle   An identifier for uniquely referencing an object.

HCI   Human–Computer Interface

HTML   HyperText Markup Language

HTTP   HyperText Transfer Protocol

IDE   Interactive Development Environment

IDL   Interface Definition Language (as defined by OMG for CORBA), but also generically

IDS   Intrusion Detection System

Interface   A description of the potential requests to which an object can respond (Snyder 1993).

I/O   Input/Output

IRM   Information Resources Management

ISO   International Standards Organization

IT   Information Technology

Java   An object-oriented programming language (developed by Sun Microsystems)

J2EE   Java 2 Enterprise Edition, a development environment and application framework.

JDBC   Java Database Connectivity

KS   Knowledge Source

KSLOC   Thousand Source Lines of Code

KSR   Kendall Square Research

LOOPS   Lisp Object-Oriented Programming System (a Xerox PARC research programming environment)

LPL   Logic Programming Language

Method   A procedure that performs a service (Snyder 1993).

MFC   Microsoft Foundation Classes

MIDL   Microsoft's IDL compiler for DCOM

MTF   Message Transforming Function

MTS   Microsoft Transaction Server

MVC   Model-View-Controller, Smalltalk-80 model

NDR   Network Data Representation (DCE)

NUMA   Non-Uniform Memory Architecture

Object   An object is an identifiable entity that plays a visible role in providing a service that a client can request (Snyder 1993).

OE   Operating Environment

O-O   Object-Oriented (my notation)

Object Reference   A value that reliably identifies an object (Snyder 1993).

ODBC   Open Data Base Connectivity (Microsoft)

ODMG   Object Data Management Group

OLE   Object Linking and Embedding (Microsoft)

OMA   Object Management Architecture

OMG   Object Management Group

Ontology   A description (like a formal specification of a program) of the concepts and relationships that can exist for a body of knowledge.

OODB   Object-Oriented Database

OOP   Object-Oriented Program

OOPL   Object-Oriented Programming Language

OOPLSA   Object-Oriented Programming Languages, Systems, and Applications

ORB   Object Request Broker

OS   Operating System

OSF   Open System Foundation

PARC   Palo Alto Research Center (Xerox Corporation)

PLoP   Pattern Languages of Program Design

POA   Portable Object Adapter

PRAM   Parallel Random Access Machine

Property   Some information about an object that you can obtain by a query method.

Proxy   An object that represents another object in some activity.

QoS   Quality of Service

RBS   Rule-Based System

RDMS   Relational Database Management System

Request   A client action to an object to perform a service (Snyder 1993).

Representation   The choice of a set of symbols to stand for an abstraction.

RMC   Remote Method Call

RMI   Remote Method Invocation (Java)

RPC   Remote Procedure Call

SADL   Software Architecture Description Language

SCM   Service Control Manager

SDK   System Development Kit

SDLC   System Development Life Cycle

SEI   Software Engineering Institute

SIMD   Single Instruction, Multiple Data

SMP   Symmetric Multiprocessor

SOM   System Object Model (IBM)

SPMD   Single Program, Multiple Data

SPP   Scalabe Parallel Processor

Sequential Programming   Sequenial programming has two characteristics: (1) the textual order of program statements defines their execution order, and (2) successive statements must be executed without any overlap in time with one another.

State Variable   A concrete realization of data associated with objects (Snyder 1993).

Structured Programming   A style of programming that emphasizes hierarchical program structures in which each command has one entry point and one exit point.

TCP/IP   Transfer Control Protocol/Internet Protocol

TPM   Transaction Processing Monitor

UDP   User Datagram Protocol

UI   User Interface

UML   Unified Modeling Language

URL   Unified Resource Locator

VM   Virtual Machine (also refers to an IBM product)

VRML   Virtual Reality Manipulation Language

Win32   An API for the 32-bit Windows Operating Systems

WSDL   Web Services Description Language

WYSIWYG   What You See Is What You Get

XML   Extensible Markup Language

INDEX